BRITAIN, RUSSIA AND THE ROAD TO THE FIRST WORLD WAR

For much of the later nineteenth-century Britain regarded Russia as its main international rival, particularly as regarded the security of its colonial possessions in India. Yet, by 1907 Russia's political revolution, financial collapse and military defeat by Japan, transformed the situation, resulting in an Anglo-Russian rapprochement. As this book makes clear, whilst international affairs lay at the root of this new relationship, personal factors also played an important role in reversing many years of mutual animosity and suspicion. In particular the study explores the influence of the liberal anglophile Count Aleksandr Benckendorff, the Russian ambassador in London between 1903 and 1916.

By 1905 Russia's multiple weaknesses required a prolonged period of external peace by eliminating frictions with the principal rival powers, Britain and Germany, while France and Britain realised that a British rapprochement with Russia would be necessary to counter Germany's power. Benckendorff, as one of the most important figures in the Russian diplomatic service, persuaded Nicholas II and his Foreign Minister, V.N. Lamsdorff, to drop their objections to various long-standing British demands in order to pave the way for a Triple Entente. Although the overarching Russian strategy was conceived as 'balancing' the imperial rivalries of Britain and Germany, numerous factors – not least Benckendorff's energetic pro-British stance – upset the scales and resulted in a stand-off with the central powers.

Demonstrating how Benckendorff's fear of losing Britain's friendship made him oppose all Russia's efforts at improving Russo-German relations, this book underlines the pro-Entente policy's role in setting Russia on the road to war. For when the Sarajevo crisis struck; there was now no hope of appealing to German goodwill to help defuse the situation. Instead Russia's status within the Entente depended on a show of determination and strength, which lead inexorably to a disaster of the Great War.

About the author

Marina Soroka, University of Western Ontario, Canada

Britain, Russia and the Road to the First World War

The Fateful Embassy of Count Aleksandr Benckendorff (1903–16)

MARINA SOROKA
University of Western Ontario, Canada

ASHGATE

Birmingham Studies in First World War History

Series Editor

John Bourne
The University of Birmingham, UK

The First World War is a subject of perennial interest to historians and is often regarded as a watershed event, marking the end of the nineteenth century and the beginning of the 'modern' industrial world. The sheer scale of the conflict and massive loss of life means that it is constantly being assessed and reassessed to examine its lasting military, political, sociological, industrial, cultural and economic impact. Run in conjunction with the Centre for First World War Studies at the University of Birmingham, this series offers a platform for the publication of international research on all aspects of the Great War. Whilst the main thrust of the series is on the military aspects of the conflict, other related areas (including cultural, political and social) are also be addressed. Books published are aimed primarily at a post-graduate academic audience, furthering exciting recent interpretations of the war, whilst still being accessible enough to appeal to a wider audience of educated lay readers.

Also in this series

British Generalship during the Great War
The Military Career of Sir Henry Horne (1861–1929)
Simon Robbins

The Ordeal of Peace: Demobilization and the Urban Experience in Britain and Germany, 1917–1921
Adam R. Seipp

Doctrine and Reform in the British Cavalry 1880–1918
Stephen Badsey

Published by
Ashgate Publishing Limited
Wey Court East
Union Road
Farnham
Surrey, GU9 7PT
England

Ashgate Publishing Company
Suite 420
101 Cherry Street
Burlington
VT 05401-4405
USA

www.ashgate.com

British Library Cataloguing in Publication Data
Soroka, Marina.
Britain, Russia and the road to the First World War : the fateful embassy of Count Aleksandr Benckendorff (1903-16).
– (Birmingham studies in First World War history)
1. Benckendorff, Aleksandr. 2. Ambassadors–Russia–Biography.
3. World War, 1914-1918–Diplomatic history. 4. Great Britain–Foreign relations–Russia.
5. Russia–Foreign relations–Great Britain. 6. Great Britain–Foreign relations–1901-1936.
7. Russia–Foreign relations–1801-1917. 8. Triple Entente, 1907.
I. Title II. Series
940.3'22-dc22

Library of Congress Cataloging-in-Publication Data
Soroka, Marina.
Britain, Russia, and the road to the First World War : the fateful embassy of of Count Aleksandr Benckendorff (1903-16) / Marina Soroka.
p. cm. -- (Birmingham studies in First World War history)
Includes bibliographical references and index.
ISBN 978-1-4094-2246-4 (hbk) -- ISBN 978-1-4094-2247-1 (ebk)
1. Benckendorff, Aleksandr Konstantinovich, Count, 1849-1917. 2. Ambassadors--Russia--Biography. 3. Russia--Foreign relations--Great Britain. 4. Great Britain--Foreign relations--Russia. 5. Russia--Foreign relations--1894-1917. 6. Great Britain--Foreign relations--1901-1936. 7. World War, 1914-1918--Causes. 8. World War, 1914-1918--Diplomatic history. I. Title. II. Series.

DK254.B428S68 2010
327.2092--dc22

2010047381

ISBN 9781409422464 (hbk)
ISBN 9781409422471 (ebk)

MIX
Paper from responsible sources
FSC® C018575
FSC
www.fsc.org

Printed and bound in Great Britain by the MPG Books Group, UK

Contents

List of Figures

Preface

> As you say we failed to prevent war, but the Balkan Conference showed that war could have been prevented. The machinery and personelle in London were effective and absolutely trustworthy. You, Cambon, Imperiali, Lichnowsky, Mensdorff and myself could and would have settled any European crisis honourably [...] and fairly [if] the difficulty had been referred to us.
>
> Lord Grey of Fallodon (Sir Edward Grey) to Count A.K. Benckendorff (22 December 1916)

The mission of the Russian ambassador in London, Count Aleksandr Konstantinovich Benckendorff, coincided with a tense, crisis-ridden time in Europe. It was also the longest period of friendly Anglo-Russian relations in the past two centuries. Since the divisions between Russia and Britain were deep and unresolved, diplomacy played a considerable part in overcoming them. And yet, from the existing books about the Anglo-Russian rapprochement of 1907 one can easily get an impression that Russia had no embassy in Britain and that the British Foreign Office dealt with the Russian foreign ministry exclusively through the British ambassadors in St Petersburg. Russian diplomacy is present only as the odds against which the British worked, as a backdrop to their brilliant maneuvering. According to the canon, ambassadors Sir Charles Hardinge and Sir Arthur Nicolson participated in the shaping of Britain's Russian policy by the Foreign Office; they also patiently and skillfully implemented this policy in Russia by neutralizing the potentially damaging initiatives of the faceless and nameless 'Russians' or 'Russian government'. A question that has never been asked: 'What was the Russian diplomatic mission doing in London during all this time?'.

The omission of Russian diplomats in pre-war diplomatic history is not surprising. Western diplomatic historians usually wrote about Anglo-Russian relations from the multitude of sources available to them in British and US archives and memoirs published in the West. Most of these historians focused on Britain's foreign policy, and learning Russian seemed a waste of time, especially because before the 1990s Russian foreign ministry archives had been practically closed to historians. The sources always manipulate historians. It is natural that in the eyes of the Edwardian diplomats the most relevant part of the pre-war European politics was their own and the only story worth telling in any detail was Britain's (and its diplomats') courageous stand against its multiple rivals.

In Russia, the Anglo-Russian convention of 1907 had never been popular, because seen from the Russian side it was a step on the way to the First World War, a test which the Russian empire did not survive. So, later historians were not interested in it. Soviet historians, besides, were trained to build their historical research on Marxist and Leninist theoretical axioms about the 'objective laws' of social development and about the answers to everything being in 'processes', not in personalities.

But had the Entente defeated the central powers before the Russian revolution broke out in February 1917, then the convention would have gone down in Russian history as a success of Russian diplomacy and Count Benckendorff as one of its heroes. Similarly, had Benckendorff's hopes for Russia's transformation into Britain's political and economic ally (or, rather, a satellite) materialized, in the course of the twentieth century a modernized Russia would have formed part of the European community and Aleksandr Benckendorff would have been hailed as a visionary. But timing and luck count for much in politics, and Benckendorff's dream was shattered by the beginning of the Great War, and once again, by the Russian revolution.

Russian historiography ignored Russian diplomatic service for a reason. As soon as the Bolsheviks seized power in 1917 they began to buttress their legitimacy by undermining and destroying what was left of the imperial Russia's prestige in the eyes of their nation and the world. Official Soviet historiography summarily referred to the old state apparatus as the lackeys of the autocracy. It did not help that Russia's foreign service with one notorious exception, turned down L. Trotsky's invitation to serve the Soviets and refused to recognize their legitimacy. From then on the study of the imperial diplomacy in the Soviet Union for a long time was an exercise in demolishing its prestige. The Tsar's diplomats were blamed for their successes, for these promoted the autocracy's rapacious designs; if they failed, they were blamed again for not looking properly after Russia's national interests.

The early official Soviet thesis, originating in M. Pokrovsky's work, was that the Russian imperial government was guilty of the seven deadly sins plus of having single-handedly instrumented the First World War. It was a clever shot at the autocracy, because the early Soviet Russia was still reeling from the wartime hardships followed by the horrors of a civil war. This fanciful version of the past was received with joy by German official historians in the 1920s, striving to erase the 'war guilt' stain from Germany's reputation. The absent always take the blame, and many veteran Western statesmen found it convenient that Russia would be the only instigator of the First World War because it exonerated them in the eyes of their own nations. The Cold War kept this myth alive in Western pop culture as a universal explanation of Russia's past, present and future behaviour.

Protests of the émigré Russian diplomats in the West were barely heard in the din of political struggles of the 1920s and 1930s. Unlike the Western statesmen, they had neither the authority to impose their views nor the leisure to work on memoirs in comfortable retirement. They did not always have the necessary documents at their disposal. But when their government and their institution were attacked many rose to defend it. In polished French, English or German they wrote again and again that despite occasional blunders Russian diplomacy had done its duty and only sought to protect Russia from war. The memoirists wandered as far back as Peter the Great's Grand Embassy and the Congress of Vienna in 1815 to explain Russia's diplomatic weaknesses and achievements, but they were vague about more recent events, to avoid maligning the dead and the absent. A further disincentive to frankness was that refugees from the Soviet Russia could not afford to offend or displease the governments of the countries which gave them asylum. No wonder that Western historians consulted these memoirs mostly as a *Who is Who* in Russian imperial foreign policy.

As a result, the story of the great powers' diplomatic relations prior to 1914 – in particular that of the Anglo-Russian convention of 1907 – has been told in English several times, but not from the Russian side. Dominic Lieven, David M. McDonald and Michael Hughes were the only Western historians who touched upon the Russian foreign ministry under Nicholas II, but the Russian diplomats remained invisible.

Before the 1960s, Soviet diplomatic historians had rarely had access to archival materials and mostly read abundant but very selectively published series of diplomatic documents from the 1920s–1930s. Soviet historians after the 1940s, for all their talent, had no first-hand knowledge of Western culture or politics and their outlook and understanding of the diplomatic relations between Russia and the West was necessarily limited. Sensibly, they did the only thing they could: write again and again about the relation between Russian foreign policy and domestic political struggle. What remained outside (Russia's presence in the West and its foreign missions' activity) they did not deem too important. The canon, adopted by Russian and Western historians, ruled that all foreign policy decisions were made in St Petersburg and ambassadors were glorified errand boys. And yet 'old diplomacy' was implemented and represented by a unique category of men that has been gradually displaced from the political scene and then extinguished. That they were from a privileged, 'elite' class only begins to describe them. The corollary is that they were their own men, for the most part, unafraid to be different or unpopular. It did not bother them to be in the minority, for they did not need a majority vote to find out what their views were. They were not more brilliant than our own contemporaries, but they did not try to win hearts by pretending to be as dumb and ignorant as the dumbest and most ignorant of their 'electorate'. Nor did they believe that being a 'team player' in politics required becoming a faceless, mindless and petty sycophant. They did not apologize for having principles and political convictions that were not popular with the tabloid press, and, because they fully believed in their own significance and individual worth, they carried out their duties with dignity and pride, fully justifying the saying that it is not the rank that makes a man prominent, but that personality lends splendour to any rank. Such ambassadors and foreign ministers, such men – such gentlemen, I venture to say, – whether bright or dim, kind or cruel, progressive or reactionary – lived and acted inspired by a definite set of values, and their personal and professional interactions left a deep imprint on the political events of the early twentieth century.

After the 1960s, access to archives became easier for Russian historians, but until the late 1980s a case study or a biography of a tsarist diplomat would never be published in the Soviet Union. It was considered inexpedient to bring the members of the former privileged classes to the attention of the Soviet people.

When finally the Soviet controls disintegrated in the 1990s, Russian historical scholarship stood in confusion over the invaluable primary sources. Many good general works on Russian foreign policy have been published, but now that the government does not issue lists of authorized national icons, historians cannot agree who among imperial diplomats qualifies as a worthy subject for a biography or a case study. As far as an outsider can gather, such a man has to be a Russian, an author of an original political doctrine and a father of at least one resounding diplomatic victory. A diplomatic victory usually follows a victorious war: there were not too many of those for Russia in the nineteenth century, and therefore, not too many candidates pass the test.

These seem to be what Marxist history calls 'objective causes' of the neglect of Russian diplomacy on all sides. I cannot say how important another 'objective factor' may have been: a very human inclination to sail in the wake of great trend-setters and pay attention only to the subjects whose validity and relevance has been recognized.

In the case of Russia's ambassador to Britain, Count Benckendorff's specific circumstances conspired to make him invisible to historians. He died suddenly, on the eve of the collapse of the Russian empire, without having written or dictated a memoir. If he had, his name would have remained at least in library catalogues.

The collection of his family papers, split between two continents, has been ignored by historians on both. And yet these documents tell a new story about triangular Anglo-Franco-Russian relations and how these played out between the ambassadors and the Foreign Office in London. The role of the London embassy in the general framework of the Entente relations reflected the administration of Russian foreign policy under Nicholas II and the workings of the 'old diplomacy'. Ultimately all this adds to the inexhaustible subject of the origins of the First World War. These issues are well-presented in Benckendorff's and his colleagues' private and personal correspondence, the French, Russian, German and British documents and memoirs.

The official exchanges between St Petersburg and the embassy have been appearing in print since the 1920s. A German spy who was on the embassy staff copied Benckendorff's correspondence in 1909–14 and had it published in Germany as part of the German Foreign Ministry's War Guilt campaign. The Soviet *Krasny Arkhiv* publications followed in the 1920s–40. In 1937–39 the daughter of the Russian foreign minister, Aleksandr Iswolsky, published most of Count Benckendorff's confidential letters to her father.

Routine correspondence between the London embassy and the Foreign Ministry is well represented in the collections of the AVPRI (The Archive of the Russian Imperial Foreign Policy) and GARF (the State Archives of the Russian Federation) in Moscow. The Royal Archive in Windsor contains numerous letters from British diplomats in Russia and from Nicholas II to King Edward VII and King George V regarding Anglo-Russian relations, as well as letters to the monarchs from the foreign secretaries and prime ministers.

Correspondence of the Foreign Office officials dealing with Anglo-Russian relations is preserved at the National Records Archive at Kew. The Surrey History Centre in Woking (UK) is the repository of the archive of the Onslow family, a member of which stood close to the emerging Anglo-Russian understanding and to the Russian embassy in London.

Most of the archival documents have come to light for the first time. Confidential letters to Benckendorff from his superiors, colleagues and subordinates by their strictly private character arrived unopened at the ambassador's desk and remained out of reach of the spy in the embassy. Later, among other family papers, they found their way to Columbia University. Benckendorff's correspondence with Empress Maria Feodorovna in the State Archives of the Russian Federation has not attracted the attention of the historians who excavate the lives of the last Romanovs. Benckendorff's correspondence with his wife in the same archives discouraged researchers: it is family correspondence of two virtually unknown persons; it is in French and the handwriting is bad. Researchers ignored it; but Countess Benckendorff was her husband's adviser and confidant, so the letters are the equivalent of diaries that they never kept.

Benckendorff's confidential letters to the foreign ministers, unlike his official reports, dealt with subjects outside his official task and presented his opinions with more force and clarity than his reports. These letters often explain the origin and evolution of the ideas formally expressed in the dispatches. Suspicions, hopes, rumours which formed part of the unofficial exchanges between the diplomats create a telling background to the actual moves of Entente diplomacy of the period.

Benckendorff's correspondence with his Russian colleagues and friends, his wife and brothers-in-law was conducted in French; his correspondence with the British was in English. His Italian brother-in-law wrote his diary in Italian. Benckendorff's sons wrote in Russian as also did Russian diarists, though many of the Russian diplomatic memoirs were published after 1917 either in English or in French. All the quotations are in my translation, unless indicated otherwise. Where Benckendorff or his correspondents inserted an English or Russian word or phrase in a French letter I wrote it in italics. 'He', 'One' or 'We' with a capital letter in Benckendorff's letters and in those of his contemporaries refer to a royal personage.

When people wrote to their superiors their handwriting was much clearer than when they dashed off notes to their underlings. Benckendorff's letters to Empress Maria Feodorovna are easier to read than her replies to him. Benckendorff's handwriting grew worse with age and his rise in the service. His later letters are almost indecipherable. The symbol [...] shows a word which cannot be read.

Letters exchanged between the Russians who lived in Russia and those who lived abroad usually had two dates: ‘the old style’ Russian date and ‘the new style’ European date. For the sake of clarity and uniformity both dates are provided in all Russian letters cited. If there is only one date in the citation it is the European one.

Marina Soroka

Acknowledgments

I am grateful to Her Majesty Queen Elizabeth II for her gracious permission to quote from papers in the Royal Archives at Windsor.

I was able to travel to Moscow, Windsor and New York thanks to the generous support of the SSHRC in 2006–2009. Research and writing has been a very happy period: I discovered interesting materials, saw beautiful places and got to know many generous and delightful people to whom I gladly acknowledge my gratitude: Professor Brock Millman, Dr Charles Ruud and Dr Neville Thompson of the University of Western Ontario; the diplomatic historians at the Russian History Institute in Moscow, and in particular, Dr Irina S. Rybachonok; Mrs Nathalie Brooke; Sir Adam Ridley; T. Chebotaryova of the Bakhmetev Archive at Columbia University, New York; Pamela Clark and Laura Hobbs of Royal Archives at Windsor; Alla V. Abramenkova of the Archives of the Foreign Policy of the Russian Empire in Moscow; Nina I. Abdullaeva at the State Archives of Russian Federation in Moscow; Elizabeth Mantz and David Murphy at Weldon Library of the University of Western Ontario, London; and last but not least, my family.

Abbreviations

AVPRI	Arkhiv Vneshnei Politiki Rossiiskoi Imperii [Archives of the Foreign Policy of the Russian Empire]
BD	*British Documents on the Origins of the War, 1898–1914*
BC2	Benckendorff Papers, Part 2 at Columbia University, Bakhmetev Archive
DDF	*Documents Diplomatiques Français, 1871–1914* (2e Serie)
FO	Foreign Office. Private Collections. Various Ministers and Officials. Public Records Office
GARF	Gosudarstvennyy Arkhiv Rossiiskoi Federatsii [State Archive of the Russian Federation]
GP	*Die Grosse Politik der Europaischen Kabinette,* 1877–1914
OP	Papers of the Earls of Onslow of Clandon Park at Surrey History Centre, Woking, UK
OR	Otdel rukopisei Rossiiskoi Gosudarstvennoi Biblioteki [Manuscripts of the Russian State Library]

Chapter 1
The Premises, 1830–1900

'Unnatural' and 'fragile' have been the traditional descriptions of the Anglo-Russian rapprochement of 1907, first in the press and later by historians. Clichéd references to imperial Russia and imperial Britain as antipodes of the 'East is East and West is West' kind served to support the idea: a political rapprochement between such dissimilar nations was bound to be fragile. But the rapprochement proved to be less fragile than some of the contemporaries hoped and others feared. It held until the beginning of the Great War and became a wartime alliance. A century of distance between us and the statesmen who were in charge of European diplomacy, puts into focus similarities of ideas, principles and reactions which the contemporaries ignored or denied. Bringing together British and Russian contemporary views of the international setting in which they acted helps to create a clearer picture of the origins of the 1907–17 understanding and to highlight the often forgotten fact that the statesmen on both sides were in many respects similar – children of the same age and products of the same cultural tradition. They understood each other only too well, even when they disagreed. Their actions were prompted by the same worldview.

In the 1900s European governments tried to implement their foreign policies without losing sight of two guiding principles. One stated that the 'man in the street never cares two damns about foreign politics until he finds himself landed in the war'.[1] The other cautioned that if a government went against the 'national feeling' too often or too openly, it might undermine the popular confidence in its foreign policy.[2] How universal these axioms were is obvious from the fact that the first one was expressed by a Foreign Office bureaucrat in parliamentary Britain and the second by the Russian autocrat Alexander III. The stereotypes dominant in the national consciousness made certain policies more palatable to the public than others. The same notions which lived in the collective mind of their nations influenced the statesmen in their choice of options. The image of the British among the educated Russian public was ambivalent: the maritime empire was admired and respected for its stability, its laws and its culture, but condemned for despoiling and exploiting the colonies and despised, as in the rest of Europe, for hypocrisy. The British government, though not the nation, was an unreliable ally and a cold friend. The ruling circles, well aware of British rivalry and its costs to Russia, tended to be Anglophobe politically, even if this feeling was mixed with admiration for Britain's cultural, social and economic achievement. They

1 D.O.M. [Dougal O. Malcolm] to Lord Cranley, 17.04.1904, OP, G173/24.100.
2 Baron B.E. Nol'de, *Dalekoie i blizkoie* (Paris, 1930), 38.

explained British Russophobia by Britain's aspirations to world supremacy, to which Russia was an obstacle. Following the Crimean war the Russian military and political circles expected that sooner or later there would be another war with Britain. In 1859 Grand Duke Konstantin during a visit to Britain wrote to his brother Alexander II:

> It is obvious that there is no sympathy or liking for Russia here, and the memories of the last war are alive. *Ce n'est qu'une trève* [It's only a truce]. What a difference with France and Sardinia where the public opinion was opposed to the war and where the governments are doing their best to move away from the past.[3]

This opinion coexisted with that expressed by N.V. Charykow, Russian deputy minister of foreign affairs (1908–11), in recalling his first visit to Britain:

> In London I was admitted to look at the narrow, uncomfortable straight-backed benches of the 'Mother of Parliaments', and felt that here liberty was neither a remote hope as in Germany, nor a vain boast, as in France, but a solid reality worth giving one's life for.[4]

The commonly accepted view of Britain as a near-paragon co-existed with uniformly negative historical associations. In 1853–55 Russia was defeated in the Crimean war by the British, French, Ottoman and Sardinian forces which attacked Russia in the Baltic, Black, White and Azov Seas, in the Pacific and in the Crimea. The 1856 Peace of Paris stripped Russia of the means of defending the Black Sea coastline and left Russia's Baltic coastline exposed to naval attacks. This first major defeat of the Russian Empire took a heavy toll of the state finances and left Russia strategically vulnerable. This lesson of the dangers of anti-Russian coalitions and on the vulnerability of Russia's territories cut deep into the national memory.

Also in 1856, after the second Anglo-Chinese Opium war, the British intensified their penetration of the Chinese Empire. As Russian and Chinese territories were not clearly delimited, the Russian government feared a British occupation of Sakhalin or the Russian maritime territories. Britain thwarted Russia's attempts to buy or lease an ice-free port on the Pacific Ocean. In the absence of a significant Russian naval force there, Britain could bomb or occupy any Russian settlement on the Pacific coast. Russian military and foreign policy officials perceived that Britain's goal in Central Asia was to take over all or some of Russian Central Asian territories bordering on the British colonies. A significant factor in the Russian forward Asian policy consisted of fears born of watching Britain's

---

3 *Perepiska Imperatora Aleksandra II s velikim kniazem Konstantinom Nikolaevichem: Dnevnik Velikogo Kniazia Konstantina Nikolaevicha* (Moscow, 1994), 119.

4 N.V. Tcharykow, *Glimpses of High Politics* (London, 1931), 79.

expansion into the Far East, Southern and Central Asia. It imposed on Russia a financially crippling program of railway and fortifications construction not only in the West but also in the Far East and in Central Asia. As Russian statesmen saw it, Britain would not allow Russia the tranquility of good relations with her Asian neighbours; in October 1878 the Amir of Afghanistan signed a draft treaty with Russia which improved Russo-Afghan relations and a month later the British began the second war on Afghanistan, converting it into Britain's springboard for threatening Russia's security. In 1885 an Afghan-Russian skirmish which Russians saw as British encroachment by proxy led to the Penjdeh crisis.

Since the 1830s Russia had regarded Persia as its sphere of interest and Britain's unceasing attempts to encroach on Persia and tie Russia's freedom of action by an Anglo-Russian agreement as a threat to Russia's predominant position in the Persian Empire. Russian rulers foresaw that an Anglo-German rapprochement would push Russia out of the Persian Gulf region altogether. In 1902 the Russian papers advised the government to use the eight years left until the completion of the Baghdad railway to reach the Persian Gulf. British government's announcement of the construction of a railway in Baluchistan prompted the Russian plan of building a line Ashabad–Meshed and then Teheran–Isphahan–Baghdad.[5]

Britain's relations with the European powers also exercised a strong influence on Russia's foreign policy in the last decade of the nineteenth century: the Mediterranean Entente of Austria-Hungary and Italy, directed against France and Russia, became a serious concern to the Russian government only after Britain joined it in 1887,[6] transforming it into a new version of the Crimean alignment. Britain's leaning towards the Triple Alliance, marked by the Anglo-German agreement of 1 July 1890 increased Russia's fears of isolation and encouraged Russia's reluctant rapprochement with France. Britain lay beyond the Channel, secure and confident but at the same time consistently able to demonstrate that Russia's territories were within its striking power. As a countermeasure, Russia feigned a threat to India. Britain's difficulties in maintaining order among the various tribes and principalities of the subcontinent would have been greatly increased by a Russian attack.

Russian political and military course in the post-Crimean years responded to the need to forestall or divert threats from Britain in these regions. Impulsive moves inspired by a momentary expediency abounded in Russian foreign policy, leaving little margin for long-term carefully-laid plans. Russian diplomats justified the need for the unprofitable and unstable rapprochement with the French Empire in the 1860s by the fear that if French overtures were rejected, Napoleon III would seek a British alliance.[7] The sale of the Aleut Isles and Alaska to the US was partly

5 Marquis de Montebello to T. Delcassé, 13.2.1902, DDF, II: 2 95–8.

6 V.N. Lamsdorff, *Dnevnik 1891–1892* (Minsk, 2003), 179.

7 Oleg Airapetov, *Vneshn'aia politika Rossiiskoi imperii, 1815–1914* (Moscow, 2006), 232.

dictated, on the Russian side, by the desire to get out of an area of confrontation with Britain.

Britain and Russia found themselves in opposition during the 1870s Balkan crisis. As Russia saw it, Britain rejected a compromise which would maintain the integrity of the Ottoman Empire and at the same time relieve the position of the Christian nations of the empire. Britain's refusal to cooperate with Russia in exerting pressure on the Ottoman Empire contributed to the situation which ultimately brought Russia to make war on Turkey. In the course of the Russo-Turkish war Britain favoured Turkey, and as a reward acquired control of the Suez Canal and Cyprus, while Russia made war and crippled her finances, only to be deprived of the main prize – the Straits – at the Berlin Congress by the powers led by Britain. Britain more than once made it known that it would oppose, if need be by armed force, the change of the Straits' regime in Russia's favour. But Russia did not give up and by the end of the nineteenth century its support of the liberation struggle of the Orthodox Slav nations stirred up anti-Turkish rebellions in the Ottoman Empire, disturbing the Balkan status quo.

British Russophobia, on the popular and political levels, encompassed the Russian government and nation. Russia was represented and imagined in Britain as the evil force looming over European civilization and progress. In his 1905 book Sir Donald Mackenzie Wallace reminded his readers that Russia's right to exist was an open question to the British: 'We need not attempt to decide whether it is better for humanity that Russia should exist as a nation'.[8] Press articles on Russia's despotic rule in the Caucasus and Poland and lurid descriptions of Siberian salt mines contributed to the repugnance with which literate Englishmen viewed the country. The Russians were regularly reminded about Britain's hostility by the press accounts of foreign policy debates in the House of Commons. MPs of both parties agreed on Britain's moral and civic right to support every move to dismember the Russian Empire.[9] Enemies of the imperial government, both intellectuals such as Prince Petr Kropotkin and terrorists such as Sergei Stepniak-Kravchinsky, found refuge and support in Britain.

The British picture of the Russian threat to the imperial interests was a mirror image of the gloomy picture that the Russian statesmen drew of Britain's inexorable enmity:

> Wherever our interests met, Russia had shown herself aggressive and ready to tread on our toes – it was the same story everywhere – in Manchuria, in China, Thibet, Afghanistan, Persia.[10]

---

8 D. Mackenzie Wallace, *Russia* (London, 1905), 2: 11.

9 Vladimir Degoev, *Bol'shaya igra na Kavkaze: Proshloe i budushee* (Moscow, 2003), 117–55.

10 The 5th Earl of Onslow, R.W.A. *Sixty Three Years: Diplomacy, the Great War and Politics, with Notes on Travel, Sports and Other Things* (London, 1944), 105.

The British concept of a safe world required weakening the Russian Empire and at the same time building up the military might of Russia's contiguous states (Afghanistan, Persia and the Ottoman Empire). By standing up to Russia in every part of the world and trying to uproot any influence Russia had beyond her borders, Britain was protecting British world supremacy from its most serious rival. Russia's expansion into Central Asia undermined Britain's prestige and authority among Muslims and Buddhists and threatened British interests in India. British imperial interests required control of the Persian Gulf ports and the Red Sea traffic and whatever Russian commerce gained in Persia was a loss to British commercial interests. Britain controlled the Suez Canal and Egypt but did not want to relinquish its influence over Constantinople and the Straits territory: if Russia succeeded in seizing control of the Bosporus, Britain would not be able to threaten the Russian Black Sea coastline and the Russian Caucasus and Russia and France could threaten Suez.

Everything that one of the rivals did could be interpreted as defensive or offensive, depending on the side from which it was seen. For example, having learned the hard lesson of the Crimean war when Russian troops could not be brought to the Crimea for lack of railroads, Russia protected her fringe territories by constructing roads, railways and telegraph lines but the British saw this as a threat because in this way Russia's military capacity increased.[11]

The British were concerned about the security of their worldwide colonial empire which alone supported their claim to world supremacy. Russian strategic and political thinking did not delineate clearly the metropolis from the borderlands of the empire. A threat to the Caucasus was a threat to Russia proper. Her push into Asia was inspired by the same motives which inspired the other powers' push into Africa but also by security considerations. Security was the priority, while status (reflected in the ability to gain advantages through diplomatic or political manoeuvring) was a close second. Russian foreign policy fended off emerging external political or military threats with scant resources and of necessity Russia's course was opportunistic. The goal of Russia's diplomacy was not a Russia-dominated globe or a Russia-dominated Europe, a dream too far removed from Russia's more pressing problems. The plundering of the Ottoman Empire on one side and of China on the other by European empires was a constant reminder to Russia's rulers of the need to be strong.

The Anglo-Russian antagonism increased as the distance which separated the territories under their control diminished. Periodic conflicts marked the stages of their colonial expansion, in which a move on one side would be matched by a move on the other. Every conflict was followed by an attempt at a peaceful compromise as both sides wanted to avoid a war.

---

11 Marina Soroka, 'Debating Russia's Choice between Great Britain and Germany: Count Benckendorff versus Count Lamsdorff, 1902–1906' in *The International History Review*, 32, 2 (2010): 2.

In the 1890s the Central Asian rivalry focused on the Pamirs where Russia claimed the western and eastern regions while Britain's advance resulted in the conquest or takeover of the mountainous principalities of north-western Hindustan. The two powers were only separated by the mountain chain and at once entered negotiations about frontier delimitation which were successfully completed in 1896. The hostility was strong but the desire to avoid a showdown prevailed. Periodically both sides declined the petitions of the local principalities or khanates to protect them against the other power. Russia refused to become involved in Baluchistan's attempt to resist British encroachment; Britain did not extend protection to the Khan of Khiva when he asked for it.[12]

Every Russian advance was matched by a British one, and vice versa, driving the two rivals to exhaustion. Colonel F.Younghusband's expedition to Lhassa in 1904 pushed the Russians to step up their pressure on the Chinese government to establish Chinese suzerainty over Tibet and Curzon's 'prancing' in the Persian Gulf had the same effect in Persia.[13] Russia and Britain each did all they could to prevent its rival from acquiring the dominant position in the regions adjacent to their borders and, as opportunities presented themselves, to continue expanding the sphere of their own influence. Still, Russia's rulers realized that further expansion in the Caucasus and Central Asia would make Russia's borders more vulnerable instead of more secure, and they accepted that in the 1880s it achieved its limits. A foothold on the Straits was the only remaining dream of Russian military strategists, but it was clearly out of bounds in the foreseeable future.[14]

The idea of an understanding periodically occurred either to one side or the other, but never simultaneously. Following the Berlin Congress of 1878, which contemporaries judged as Britain's great bloodless triumph over Russia, it turned out that in the changing European situation Disraeli's achievements did not put Britain that far ahead of its rival and in some cases were even counterproductive in the long run. Absorbed by his contest with Russia, Disraeli did not foresee the consequences of the rise of the German Empire. The Ottoman Empire, which paid for British support by giving up Cyprus and Egypt (Britain occupied it in 1882), retained a vindictive memory of these losses and Germany's advances were soon welcomed at Constantinople. Russia was recovering despite its difficulties and becoming more active in the Far East and Central Asia. The contest seemed endless and, to some statesmen, hopeless. As the balance of power in Europe shifted, statesmen realized that old rules did not apply to the new situation. The colonial issues and the Straits question still divided them, but now growing German involvement in both complicated the situation. Britain and Russia had a better chance of keeping what they had already acquired if they did not have to

12 L.N. Khariukov, *Anglo-russkoie sopernichestvo v Tsentral'noi Azii i ismailism* (Moscow, 1995), 31–2.

13 Russian foreign ministry, Instructions to A.N. Speyer, Russian minister in Teheran, in *Korennye interesy Rossii* (Moscow, 2004), 366.

14 Marina Soroka 'Debating Russia's Choice', 3.

share with Germany, and opposing Germany was easier if they joined forces. By the end of the 1880s the railroad construction boom was mostly over in Europe and European railway builders invaded the Near and Far East. The success of German entrepreneurs in obtaining concessions from the Ottoman Empire affected Russia and Britain commercially and strategically as German businesses began to move into Persia. Russians saw by the 1900s that the Anglo-Russian antagonism resulted in Germany gaining ground in Constantinople.[15] It reawakened the Eastern Question because the idea of the Straits under German control was equally unacceptable to both Britain and Russia.

There were signs of new thinking. Alexander III's foreign minister Nikolai Giers instructed the ambassador to Britain in 1883:

> British interests are mostly focused on Egypt and the Suez Canal. Ours are mostly in the Balkan Peninsula and the Straits, not because of ambition, but as a guarantee of our security and to advance our interests. This situation favours a rapprochement between the policies of the two countries.[16]

British and Russian diplomats posted in the parts of Asia where the rivalry was at its highest saw its costs and the potential for a settlement. Sir Robert Morier was the first British ambassador in Russia to suggest in 1884 an understanding with Russia in Asia and in Europe to maintain the Ottoman Empire and to share its inheritance when it collapsed. He believed that a long period of trading and cooperating with Russia and eventually joining Russian and Indian railways would overcome the British public hostility to Russia.[17] The Foreign Secretary, Lord Salisbury, rejected the suggestions because he hoped Russia would be pushed into bankruptcy and revolution by the strain of military expense into which Britain was driving her. [18] Morier reported on overtures from Giers in the autumn of 1886 about an understanding regarding the Ottoman Empire.[19] In 1887 Giers spoke to Morier of a general Anglo-Russian entente, because of Franco-German tensions which made it reasonable for the two powers opposed to changes of European status quo to draw together.[20] Salisbury replied that, on the contrary, British policy was identical to that of the central powers who were 'satisfied' while France and Russia were 'hungry'.[21] When in 1888 Salisbury thought of economic cooperation with Russia in Persia, it was not a change of heart. To

15 A.N. Svetchin to A.K. Benckendorff, 18.04/01.05.1903, BC2, box 14.

16 A.F. Meyendorff (ed.) *Correspondance diplomatique de M. de Staal (1884–1900)* (Paris, 1929), 1: 27.

17 Agatha Ramm, *Sir Robert Morier; envoy and ambassador in the age of imperialism. 1876–1893* (Oxford, 1973), 207.

18 Ibid., 209.

19 Ibid., 226.

20 Ibid., 247–9.

21 Ibid., 251.

him a settlement with Russia was a protracted truce marked by isolated cases of limited cooperation in specific issues of practical interest to Britain.[22] They would not subtract from the sum total of the incompatibility of British and Russian interests. This would be the position of the Russian foreign minister Vladimir N. Lamsdorff in the 1900s. Morier thought that a fundamental settlement with Russia was possible and a period of consistent cooperation would open the door to smoothing out the conflicts which then would be viewed not as manifestations of incompatibility, but as specific cases to be solved in order to maintain the general harmony, a position which the Russian and British ambassadors, Benckendorff and Nicolson, shared two decades later.

In October 1889 the British minister to Teheran, Sir Hugh Drummond-Wolff visited St Petersburg and was received by Alexander III. As soon the emperor heard the word 'cooperation' he formulated his terms, as something that he had given much thought: reciprocity in railroad concessions and in the use of waterways, but no partition of Persia.[23] Then a Russian force expelled Colonel Younghusband from the Pamirs and all thought of a rapprochement was postponed until a better moment. Still, in the last two decades of the nineteenth century, Russia and Britain signed seven diplomatic acts dealing with frontier delimitation, extradition of criminals and partition of spheres of interest in Central Asia and the Far East. They pointed to a tendency to reduce tensions even as the press on both sides was spoiling for a fight. At the time of the worst Anglo-Russian crisis in Penjdeh, in the spring of 1885, a Russian diplomat wrote to a colleague: '… a war on account of Afghanistan would be an unpardonable mistake considering our domestic and financial state'.[24]

In 1896–97, during the Near Eastern crisis, and in the following years Russia was alarmed by the possibility of the appearance of the British navy in the Straits. Repeated studies of Russian military capacities available for seizing the Bosporus, demonstrated again that they were insufficient.[25] The status quo was all that Russia could hope for. The British government at the same time accepted the impossibility for the British navy of stopping Russia from seizing the Straits if she tried.[26]

Outsiders tend to see things earlier than the parties involved, so in 1889 a French diplomat Count Chaudordy remarked that in pursuit of industrial and economic goals the British had allowed Germany to defeat their only worthwhile potential

22 Ibid., 330.

23 Sir H. Drummond Wolff to Marquess Salisbury, 14.10.1889, BC2, box 15.

24 S.S. Tatishchev to I.A. Zinoviev, 04/17.04.1885, GARF, f.597, op.1, ed.hr 727, l.1.

25 V.M. Hevrolina and E.A. Chirkova, Prolivy vo vneshnei politike Rossii v 80–90 gg.XIX v., *Rossi'ia i tchernomorskiie prolivy (XVIII–XIX stoleti'ia)* (Moscow, 1999), 243.

26 Keith M. Wilson, 'Constantinople and Cairo: Lord Salisbury and the Partition of the Ottoman Empire 1886–97', in *Empire and Continent: Studies in British Foreign Policy from the 1880 to the First World War* (London, 1987), 1–30.

ally, France and their position in Europe became weakened,[27] while Russia lost her dominant role in her traditional political partnership with Prussia[28] and would not easily adapt to her new role as a follower. A foreign policy shift was imminent. Chaudordy listed Russia's foreign liabilities: Turkey, Persia, Central Asia and Poland. Neither France nor Britain had interests in Turkey any more. France had only commercial interests in Asia and Persia. As for Poland, French and British sympathy would remain confined to words. France and Russia had reached an unspoken understanding and if Russia and Britain settled their proverbial rivalry in Central Asia, they would 'give to Europe the tranquility which she is lacking'.[29] The new situation in Europe dictated to Britain and Russia the need to put their imperial ambitions aside for the sake of higher interests.

Ivan A. Zinoviev, the head of the Asiatic Department of the foreign ministry, urged the minister in 1891 to concentrate all efforts on reaching an agreement with London, as soon as Russia had strengthened her position in Central Asia by building railroads and accumulating resources.[30] In 1897 Baron Roman R. Rosen, Russian minister in Japan, called the minister's attention to the danger created by Russia's actions after the Peace of Shimonseki and suggested that only an entente with Britain could help Russia protect her interests in the Far East; but he did not insist on it, knowing that prejudice was too strong.[31]

After the expiry of the Russo-German Reinsurance Treaty and Germany's refusal to renew it, events evolved as Count Chaudordy had foreseen. The Straits issue and antagonism with Russia began to lose their predominance in British political thinking at the same time as Germany's growing might became a concern.[32] A Russian rapprochement with France in 1892 changed the situation in Europe not only for Berlin but also for Britain where it created fears that the new grouping would make difficulties for the empire in the Far East (France pushing towards the Bay of Bengal), in Egypt, in Central Asia and also make the control of the Straits practically out of reach for the British navy owing to the presence of the French navy in the Mediterranean. But the French had no intention of allowing the situation to develop; in 1896 and again in 1899 the French government refused to support Russia in pressing the Sultan to keep the British out of the Straits.[33]

In 1894–95 Anglo-Russian rivalry found another venue when Russia began the construction of the Trans-Siberian railway, aiming at expansion into Manchuria and Korea. Britain and France followed suit and encroached on Chinese territory

27 Cte. Jean Baptiste Alexandre Damaze de Chaudordy, *La France en 1889* (Paris, 1889), 162.

28 Ibid., 182.

29 Ibid., 240.

30 V.N. Lamsdorff, *Dnevnik 1891–1892* (Minsk, 2003), 124.

31 R.R. Rosen to A.K. Benckendorff. 11/24.12.1905. BC2, box 14.

32 V.N. Lamsdorff, *Dnevnik 1894–1896* (Moscow, 1991), 333–5.

33 Charles Zorgbibe, *Delcassé: Le grand ministre des Affaires Etrangères de la IIIe République* (Paris, 2001), 134–7.

from their previously acquired possessions in India and South-East Asia. When Japan joined them, invading China, and later Germany and the US also entered the scramble, each of the contenders hoped to reap the fruits of the others' disputes. Lord Rosebery had a dream of neutralizing Russia's threat to India by dividing Russia and France: he took a strong position with France while being conciliatory to Russia.[34] This ruse failed when Britain refused to support Russia's opposition to Japanese expansion in China and later violated the Pamirs Treaty.[35]

After a quarter of a century of peace the Russian government and its contenders forgot that Russia was weak, while the Boer war shocked European governments as much as it did the British. Suddenly Russia seemed the up-and-coming power and Paul Cambon, a prominent French diplomat, believed in 1900 that France had been extremely clever in getting the Russian alliance because Britain was on the decline: India was escaping from British control and Britain 'knows that before the end of the new century Russia will establish her dominion there; hence her [British] haste in Africa'.[36]

On the Russian side the desirability of an Anglo-Russian detente increased because the strain of rivalry with Britain might push Russia into a formal alliance with France,[37] a step which the Russian government, unless menaced, was averse to make. After Salisbury returned to office in 1895 an Anglo-German coalition, favoured by Joseph Chamberlain, seemed to St Petersburg a frightening possibility[38] which also could only be averted by a Russian rapprochement with Britain.

In the process of colonial expansion, old continental rivalries were combining with new ones, creating premises for often unexpected and mostly short-lived combinations.[39] An Anglo-German, a Franco-Russo-German and even an Anglo-Russian Far Eastern settlement of the 1890s were limited to a specific short-term goal (resisting the other great powers' encroachments) and fell apart when one of the sides attempted to extend it.

An Anglo-Russian settlement increasingly seemed the solution to existing problems. After Queen Victoria's death and Salisbury's retirement in 1901 and 1902 respectively, the French expected that British foreign policy was about to change, since the three men who, the French believed, were in charge of it, Edward VII, Joseph Chamberlain and Lord Lansdowne, wanted a dialogue with France.

34 Gordon Martel, *Imperial Diplomacy: Rosebery and the Failure of Foreign Policy* (Kingston, Ontario, 1986), 257–61.

35 Ibid., 240, 247.

36 Paul Cambon to Jules Cambon, 19.03.1900, *Correspondance 1870–1924* (Paris, 1940), 2: 40.

37 V.N. Lamsdorff, *Dnevnik 1891–1892*, 180.

38 V.N. Lamsdorff, *Dnevnik 1891–1892*, 218.

39 Irina S. Rybachonok, 'Russia's National Interests through the Eyes of Russian Statesmen, Diplomats and Military in Late Nineteenth and Early Twentieth Century', in *Geopoliticheskie factory vo vneshnei politike Rossii: Vtora'ia polovina XVI–nachalo XX veka* (Moscow, 2007), 268.

The French ascribed to these three men an idea of a triple Franco-Russo-British (or English, as they said in those times) entente.[40]

Russia's acquisitions in Manchuria and Korea, after the beginning of the construction of the Trans-Siberian railway, threatened Britain's dominant position in China[41] and after the Boxer rising of 1900, Salisbury's policy of free hand ceased to satisfy his younger colleagues.[42] Admiral Sir John Fisher, a member of the king's intimate circle, summarized his view of Russia in a letter to a journalist known for his pro-Russian sympathies:

> … Russia does not affect our trade and commerce in any degree whatever, and the Afghan bogey has become ludicrous, simply because we can overrun the country far sooner than Russia can. I do sincerely hope you may have time to give thought and consideration to this very big question; and … you want some great political authority like Sir C. Dilke (or Sir E. Grey failing him) to godfather the scheme.[43]

In 1903–4 the French foreign minister Théophile Delcassé took it for a fact that in settling with France the British also hoped to neutralize Russia's threat, and he maintained the pressure on the British during the Anglo-French rapprochement, never asking the Russians to abandon their decision to build the Orenburg–Tashkent railway line which alarmed the Indian government.[44] He saw the settlement with Britain as part of his plan to 'lean simultaneously on Russia and England against Germany!'.[45] To the rational French, the main impediment to an Anglo-Russian rapprochement in 1902 was psychological: it was impossible to improve relations between two powers 'each of which was convinced that the other was a liar and a thief'.[46]

Even so, Edward VII's personal attentions to Nicholas II somewhat improved the latter's attitude towards Britain. In Russia, the powerful finance minister Sergei Witte welcomed the favourable comments on an Anglo-Russian rapprochement in the British press and hoped that economic cooperation with Britain would lead to a political rapprochement.[47] With Russian finance in mind, when he referred to

---

40 Zorgbibe, 176.

41 T.G. Otte, 'The Boxer Uprising and British Foreign Policy: The End of Isolation' in *The Boxers, China and the World* (eds R. Bickers and R.G. Tiedemann) (New York, 2007), 163.

42 Ibid.,170.

43 Fisher to Arnold White, 06.08.1902, *Fear God and Dread Nought: The Correspondence of Admiral of the Fleet Lord Fisher of Kilverstone* (London, 1952), 1: 259–62.

44 Zorgbibe, 183.

45 Ibid., 184.

46 Spring Rice to Bertie, 23.11.1902, FO 800/176, 153–9.

47 S. Yu. Witte to S.S. Tatishchev, 24.12.1898/06.01.1899, GARF, f.597, op.1, ed.hr.107, l.5 ob.

the rivalry between the two empires, he said bluntly: 'Belligerence will hurt the pocket'.[48] St John Brodrick, the secretary of state for India in 1903–5 echoed the idea, when he wrote: 'India is calling out loudly for a rest'.[49] Russia and Britain had repeatedly tried, each in its own way, to reach an understanding with Germany, the dominant power in Europe in the 1890s, and failed to obtain the guarantees they wanted. The view at the Foreign Office was that a German alliance was unnecessary since in case of a war with France and Russia, Germany would come to Britain's aid in order to protect the balance of power in Europe.[50]

By the 1900s, after so many aborted initiatives and tentative *sondages*, the areas of Anglo-Russian friction, the sources of mutual dissatisfaction and therefore, the prizes to be obtained by a settlement, had become obvious to some political observers in France, Britain and even Russia. But Count Vladimir N. Lamsdorff, the foreign minister from 1900 to 1906, like Lord Salisbury earlier, did not believe that Britain and Russia could achieve more than limited cooperation.[51] Russia therefore did not want an entente with Britain, while British diplomats considered that a specific agreement with Russia would not be a reliable enough guarantee.[52] The Conservative Foreign Secretary, Lord Lansdowne, attempted a rapprochement with Russia as late as October 1901 but met with no success.[53] Russia's confidence gave no grounds for Britain to hope for a beneficial settlement.[54]

48 S. Yu. Witte to S.S. Tatishchev, 19.10/01.11.1898, GARF, f.597, op.1, ed.hr.107, l.20–21 ob.

49 St. John Brodrick to Viscount Cranley, 31.08.1905, OP, G 173/24/9.

50 Francis Bertie, *Memorandum*, 9.11.1901, BD, 2: 73–6.

51 V.N. Lamsdorff to P.A. Kapnist, 22.01/04.02.1904, A[rkniv] V[neshnei] P[olitiki] R[ossiiskoi] I[mperii], f. 151, op.482, ed.hr. 63, ll. 18–22 ob. Courtesy of Dr Irina Rybachonok.

52 Spring Rice to Louis Mallet, 29.10.1903, FO 800/140, 183–9.

53 Lansdowne to Knollys, 25.07.1902, RA VIC/ADDC 7/2/Q.

54 Hardinge of Penshurst, *Old Diplomacy*, 84.

Chapter 2
Old Diplomacy *à la Russe*, 1868–1902

The Riga Benckendorff family, says *Almanach de Gotha*, were of bourgeois Swedish origin and became ennobled in the sixteenth century. They never used the German nobility's prefix 'von' which some historians later attached to the Russian ambassador's name by association with the German family the von Benckendorff-Hindenburgs, to which the Petersburg courtiers had no ties.[1] A Benckendorff became an officer in Peter I's army and a member of the Russian service nobility. The family rose at the imperial court at the end of the eighteenth century. Grand Duchess Maria, the daughter-in-law to Catherine II, was greatly attached to her maid of honour, Juliana Schilling von Kanstadt, who had come with her to Russia from her native Würtemberg. For political and domestic reasons Catherine II wanted Fraulein Schilling von Kanstadt to return to Germany. The young grand duchess countered by marrying off her favourite to an officer from the grand duke's retinue, Christoph (Khristofor Ivanovich) Benckendorff. Juliana Schilling remained in Russia, and her husband became a general. When Maria became empress-consort (1796–1801) the Benckendorff couple remained close to her, and their children's fortunes were made.[2] Even the Russian names of their sons (they also had baptismal Germanic names), Aleksandr and Konstantin, were also those of the sons of the imperial couple, pointing to the Benckendorffs' ties to the Romanovs. One of their daughters married General Shevich; their descendant was Russia's ambassador to Vienna in the 1890s; another married Prince von Lieven, Russia's ambassador to Britain, and became known as a confidante of British and French statesmen and an agent of the Russian government.

After their mother's early death, Dowager Empress Maria took the Benckendorff brothers under her protection. They were educated at a French Jesuit college in St Petersburg, entered the army and had honourable military careers during the Napoleonic wars. Aleksandr and Konstantin, owed their fortune and careers entirely to the Russian monarchs. Their father joined the Baltic landowning nobility when Paul I sent him to serve in Estonia and gave him an estate there. Aleksandr Benckendorff inherited the estate, Fall, on the Baltic coast. But Konstantin's estate, Sosnovka, also a gift from Paul I, was in the heart of Russia.

Aleksandr Khristoforovich (1783–1844), the best known of the Benckendorffs, was a personal friend to the most hated Russian emperor, Nicholas I. As the founder of the Russian political police (The Third Section and the Gendarme

---

1 Prince von Bülow, *Memoirs 1903–1909* (London, 1931–1932), 2: 38.

2 P. Dolgorukov, *Peterburgskie ocherki: Pamflety emigranta, 1860–1867* (Moscow, 1992), 258.

Corps) he achieved a unique notoriety in Russian history. Lately, the rehabilitation of Nicholas I has led to a re-examination of the Chief of Gendarmes' reputation and his first biography presents him as a hero of the Napoleonic wars and a competent civil servant. Nicholas I rewarded Aleksandr Benckendorff's services with the title of count. (After his death, the title passed to the remaining male Benckendorff, his nephew.) His daughters' marriages linked the Benckendorffs to the Austro-Hungarian and Italian aristocracy as well as the oldest Russian nobility.

Russian Europeans

Konstantin Khristoforovich Benckendorff, who married the daughter of a Russian diplomat Nathalie Alopeus, died early. His son, Konstantin, the second Count Benckendorff was born in Berlin in 1817 where his father was serving as a military agent. After a period in the Russian Caucasian army he joined the diplomatic service, serving at German courts and married Princess Louise von Croy-Dülmen. The Catholic von Croys were the German branch of an ancient French family de Croy which also had branches in Austria, Hungary, Bohemia and Belgium.[3] Konstantin Benckendorff died in 1858. His four children – Aleksandr, Pavel, Nathalie and Olga – were brought up by their mother as Catholics, mostly in France, though she regularly returned to Russia to attend to the estate and maintained the connection to the Court.

Nathalie and Olga Benckendorff severed their tenuous ties to Russia after they married a German and an Italian nobleman respectively, but Aleksandr Konstantinovich Benckendorff (1849–1916) and his brother Pavel Konstantinovich (1853–1921) settled in Russia when they reached the age of service. Their background and family tradition determined their allegiance, without causing a conflict with their foreign upbringing. Aleksandr Benckendorff, whose career took him away from Russia for most of his life, nevertheless considered himself a Tambov landowner and the estate of Sosnovka, which he owned jointly with his brother, his home.

Pavel K. Benckendorff became a guards officer and under Nicholas II rose to the position of court marshal. He married Princess Maria Dolgorouky, a close friend of the Dowager Empress Maria Feodorovna. Aleksandr Benckendorff married Countess Sofia Petrovna Shuvalova. One of her sisters was married to Alexander III's grand master of ceremonies, and another to a grandson of Catherine II. The Shuvalov family also had European relatives: the Austrian Princes von Dietrichstein and, more unusually, the English Earls of Pembroke.

Every one of the Benckendorff alliances in the nineteenth century helped this Baltic family to rise in Russian high society and brought with it a plethora

3 The Russian ambassador to London was related to the Austro-Hungarian ambassador and a first cousin to the German ambassador.

of connections outside Russia. The connections were documented, remembered and kept alive by regular correspondence and meetings. They established the Benckendorffs' position in the hierarchy of European nobility and made them welcome in any European capital. Letters which Aleksandr Benckendorff received and answered during the Great War came not only from France, Belgium and Italy, but also from the Triple Alliance enemies. The Borgheses, Rohans, von Croys, Salm-Salms, Hatzfeldts and Metternichs asked 'Cher Sacha' or 'Liebe Vetter' to see to the well-being of French and Belgian relatives captured by the Germans and German or Austrian nephews or cousins taken prisoner by the Russians. The Benckendorffs continued to carry out these requests after their own son, a Russian officer, was killed in combat. The 'old diplomacy' and European nobility deliberately kept personal honour and ties of affection separate from political or national considerations.

Aleksandr Konstantinovich Benckendorff was 19 years old in 1868 when he entered the foreign ministry under Prince Aleksandr Gorchakov (1856–82). Those who wanted to join the ministry had to have a university education (usually in languages or in law) and speak and write Russian and French. Knowledge of Latin, German, English or Oriental languages was a bonus. The requirements also included a general knowledge of diplomatic history, international and maritime law and the history of international treaties and political economy related to foreign trade and state economy as well as statistics. Those who were accepted signed an oath of allegiance to the emperor and a statement that they did not belong to a secret society. The examination was modified in 1875 because the senior officials realized that the content of the diplomats' work had changed, but nepotism and personal favour still ruled in the choice of suitable candidates, as well in their subsequent postings. A contemporary ironically compared the pattern of diplomats' appointments to those of Orthodox priests, who often took 'livings' over from their retired fathers. A certain diplomatic dynasty monopolized the posts at the Russian embassy in Spain.[4] In Benckendorff's case, even the formal requirement of a university degree was waived: he had been educated at home.[5] A disgruntled contemporary wrote about the successful applicants for Russian foreign service in Benckendorff's youth:

> The requirements for joining the blessed institution were few. The examination was more than easy: knowledge of languages, especially French, easy wit, elegant and polished manners. They could be – and often were – absolute ignoramuses, illiterate in Russian, ignorant and uninterested in anything relating to Russia, and none of this was an impediment. On the contrary, the less they resembled Russians, the better ...[6]

4 N.S. Leskov to A.S. Suvorin, 08/20.10.1886, No 54. Available at: http://az.lib.ru/L/leskow_n_s/.

5 A.K. Benckendorff's service record, AVPRI, f.159, op.464, d.295a, ll.1–11 ob.

6 *Memuary grafa S.D. Sheremeteva* (Moscow: INDRIK, 2001), 81.

The last reproach seems aimed at Benckendorff who grew up in France but it confirms that he was not an exception among his colleagues. Every mention of Benckendorff by Russian memoirists includes a reference to the ambassador's ignorance of Russian, the implication being that he was entirely alien to everything Russian. It was a painful issue for the Russians and it remains a point of debate among historians to this day: did a 'Germanic elite' rule over the great Russia? There is no universally accepted criterion for judging anyone's national identity: should it be by the last name, by the amount of Russian blood in the veins, by religion, by the maternal language, by the place of birth or by the individual's declared allegiance? A French historian judged by a list of the officials' last names that 57 per cent of the foreign ministry's officials were of Germanic origin, and juxtaposed it to the proportion of Germans in the Russian population (1.4 per cent).[7] But statistical approach becomes misleading when it places fervent Russian Orthodox patriots Vladimir Lamsdorff and Nikolay Hartwig among 'the German element'. Aleksandr Benckendorff, a Catholic with not a drop of Russian blood in his veins, always referred to himself as a Russian. Now, it must also be pointed out that there were many different ways of being Russian.

To the repeated reproaches from the ministry that all despatches from the London embassy were in French, the ambassador's wife expressed her indignant incomprehension. She vehemently defended her husband's embassy from the recurrent accusation of being a place where ethnic Russian diplomats were unwelcome. She argued that one of the embassy secretaries, although Polish, had been brought up and educated in Russia, and the other, a Greek, was not only educated in Russia, but of Orthodox faith. As far as she was concerned, they were Russian.[8] This view, common in Russian upper class, periodically came under attack from the chauvinist press.

Benckendorff was not the only one at the ministry whose first language was French: the Russian minister in Greece, Elim P. Demidov, felt profoundly hurt when, during the First World War the government demanded from its officials to write their despatches in Russian. His reaction in a private (French) letter to the foreign minister was dramatic:

> Your telegram telling me to use only Russian in official correspondence has raised a storm in my heart … What happened? Why, after so many years of 'tacit consent'… should suddenly an impediment be set to the free flow of my thought?[9]

If there is truth in the assumptions of Benckendorff's non-Russianness, it is because the earliest influences leave the deepest imprint on a personality. Brought up as a Catholic by a German mother in France, Benckendorff must have felt

7 Marie Eve Rakosin, *Les diplomates russes entre 1890 et 1914: Perception identitaire, activité professionelle et reflexions politiques PhD* (Paris, 2003), 185.

8 S.P. Benckendorff to A.K. Benckendorff, 29.03/11.04.1906, BC2, box 21.

9 E. Demidov to S.D. Sazonov, 12/25.08.1915, AVPRI, F.340, op.812, d.47, ll.37–8.

strong cultural affinity to Western Europe. As for Benckendorff's Russian, even if not fluent, it sufficed for him to read the press, his correspondence[10] and the ministerial documents. French was his language of choice for conversation and official and personal letters; he wrote to British acquaintances in English. But he made a point of writing to his children in Russian until they grew up and they continued writing to him in Russian as adults. He also sent his sons to St Petersburg exclusive military schools when they were in their teens, and their stays abroad were no more than sporadic vacations. He was determined to spare them his own lot of growing up as an expatriate.

The Benckendorffs' daughter's English fiancé wrote to the count: 'I can only hope that you are not very disappointed that Nathalie has married out of Russia',[11] and, indeed, giving the news of his daughter's engagement, Benckendorff wrote: 'She is marrying an Englishman, it is the only negative side' and added that it made Nathalie hesitate for a long time. He concluded:

> I always thought it quite probable – considering the conditions of our life – but I regret it. It is not that I am against the English, on the contrary. But I hoped she would settle in Russia.[12]

The Imperial Foreign Ministry

When the young Benckendorff joined the ministry (see Fig. 2.1), it consisted of the Chancellery responsible for political correspondence, and three departments. The Asiatic Department dealt with the political affairs of the Orient. The Internal Department dealt with matters related to foreign subjects on Russian territory and Russian subjects abroad, treaties, consular, border, trade and immigration issues. The Staff and Household Department looked after the personnel of the ministry, administered the property of the Russian state abroad, ministerial finance and the budget. The Chancellery was the closest to the minister because only its employees had diplomatic ranks; the others were ordinary bureaucrats.

Formally, there was a rigorous internal hierarchy: the clerk reported to his office manager, the office manager to his departmental director; the departmental director to the minister. But the minister consulted only a chosen adviser or two. In the last five years of Nikolai Karlovich Giers' ministry (1882–94), Count Vladimir N. Lamsdorff became practically the only adviser to the minister, bypassing the deputy minister. When Giers died soon after his master, Alexander III, Lamsdorff was amazed to find himself the only man in the whole ministry and even the

10 K.A. Benckendorff to A.K. Benckendorff, 26.6/09.7.1903, GARF, 1126, op.1, ed.hr.26, ll.75–8 ob.

11 Jasper Ridley to A.K. Benckendorff, 02.05.1910, BC2, box 14.

12 A.K. Benckendorff to Empress Maria Feodorovna, 10/23.11.1910, GARF, f.642, op.1, ed.hr.918, ll.19–22.

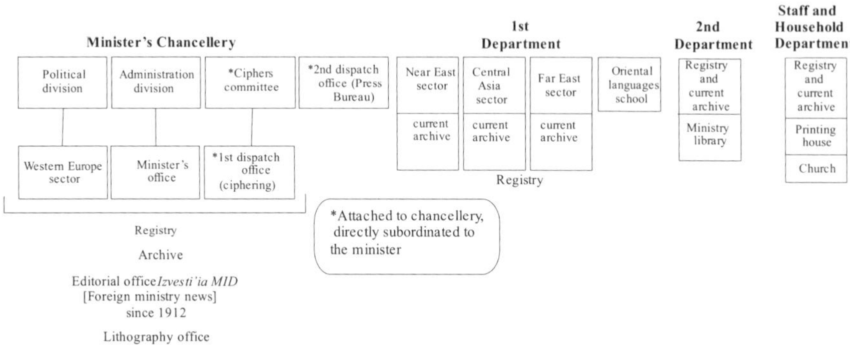

Fig. 2.1 Russian Imperial Foreign Ministry: The Structure

whole government who knew the whereabouts of all the secret papers and held all the information relating to the foreign policy of the previous reign.[13] Lamsdorff wrote and edited most of documents issuing from the ministry, including the correspondence with other ministries. Only specific issues of the Asiatic policy remained outside of his domain.

This illustrates the problem for modern historians and especially political scientists who deduce from the ideal schemes of institutional or departmental line of command a comfortingly rational picture of how the Russian imperial government arrived at and implemented its decisions. In reality the decision-making was muddled by the lack of a strictly followed procedure within a ministry and of coordination between ministries. The contribution or impact of each institution depended more on the personality of the minister than the functions attributed to it. The apparent extreme centralization of the foreign ministry apparatus did not prevent confidential information being leaked regularly by the minister's closest assistants to their subordinates and friends. Gossip was rampant and nothing remained secret, as diplomats' private correspondence amply testifies. Benckendorff's wife in the 1900s regularly summoned the timid deputy minister, Prince Valerian Obolensky, to her house to demand explanations of the state of Russo-Japanese negotiations or Russia's position in the Algeciras conference – and she got them.[14]

After the 1897 reform the Chancellery maintained all political correspondence with European, Asian, American and African states. The Internal Department became 'the Second Department'. The Asiatic Department became 'the First Department' and political affairs were partly removed from its mandate. But the reform failed to separate clearly the functions of the Chancellery and the First Department and in the 1900s there was much interdepartmental fighting about who had the final say in the matters concerning the great power relations in the Far and Near East, the more so because in these years the former 'Asiatic Department'

13 *Ministerska'ia sistema v Rossiiskoi imperii* (ed. D.I. Raskin) (Moscow, 2007), 302.
14 S.P. Benckendorff to A.K. Benckendorff, 1903–1907, BC2, box 21.

became busier and therefore more influential. All this worked against the foreign minister in 1903–4 when he attempted to devise a coordinated and consistent political course to counter the influence of the court clique which promoted an aggressive policy in the Far East. It also led to mutual accusations of intrigues and incompetence between the minister and the London embassy on one side and the First Department on the other during the Anglo-Russian negotiations in 1906–7.

Like the military, the naval and the imperial household administration, the foreign ministry was under the emperor's direct control. Hence its second name, 'His Imperial Majesty's Chancery of Foreign Affairs'. Only after 1906 did the State Council begin to exercise the right of discussing foreign policy which it had formally had for a century.[15] The foreign ministry's pivotal role in planning, adopting and implementing the most important foreign policy decisions had remained unchanged since its formation in 1802, but in the second half of the nineteenth century new institutions began to claim part in decision making: the military, the finance ministry and, in the late imperial period, the emperor's favourites.

For all its incompleteness, the transformation of the autocracy into a constitutional monarchy in 1905 brought about changes in the administration of foreign policy. The Duma, the reformed State Council, the United Government and the freedom of press brought into being new pressure groups and complicated the process of coordinating foreign policy. The Fundamental Law of 1906 confirmed and reinforced the emperor's sole authority in the sphere of foreign relations, but caveats in Article 13 of the Fundamental Law allowed for a degree of governmental influence over the foreign ministry.

Lamsdorff's successor A.P. Iswolsky (1906–10) wanted to preserve the ministry's unique position of independence within the government; but, when he acted rashly without informing the government in September 1908 and provoked the Bosnian crisis, the prime minister, Petr A. Stolypin, got Nicholas II's authorization for the council of ministers to control the ministry. Nicholas II, discouraged by a series of failures in his personal diplomacy, somewhat distanced himself from foreign policy. It became subject to discussions by the council of ministers and ministerial conferences. Under Sergei Dmitrievich Sazonov (1911–16) the ministry became, in fact, subordinated to the chairman of the council of ministers.[16] By 1914 the foreign ministry recovered its autonomy within the government because the new chairman of the council of ministers, Ivan L. Goremykin, with the emperor's approval tried to bring foreign policy back under the monarch's prerogative. When in 1915 Nicholas became commander-in-chief, his headquarters, the *Stavka*, practically became a skeleton government and 'the Emperor's Own Chancellery' duplicated the foreign ministry's functions. Between them they implemented foreign policy outside governmental control.[17]

15 *Ministerska'ia sistema*, 291–312.

16 Ibid., 307–8.

17 Ibid., 310.

As stipulated by the Vienna Reglament of 1815, Russia had four categories of diplomatic representatives: ambassadors to the great powers,[18] ministers and ministers plenipotentiary, chargés d'affaires and resident ministers who ranked between ministers and chargés d'affaires. Russia's extraordinary and plenipotentiary ambassadors were the emperor's personal envoys with the right of direct access to the heads of foreign states. The ambassador's rank was equivalent to ministerial; in the Table of Ranks of the Russian Empire it was in the highest class (chancellor) and the salary of an ambassador was double or triple that of the foreign minister. In 1900 the foreign minister drew a salary of 30,000 roubles, including the expenses for representation. A Russian ambassador's salary was 75–85,000 roubles, the highest in Europe. All of the above explains why Witte asked Nicholas II to appoint him ambassador after he had been forced to resign as head of the government in 1906. To Nicholas II's question: 'Will it not embarrass you that the foreign minister will be much younger than you?', he replied that '… ambassadors are not subordinated to the foreign minister, they are directly responsible to Your Majesty'.[19] This situation affected the discipline and cohesion of Russian diplomacy, especially when an ambassador was as self-confident as Benckendorff.

Formally, the role of Russian diplomatic legations was to supply information and to implement the decisions made in St Petersburg. In theory, St Petersburg expected and received absolute compliance from its envoys.[20] Tradition also has it that only the most respected veteran ambassadors ventured to express their opinions to their St Petersburg chiefs. But archival documents show that under Nicholas II Russian diplomatic agents freely offered opinions to the ministers in their confidential letters and 'absolute compliance' was an ideal, no more.

Russian diplomats of the late nineteenth century formed their ideas under the influence of a largely westernized upbringing and education, the general mood in Russian high society which staffed the foreign ministry and the peculiar atmosphere of this institution. A contemporary spoke of three rival political factions in Petersburg high society beginning in the 1860s: 'the cosmopolitan bureaucratic faction', the Slavophiles and 'the Russian faction'.[21] After the Crimean war the so-called 'cosmopolitan-bureaucratic' group, who shared the Vienna Congress and Holy Alliance ideas, was temporarily in abeyance. The Slavophile faction then acquired a certain ascendance, though it never found many partisans among the Russian nobility, and even fewer in the foreign ministry. The West was hostile to it because the doctrine insisted on religious and ethnic affinity between Russia and other Slav nations and, by extension, propounded the idea of a great Slav federation or empire. The importance given to it by Western sources reflects Western apprehensions rather than the scope of their influence in Russia. The 'Pan-Slavs' were popular in Russian

---

18 Austria-Hungary, Great Britain, France, Germany, Italy, Russia and, in the twentieth century, the US.

19 S. Yu. Witte, *Vospominani'ia* (Tallinn, 1994), 3: 329.

20 *Ministerska'ia sistema v Rossiiskoi imperii*, 301.

21 *Memuary grafa S.D. Sheremeteva* (Moscow, 2001), 297.

intelligentsia circles (small and with little political weight) and only during the 1870s were they heard by the government because their dreams temporarily coincided with the interests of imperial foreign policy. Pan-Slavism was no more a political program in Russia than Polish independence was in France and Britain.

The 'Russian' faction did not believe in mixing sentimental, religious or nationalist issues with politics. It was equally sceptical of the European concert's benefits for Russia and of the selfless love of the lesser Slav brothers for Russia. At the foreign ministry the traditional 'concert of Europe' and 'balance of powers' ideas usually prevailed over specific circumstances because they were most readily associated with the maintenance of peace. As for the general principles to which most Russian diplomats adhered, they were the same as elsewhere in European chancelleries: only the great powers' interests counted and the lesser players, in and out of Europe, were destined to be their political pawns. The foreign ministry regarded itself as the voice of reason in Russia. One of Benckendorff's subordinates put it in a letter to his chief: 'I am absolutely convinced that if our ministry were more listened to we would have nothing to fear in the future'.[22] They had a strong belief in the international community of diplomats, in its skill and its authority, and in its professional code based, when all was said and done, on the rejection of impulsive and violent policies in favour of peace and cooperation. They certainly believed that '… diplomacy is a dialogue among people assigned to the job – the diplomats'.[23]

Posted abroad, Russian diplomats mostly relied on the Western press for news because the Russian press prior to 1905 was under censorship and its coverage of the Russian domestic situation was not reliable, though that of the foreign news was usually tolerably open. This, coupled with the fact that they spent their lives outside Russia, meant that Russian diplomats' ideas were coloured by the western worldview. They also learned some news through the correspondence with their colleagues and family back in Russia. This rather detached attitude to Russian internal events in many Russian envoys reflected and reinforced the tradition, noticed by foreign observers: in the Russian Empire foreign policy course had little or nothing to do with domestic circumstances.[24] Russian diplomats exchanged their ideas openly, notwithstanding the difference in the official ranks. All the officials of the ministry belonged to the noble class, either by birth or by service, and the subordination required in formal dealings coexisted with a concept of social equality and a traditional corporate spirit. Such an atmosphere allowed for an outspoken and friendly dialogue between subordinates and their chiefs, as in Count Benckendorff's correspondence with his ministers and his subordinates. Besides, the ambassador picked the embassy staff from diplomats with congenial ideas, so it is not surprising that the correspondence between him and his secretaries was so frank.

---

22 S.A. Poklevsky to A.K. Benckendorff, 27/08/9.09.1904, BC2, box 14.

23 Mai'ia K. Davis Cross, *The European Diplomatic Corps: Diplomats and International Cooperation from Westphalia to Maastricht* (Basingstoke, 2007), 3.

24 Bompard to Bourgeois, 31.05.1906, DDF, X: 128–30.

The tradition of leaving a diplomat in the same European country for most of his career, which was specifically avoided by the Foreign Office for fear of diplomatic representatives 'going native', was common in the Russian diplomatic service, partly because of the nepotism and partly because of the commonly acknowledged scarcity of qualified personnel.[25] Russian diplomats often fell under the spell of western cultures. Without being entirely 'Germanized' or 'Frenchified' or 'Anglicized' as their detractors believed, they ceased to see the world in the same way as their countrymen in Russia. They stood on the unsteady middle ground between the clashing cultures and political interests, seeing both sides and receiving blows from both. One of these wrote: 'The king [Edward VII] told me that in London I had a reputation as an Anglophobe … I told the king that in Russia I was considered Anglophile'.[26] Russians were not the only ones who criticized their diplomats for being 'foreign', it was the widespread politico-tabloid accusation aimed at them throughout the nineteenth century, whenever a state suffered what it saw as a humiliating defeat. This reputation of 'foreignness' was the inevitable result of exercising continued contact with other diplomats, developing a professional network and sharing common professional standards. Their manners and knowledge of foreign languages, as well as their professional inclination to look for common ground rather than defy and challenge their foreign counterparts,[27] made them a group both envied and admired.

Not unexpectedly a book about Russian Freemasonry lists many diplomats, with Benckendorff's subordinates (Elim Demidov, Stanislav Poklevsky-Koziell and Konstantin Nabokov),[28] relatives (the Bobrinsky family) and colleagues prominent among them. Their outlook made them ideally suited to an international organization with a supra-national doctrine and the fact that in joining it they violated their oath of allegiance did not cause them undue concern.

Looking back from the perspective of the 1950s, a former Benckendorff's subordinate thought that a long stay abroad incapacitated his colleagues for 'any serious role' in their own country. According to him the Russian upper classes lived in the twentieth century while the majority of the Russian people remained in the fifteenth or sixteenth, 'so that a diplomat who abroad might be considered clever and charming would be taken seriously by hardly anyone upon his return to Russia'.[29] He placed Count Benckendoff in this category of diplomats whose clear vision and advanced ideas were not understood by their countrymen. To say that the Russian nation and its diplomatic agents lived in different centuries was to bring up the eternal issue of the cultural distance between Russia and Europe and the effects of westernization on Russians. This memoirist confirms the difficulty of harmonizing the world views of those who saw Russia and Russia's national

25 Prince von Bülow, *Memoirs 1903–1909* (London, 1931–1932), 2: 38.
26 P. Lessar to A.K. Benckendorff, 28.08/09.09.1903, BC2, box 13.
27 Mai'ia K. Davis Cross, *The European Diplomatic Corps*, 36–8.
28 Nina Berberova, *Liudi i lozhi. Russkie mason'y XX stoleti'ia* (Kharkov, 1997), 24–5.
29 D.I. Abrikossov, *Revelations of a Russian Diplomat* (Seattle, 1964), 106.

interests from within and from without, a difficulty which was perceived on both sides and produced the mutual recriminations of Russian diplomacy and the Russian parliament and press. It was also an indication of the gap between the retrograde political views of the emperor, imposed on the foreign ministry, and the liberal, modern in the Western sense, worldview of most Russian diplomats shaped by their westernized education and environment.

Benckendorff's Career

Benckendorff's (Fig. 2.2) first posting in 1869 was as an unpaid attaché to the Russian legation in Florence, an appointment for which he must have qualified by his Catholicism and by his familiarity with the country and its upper class.

Fig. 2.2 Count A.K. Benckendorff
Source: By kind permission of Mrs Nathalie Brooke.

Fig. 2.3 Countess S.P. Benckendorff
Source: By kind permission of Mrs Nathalie Brooke.

Four years later he became the second secretary at the embassy at Rome. In 1878–86 he was back at the foreign ministry and during this period he fell in love with and married Countess Sofia Petrovna Shuvalova (Fig. 2.3), entering a powerful St Petersburg clan. As he was Catholic and she was Orthodox, there were serious obstacles to their marriage and his initial attempts to obtain authorization from the Holy Synod failed, driving Benckendorff and his fiancée into despair. They were married in the summer of 1879 and were happy ever after. Benckendorff admired his wife's logic, intellectual curiosity and forceful personality; she deferred to his intellect and erudition. They wrote to each other daily when one of them was away, and this correspondence testifies to their wide scope of interests and the habit of discussing everything, from family matters to politics. From their debates over the Balkan wars or the Russian Duma, there gradually emerges a touching picture of a singularly united and devoted couple.

After the assassination of Alexander II in 1881, violating his oath, the count joined a secret monarchist society founded by his brother-in-law, Count Pavel Petrovich Shuvalov. At the peak of terrorist activity in Russia, the Holy Host (1881–83) tried to counter the violence against the government through their own secret network. Sergei Witte, himself a member in his youth, described it ironically in his old age as a conspiracy of young courtiers and guardsmen who had more money than brains. They published anti-revolutionary Russian newspapers and raided a few clandestine printing-houses of the revolutionary groups. Cloak and dagger games apart, the young monarchists, who under a parliamentary regime would have joined a political party, sought an outlet for their energy and ambitions. A memoirist says that the Holy Host even elected a shadow government, with a 'foreign minister' (not Benckendorff).[30] Benckendorff's papers contain his unfinished draft of an essay titled *Origine du C.D.* [Franco-Russian: The origin of the Holy Host]. He wrote that the police alone did not suffice to fight against the growing occult power of nihilism and its European network of terrorist organizations. The Holy Host united those who professed an absolute loyalty to the emperor and the dynasty. It opposed all internal reforms unless they originated in the emperor's will.[31] These remained Benckendorff's political convictions until the ascension of the disappointing Nicholas II. In the early 1880s his views were extreme right monarchist. He referred scathingly to the ministers who proposed modest liberal reforms, like Count Mikhail T. Loris-Melikov and Dmitry Miliutin, rejoicing when Alexander III ousted them,[32] and described his brief contacts with the Russian royalty in a gushing tone which in his later years he reserved for Edward VII only.[33]

He also admired Bismarck, entirely disagreeing with those who grumbled that the German chancellor owed to Russia his success in creating the German Empire and showed his ingratitude at the Berlin Congress:

> we are abominably ill-informed about Berlin … What a pigmy this country [Russia] is next to it … It is easy to say that all our misfortunes come from someone else's betrayal and all their successes are due to our support. What we forget is … that they have not ceased to work seriously and intelligently, and that we have not made anything but blunders …[34]

30 M.E. Kleinmikhel, *Za kulisami istorii, 1840–1914* (Moscow, 2004), 458.

31 GARF, f.1126, op.1, d.10.

32 A.K. Benckendorff to S.P. Benckendorff, [n/d, 1881], GARF, 1126, op.1 ed.hr.158, ll.8–11.

33 Ibid.

34 A.K. Benckendorff to S.P. Benckendorff, 31.12. [?], GARF, f.1126, op.1, ed.hr.154, ll.29–31.

This was a moment when Benckendorff felt that his career was stalled and he was impatient for a posting,[35] but in 1886 he went to the Vienna embassy as the first secretary,[36] leaving his younger brother to take care of the jointly-owned Benckendorff estate.

A look at the Benckendorff brothers' correspondence, full of neat columns of numbers, shows how difficult it was for a man who spent his life away from his properties, to look after his finances. Pavel Benckendorff, although pursuing his own career at St Petersburg, took great pains to attend to the complicated family financial affairs and sent regular reports, such as the one of summer 1886, when he reported on the state of affairs at Monticello, the Benckendorff villa in Nice, and listed the expenses and revenue which the count could expect: one of his bank deposits of 445,000 roubles at 3 per cent would give quarterly interest of 8,900 roubles.[37] The sums give some idea of the financial situation of the Benckendorff family, but it was not without its difficulties, as Pavel Benckendorff explained to his absent-minded brother:

> I have just written to you more calmly than the other day. I hope that you have received my letter and that you have sent back the document [which Benckendorff had taken with him abroad by mistake] at once ... Selling the house seems impossible. In the meanwhile we have to send money to Mama and there is not any. Debts again ... I am beginning to be seriously preoccupied ...[38]

Besides the income from the crops and the factories in Sosnovka, the countess's shares in Siberian platinum mines, the Benckendorffs had some investments abroad, mostly through Barings bank owned by their close friend Lord Revelstoke. Nevertheless, financial problems haunted them and, if Witte is to be believed, the count resolved them by throwing himself on the mercy of his friend Empress Maria Feodorovna and she had his debts paid by the treasury.[39]

In 1905–6, probably because of the revolution in Russia, the Benckendorffs again experienced financial problems and borrowed a large sum of money from Revelstoke.[40] Later, family finances were further strained by the need to pay the considerable expenses of keeping young Petr Benckendorff in the prestigious

35 A.K. Benckendorff to S.P. Benckendorff, 30.7.s.a. GARF, f.1126, op.1, ed.hr.154, ll.135–6.

36 A.K. Benckendorff's service record, AVPRI, f.159, op.464, d.295a, ll.1–11 ob.

37 P.K. Benckendorff to A.K. Benckendorff, 12/24.06.1886, GARF, f.1126, op.1, ed.hr.47, ll.34–6.

38 P.K. Benckendorff to A.K. Benckendorff, 07/19.08.1884, GARF, f.1126, op.1, ed.hr.47, ll.12–14.

39 Prince von Bülow, *Memoirs 1903–1909*, 2: 38.

40 S.P. Benckendorff to A.K. Benckendorff, 09.10.1906, BC2, box 21.

Horse Guards. In 1910 the count decided to put their Mediterranean villa up for sale.[41]

At the age of 44, in 1893, Benckendorff became the counsellor at the Vienna embassy. This hardly gave him much experience, as 'there is never anything to do at Vienna', as Sir Charles Hardinge wrote.[42] The next year he travelled to St Petersburg for the funeral of Alexander III and shared his impressions with his wife. The criticism in the ministry and in Benckendorff's family circle was that the ministers of Alexander III whom his son retained after accession, were low-born retrogrades and opportunists, who would meekly follow any forceful personality. It is hard to think of someone more intelligent or with a more forceful personality than Witte in the Russian government of the time, and it is a measure of Benckendorff's ignorance of Russia's political life that he accepted the judgments of disgruntled courtiers.

Benckendorff's sources were more competent to judge the new emperor, and the early consensus was that he had no character and followed his mother's advice, inspired by the reactionary Procurator of the Holy Synod, K.P. Pobiedonostsev.[43] Today's historians share this opinion. Like many members of their circle, the Benckendorffs considered that political reform was long overdue[44] and the personality of Nicholas II mattered largely because it would either ease or block the evolution of the Russian political system.

At this time deputy minister Vladimir Lamsdorff wrote with typical melancholy:

> The good side of the past reign was, undoubtedly the foreign policy which restored calm in everyone's mind. Through the use of very clever and adequate means it managed to block every move which might have disturbed this calm … The empire worked to develop its own prosperity and power and used both as tools of pacification rather than destruction and adventurism.[45]

The meaning of Lamsdorff's (Fig. 2.4) paean to the past becomes evident as he describes further the new trends in the Russian foreign ministry. Nicholas II's friends among the Petersburg guardsmen and his ambitious brother-in-law Grand Duke Aleksandr formed the circle which influenced the emperor's views on Russia's domestic and foreign policy, strongly reducing the weight of the advice which members of the government (the foreign minister among them) offered.

41 A.K. Benckendorff to S.P. Benckendorff, n.d. [1910], GARF, f.1126, op.1, ed.hr.153, ll.6–9.

42 Sir C. Hardinge to Sir F. Bertie, 14.03.1905, FO 800/176, 216–7.

43 *S.P. Benckendorff's memoir*, Russian State Library, Manuscripts Department, f.30, d.42, ed.hr.51.

44 S.P. Benckendorff to A.K. Benckendorff, 21.06.1905 and 16/29.11.1906, BC2, box 21.

45 V.N. Lamsdorff, *Dnevnik 1894–1896* (Moscow, 1991), 76.

Fig. 2.4 Count Vladimir N. Lamsdorff
Source: By kind permission of the Archive of Russian Imperial Foreign Policy.

The emperor's uncles and cousins, as well as his wife, began to press their advice and wishes on him.[46] The minister's views were swept aside. Instead of trying to catch up with modern times, the Russian state system was returning to obsolete practices.

But Benckendorff profited from this situation. The old foreign minister Giers died in 1895 and, after a difficult search, Nicholas II replaced him with Benckendorff's chief, the elderly ambassador to Vienna Prince Aleksei Borisovich Lobanov-Rostovsky. The prince died in mid-1896 and on 1 January 1897 Nicholas II appointed Mikhail N. Muraviov, the minister to Copenhagen. The appointment of another minister from the diplomatic service ranks meant a reshuffle. After a

46 Ibid., 141.

decade in Vienna which Benckendorff had been fretting to leave[47] he replaced Muraviov in Denmark in February 1897.[48]

Copenhagen postings were coveted by the courtier type of European diplomats because the Danish king was 'the father-in-law' of Europe and the most onerous task the diplomats performed there was to organize and assist at welcoming ceremonies for the visiting European royalty.[49] The diplomats became personally known to the Danish-born Russian dowager empress, her sister and brother-in-law the Princess and Prince of Wales (soon-to-be Queen Alexandra and Edward VII). This was useful socially in the case of European diplomats and all-important for the Russians. Appointments to the Russian legation in her native Denmark were the domain of Empress Maria Feodorovna. She had known Count Benckendorff since the 1870s when he helped organize her trips abroad and had been her mazurka partner[50] and he could count on her for promotion. During the first ten years of Nicholas II's reign when Maria Feodorovna's influence on her son was very considerable, Benckendorff's correspondence with the dowager empress was at its most intense. She tried to be informed about foreign policy so as to be able to give her son advice and relied on Benckendorff to explain to her the political events of the day.[51] All the Benckendorff family regularly visited her and discussed political issues with her. After 1906 the Benckendorffs began to comment on the empress's loss of interest in politics and the count's correspondence with Maria Feodorovna dwindled. Thanks to this connection, and probably also to his brother's proximity to the emperor, Benckendorff became the only Russian ambassador whose name appears in Nicholas II's diary as a family guest.

Benckendorff's confidential letters to Lamsdorff by 1899 already convey his boredom with the rustic pleasures of the Danish capital. The greater part of every letter was devoted to the empress's movements in her homeland, to her health and that of her retinue. A letter of his opened with 'Even considering the current troubled times I cannot report to you anything from here which could interest you in the least'.[52]

After an interregnum following the sudden death of M.N. Mouraviev, Count Lamsdorff, the veteran adviser of the ministers, a retiring, shy and nervous little man, was appointed to head the ministry in the summer of 1900. Benckendorff welcomed his appointment: '… you, who have long been observing everything

47 A.K. Benckendorff to S.P. Benckendorff, n.d., GARF, f.1126, op.1, ed.hr.154, ll.34–5.

48 AVPRI, f.137, op.464, ed.hr.295a, ll.1–11 ob.

49 Maurice Baring, *The Puppet Show of Memory* (London, [1937] 1987), 209.

50 Prince von Bülow, *Memoirs 1903–1909* (London, 1931–2), 2: 153.

51 A.K. Benckendorff to Empress Maria Feodorovna, n.d., GARF, f.642, op.1, ed.hr.916, ll.17–18 ob.

52 A.K. Benckendorff to V.N. Lamsdorff, 23.10/5.11.1900, GARF, f.568, op.1, ed. hr.326, l.17.

and doing everything, are the best person to assist our August Master in seeing in the future without losing sight of the past'.[53] The minister was five years older than Benckendorff, but his extreme prudence, discretion and scepticism were those of a much older man. He was the Cassandra of the foreign ministry, an adviser whose good advice was neglected all too often. The count had never served abroad, but his intelligence and experience made him Russia's best judge of European diplomacy. He was convinced that Russia's foreign policy should, inasmuch as possible, continue the cautious course adopted by Alexander III and Giers, which had preserved Russia from diplomatic or military disasters. He considered that the Russo-French alliance and the traditional friendship with Germany sufficed to keep Russia out of conflicts, provided Nicholas II steered clear of adventures.[54] The bold manoeuvres of his two predecessors and the interventions of the war and finance ministers in the foreign policy filled him with apprehensions. He managed to bring Sergei Witte and General Aleksei Kuropatkin, the finance and war ministers respectively, over to his side and did his best to moderate the foreign policy course which in the late 1890s began to turn aggressive under the influence of Nicholas II's ambitious extra-governmental advisers. They included the group of military and financiers called Bezobrazovtsy ('the Bezobrazov clique') after their leader and Nicholas II's favourite, Aleksandr Bezobrazov. The group was supported by the minister of interior Viacheslav Plehve and the emperor's friend and brother-in-law, Grand Duke Aleksandr.

Benckendorff's letters were not shorter for all that he did not have much to report. He philosophized, commented on the events of the day and periodically dropped hints regarding his abiding interest in Russia's relations with Britain, but, above all, with Germany.[55] He was interested in combinations of the powers which were springing up around Russia: a possible Anglo-German alliance which would inevitably make war against Russia.[56] Regarding Britain, he was at one with Lamsdorff and most of his colleagues in resenting empty gestures of defiance. Baiting the British was inappropriate and counterproductive.[57] Russian popular opinion, including Nicholas II, was pro-Boer during the Anglo-Boer war, but the foreign ministry did its best to present to the world a correct neutral position and rejected William II's idea of intervening in the Boer war.[58] On

53 A.K. Benckendorff to V.N. Lamsdorff, 27.7/9.8.1900, GARF, f.568, op.1, ed. hr.326, l.13.

54 I.S. Rybachonok, 'V.N.Lamsdorff' in *Rossiiskaia diplomati'ia v portretakh* (Moscow, 1992), 288–9.

55 A.K. Benckendorff to V.N. Lamsdorff, 11/25.9.1900, GARF, f.568, op.1, ed.hr. 326, ll.15–16.

56 A.K. Benckendorff to S.P. Benckendorff, n.d., GARF, 1126, op.1, ed.hr. 154, l.129.

57 A.K. Benckendorff to S.P. Benckendorff, n.d., GARF, 1126, op.1, ed.hr.156, ll.37–8.

58 C. Spring Rice to Knollys, 02.11.1908, RA VIC/ADDC 7/2/Q.

his return from St Petersburg Benckendorff told his British colleagues that the emperor wished to allay hostility to Britain in regard to the Boer war, and that Russia would not be drawn into any interference with Britain.[59] Benckendorff spoke of the foreign ministry's position to which he hoped the emperor would be forced to adhere. Like Maria Feodorovna, the count deprecated the Russian initiatives in favour of the Boers which would only result in more bad blood between Russia and Britain.[60] These repeated expressions of political sympathy, so unusual in a Russian diplomat, were noticed by the British. Edward VII heard nothing but good about Benckendorff from his Russian sister-in-law and his wife; the Foreign Office received favourable accounts of him from the members of the British legation; after Copenhagen, Sir Edward Goschen, Sir Alan Vanden Bempde Johnstone and Maurice Baring became lifelong friends of the Benckendorff couple.[61] Goschen must have given glowing references to the Benckendorffs in December of 1902 when for 15 minutes Lord Lansdowne interrogated him about them.[62]

Copenhagen Origins of the Anglo-Russian Rapprochement

Russia's forward policy in the Far East obeyed its own logic and reflected the political influences which prevailed at St Petersburg, but, like other powers' reawakened colonial ambitions, it was also encouraged by Britain's involvement in South Africa. Between 1898 and 1900 Russia leased from China ice-free naval bases, Port-Arthur and Dalian-Van (Dalny) and succeeded in uniting its force to that of Germany and France to make Japan roll back its intervention in China. In July 1900 Russia invaded Manchuria in order to protect the construction of her railroad and the Russian subjects employed in the construction. In August, in retaliation for the Chinese attacks on Russian interests, Russians moved into the treaty port of Niuchuang (Newchwang). The 9 November 1900 Russia and the Chinese viceroy of the north-eastern provinces signed a secret agreement to allow Russia to control the provinces. When it became known in January 1901, the Japanese government declared that they would not negotiate with Russia about Korea until Russia evacuated Manchuria. Even without knowing that in September of 1901 secret Anglo-Japanese treaty talks were advancing, the Russian government, under Lamsdorff's pressure, made attempts to conciliate Japan, the USA and Britain. In August 1901, the foreign ministry suggested that Manchuria would be evacuated in exchange for mining concessions there. Lamsdorff was

59 Sir Edward Fane to Lord Salisbury, 1.1.1900, BD, 1: 244.

60 A.K. Benckendorff to Empress Maria Feodorovna, 06/19.10.1901, GARF, f.642, op.1, ed.hr.916, ll.20–1 ob.

61 Edward Goschen, *The Diary of Edward Goschen 1900–1914* (London, 1980), 72.

62 Ibid., 73.

concerned about Japan's war preparations, but he and the finance minister Witte faced the opposition of the military and the Bezobrazovtsy.[63]

Tired of watching from the Copenhagen sidelines, Benckendorff took to writing to his minister extensive letter-essays on European politics. Regarding the powers' demands for Russia to evacuate Manchuria, he admitted that Russia's interests demanded her push in the Far East, but he deplored the discordance between Russia's declarations and her conduct in the Far East: 'In my eyes, the first foundation of our prestige is always the emperor's word, our strength is the second'.[64] In an autocracy, national honour or dishonour is identified with the personal honour of the autocrat, and they became a recurrent theme in Benckendorff's correspondence with his colleagues and chiefs. He insisted that honour was the strongest motive Russia could possibly have in pursuing this or that course – usually, when the course was detrimental to Russia's interests. His later frequent reminders of Russia's debt of gratitude and loyalty imply that Russia had to deserve British goodwill and to repay the British trust which had been advanced to it when the Anglo-Russian convention was signed. Despite his periodic scathing remarks about Russian statesmen's moral standards[65] he obviously believed in appealing to their honour.

A contemporary of Benckendorff remarked that it is futile to look for Christ-like virtues in the wrong places: purity of motive and forthrightness do not go with politics.[66] Still, Benckendorff, when scolding Russians, usually pointed to the high ethical standards of the British. British diplomats and the British press of the time often remarked that Russians (and other foreigners) were congenital liars and schemers. Sir Charles Hardinge was quick to qualify his Russian colleagues as 'hopelessly untruthful' or 'like all Russians … slippery in his dealings'[67] while he saw his own spying on Turkish and Russian military and diplomatic secrets[68] and lying his way out as humorous incidents in the career of a patriot.[69] Russians were less inclined to cast stones. Lamsdorff, even though annoyed by the British success in China, wrote: 'Yes, what an intriguer this O'Conor is! Actually, we cannot qualify a diplomat's actions to protect his country's interests as intrigues. Seen from this angle everybody has been intriguing'.[70]

63 Ian Nish, *The Origins of the Russo-Japanese War* (London and New York, 1985), 108.

64 A.K. Benckendorff to V.N. Lamsdorff, 27.3/9.4 1901, GARF, f. 568, op.1, ed.hr. 326, ll.25–6 ob.

65 A.K. Benckendorff to Empress Maria Feodorovna, 05.10.1906, GARF, f.642 op.1, ed.hr. 917, ll.72–7 ob.

66 Vasily Rozanov, *Literaturny'ie izgnanniki: Vospominani'ia.Pis'ma* (Moscow, 2000), 277.

67 Lord Hardinge of Penshurst, *Old Diplomacy: The Reminiscences of Lord Hardinge of Penshurst* (London, 1947), 69–70.

68 Ibid., 107.

69 Ibid., 48.

70 V.N. Lamsdorff, *Dnevnik 1894–1896* (Moscow, 1991), 257.

Everybody, except Benckendorff. Given the choice between a spotless reputation and a successful diplomatic coup, Benckendorff opted for the first and it is a testimony to the Russian foreign ministry's sympathy with this noble principle or to its happy-go-lucky ways that not only was he kept on but promoted to a high position. He acted on the principle formulated by his wife: '… there are moments when conscience and personal honour are above the code of honour based on prejudices [that is, professional responsibility] and … at such moments you abandon what prevents you from being yourself'.[71] This attitude, coupled to his low opinion of the competence of most Russian diplomats, statesmen, military and journalists, made him feel justified in contravening his instructions and relying on his pacts with the Foreign Office made behind his ministers' backs: he was saving Russia despite herself. Coupled with his proverbial absent-mindedness and docility with regard to the Foreign Office his behaviour caused affectionate smiles from the British, but earned him French scorn and Russian resentment.[72]

His brother's closeness to Nicholas II was a mixed blessing for the ambassador. On the one hand he received frequent reports from the court, describing the emperor's mood, actions and words. It made him one of the few persons who 'saw' in Nicholas II's heart and added certain weight to his words. On the other hand, this constant flow of gossip walled him off from other sources of information about Russia's internal events because it created an illusion of knowing everything worth knowing.

His view of the ultimate purpose and rationale of diplomatic activity was lofty and his principles, when formulated, were highly quotable; his favourite theories would have made interesting lectures for students of political science or history. But when it came to applying them, he was at sea. His wife, better at separating ideals from reality, gave him a piece of advice which he ignored: 'It is good to be liberal, but it is also necessary to be patriotic and I believe that Russians must above all think of Russia. I, in my boudoir, can afford to think of humanity but men of action must have a more specific ideal and goal'.[73]

Benckendorff's letter to Lamsdorff of 27 March/9 April 1901 developed the idea that, with Japan now a global factor in politics, and with the scramble for China gathering momentum, Russia might be in need of an ally. In his opinion only Germany and Britain counted as great powers. France could not counterbalance either of the above, and her only usefulness to Russia would be in the case of a European war 'from which may Lord preserve us'. Benckendorff then looked at Britain. At this moment, weakened by the Boer war and isolated, Britain nevertheless would find Germany of no use, because they could not expect William II to make a serious commitment against Russia. They might want his

71 S.P. Benckendorff to A.K. Benckendorff, 03/16.04.1906, BC2, box 21.

72 Lady Juliet Duff to A.A. Savinsky, 25.11.1911, AVPRI, f.340, op.706, d.19, ll. 155–7; Paul Cambon to T. Delcassé, 06.08.1903, DDF, 2: 520–22; Prince von Bülow, *Memoirs 1903–1909*, 2: 38.

73 S.P. Benckendorff to A.K. Benckendorff, 10.10.1905, BC2, box 21.

favourable neutrality to keep him from doing favours to Russia, but this would not be enough for a convention. Russia's and Britain's frontiers were proximate and a discussion would help to avoid dangerous collisions. At that point he believed that both Germany and Britain would welcome an understanding with Russia: 'Owing to the position which we occupy, all eyes continue to watch us and it seems to me that we could always extend to one or maybe even to the other power, as many or as few fingers as we deem convenient …' Russia could initiate talks for a political rapprochement with Britain or/and Germany based on the Far Eastern affairs and, following that, based on European issues. Then followed a suggestion which in the years to come would become a recurrent theme in the count's letters to his chiefs: Russia should explain her behaviour, the sooner the better.[74]

Lamsdorff made vague overtures to Sir Charles Scott, British ambassador to Russia, in the summer of 1901 about an understanding over China,[75] but nothing came out of them. The subject of an Anglo-Russian détente came up in Benckendorff's correspondence with the minister after Lamsdorff accompanied Nicholas II to France in September of 1901. The Conservative Foreign Secretary, Lord Lansdowne, attempted to achieve a compromise with Russia as late as October 1901 but met with no success.[76] Russia's confidence gave no grounds for Britain to hope for a beneficial settlement.[77] Then circumstances began to combine in a way which eventually brought about the result desired by Lansdowne.

The painful blow of the Anglo-Japanese treaty came in January 1902. Lamsdorff looked for ways to secure Russia's position in the changing circumstances. Lord Lansdowne's words in the winter of 1902 on several occasions seemed to invite overtures from other interested powers.[78] Tentative approaches to Lansdowne were made simultaneously in St Petersburg and London. The Russian foreign minister spoke to Sir Charles Scott about the possibility of an Asiatic understanding as early as February 1902.[79] The French ambassador to Britain, Paul Cambon, spoke to Lansdowne ten days later in the same spirit. Lansdowne's reply, reported to Lamsdorff, was that he had repeatedly offered the Russian ambassador, Baron E.E. Staal, to begin talks about all the points of common interest: China, Korea, Persia and the Indian border but the lack of interest on the Russian part led to the treaty with Japan.[80] In May 1902 the first secretary of the Russian embassy in London, Stanislav Poklevsky reported that the British government did not quite trust

74 A.K. Benckendorff to Lamsdorff, 27.03/09.04.1901, GARF, f.568, op.1, ed.hr.326, ll.25–6.

75 Ian Nish, 104.

76 Lansdowne to Knollys, 25.07.1902, RA VIC/ADDC 7/2/Q.

77 Hardinge of Penshurst, *Old Diplomacy*, 84.

78 Paul Cambon to T. Delcassé, 14.2.1902, DDF, 2: 100–102.

79 Sir Charles Scott to Lansdowne, 2.2.1902, BD, 1: 272–3.

80 P. Cambon to T. Delcassé, 12.2.1902, DDF, 2: 88–9.

Japan's peaceful intentions with regard to Russia[81] and might be interested in a settlement with the latter in order to avoid being drawn into a Russo-Japanese conflict. To Lamsdorff an improvement in Anglo-Russian relations would reduce the danger of a Russo-Japanese conflict.

A biographer ascribed to the French foreign minister Théophile Delcassé the initial idea of having Benckendorff go to London to work for an Anglo-Russian settlement.[82] A man of Benckendorff's characteristics would, indeed, serve the French purpose in London well. By the summer of 1902 French diplomacy began to work on a strategy to lock France firmly into a system of protective international agreements that at the same time would isolate Germany just as effectively as Bismarck had isolated France in 1870. A contemporary observer called its first stage 'le mouvement camboniste', because it was marked by a series of appointments to the key capitals of the closest friends and partisans of the energetic Paul Cambon and his brother Jules. Théophile Delcassé in tandem with Paul Cambon was tirelessly working at what would become the Entente cordiale with Britain. Cambon's close friend Camille Barrère went to the Rome embassy to smooth out Franco-Italian differences; Cambon's right-hand man Maurice Bompard was appointed to St Petersburg; Cambon's friend Georges Bihourd went to Berlin, his former secretary Jean Jusserand to Washington, his younger brother Jules became the ambassador to Spain and his protégé, Jules de La Boulinière, was posted to Cairo,[83] where British and French interests converged. It was from Egypt that the confirmation of the existence of the French plan and its far-reaching goals came. During the Anglo-French entente negotiations of 1903–4 the viceroy of Egypt Lord Cromer repeatedly wrote to Lansdowne that he heard from his French colleague, La Boulinière that 'Delcassé hopes that eventually we shall come to terms with Russia and thus isolate Germany'. Cromer added: 'Indeed, I cannot help thinking that to the French Government, this is one of the main attractions of the whole scheme'.[84]

Prior to Washington, Jusserand was Benckendorff's colleague at Copenhagen. He remembered his Russian colleague and his wife as being unusually free spoken in their criticism of the political system and the rulers of Russia. The emperor's envoy called Nicholas II 'a flounderer', comparing his position in the nation to that of Louis XVI; his wife, as a true Russian liberal, declared that the greatest crime in history had been the partition of Poland.[85] Jusserand found it unusual, because other Russian officials kept their identical opinions to themselves, remembering at all times that they were the personal representatives of Nicholas II. Benckendorff

81 S. Poklevsky, *Report*, 8/21.5.1902, AVPRI, f.184, op.520, d.1086, l. 91.

82 Alberic Neton, *Delcassé (1852–1923)* (Paris, 1952), 324.

83 F. Masson to Grand Duke Nikolai Mikhailovich, 08.09.1902, *Au temps de l'alliance franco-russe: Correspondance entre le grand-duc Nicolas Mikhailovitch de Russie et Frédéric Masson* (Paris, 2005), 195–7.

84 Cromer to Lansdowne, 27.11.1903, FO 800/124, 144–6.

85 Marina Soroka, 'Debating Russia's Choice', 3–4.

propped up his personal reputation of a frank and impartial man at the expense of his government's prestige. His behaviour stands in sharp contrast to that of other European diplomats and even to Benckendorff's own position with regard to the line of conduct he later prescribed for Russian diplomacy: its main goal, he insisted for ten years, was not to allow Germany suspect a rift between Russia and the Entente, for it weakened the bloc's position. His open contempt for his own government and its policies undermined Russian foreign policy by disclosing the disaffection in the Russian political circles.

Paul Cambon could expect to dominate Benckendorff in a sense favourable to the French interests, and, as it happens, later the French diplomat, according to his son, 'used his relations of trust with Benckendorff to plant ideas in [the Russian foreign minister] Iswolsky's head' because the two Russians were friends. Planting ideas in Benckendorff's head was not a difficult task, as his reports and, especially private letters show. He habitually passed on Grey's or other British officials' words as his own opinions. Perhaps he thought they were his own. While the Foreign Office put aside the idea of an Anglo-Russian arrangement until a better moment, a Russian ambassador like Benckendorff was welcome. At the same time Staal resigned for age and health reasons and King Edward VII asked Nicholas II to appoint Benckendorff to London. Lamsdorff did not oppose the idea because it was a time-honoured tradition of the Russian monarchy to post courtiers, rather than competent diplomats, to the Great Powers. Lamsdorff's diary refers several times, rather dismissively, to the criteria which a Russian ambassador had to meet: a certain rank in the service, a title, a fortune and a well-mannered wife.[86] The characteristic of utmost importance was discipline: Baron Osten-Sacken, the Russian ambassador in Berlin, was a simpleton whom Holstein led by the nose, but a simpleton who followed his instructions to the letter was safer than a smart daredevil at the head of an embassy.[87] Lamsdorff was certain of being able to keep Benckendorff in line.

Benckendorff received the news of his promotion with enthusiasm. In early August 1902 while on leave in Sosnovka, he wrote to Lamsdorff about his eagerness to talk to his predecessor when the latter passed through St Petersburg. He flattered the minister by saying that he was not nervous because the political programme which Lamsdorff had explained to him was perfectly clear, and added: 'Maybe precisely thanks to this and only because of this, I might be useful and might render a service to our August Sovereign and to Russia'.[88] Lamsdorff considered that discussions between Staal and his yet unofficial successor were premature, and Benckendorff returned to Copenhagen at the end of August, champing at the bit. He wrote from there at once: 'I am waiting. Before going to London I would like to visit you in Petersburg, then return here and present my

86 Marina Soroka, 'Debating Russia's Choice', 3–4.

87 Ibid., 4.

88 A.K. Benckendorff to V.N. Lamsdorff, 3/16.8.1902, GARF, f.568, op.1, ed.hr.326, ll.57–8 ob.

letters of recall … I need to have an interview with Staal …'.[89] Unable to restrain his eagerness, the count began to prepare the ground for his mission while still in Denmark.

In September he had a letter from the British diplomat Sir Alan Vanden Bempde Johnstone, his Copenhagen friend:

> I wrote to Sanderson,[90] asking that no one but he and Lord Lansdowne should know what I said – about your mission being to clear away difficulties by avoiding all misunderstandings – quoting, in fact, your French phrase. Sanderson has thanked me for my letter and has promised that no one but Lord Lansdowne shall know of it. So you start with the character of an honest gentleman genuinely anxious to avoid any misunderstandings with England – thoroughly Russian and yet determined if possible that there shall be an entente cordiale between the two countries. I can only trust that your mission will succeed.[91]

The letter, reproducing Benckendorff's own interpretation of his mission, predates by three months the official instructions which he was to receive on his departure to London. It is a sample of what would become Benckendorff's *modus operandi* of an 'honest gentleman': in secret from his minister he forestalled Russian official declarations by his own advances. Staal congratulated his successor on the appointment and assured him that he would be happy in Chesham House. The postscript to Staal's letter makes it obvious that his state of health and age made his retirement long overdue:

> P.S. I apologise for not using the code – I cannot do so unaided. My blindness is getting worse with every day that passes. I am waiting for it to be complete in order to risk an operation.[92]

A week later he wrote, with the same unaffected amiability that characterizes the correspondence of the Russian diplomats of the time:

> The king will return around the 22 of October to Buckingham Palace in order to attend on the 25th the St Paul's ceremony. On the following day I will hand in my letters of recall. So come by the twentieth, to inspect the embassy and decide on the issues of change, repairs, arrangement and hiring. I must warn you that

---

89 A.K. Benckendorff to V.N. Lamsdorff, 27.8/9.9.1902, GARF, f.568, op.1, ed.hr. 326, ll.60–62 ob.

90 Sir Thomas Sanderson (later Lord), Permanent Under-Secretary of the Foreign Office.

91 Sir Alan Vanden Bempde Johnstone to A.K. Benckendorff, 20.9.1902, BC 2, box 13.

92 E.E. Staal to A.K. Benckendorff, 5.10.1902, BC2, box 14.

the 'kazennyi' [state-property] furniture is deficient, or rather, insufficient. The same refers to pictures. You will see for yourself.

As for me, dear colleague, your visit will provide me with the occasion and the joy of shaking your hand and personally offering you my most sincere good wishes before I sink into the anonymity of retirement.[93]

In October 1902 the impatient Benckendorff was, at last, authorized to visit unofficially the departing ambassador. He warned Maria Feodorovna who was on her routine holiday in Denmark, that he would secretly go to London on the weekend and asked her not to contradict the rumour that he was in Paris.[94] In this way he made sure that Queen Alexandra and Edward VII would also know.

Benckendorff wrote to his wife daily reports from London. On October 22: 'I became tired of listening to the upholsterers' hammering and went to the British Museum'. The Elgin Marbles, which he had seen in reproductions, were much more impressive that he expected: 'Nothing to rival them in Paris, nor in Berlin. Nothing, nothing'. Then he turned to the state in which he found the embassy. The first floor was very pretty, with fine Turkish rugs. 'If the state compensates us, we will do the upper floor nicely. We have everything for the bedrooms. I have answered all your questions: I have the inventory ready. I will have the layout [of the house] tomorrow'. He described Staal and other embassy officials in a patronizing tone:

Staal is charming but lacks shrewdness … The military agent – Europeanized, excellent English and French, intelligent, even pleasant … Staal … despite all, is intelligent. He talks politics like Darwin talks science, he speaks the vernacular, any child would understand him …[95]

On his arrival, he at once found himself surrounded by friends and acquaintances.

He dined at the Carlton hotel, in the company of a distant relative of the Shouvalov family, Lady Gladys de Grey, also Lady Granby (the future Duchess of Rutland), Lady Westmorland and a Russian diplomat and Prince Belosselsky, Benckendorff's old acquaintance and a fellow-conspirator of the Holy Host.

Then, he wrote to the countess, Edward VII heard of his arrival through Belosselsky and sent a word that he wanted to see him privately, without any official notice, which the proud Benckendorff called 'charming but embarrassing'. Staal told him that it did not matter in the least that Benckendorff was not in London officially:

93 E.E. Staal to A.K. Benckendorff, 13.10.1902, BC2, box 14.

94 A.K. Benckendorff to Empress Maria Feodorovna, n.d.[October 1902], GARF, F. 642, op.1, ed.hr.642, ll.24 ob.

95 A.K. Benckendorff to S.P. Benckendorff, 22.10. [1902], GARF, 1126, op.1, ed. hr. 156, ll. 96–100.

> Staal says, forget about Germany, here nothing matters ... The king is very grateful for having got the ambassador of his choice (he said to Kostia [Belosselsky]). Staal advises me to use it to the advantage of the mission.[96]

The formalities were settled by a letter from the king's private secretary Lord Knollys, promising that there would be no official notice of Benckendorff's being received by the king.[97] On his return to Copenhagen he reported to the minister. The embassy house was in a bad condition. Benckendorff wrote: 'I am not sure to what extent the ministry usually helps [financially] new ambassadors, but in any case, all that is necessary will be done'. He explained that Queen Alexandra had known about his arrival and the king had expressed a desire to see him. The count hastened to position himself as a member of the king's private circle before he became known as the ambassador of Russia to Britain.

He told Lamsdorff that Edward VII was pleased because Nicholas II had sent him the diplomat of his personal choice. The king said that Nicholas II's gesture was a good omen for Anglo-Russian relations. As for his task, Benckendorff wrote: 'I know there will be difficulties, but I will not further complicate things by prejudices. I will try to treat official matters as business and nothing more'.[98] He promised to remember that an Anglo-Russian rupture would affect the European peace, to avoid prejudice in interpreting British actions; and to keep the affairs as clear as possible, by explaining Russia's policy to the British.

It seemed to the count that his mission to London was off to a brilliant start. He did not grasp the whole meaning of Staal's words that London was not Germany. Edward VII did not direct foreign policy. The king's personal sympathy for a diplomat did not change the political course, though it sometimes reflected the change in the Foreign Office's attitude.

It is true that the king favoured an Asian understanding with Russia and in 1902 had told Lansdowne that instead of trying to bribe the Persian Shah away from the Russians it was preferable to settle with them.[99] In the autocratic Russian court, hopes of better relations with Britain derived from the less significant fact that Edward VII was an uncle to both the Russian emperor and the empress.

Lamsdorff did not believe in such diplomacy but as long as he would be in charge of political relations, he was pleased with Benckendorff's friendship with the British royalty. Some of Benckendorff's contemporaries, like his subordinate Dmitry Abrikossov, believed till the end of their days in the 1960s that Benckendorff's friendship with the king had been an important asset to Russian policies. If anything, it worked in reverse: Benckendorff was so fascinated by

---

96 A.K. Benckendorff to S.P. Benckendorff, 22.10. [1902], GARF, f.1126, op.1, ed.hr. 156, ll.94–5.

97 Knollys to A.K. Benckendorff, 22.10.1902, BC2, box 13.

98 A.K. Benckendorff to V.N. Lamsdorff, 19.10/1.11.1902, GARF, f.568, op.1, ed.hr.326, ll.71–3 ob.

99 Lansdowne to Knollys, 25.07.1902, RA VIC/ADDC 7/2/Q.

the king that the latter's opinions had a strong influence on the ambassador. One instance was the ambassador's anti-German stance[100] which, after a year in London, outdistanced any such sentiment among his Russian colleagues, imitating Edward VII.[101] In 1901 the count still thought that Russia could benefit from a rapprochement with either Germany or Britain, or both,[102] but when he adopted his British and French friends' views of Germany as a menace to Europe, he also accepted their foreign policy rationales.

100 Paul von Metternich to Chancellor von Bülow, 09.07.1904, in Prince von Bülow, *Memoirs*, 34–5.

101 Sydney Lee, *King Edward VII: A Biography* (London, 1925), 1: 729.

102 A.K. Benckendorff to Lamsdorff, 27.3/09.1901, GARF, f.568, op.1, ed.hr.326, 25–6.

Chapter 3
The New Ambassador and his Objectives, 1902–1904

Chesham House, Chesham Place, (Fig. 3.1) the Russian embassy, was in a quiet tree-lined street in Belgravia to which the officials walked from their equally imposing addresses. There are still many embassies and consulates in the Georgian houses facing the streets between Buckingham Palace Gardens and Chesham

Fig 3.1 The Benckendorffs in their private apartment in Chesham House
Source: By kind permission of Mrs Nathalie Brooke.

Fig. 3.2 The Ambassador's Coach in Front of Chesham House
Source: By kind permission of Mrs Nathalie Brooke.

Place. The Russian embassy consisted of two houses, with a corner house between them which was the private residence of a gentleman who refused to sell. The two embassy buildings were therefore connected by a strange system of added-on corridors. The stubborn owner of the house-in-between suffered the inconvenience of having to answer the door to the visitors who mistook it for the entrance to the embassy. The embassy was a reasonably comfortable place, with electricity and a lift installed by Baron de Staal in the beginning of his term, in the 1880s. Benckendorff had the lift repaired and asked the ministry to provide the money for renovations of the reception rooms[1] but even renovated, they did not look as imposing as the Benckendorffs' private apartment on the third floor (Fig. 3.2) which they filled with their own furniture. A British visitor praised the Benckendorffs' 'fine taste … which was reflected in the appointments of the embassy'.[2]

The chancery occupied two small rooms on the fourth floor, and access to them was gained by a back staircase. Three clerks ciphered and deciphered the telegrams and copied the ambassador's dispatches, written in French and in a spidery handwriting. There was an old typewriter in the office and several telephones which constantly rang; calls came in from the ambassador's study, from the Foreign Office or from the acquaintances of the staff. A junior staff

1 G. Graevenitz to A.K. Benckendorff, 26.6/9.7.1903, BC2, box 12.
2 J.A. Spender, *Life, Journalism and Politics* (London, 1927), 2: 176.

member during Benckendorff's ambassadorship, Dmitry I. Abrikossov, recalled that when he arrived in 1904 the archives of the embassy were disorganized and he volunteered to put them in order. In the fine ministerial tradition of withholding knowledge as the key to power, young Abrikossov became important as the only person who could tell where a particular document was.[3]

At the end of 1902 a list of the embassy staff and domestics who enjoyed diplomatic privileges was sent to the Foreign Office.[4] The embassy counted nine domestic servants, some British, other 'continentals', an Orthodox priest, a deacon and six cantors of the embassy church. The countess even tried to have 'diplomatic privileges' extended to her dog, but after a good deal of correspondence the Benckendorffs complied with the British quarantine regulations. Lansdowne declared that he always believed it would be easier to get the Russians out of Manchuria than 'that dog' out of the Russian embassy.[5]

The Embassy Staff

The new ambassador interviewed all the officials to determine whom he wanted to keep. He wanted young and active people, good workers 'with sufficient means to lead a life befitting a member of the embassy'.[6] Staal's counsellor, Pavel M. Lessar, became Russia's minister in China; Staal's second secretary Elim P. Demidov was transferred to Madrid. Staal's first secretary, Baron Grigorii A. von Graevenitz, became Benckendorff's counsellor. Stanislav A. Poklevsky-Koziell was the first secretary. Prince Petr Volkonsky and Matvei M. Sevastopoulo were second secretaries. Sergei S. Tatishchev represented the finance ministry. A diplomat expelled from the service for indiscretion, a well-known historian and political commentator, he was Witte's protégé and Lamsdorff's sworn enemy. There was also a naval agent with an assistant, and a military agent, Colonel Nikolai Sergeevich Yermolov, who worked alone but accomplished more than his naval colleagues.

Russian diplomats posted to imperial Berlin or Vienna had to belong to *très von und zu* families, but wealth was the most important qualification for a London posting.[7] The materialistic side became particularly prominent in the British upper class's minds because of Edward VII's well-known appetite for luxury, and diplomats posted to London had to hold their own with the British aristocracy. When a colleague informed Benckendorff in 1904 that Sergei Sazonov was posted to the embassy, he pointed out that the Sazonovs are '... not as wealthy

3 D.I. Abrikossov, 104.

4 Russian embassy in London, *List of Embassy Staff and Domestics Enjoying Diplomatic Privileges*, 23.12.1902. AVPRI, f.184. op.520, d.1037, ll.79–81.

5 4th Earl of Onslow to Cranley, 09.03.1904, OP, G173/24/80.

6 D.I. Abrikossov, 93.

7 Ibid.

as Graevenitz and Poklevsky, but they are well-off'.[8] Demidov, Abrikossov and Poklevsky were millionaires whose fortunes had been made between the beginning and the end of the nineteenth century in industry and trade. A Urals' merchant dynasty, the Demidovs bought from the Pope the title of the Princes of San Donato, a title never recognized in Russia. This circumstance, and the marriage of one of them to Napoleon's niece, Princess Mathilde Bonaparte, led to the Demidovs' spending more and more time outside of Russia and becoming to a great degree expatriates. Their charitable foundations, their generous patronage of arts and sciences (le Prix Demidoff) were established in France and Russia; their official family seat was Villa Pratolino, near Florence. Elim Demidov, Eton-educated and married to a relative of Countess Benckendorff, had arrived in London during the ambassadorship of Baron Staal. Disregarding the rule that junior officials should be introduced in society by the ambassador, the Demidovs quickly joined the Marlborough set of the then Prince of Wales and as soon incurred the prince's anger. On his order they were dropped by all their mutual friends. Prior to Benckendorff's arrival the unpleasantness had been patched up but Demidov was transferred from London.

Poklevsky's grandfather was a member of Polish gentry. For his involvement in the 1830 rebellion he was exiled to Siberia where he settled and the family made millions in mining and the liquor industry. Stanislav Poklevsky was educated at Petersburg, joined the foreign ministry and came to London after four years in the Russian legation in Tokyo. A merry bachelor who spent money like water, he achieved almost as grand a standing in the London society as the Benckendorffs; he financed the Duchess of Manchester's receptions in exchange for the introduction into Edward VII's intimate circle.[9]

Abrikossov was an ambitious and clever youth from a Moscow merchant dynasty who set out to breach the obstacles placed to the non-nobles in the foreign ministry. An orphan, he had an enormous fortune at his disposal and had traveled and lived abroad before becoming a diplomat.

The military agent Yermolov was of a different breed to the empire's servants. A graduate of the St Petersburg Military Academy, he also held a diploma from the Petersburg School of Oriental Languages. Prior to coming to Britain in 1891, he had explored Central Asia and India and published work about the Indian frontier and the military potential of the Indian army. Sergei Yu. Witte characterized Yermolov as 'an intelligent, kind, cultivated and decent man, but somewhat weak-willed'.[10] Benckendorff looked down on the agents of other ministries, but he lamented Yermolov's transfer during the Russo-Japanese war,[11] when his friendly

8 K.A. Gubastov to A.K. Benckendorff, 17/30.07.1904, BC2, box 16.

9 D.I. Abrikossov, 102–3.

10 S. Yu.Witte, 2: 385.

11 M.K. Baskhanov, *Russkie voennye vostokovedy do 1917 goda: Bibliograficheski'i slovar* (Moscow, 2005), 85–8.

connections in the British War Office were particularly useful.[12] The ambassador was exasperated with Yermolov's successor Colonel Polovtsev:

> P[olovtsev] is an impulsive … and scatterbrained fellow. Assuming conspiratorial airs, hinting at hidden agendas … all this … is … one of those symptoms by which the English and other nations judge us … I shall take Yermolov [back] with both hands. What I need here, above all, is a perfectly decent man without a shady past in the *far* [sic] *East.*[13]

Benckendorff triumphed over the military, and Major General Yermolov was posted back to Britain where he remained until 1917 as the military agent and later as a refugee.

Dmitry Abrikossov, after a while in London, felt that he needed to see more of Russians because he 'already suffered from too much admiration for everything English'. He found that, unlike the continent, where Russian colonies consisted of holidaying aristocrats, students, artists and business people, most of the Russians in London were political exiles,[14] so in London the embassy staff spent their time among the British and in the diplomatic set. But they relished it. This was another qualification which Count Benckendorff found essential in his subordinates: absence of anti-British prejudice. Sergei Sazonov came with the following characteristic: he had already served in London and 'he still retains a good dose of Anglophilia. I do not know whether it is a quality or a defect'.[15] In Benckendorff's eyes it was definitely a quality.

Benckendorff usually began his campaign against any latent Anglophobic sentiment among his staff by reminding them that Russians had no right to blame Britain for its successful advancement of its interests.[16] True as this was, anything less than unconditional recognition of British moral and intellectual superiority was Anglophobia in his eyes. When King Edward reproached him for Anglophobia, Staal's counsellor Pavel Lessar said: 'By putting the interests of my country first I only do what His Majesty expects from His subjects'. This was not an attitude which Benckendorff found useful and Lessar's later request to the ambassador to help him return to London from Peking[17] remained unfulfilled.

Lamsdorff forced on Benckendorff Lessar's friend, the intelligent and energetic Petr S. Botkin, as the first secretary because, after Lessar's transfer to China, not one of the ambassador's hand-picked staff knew how to write a serious political or

12 A.K. Benckendorff to N.G. Hartwig, 09.05.1905, GARF, 1126, op.1, ed.hr.1, ll.1–2.

13 A.K. Benckendorff to Iswolsky, 12/25.12.1906, *Au service de la Russie: Alexandre Isvolsky – Correspondance diplomatique, 1906–1911* (ed. G. Chklaver and Helene Iswolsky) (Paris, 1937), 1: 413.

14 D.I. Abrikossov, 107.

15 K.A. Gubastov to A.K. Benckendorff, 17.7.1904, BC2, box 16.

16 D.I. Abrikossov, 117.

17 P.M. Lessar to A.K. Benckendorff, 28.08/09.09.1903, BC2, box 13.

economic report. Botkin was a professional who did it well and besides could write in Russian![18] The Benckendorffs (for the countess took an active part in fighting the ministry's decision) even threatened the ambassador's resignation unless he was allowed to keep his favourites and have Botkin transferred from London[19] but achieved only a compromise: the Benckendorffs' pet Sevastopoulo remained in London while Botkin for the time being replaced Poklevsky.

Like most of those who had begun service in the Asiatic Department[20] and was well familiar with the Anglo-Russian rivalry outside Europe, Botkin was skeptical of the rapprochement with Britain, he gave priority to good Russo-German relations which alone, he felt, could help Russia preserve the status quo in the Balkan Peninsula.[21] Besides, his personal relations with the ambassador had started off on the wrong foot – perhaps because he knew that he was not welcome.

Botkin's one advantage in his conflict with the ambassador was the backing of Prince Vladimir N. Orlov, a childhood friend of Nicholas II and chief of the Emperor's Military Chancery. The prince gave to the emperor the political letters that Botkin regularly wrote to him. Botkin had the imprudence to boast to his colleagues that his letters reached the emperor's desk before the ambassador's dispatches,[22] which made him a declared antagonist of his chief. Under Lamsdorff's successor, A.P. Iswolsky who was the ambassador's friend and fellow-thinker, Benckendorff got rid of Botkin. Referring to Botkin's reports as 'political views of an indescribable silliness', Iswolsky wrote: 'I understand why you do not want him in your staff and promise to spare you this nuisance'.[23] Iswolsky had Botkin posted to Tangiers where Russia had no interests. The minister reported to his friend the ambassador: 'I know you want Sevastopoulo and I do my best to please you'.[24] The second secretary of the embassy, Sevastopoulo, was promoted to Botkin's position.

Benckendorff also curbed the initiatives of other partisans of Anglo-Russian rapprochement and put an end to what he called the 'excessive decentralization of our representation' which complicated his task.[25] The ambitious financial agent, Tatishchev, had been working for an Anglo-Russian understanding prior to Benckendorff's arrival, but Tatishchev's status as the black sheep of the foreign ministry and his personal contacts with the press and European diplomats made

18 S.P. Benckendorff to A.K. Benckendorff, 29.03/11.04.1906, BC2, box 21.

19 S.P. Benckendorff to A.K. Benckendorff, 07/20.04.1906, BC2, box 22.

20 P.S. Botkin, *Kartinki diplomaticheskoi zhizni* (Paris, 1930), 17.

21 I.V. Bestuzhev, *Bor'ba v Rossii po voprosam vneshnei politiki 1909–1910 gg.* (Moscow, 1961), 223.

22 D.I. Abrikossov, 135.

23 A.P. Iswolsky to A.K. Benckendorff, 25.4/8.5.1907, BC2, box 13.

24 A.P. Iswolsky to A.K. Benckendorff, 4/17.7.1907, BC2, box 13.

25 A.K. Benckendorff to V.N. Lamsdorff, 14/27.01.1904, GARF, f.568, op.1, ed.hr.326, l.90.

him both a rival and a threat to Benckendorff's mission. On his request, Tatishchev was recalled from London.[26]

Through systematic selection he filled his embassy with wealthy bachelors with a taste for social life. His most unfortunate choice was Sevastopoulo's successor as the second secretary. A Baltic landowner, Baron Benno von Siebert, arrived from the Russian legation in Washington in the spring of 1908 preceded by a letter of thanks to Count Benckendorff. He wrote: 'I will not fail to employ all of my zeal in carrying out my obligations so as to justify the confidence your Excellency has placed in me'.[27] In 1909–14 Siebert employed his zeal in passing to the Germans copies of the correspondence between the Russian foreign ministry and the embassy.[28]

For all the German-spy fever of the First World War, von Siebert's name never got into the press after his defection in 1918, owing to the discretion of the German foreign ministry and his own quick thinking. Neither Abrikossov nor Harold Nicolson who mentioned a German spy at the Russian embassy, spelled out his name, which points to another feature of the old diplomacy: it did its laundry at home.

London Début

From Copenhagen, Sir Edward Goschen congratulated Benckendorff on his success in London.[29] It could hardly been otherwise, since he entered London society as a member of Edward VII's intimate circle. Social success implied more engagements. The empress mother hardly missed a year without a visit to her sister Alexandra and attending to her took up much of Benckendorff's time, though it also allowed him to feed her ideas which he wanted to reach Nicholas II. Neither of the Benckendorffs enjoyed strong health, and the countess often used it as a pretext to avoid official functions. Her letters from Cowes, written on board the *Britannia*, speak of boredom. She looked forward to leaving it behind and 'enjoying a little simple life and seeing the countryside from the motor car'.[30] She replied to the ambassador's report about his visit to Lord Lansdowne's country house: 'The Bowood party seem uninteresting … too

26 S.S. Tatischev to S. Yu. Witte, 10/23.03.1903, GARF, f.597; op.1, ed.hr.701, l.13 ob.

27 B.A. von Siebert to A.K. Benckendorff, 16/29.04.1908, AVPRI, f.184, op.520, d.1245, ll.11–12.

28 Stephen Schroeder, 'Ausgedehnte Spionage' – Benno von Sieberts geheime Zusammenarbeit mit dem Auswaertigen Amt (1909–1926)' in *Militargeschitchliche zeitschrift*, 65 (2005): 425–63.

29 Edward Goschen to A.K. Benckendorff, 20.3.1903, BC2, box 12.

30 S.P. Benckendorff to A.K. Benckendorff, 10.8.1907, BC2, box 22.

many F[oreign] O[ffice officials] – the most boring for me. I like … politicians, but not officials'.[31]

Once she was happily installed in Sosnovka, nothing could make her interrupt the stay and honour an official or private engagement in Britain. The ambassador wistfully wrote from London: 'You do not know how envious I feel that you are going to be in Sosnovka'.[32] It usually fell to him to suffer boredom for Russia's sake at the country homes of Foreign Office officials. From the Wiltshire home of Sir Louis Mallet, Benckendorff complained: 'Malet [sic] does not utter a word, no one talks; it is one long ceremony … a royal progress. I hate to criticize the hosts who are doing their best, but …'.[33]

His social diary was strenuous: 'Yesterday I dined at Curzon's, a magnificent and very entertaining affair, eight tables of 14 people. [Today] lunch at Harry Cust [a journalist] with the literature, Lady Horner, Margot [Asquith] … Tonight – a dinner at Rosebery's in knee-breeches …'.[34] An enthusiastic hunter and fisherman, amiable, garrulous and argumentative,[35] Benckendorff was well-liked. Although in his letters he makes approving references to crowds of young beauties present at some of the social functions, he especially enjoyed men's parties because of the sports and relaxed atmosphere. He described his favourite kind of party: after an improvised beefsteak dinner at the house of Lord Revelstoke, Arthur Balfour appeared, then Lady Desborough dropped in and left after dinner; '… we chatted till midnight. Very little politics but all sorts of other topics'.[36]

His leaves in Sosnovka were often cut short or delayed by emergencies, so when he needed a short break, he went to Duart Castle, on the Isle of Mull in Scotland, for fishing and hunting, sometimes in the company of other members of the London diplomatic corps. He rarely managed to see his sisters Marchioness Guiccioli and Duchess of Trachenberg, especially after his Italian brother-in-law was appointed ambassador to Japan, frustrating the Benckendorff-Trachenberg-Guiccioli hopes to bring the family together by having 'Sandro' posted to Germany.[37]

His new position brought Count Aleksandr Konstantinovich to the attention of the press and all sorts of people who followed the news in Europe. The editor of *La Revue Diplomatique*, M. Jules Muelmans, reminded Count Benckendorff that he wrote the ambassador's biographical essay and asked for a loan of money

31 S.P. Benckendorff to A.K. Benckendorff, 30.11.1903, BC2, box 21.

32 A.K. Benckendorff to S.P. Benckendorff, n.d., GARF, f.1126, op.1, ed.hr.156, ll.137–8.

33 A.K. Benckendorff to S.P. Benckendorff, n.d., GARF, f.1126, op.1, ed.hr.156, ll.84–85.

34 A.K. Benckendorff to S.P. Benckendorff, 18.6/1.7.1912, GARF, f.1126, op.1, ed.hr.153, ll.58–9.

35 Maurice Baring, *The Puppet Show of Memory* (London, 1987), 213.

36 A.K. Benckendorff to S.P. Benckendorff, 7.1.1910, GARF, f.1126, d.152, ll.21–2.

37 Nathalie Hatzfeldt, Duchess of Trachenberg to A.K. Benckendorff, 25.07.1894, GARF, 1126, op.1, ed.hr.42, ll.29–32 ob. and 01.08.1912, GARF, 1126, op.1, ed.hr.42, ll.41–2 ob.

to send his invalid daughter to the south.[38] A London theatrical agency wanted his patronage to bring the Moscow Art Theatre to London. A Russian political emigrant asked him to send a petition for pardon to the emperor.[39] The embassy provided travelling permits in Central Asia to British big game hunters[40] and received unsolicited proposals from enterprising businessmen, such as a Mr Johimsen who asked the count to pass on to the empress mother his scheme which would enable Russia to sustain German pressure and put an end to 'the exploitation of the country by foreigners and Jews'.[41] At the time of international crises and later during the Great War the flow of British letters to the embassy proposing financial or military schemes and soliciting money for promoting Anglo-Russian friendship sharply rose.

When Russian subjects who had either witnessed or committed a crime found asylum in Britain the embassy was charged with requesting the British side to comply with the Russian court's request to extradite that person.[42] Obtaining British compliance was as tricky as it is today, and for the same reasons: a Russian subject who claimed to be a victim of political persecution rather than a suspect in a common crime was given the benefit of the doubt. Count Benckendorff found this side of his duties extremely distasteful. In pursuing these matters, which he considered insignificant, he was afraid of damaging the easy friendship between his embassy and the Foreign Office which he hoped to use for settling grand political issues. It was a great but rare relief to him when he could simply telegraph to St Petersburg as he did in 1914:

> Karl Seemel (born in Riga 1876, post office employee) stole 5,000 roubles in October 1907. Today has surrendered himself to the local justice. Benckendorff.[43]

The peculiar reputation which the Russian state had among the British led to the idea that Russian institutions of all kinds were in permanent need of more secret agents. A veteran of the British South African police applied to the embassy to join Russian 'Secret Service Police attached to this country'. The answer from the embassy was that they did not have secret police on the staff.[44] The embassy had no contacts with Russian political police agents whose task was

38 Jules Muelmans to A.K. Benckendorff, 25.08.1913, BC2, box 13.

39 V. Danchich to A.K. Benckendorff, 1911, BC2, box 12.

40 G. Gardyne to A.K. Benckendorff, 18.11.1910, BC2, box 12.

41 I.W.H. Johimsen to A.K. Benckendorff, 10.4.1909. BC2, box 13.

42 Russian foreign ministry to Russian embassy in London, [n.d.], AVPRI, f.184, op.520, d.1104, l.2

43 A.K. Benckendorff to Russian foreign ministry, [1914], AVPRI, f.184, op.520, d.1481, l.5.

44 Frank Colliard to Russian ambassador to Great Britain, 22.03.1914, AVPRI, f.184, op.520, d.1481, l.20

to report on the Russian political exiles, from anarchists to Bolsheviks. Most of these agents were recruited by the St Petersburg secret police among those who came to Britain as victims of political or anti-Semite persecutions in the Russian Empire.[45]

The latter issue, persecutions of Jews in the Russian Empire, hounded Count Benckendorff throughout his stay in Britain. The count was exasperated by the way the Russian government brought grave political problems on itself through the mismanagement of the Jewish issue. From his point of view the obsolete discriminatory Russian Jewish legislation needlessly complicated the domestic situation in Russia. The publicity given in Britain to the pogroms in the Polish, Ukrainian, Bessarabian and Byelorussian provinces of the empire, where most of Russia's Jewish subjects resided, and the protests and incriminations against the Russian government's attitude in the British and US press, worked against Russia's interests abroad and against his task of building up and maintaining good Anglo-Russian relations. He pleaded with the dowager empress to persuade Nicholas II to adopt a more modern and pragmatic attitude.[46] To his friend the foreign minister he wrote:

> As for the Jews, to look for remedies or palliatives ignoring the only existing effective remedy [removal of discriminatory legislation] because we do not like it, seems to me absolutely pointless. As long as this cause persists the Jewish poor will be at the head of terrorism despite the police, the security and the repression, and the Jewish rich, unable to find an alternative to these desperate measures, will wage a financial war on us.[47]

London Society

Benckendorff hoped to accomplish a turnaround in Anglo-Russian relations by influencing public opinion through his personal relations with influential Britons and through the press. The former was a tradition among aristocracy and diplomats: maintaining a wide circle of acquaintances in the best society by entertaining, visiting and joining associations. The count never failed to remind the Russian foreign ministry to extend the Petersburg Yacht Club membership to the British diplomats and made sure that his staff became members of the best London clubs, like White's or the Travellers' and were treated with due respect there. He advised

45 S.G. Svatikov, *Russkii politicheskii sysk za granitsei* (Moscow, 2002[1930]), 120–54.

46 A.K. Benckendorff to Empress Maria Feodorovna (draft), 25.11/8.12.1905, GARF, f.1126, op.1, ed.hr.1, d.4, ll.5–8.

47 A.K. Benckendorff to Iswolsky, 17/30.03.1908; *Au service de la Russie*, 2: 145–50.

the Russians to accept philosophically attacks on Russia in British newspapers.[48] The count argued that '[protests] would only very inadequately correspond to the principles of national dignity'.

Yet he reacted strongly to a slight to the personal dignity of a Russian gentleman. When an official at the Ascot Horse Show treated a visiting Russian officer rudely, the episode produced a flurry of letters between Benckendorff, the French ambassador, as the doyen of the diplomatic corps, and the president of the show.[49]

He applied great effort to meeting many people in the small social group which held a near monopoly on political power in Britain. He may have learned from them or about them much that would have helped him in his professional activity, but Benckendorff was not a man to take advantage of private relations for professional purposes. This reduced his busy social life to a pursuit of personal popularity largely for its own sake. The personal acceptance he achieved in the British upper class was not translated into influence on the British statesmen. In fact it was the reverse. The people who befriended him – Asquith, Hardinge, Grey, Haldane, Cassel, Revelstoke, Curzon, Churchill and Cambon – had stronger personalities than he did. Many professional politicians, financiers or officials of a parliamentary state had the toughness and single-mindedness required and tested by their career. Compared to the obstacles they had had to overcome in rising through the ranks, the Russian ambassador drifted into his high position with many illusions intact, and as a result he was much more prone to treat his post as the British aristocracy were said to do: as part of a 'giant system of outdoor relief'.

Two circumstances contributed to Benckendorff's considerable personal success: personality and pedigree. He and his wife were 'an extraordinarily exhilarating and encouraging public',[50] and Chatsworth, Tring, Bowood, or Coombe were the natural places for the Benckendorffs to be seen. If ever the count looked down on the clever bourgeois Paul Cambon it would have been when he wrote to his wife that he was going to Windsor for what seemed a very grand party, with the Austrian ambassador Count von Mensdorff (the king's third cousin) and himself being 'the only ones to have crossed the bridge'.[51]

Benckendorff's tastes and sympathies drove him socially towards the Conservatives. The Duke of Devonshire, Lord Lansdowne, the ex-prime minister Arthur Balfour and other Cecils were his lifelong friends. He relied much on

48 A.K. Benckendorff to Maria Feodorovna, 06/19.04.1904, GARF, f.642, op.1, ed.hr.917, ll.35–42 ob. and A.K. Benckendorff to S.D. Sazonov, [n.d.], AVPRI, f.184, op.520, d.1481, l.16.

49 A.K. Benckendorff to Lonsdale, 13.06.1910, BC2, box 13; Lonsdale to A.K. Benckendorff, 18.06.1910, BC2, box 13.

50 Maurice Baring, 213.

51 A.K. Benckendorff to S.P. Benckendorff, 3/15.6.1912, GARF, f.1126, op.1, d.178, l.50

their political opinions. He also made friends with the Churchills, the Liberal Prime Minister H.H. Asquith, his wife Margot, their children and in-laws.[52] The ties proved so lasting that in the 1930s Asquith's granddaughter married Benckendorff's grandson. Mrs Asquith's friends, the Souls Lady Horner, Lady Desborough and the Duchess of Rutland figure regularly in the ambassador's letters. At the house of Harry Cust, a journalist and also a member of the Souls, Benckendorff met political figures and journalists. On the Windsor weekends Benckendorff talked to the King's friend and financier Sir Ernest Cassel about the Baghdad railway enterprise.[53] The Benckendorffs regularly exchanged visits with the Sassoons and the Rothschilds.

He had a wonderful time as he endeavoured to translate the British aristocracy's liking and interest in himself to Russia, but the ultimate political effect was minimal. At most, he made the Japanese legation jealous during the Russo-Japanese war: they complained about being neglected by London society. Lansdowne realized that this was only because Benckendorff was outgoing and made friends easily, and to correct the impression the Foreign Secretary imposed on himself and on the king, the duty 'to make more fuss' over the Japanese ambassador.[54] No matter how many shoots Benckendorff attended at ducal country seats, the Japanese were still Britain's allies and the Russians were their antagonists. Benckendorff's expectations and Hayashi's touchiness were a common mistake which Sir Edward Grey pointed out to the German ambassador in August 1914: one should not draw political conclusions from British personal friendliness.[55] In 1906, during the Anglo-Russian rapprochement, Lord Revelstoke flattered Benckendorff by saying that the latter's personal popularity helped Barings Bank place the Russian loan in the City,[56] but it is hard to measure how many millions of pounds sterling personal popularity was worth in the City. The Japanese had placed their loans without much courting of London society.

The count, who spent most of his own life outside Russia, encouraged his British friends to travel there to learn 'something new about Russia in the good sense'.[57] In 1902–14 the name of Benckendorff's estate Sosnovka was well-known among their London acquaintances. Those who enjoyed the Benckendorffs' hospitality and toured Russia under the guidance of the count's numerous in-laws often returned with a keen desire 'to remove erroneous ideas that exist in regard to

52 H.H. Asquith, *Letters to Venetia Stanley* (Oxford, 1982).

53 A.K. Benckendorff to S.P. Benckendorff, 05/18.12.1909, GARF, f.1126, op.1, ed.hr.152, ll.107–12.

54 Lansdowne to Knollys, 09.12.1904, RA VIC/ADDC 7/2/Q.

55 *Perepiska Vilgel'ma II s Nikolaem II, 1894–1914* (Moscow, 2007[1923]), 228.

56 Revelstoke to A.K. Benckendorff, 10.04.1906, BC2, box 14.

57 A.K. Benckendorff to S.P. Benckendorff, 25.7/8.8.1912, GARF, f.1126, op.1, ed.hr.153, ll.87–8.

all things Russian'.[58] But if any benefit for Russia's image came out of these visits, it was from Countess Benckendorff's literary and artistic friends. Even minor literary figures, like Maurice Baring or Hilaire Belloc, had a wider audience and more persuasive power than a society figure, like Evan Charteris. The composer Ethel Smyth, one of the visitors to Sosnovka, wrote to Countess Benckendorff that she wanted to open her countrymen's eyes because 'the English seem to know nothing whatever about the Russians … or rather, they know the Russian ballet … then comes a hiatus … then wild words – 'Siberia! Cossacks!'[59] Her words indicate that by sheer luck the count's efforts to improve Russia's public image coincided with a fashion for everything Russian, which swept Europe between 1907 and 1914 thanks to the *Ballets Russes*, but the general opinion still veered wildly between the extremes and ignored the un-dramatic everyday Russia.

Public Relations

Another element which the ambassador cultivated in creating a favourable climate for Anglo-Russian political relations was the press. He went to great lengths to be well informed and also to provide information to the press, both in Russia and in Britain. He had a lifetime habit of reading the Russian and European press and usually discussed the most interesting items with his wife. Benckendorff preferred the British conservative press as being considerably more level-headed than the 'liberal papers' such as the *Daily News* and the *Westminster Gazette*. He had contacts with the conservative *Daily Telegraph* and the *Standard*, and to a lesser degree with the *Westminster Gazette* and the *Morning Post*. He made a point of frequent confidential talks with the Foreign Office officials to reassure them regarding Russia's position and intentions and he did as much for the journalists because, as he wrote to the countess:

> The press does not understand that governments change their opinions every day because events are galloping and views are following them, and the press is still attacking the [Russian] government for the position which it abandoned long ago.[60]

Whenever possible, the ambassador enlisted well-disposed British politicians to curb British newspapers' anti-Russian attitudes. On at least one occasion H.H. Asquith had an explanation regarding a Russian issue with J.A. Spender, the editor of the 'well-intentioned but mischievous' *Westminster Gazette*.[61]

58 Lawrence Troing to A.K. Benckendorff, 19.2.1905, BC2, box 15.

59 Ethel Smyth to S.P. Benckendorff, 10.09.1916, BC2, box 14.

60 A.K. Benckendorff to S.P. Benckendorff, 23.10/6.11.1912, GARF, f.1126, op.1, 153, ll.165–8.

61 H.H. Asquith to A.K. Benckendorff, 15.5.1910, BC2, box 12.

Benckendorff found a strong supporter in Gavriil Wesselitsky[-Božidarović]. This London correspondent of the *Novoye Vremya* [New Times] and a longtime president of the London section of the Foreign Press Association (FPA) also wrote under the pen name 'Argus'. Wesselitsky was an influential figure in the European journalistic world, with ties to many European statesmen and to the British Balkan Committee. He settled in London in 1892 when he was expelled from Prussia for his hostile correspondences to Petersburg. He had preached an alliance of Britain, Russia and France since then and was considered by the Kaiser, one of Germany's worst enemies along with two other Benckendorff collaborators, Poklevsky and Tatishchev.[62] He provided the ambassador with news and wrote his political comments for the press along the guidelines supplied by Benckendorff.[63]

Wesselitsky's presidency of the FPA was useful to the Russian embassy in indirect ways: wide acquaintance among foreign journalists in London kept him well-informed about the situation in their home countries and his re-election in 1910 was a little bonus for Russian foreign policy.[64] Wesselitsky invited Benckendorff and his staff to attend the FPA banquets in order to mix with the journalists and diplomats of other countries.[65] Through Wesselitsky the ambassador met some London journalists. In the midst of an anti-Russian campaign, provoked by the Russo-Japanese war, the editor of the *Westminster Gazette* J.A. Spender wrote to the ambassador:

> Wesselitsky suggests that I come and see you. I need not say that I understand perfectly well what M. Wesselitsky tells me about Your Excellency's position in respect to English politics ...[66]

The Anglo-Russian rapprochement considerably mellowed *The Times*' attitude to Russia, and the tone of the paper changed in 1906. The ambassador undertook to improve the embassy's relations with *The Times* and in April 1907 Valentine Chirol, the foreign editor, wrote to Benckendorff to say that he was glad that 'what we said so completely met your views' and added that he would be glad to avail himself of Benckendorff's invitation to come and talk.[67] J.A. Spender left a portrait of Benckendorff in his memoirs which explains why his invitations were popular:

> He told me that if I would come to the embassy soon after twelve any morning I should nearly always find him there and ready for a talk. I did go pretty often and sometimes, I will confess, for the mere pleasure of hearing him talk. He gave

62 *The History of the Times: The 20th Century Test, 1884–1912* (London, 1947), 461.
63 G. Wesselitsky to A.K. Benckendorff, 1903, BC2, box 15.
64 G. Wesselitsky to A.K. Benckendorff, 02.05.1910, BC2, box 15.
65 G. Wesselitsky to A.K. Benckendorff, 20.06.1910, BC2, box 15.
66 J.A. Spender to A.K. Benckendorff, 24.3.1904, BC2, box 14.
67 Valentine Chirol to A.K. Benckendorff, 10.4.1907, BC2, box 12.

> me whimsical but kindly descriptions of the Russian people, and of the political ideas which ran through a million villages across the great expanse of Russia. He threw up his hands in a comic despair when I asked him how I was to justify the ways of the Czardom to the Liberal readers of the *Westminster Gazette* ... He painted rapid and vigorous sketches of the relations of the powers and the play of personalities among them, and was generally clear and sagacious in his forecasts.[68]

In the earlier years Benckendorff complained that the popular *Tribune* and *Daily News* harmed Russia's image in British public opinion, but he regarded the British press as the best and the most independent there was.[69] In the case of anti-Russian publicity, the ambassador rather unconvincingly excused the British papers on the grounds that they did no more than pick up the gossip originally spread by the French.[70]

Benckendorff courted the British press but expected obedience from the Russian press.[71] In his low opinion of Russian journalists, Benckendorff was at one with his colleagues. Lamsdorff habitually referred to one or another paper as 'the notorious organ of our pathetic press'.[72] The minister scorned their claim to independence, knowing that although he could not dictate to the papers, he could have them fined or closed. On such terms collaboration between the press and the foreign ministry was impossible. Lamsdorff's only way of influencing public opinion was through articles written by his officials and inserted in the press.[73]

Nevertheless the British embassy found Russian newspapers to be 'a useful index of public opinion' precisely because they had no general political direction from above and the government's desires carried little weight with the journalists.[74] After 1905, reflecting the attitude of Russian society, the papers of all political persuasions were, to varying degrees, hostile to Russian diplomacy: from the right and from the left the diplomats were accused of sabotaging Russia's national interests. Much as Benckendorff derided the tone and ignorance of the Russian papers he admitted bitterly that the right-wing *Novoye Vremya* and the liberal *Rech* [Speech] between them 'yield enough power to ruin the empire of Alexander the

68 J.A. Spender, 2: 176.

69 A.K. Benckendorff to Iswolsky, 09/22.08.1906, *Au service de la Russie*, 1: 357–8.

70 A.K. Benckendorff to V.N. Lamsdorff, 22.9/5.10.1904, GARF, f.601, op.1, d.739–40, ll. 11–12.

71 S.P. Benckendorff to A.K. Benckendorff, 22.11/4.12.1908, BC2, box 22.

72 V.N. Lamsdorff to A.K. Benckendorff, 13.2.1904, BC2, box 13.

73 Scott to Lansdowne, 02.02.1902, BD, 1: 272–3.

74 Spring Rice to Grey, 26.04.1906, *British Documents on Foreign Affairs – Reports and Papers from the Foreign Office Confidential Print. Part I, from the mid-nineteenth century to the First World War. Series A, Russia, 1859–1914* (ed. Dominic Lieven) (Frederick, c.1983), 4: 53.

Great and the Roman Empire'.[75] In his eyes the influence of the press undermined diplomacy's efforts to maintain peace by inflaming low passions with their 'cheap patriotism'.[76] Whenever there was a political crisis in Europe, Benckendorff's letters were filled with scathing references to the Russian press:

> When you read them attentively, it is as if this press did not realize that they are pushing straight for a war under the worst conditions. It is the disgrace of these 'grassroots movements' that they are stimulated by … [irresponsible] hacks.[77]

Nor was the ambassador in London the Russian press's hero. During the Russo-Japanese war, the press attacked Russian diplomacy for having failed to avert the war. The atmosphere was so heated that, breaking with the ministry's tradition of contemptuous silence, the director of the First Department, Hartwig, sent a letter to the owner-editor of the *Novoye Vremya* A.S. Suvorin, protesting against the libelous accusations of betrayal.[78] Benckendorff never desisted from his attempts to get the *Novoye Vremya* to abandon its anti-British tone. He attempted to meet Suvorin in order to 'open his eyes' and made other contacts with his journalists. A personal meeting helped him to win over to his views a *Novoye Vremya* political analyst A.A. Pilenko, who had been attacking Benckendorff's activity.[79] But the hostility of the newspaper to the pro-Entente course of the foreign ministry remained unabated. In 1911 Suvorin refused to publish Wesselitsky's correspondences inspired by Benckendorff, and the ambassador had his unofficial assistant reinstated through the ministry's informal contacts at the newspaper.[80] Benckendorff's archive contains a letter from a *Novoye Vremya* journalist describing his efforts to persuade his colleagues of the need for a more conciliatory attitude towards Britain and promising to continue acting in accordance with 'the obligations which I undertook with respect to Your Excellency'.[81]

Former Russian diplomats, especially those who became journalists and crossed to the enemy side with all their contacts and knowledge, were the most dangerous enemies in the foreign ministry's eyes. Sergei S. Tatishchev, after leaving the London embassy, became the head of a newly formed department

75 A.K. Benckendorff to S.P. Benckendorff, 27.09/10.10.1912, GARF, f.1126, op.1, ed.hr.153, ll.127–9.

76 A.K. Benckendorff to S.P. Benckendorff, 07/20.10.1912, GARF, f.1126, op.1, ed.hr.153, ll.148–9.

77 A.K. Benckendorff to S.P. Benckendorff, 07/20.10.1912, GARF, f.1126, op.1, ed.hr.153, ll.148–9.

78 N.K. Hartwig to A.K. Benckendorff, 08/21.07.1904, GARF, f.1126, op.1, ed.hr. 11, l.1.

79 *Les Carnets de Georges Louis (directeur des affaires politiques au ministère des affaires étrangères, ambassadeur en Russie) tome premier 1908–1912* (Paris, 1926), 1: 221.

80 A.A. Neratov to A.K. Benckendorff, 25.08/07.09.1911, BC2, box 13.

81 N.A. Komarov to A.K. Benckendorff, 21.07/03.08.1904, BC2, box 13.

of the interior ministry which encroached on the foreign ministry's monopoly of providing official information to foreign journalists. During the Russo-Japanese war his task was to influence the coverage of Russia in the foreign press. His 1904 tour of European capitals unnerved Lamsdorff and caused Benckendorff's protest against Tatishchev's planned arrival in London on the grounds that it would create the impression that he, the ambassador, was trying to interfere with the freedom of British press. He wrote:

> … the attitude I am trying to maintain, ineffectual though it might be, is that I never interfere. Influencing the press is possible, I believe, in Germany, probably in France, less so in Italy, but in England it is impossible, unless there are special circumstances and resources which the Japanese have used but I cannot.

As the interior minister, Vyacheslav Plehve, was high in the emperor's favour, he disregarded Lamsdorff's request to cancel Tatishchev's tour or to make him skip London.[82] Lamsdorff warned the ambassador to be cautious with 'this perfidious man' who would travel through Paris and Berlin 'spreading rumours ahead of the official information by our diplomatic channels'.[83] Witte's intervention brought Tatishchev's enterprise to an end during his first stop at Berlin.[84] The inter-ministerial struggle for authority undermined everybody's work. Benckendorff attempted to maintain unity of command at least in London, and banned unauthorized contacts between his subordinates and British officials or press.

Ambassador's First Steps

Lamsdorff's instructions to Count Benckendorff in December 1902 summed up Russia's position: British and Russian interests were threatened in Crete, Macedonia, Turkish finance and the Baghdad railway project. The *status quo* in the Ottoman Empire suited Russia's interests, and Russia would always oppose the emergence of a strong foreign influence in Constantinople. The German Baghdad railway project, if implemented, would be pernicious to Russia's interests. Since the railway would affect Britain's control of the shortest route to India, it would be logical to assume that Britain would also oppose the project. Lamsdorff pointed out that even a rumour of a pending Anglo-Russian understanding would help to delay the implementation of the project by Turkey and Germany. Knowing the traditional British fear of becoming an unwilling instrument of Russia's seizure of the Straits, Lamsdorff wanted the ambassador to tell them that if the situation

82 A.K. Benckendorff to V.N. Lamsdorff, 19.04/01.05.1904, GARF, f.597, op.1, ed.hr. 822, ll.1–2 ob.

83 V.N. Lamsdorff to A.K. Benckendorff, 24.05.1904, BC2, box 13.

84 V.N. Plehve – S.S. Tatischev, 28.05/10.06.1904, (Telegram), GARF, f.597, op.1, ed.hr.770, l.41.

in Constantinople became truly unfavourable to Russia, the imperial government might act to protect its interests on the Bosporus with or without British consent. Such a perspective should convince the London cabinet that Ottoman status quo was in their interest as well.

Lamsdorff explained that Anglo-Russian interests were opposed in the Mediterranean basin and Egypt. The French had resigned themselves to Britain's growing presence in Morocco and Egypt, but, if Britain achieved complete control of these countries, then both exits from the Mediterranean would be in British hands and Russia could not accept that.

Still, Britain's political and economic rivalry with the US and Germany might become a base for a rapprochement with Russia. Russia and Britain could achieve a compromise because Britain had lost her predominant position in the Ottoman Empire. Anglo-Russian rivalry in Persia was inevitable. Russia acknowledged Britain's strong positions in Kuwait, Masqat, Bahrain and partly in Persian ports, but the British presence in continental Persia was comparatively insignificant and British proposals for a partition of spheres of influence would put Russia at a disadvantage. Russia and Britain had made an agreement on the inviolability and integrity of Persia, but the British at one time violated it by occupying part of Persian Baluchistan, and the Russian government had to pressure the Shah's government to demand their withdrawal. The British, said Lamsdorff, encouraged the Afghanis to claim parts of Seistan, the only fertile region on the crossroads from India and Central Asia to Persia, and even provoked hostilities between the two, so as to take advantage of the 1857 Anglo-Persian treaty and act as the mediator. Russia took steps to establish maritime communications with Persia via the Persian Gulf ports. This was designed to put an end to the frequent British claim that the Gulf was their exclusive property.

In Central Asia, Lamsdorff continued, Russia's expansion was driven by the need to protect her frontiers from the stateless tribes eternally engaged in internecine wars. By the treaty of 1872–3, the Russian government agreed to abstain from direct political relations with Afghanistan in exchange for the British commitment not to expand their domains in the Pamirs. In 1885 a border agreement *de facto* delimited Russian and Afghan territories. In 1900 Russia communicated to London that there was a need to modify the existing procedure because of the need for the Russian administration of the border provinces to settle routine non-political issues with the Afghan authorities. London agreed in principle, but suggested defining the issues on which direct Afghan-Russian contacts could take place. The Russian government left this suggestion unanswered because the issue of principle was settled and only time would tell what concrete issues should be discussed. Benckendorff was to observe the trends in Anglo-Afghan relations under the new Amir. Lord Curzon's measures to raise the military potential of the Indian army intensified British activity on the north-western border of India. If Britain seized the strategic routes to India, it would hurt Russia's interests.

The foreign ministry held that in China, as in Persia, Britain was trying to make headway by encouraging separatist rulers of the frontier regions. Russia, on the contrary, supported the legitimate rulers who ensured stability in their countries. In 1899 Britain and Russia agreed on spheres of interests in China. From St Petersburg's point of view, Britain was not holding too strictly to the agreement and, taking advantage of China's weakness after the uprising of 1900, along with Japan, Germany and the United States, tried to force from the Chinese government railway concessions to the north of Peking and appointment of a British director on the Peking–Shanghai–Guan railway, which Russia managed to prevent. Britain also attempted to create international combinations to oppose Russia's alleged ambitions, including the alliance with Japan which became Russia's regional adversary after the Sino-Japanese war.[85]

The Anglo-Japanese alliance treaty, did not alarm Russia, the foreign minister wrote, because the parties agreed that each of them would remain neutral in case of the other one's war with a third power. Benckendorff was to insist, in his discussions with the British, that in March 1902 Russia signed a treaty with China about a conditional evacuation of Manchuria, thus demonstrating her absolute disinterest.

Britain's attempts to get all-encompassing and exclusive rights in China (as confirmed by the text of the Anglo-Chinese treaty of 25 August 1901) might potentially affect Russia's interests confirmed by various Russo-Chinese treaties. But in the Far East, as almost everywhere else, British interests were coming into collision with Germany's, which could have favourable consequences for Russia.

Lamsdorff emphasized Britain's recent readiness to enter not only specific agreements but even formal alliances with restrictive obligations because she could not obtain the desired goals by her own means. Britain's relations with the Triple Alliance therefore were of particular interest. A permanent arrangement between England and Germany would be very dangerous for Russia, and Russian policy was to discourage their rapprochement. Benckendorff was instructed to persuade the British government that it was possible for Britain and Russia to reconcile their interests, as long as 'the historic tasks of the two nations were not brought into play'. Lamsdorff did not believe in a broad and lasting Anglo-Russian understanding, even less an alliance.[86]

The correctness of Lamsdorff's estimates is confirmed by historians who write that after Lansdowne's unsuccessful attempt at achieving an Anglo-German combination to oppose Russia in the Far East early in 1901, Britain and Germany began to drift apart.[87] Alfred Lyall, a veteran expert on Central Asian issues, wrote in November 1902 to the Secretary for India Lord George Hamilton that if the viceroy's report about the new Afghan Amir's intention to make a frontier

85 T.G. Otte, 'The Boxer Uprising and British Foreign Policy: The End of Isolation' in *The Boxers*, 163.

86 Russian foreign ministry, *Instructions to A.K. Benckendorff, Russia's ambassador to London*, 01/13.12.1902, in *Korennye interesy Rossii*, 332–8.

87 Keith Neilson and T.G. Otte, *The Permanent Under-Secretary for Foreign Affairs, 1854–1946* (New York, 2009), 14–16.

arrangement with Russians was true, then Britain's policy regarding Afghanistan would have to be reviewed. Britain would be free from any obligations towards the Amir and it would make sense to ascertain whether an understanding with Russia was possible.[88] The newly formed Committee for Imperial Defence (CID) wanted to hear about the effects on Britain's strategic position in the Mediterranean, of a Russian occupation of Constantinople and the Straits, and the reinforcements required in India in case of a war against the Franco-Russian alliance,[89] Britain's perennial concern. Two months later Prime Minister Balfour explained to the king that an arrangement with Russia was desirable, so it was better not to annoy it unnecessarily in Tibet.[90]

But before he left for London with instructions, Benckendorff made it his business to visit his old friend Sir Charles Scott, the British ambassador at Petersburg, and set the tone for the next ten years of his cooperation with the Foreign Office. Scott wrote to Lansdowne that Benckendorff gave him information which was to be kept 'strictly secret, for he [Benckendorff] has seen neither the emperor nor Lamsdorff since his nomination' and did not want to be named as the source. To Scott's complaint about Lamsdorff's silence regarding Britain's protest against Russo-Afghan border contacts, Benckendorff replied that although he had no instructions as yet to discuss Afghanistan he could tell him a secret: Hartwig told him that Russia had 'no intention to enter any new relations with Afghanistan without the consent of Britain'. Lamsdorff's delay in replying was only due to the difficulty of formulating practical proposals. Then Benckendorff asked Scott: 'What will your government consider acceptable and practicable terms?' Scott prudently answered that he had no idea, but they would not agree to diplomatic relations between Russia and Afghanistan. Benckendorff reassured him again that no missions would be sent to Kabul or Herat and suggested to Scott to pass this information on to London without mentioning his name.[91]

Lansdowne's answer was enthusiastic.[92] But when Scott went to see Lamsdorff, he heard the opposite of what Benckendorff told him.[93] In this manner, even before the chivalrous count presented his credentials in London, Lansdowne knew that his soul was pure, but that he was prone to speak without authority. The British eventually ceased to listen to the ambassador but instead supplied him with ideas which they wanted the Russian foreign ministers to hear.

Benckendorff's French colleague, Paul Cambon, who was to assist him in his mission,[94] took the view that if Anglo-Russian relations were to improve, Cambon himself would have to do all the work, because the Russian was

88 Alfred Lyall to George Hamilton, 19.11.1902, RA VIC/MAIN/X/14/9.
89 Minutes of the 1st Secret CID session, 18.12.1902, RA VIC/MAIN/W/32/1.
90 A. Balfour to Edward VII, 19.02.1903, RA VIC/MAIN/R/23/43.
91 Scott to Lansdowne, 25.12.1902, FO 800/140, 123–41.
92 Lansdowne to Scott, 29.12.1902, FO 800/140, 142.
93 Scott to Lansdowne, 22.01.1903, FO 800/140, 92.
94 Russian Foreign Ministry, *Instructions*, 332–8.

a nonentity. He summed up his opinion in a letter to his minister: up to 1902 Benckendorff had occupied junior posts and he owed his ambassadorship and his success in society to Queen Alexandra's friendship. He was nearly ignorant of the economic interests of the nations, of British global policies and knew even less about the British political system and parties. He would base his judgments on gossip and petty considerations.[95] To serve French interests Cambon took it on himself to persuade Lansdowne that Russia had no annexionist designs.[96] At the same time, he explained to the Russian ambassador that Britain was on the defensive in Asia and Lansdowne wanted an arrangement with Russia if the latter would accept a compromise. Benckendorff said he would like to hear this directly from Lansdowne, as he was afraid to start the conversation because he might he disavowed from Petersburg.[97] Since the autumn of 1902 Lord Lansdowne had known that Benckendorff was eager to work for an entente and he waited for Russia to make the first move. Benckendorff hoped to avoid it by using the French ambassador as a go-between. In the meanwhile the count busied himself with the current issues of bilateral relations, and his efforts did not go unnoticed. The German chargé d'affaires reported in the spring of 1903 that London financial circles including the Rothschild family, which used to be anti-Russian, seemed now to be more favourable to Russia. He attributed this to the efforts of the new ambassador and his first secretary, Poklevsky.[98] Overtures from the embassy led the Rothschilds to expect a change in the attitude of the Russian government to the Jewish problem in Russia. Benckendorff supported a proposal from the new Russian financial agent to the responsible ministries (finance and interior) to accelerate the revision of the 'Jewish legislation' and to keep the Jewish press in the US and Britain (the most hostile to the Russian government) informed about the progress. All this was presented as a way to diminish the anti-Russian propaganda in the news.[99]

One of Lamsdorff's first letters to the new ambassador came accompanied by the file relating to Russia's relations with Afghanistan.[100] The minister painstakingly explained to Benckendorff that, given Britain's weak position, a negative understanding in the Afghan issue suggested by the ambassador would be a bad bargain: the Amir forbade his officials to have direct contacts either with the Russian or the Anglo-Indian border agents. Benckendorff was instructed to tell Lansdowne that direct contacts between Russian and Afghan border agents were already taking place and would be impossible to prevent. In April there were border frictions between the peasants on the Russian side of the border and

95 Paul Cambon to T. Delcassé, 06.08. 1903, DDF, 2: 520–2.

96 Lansdowne to E. Monson, 12.02.1902, BD, 2: 124–5.

97 Paul Cambon to T. Delcassé, 06.08.1903, DDF, 2: 520–2.

98 Eckardstein to Bülow, 10.05.1903, *Die Grosse Politik der Europaischen Kabinette. 1877–1914* (Berlin, 1924), 17: 567–70.

99 I.V. Rutkovsky to V.N. Kokovtsev, 18/31.07.1904 (draft), BC2, box 14.

100 Lamsdorff to A.K. Benckendorff, 23.01/05.02.1903, BC2, box 13.

the Afghanis; the boundary pillars were broken near Herat and the local Russian authorities wrote to the governor of Herat about the repair. The Indian government considered it a political issue on which Russia should communicate with them. Russia treated it as a local issue to be settled directly by Russian and Afghan local authorities. The Indian government interpreted this as Russia's foray against Britain's control of Afghan foreign relations.[101] The Russian foreign ministry did not attempt to allay British suspicions.

China's weakness left a power vacuum in Tibet and since the autumn of 1902, on both sides rumours were rife of the rival's pending move into Tibet. Lamsdorff authorized the Russian minister in Peking to assure the Chinese government that there were no Russians in Tibet and that the rumours were spread by the British.[102] He also instructed Benckendorff to warn the British that Russia disapproved of their moves in the region. Lamsdorff demanded that the ambassador warn Lansdowne 'in a categorical manner' that unless the British desisted, Russia would also take measures,[103] in the tradition of the Great Game.

The Foreign Office began by disclaiming any intention of sending troops into Tibet or adjoining provinces;[104] then claimed the need to secure compliance in a frontier dispute between Tibet and Sikkim,[105] and finally Lansdowne counter-attacked, accusing Russia of having made secret agreements with China and with Tibet to post a Russian agent in Lhassa.[106] Lansdowne said that Britain would send an agent if Russia did. In February Balfour resisted the pressure from Lord Curzon to deter Russia from placing a consul in Lhassa by sending a large military escort there.[107] Benckendorff received orders to question Lansdowne's statements and make representations about the forward policy of the British minister in Persia. He complained to Maria Feodorovna that Russia's relations with Britain would be better with a little less suspicion on the Russian side.[108] Lamsdorff insisted that the ambassador had to get the truth out of the British, for they were reconnoitring the area near the Tibetan border and marching on Chumbi. Benckendorff was free to tell the British that there was no Russo-Chinese convention, but that Russia considered the status quo in Tibet a matter of necessity. If the British violated it, Russia would protect its interests, the

---

101 Foreign Office, *Memorandum*, 14.10.1903, BD, 4: 512–21.

102 Lamsdorff to P.M. Lessar, 03.07.1903, *Rossi'ia i Tibet: Sbornik russkikh arkhivnykh dokumentov, 1900–1914* (Moscow, 2005), 45.

103 Lamsdorff to A.K. Benckendorff, 18/31.01.1903 (Telegram), AVPRI, f.184, op.520, d.1005, l.4.

104 T. Sanderson to G.A. Graevenitz, 12.10.1902, AVPRI, f.184, op.520, d.1005, l.1.

105 Foreign Office, *Memorandum*, 14.02.1903, AVPRI, f.184, op.520, d.1005, ll.11–12.

106 Lansdowne to A.K. Benckendorff, 19.02.1903, BC2, box 15.

107 A. Balfour to Edward VII, 19.02.1903, RA VIC/MAIN/R/23/43.

108 A.K. Benckendorff to Maria Feodorovna, 16/29.03.1904, GARF, f.642, op.1, ed.hr.916, ll.44–7 ob.

minister wrote, adding in a footnote: not in Tibet but in another area of Asia[109] – a hint which had never failed to get Britain's attention.

Benckendorff reported that the Foreign Secretary was extremely pleased to hear that there was no Russo-Tibetan convention. He omitted to write that he had also reassured Lansdowne that Russia had no intention of sending agents there.[110] In return, Lansdowne reiterated that England had no interest in annexation or aggression in the area[111] but did not tell the Russian ambassador that he had authorized an 'armed mission'. So, at the same time with Benckendorff's reassurances, throughout the summer and the autumn Lamsdorff received reports about the imminent British advance.[112]

In 1903 Lamsdorff lost his hold on the foreign policy to the Bezobrazovtsy, a clique of Nicholas II's personal friends, guardsmen, some of them still in service, others retired and involved in business. They got the nickname from their most active member and head of the ad hoc Far Eastern Committee (1903–5), General Aleksandr M. Bezobrazov. At the time, this inexperienced but bold and reckless man was close to Nicholas II. Initially their expansionist plans in the Far East had the support of some government ministers, but by 1903 Witte and Aleksei N. Kuropatkin, the finance and war ministers respectively, joined forces with Lamsdorff to avert war with Japan.

In February 1902 the war minister recorded in his diary that Nicholas II had plans to annex Manchuria and Korea, to establish Russian protectorate over Tibet, take over Persia and proceed to establishing Russian control over the Straits.[113] The Bezobrazovtsy persuaded Nicholas II to keep Lamsdorff in the dark regarding these plans and simply present him (and the world) with a *fait accompli*.[114] They treated Witte and Lamsdorff as timid and unimaginative bureaucrats who did not care about Russia's national greatness. General A. Bezobrazov visited the shocked Japanese ambassador to tell him that Witte and Lamsdorff were to be ignored because it was he, Bezobrazov, who made the decisions.[115] The emperor, as was his habit, set one side against the other and undermined the authority of his foreign ministry in the eyes of the world.

After the emperor ordered him to pass all the Far Eastern political issues to the 'Emperor's Lieutenant in the Far East', Admiral Evgueni I. Alekseev, formally putting two institutions in charge of Russia's foreign policy, in May 1903 Lamsdorff

109 Lamsdorff to A.K. Benckendorff, 20.03.1903, AVPRI, f.184, op.520, d.1005, ll.13–14.

110 Note, BD, 4: 305.

111 A.K. Benckendorff to Lamsdorff, 28.03/10.04.1903, AVPRI, f.184, op.520, d.1005, l.16.

112 V.O. Klemm to N.G. Hartwig, 20.10.1903, *Rossi'ia i Tibet*, 47.

113 V. Shatsillo, L. Shatsillo *Russko-I'aponskai'a voina 1904–1905* (Moscow, 2004), 191.

114 V. Shatsillo, L. Shatsillo, 154.

115 Scott to Lansdowne, 06.01.1904, RA VIC/ADDC 7/2/Q.

sent in his resignation. Nicholas II refused to accept it, angrily telling his minister that he entrusted Alekseev with the Russian interests in the Far East because 'neither you nor I can grasp the daily changes there from reading fragmented and often contradictory bits of information'.[116] He seems to have found convincing the Bezobrazovtsy's idea that a foreign minister knew less of foreign affairs than the colonels and admirals in the Far East. The minister unhappily continued in his post, unable to change the dangerous direction of the Far Eastern policy.

In London, to Benckendorff's disappointment, Lansdowne did not make any moves towards negotiating an understanding. The Foreign Secretary was interested in an agreement that would include Afghanistan, Seistan in Persia, and a coordinated position regarding the Baghdad railway. If the Russians decided to build a Caspian Sea–Persian Gulf railway to counter the Baghdad one, Lansdowne would not object to it, provided the southern end was under British control,[117] but he would not be the first to speak to Russia. Lamsdorff's future was uncertain and so was Russia's foreign policy course.

Nevertheless, Lansdowne's speech outlining the British position in the Baghdad railway project and the Persian Gulf, and the subsequent debates at the House of Lords were received in Europe as an indication that Arthur Balfour's government might be inclined to achieve an understanding with Russia.[118] In the summer Benckendorff wrote to the minister that Cecil Spring Rice was posted to Russia because he was from a political group favourable to better Anglo-Russian relations.[119] Spring-Rice, who became the first secretary and later the counsellor of the British embassy, was an enemy of Germany more than he was a friend of Russia.[120] Benckendorff, naively or disingenuously, always referred to the British Germanophobes as Russia's friends because they tended to see an understanding with Russia as the best counterweight to Germany. In any case, Spring-Rice, to whom the Benckendorffs in their semi-coded letters referred as 'Printemps', became a friend of the family and supplier of diplomatic gossip to the countess. His political opinion and advice were welcome on the strength of this friendship.

Benckendorff's counsellor, Graevenitz, on a visit to Petersburg in July complained to Lamsdorff that there was a marked coldness towards the Russian embassy in London official circles, because the British were disappointed at seeing no overtures from Russia. Lamsdorff retorted that he could not understand the British: they had spoken to the French of their wish to settle with Russia, and Russia was all for reconciliation, but she must also look out for her interests. Graevenitz reported to the ambassador that Lamsdorff's position at the ministry

116 Published by I.S. Rybachonok in *Istochnik*, 1 (1999): 38–9.

117 Lansdowne to Hardinge, 23.03.1903, FO 800/140, 158–9.

118 *The Times*, 06.05.1903.

119 A.K. Benckendorff to V.N. Lamsdorff, 04/17.06. 1903, GARF, f.568, op.1, ed.hr. 326, ll.80–81 ob.

120 For the characteristics of the British diplomats in Russia, see: Keith Neilson's *Britain and the Last Tsar.*

seemed uncertain; a change of political course was expected and Witte's dismissal confirmed this impression.[121]

But it was not yet clear what the change might entail. Insisting on Russia's evacuation of Manchuria and on curtailing the Bezobrazovtsy-led penetration of Korea, Lamsdorff warned his agents and the viceroy of the Far East that '... gaining new advantages for Russia always and everywhere is to be welcomed, provided ... the consequences of such acquisitions will not be the reverse of those desired'.[122] Lamsdorff persuaded Nicholas II to instruct the Russian minister in Peking to negotiate Russia's withdrawal.[123] The Bezobrazovtsy decried this as a humiliating concession. Lamsdorff retorted: 'In general, we can only concede something which is either ours by right or which we lay claims to; this is a case of neither ...'.[124] But almost the next day Nicholas II reiterated that Russia's three envoys (in Korea, Japan and China) were to follow the viceroy's instructions, as he was 'the principal guarantor of Russia's dignity and interests in the Far East'.[125]

A Russo-Japanese conflict would endanger France, and Delcassé instructed his ambassadors to obtain Britain's cooperation to avert it. Maurice Bompard, the French ambassador in Petersburg, failed to enlist the support of his British colleague; Paul Cambon attempted to get Lansdowne's or even Edward VII's intervention, but with scant results. Loubet and Delcassé encouraged Benckendorff to try and get Britain to exercise a moderating influence on Japan.[126]

Soon afterwards, Benckendorff made an indirect overture to Lansdowne. He said that according to Théophile Delcassé the English would welcome an understanding if Russia did not oppose Britain in Yang Tse Valley, but, he said, Lamsdorff was astonished to hear this, because Russia had not opposed Britain there. So, what were the Foreign Secretary's exact words to Delcassé? Lansdowne said that he wanted an agreement in Newchwang and Manchuria but first Russia would have to state its terms and reciprocate Britain's concessions.[127]

Two weeks later, Benckendorff came to inform Lansdowne that Russia would soon evacuate Manchuria and asked if a general understanding between Russia and Britain was possible in this case. Lansdowne answered in the affirmative

---

121 G. Graevenitz to A.K. Benckendorff, 26.06/09.07. 1903, BC2, box 12.

122 Foreign ministry to P.M. Lessar (a telegram) 24.08/06.09.1903, in V.V. Glushkov and K.E. Cherevko, *Russko-iaponska'ia voina 1904–1905 gg. v dokumentakh vneshnepoliticheskogo vedomstva Rossii: Fakty i kommentarii* (Moscow, 2006), 60.

123 E.I. Alekseev to foreign ministry, 23.08/05.09.1903, in V.V. Glushkov and K.E. Cherevko, *Russko-iaponska'ia voina 1904–1905 gg. v dokumentakh vneshnepoliticheskogo vedomstva Rossii: Fakty i kommentarii* (Moscow, 2006) 59.

124 Foreign ministry to General-Adjutant E.I. Alekseev, copied to P.M. Lessar, 26–29 August 1903, in V.V. Glushkov and K.E. Cherevko *Russko-iaponska'ia voina 1904–1905*, 61.

125 Nicholas II's resolution, 30.08/12.09.1903, in V.V. Glushkov and K.E. Cherevko *Russko-iaponska'ia voina 1904–1905*, 61.

126 Maurice Bompard, *Mon ambassade en Russie, 1903–1908* (Paris, 1937), 7–8.

127 Lansdowne to Scott, 29.07.1903, BD, 2: 212.

and repeated that he wanted to know Russia's full terms.[128] Soon after, Cambon complained to Delcassé about Benckendorff's inability to establish a rapport with Lansdowne. The count hoped that the French might influence Lamsdorff or Lansdowne to initiate talks. Bompard advised Delcassé to keep out of these exchanges until there was a formal request for French mediation; Benckendorff's overtures might be a Russian ruse to distract Britain because the two sides were not talking about Persia, the most important issue dividing them.[129]

In September, Benckendorff went on leave. He was not certain of returning to London. Still on leave in Russia, he had a letter from his well-informed brother:

> I do not know whether your chief will stay in office, particularly since he is begging to be allowed to quit. He will be missed, because the outside influences are growing stronger and they have already imposed one resignation [Witte's] and are preparing another for the autumn. Yours will be the third one. [130]

The Besobrasovtsy's policy entailed a confrontation with Britain, so they criticized Witte, Lamsdorff and his staff for being too conciliatory with the Japanese and the British. Witte's fall had been predicted for so long that when it came at the end of the summer, following his recommendation to accept the Japanese terms, it caught Witte himself by surprise. The French ambassador reported that the foreign ministry was terrified[131] because now there was no one left to side with them against Nicholas II and the Bezobrazovtsy. Benckendorff tried to influence the events through Maria Feodorovna. He wrote to her that Lamsdorff's dismissal would doom the prospects of better relations with Britain. The count's references to the subject leave no doubt that he had discussed the subject with the empress mother before and that he blamed the lack of progress on Russia: 'I am not discouraged regarding London … but I have not found anything here [in St Petersburg] to give me any confidence and *Ermutigung* [encouragement]'.[132]

He wrote to Lamsdorff about the desirability of a partnership with the strong and successful Britain which would save Russia from a conflict with Germany or Japan. Britain's behaviour during the crises bore witness to her wish to improve relations with Russia. After the general statements, Benckendorff made practical suggestions. The British were disappointed by the absence of firm proposals from Russia, and the autumn of 1903, he thought, was the critical moment when Anglo-Russian relations could either worsen or improve at the cost of 'relatively insignificant concessions', such as Afghanistan. Benckendorff suggested again that

---

128 Lansdowne to Scott, 12.08.1903, BD, 2: 213.

129 Bompard to Delcassé, 28.08. 1903, DDF, 3: 546–51.

130 P.K. Benckendorff to A.K. Benckendorff, 15/28.09.1903, GARF, f.559, op.l, ed.hr.87, ll.56–7.

131 Bompard to Delcassé, 02.09.1903, DDF, III: 556–9.

132 A.K. Benckendorff to Maria Feodorovna, 06/19.09.1903, GARF, f.642, op.1, ed.hr.916, ll.49–51 ob.

he should allay the Foreign Office's suspicions regarding the extent of Russia's interests there. Afghanistan was useless to Russia as a means of pressure on Britain. It was easier for Britain to exert pressure on Russia through Afghanistan[133] so it followed that an arrangement in the region would benefit Russia more than it would Britain.

In July and August, the Bezobrazovtsy promoted the idea of a continental Russo-German agreement which would allow Russia to increase the pressure on Japan and Britain in the Far East after having secured the western frontier.[134] The memorandum which they presented to Nicholas II was confidential, but the observers, experienced in guessing the imperial will from his actions and randomly dropped remarks, read Nicholas II as an open book: he turned down invitations to France and Italy but met with the Austrian and German emperors.

To general surprise, none other than Lamsdorff accompanied the emperor on his visits to Vienna and Germany. In fact it was on Lamsdorff's insistence that the emperor went there and signed the Mürzsteg Punctation of 2 October 1903 with Austria-Hungary. The two empires agreed to preserve the status quo in Macedonia through jointly supervised reforms. It was all Lamsdorff could do: safeguard Russia's interests in Europe during the Far Eastern war which he despaired of averting. During the stay in Mürzsteg, Nicholas II received and approved of the viceroy's report that he thought that negotiations with China regarding Manchuria should be dropped because of the Chinese government's recalcitrance, but new proposals should be presented to Japan.[135] Nicholas II and Alexandra stayed for a long vacation among her German relatives in Darmstadt where William II visited them. This made the alarmist Cecil Spring Rice imagine 'a Baltic agreement' of Russia, Denmark and Germany and probably France. He wrote that Russian overtures to Britain for specific settlements might follow but Britain had no use for those. Only a treaty would solve all the issues, but in exchange Russia would demand 'that which we cannot give her – a betrayal of Japan in the dark moment'.[136]

Nevertheless, Lamsdorff's desire to make progress in the negotiations with Japan combined to produce the effect which Benckendorff had desired. Later Benckendorff told Paul Cambon that in 1903 he approached first the king and then Lord Lansdowne without instructions. When he took what he considered encouraging news to Lamsdorff at Darmstadt, he obtained permission to ask the British if they wanted to begin exchanges. Later, he met Lamsdorff in Paris and reported that they did, and got his authorization to speak to Lansdowne.[137]

---

133 A.K. Benckendorff to V.N. Lamsdorff, 08/22 October 1903, GARF, f.568, op.1, ed.hr.326, ll.81a–d.

134 Ibid., 171–2.

135 Lamsdorff to E.I. Alekseev, 18.09.1903, in V.V. Glushkov and K.E. Cherevko *Russko-iaponska'ia voina 1904–1905*, 62.

136 Spring Rice to Mallet, 29.10.1903, FO 800/140, 183–9.

137 Paul Cambon to Rouvier, 20.10.1905, DDF, VIII: 91–6.

Benckendorff's shuttling between Darmstadt, London and Paris took place after Russia had let the third deadline for the evacuation of Manchuria pass and Japan had stepped up its war preparations. Lamsdorff came to Paris in October 1903 with a letter from Nicholas II to the French president. It was an attempt to seek the help of France and Britain to settle with Japan and Lamsdorff announced his arrival to the Russian ambassador in France with the solemn words: 'The die is cast'. During his three-day stay in Paris, Lamsdorff had a meeting with the Russian diplomats who came to Paris: Count Cassini, (Russia's minister in the US, formerly ambassador in China), his favourite assistant N. Hartwig, the ministry's renowned legal adviser F. Martens and count Benckendorff.[138]

Lamsdorff told the French foreign minister that he hoped that the imminent Anglo-French rapprochement would improve Anglo-Russian relations.[139] He listened to the French exhortations to be more open with the British government regarding Russia's intentions in Manchuria, if Russia wanted Lansdowne's favourable influence on the Japanese.[140] Then the minister told Benckendorff to talk to Lansdowne. Benckendorff's instructions were urgent for all that they lacked in specifics. He wrote a hasty letter to Maria Feodorovna that he would not be able to visit her in Denmark as promised because 'the upsetting of Lamsdorff's plans upset mine', and added:

> I am charged with transmitting a conciliating message to England, which I believe to be 'prudent', but what are all assurances in the world if the facts disprove them … Lamsdorff's views clash with those of Alexeev and both speak for the emperor.

Again the count threw in a plea for Lamsdorff who, he said, was the only one to support him wholeheartedly in his task of averting a war with Japan. He added: 'I hope he will remain in his post … I do not see anyone better'.[141] When Lamsdorff left for St Petersburg, Russian diplomats in Paris were anxiously waiting for the news from London.[142] Everyone was aware that Russia's prospects in the Far East were not good. Lessar reported to the foreign minister from Peking:

> Germany is trying its best to get us involved [in a conflict] in the Far East, and of course, does not promise China to support it against us, but constantly reminds them that any concession to Russia in Manchuria will have to be also granted to Germany in Shandong. England is the calmest of all. It understands

---

138 Lamsdorff to Urusov, 11/24.10.1903, Bachmet'ev Archive, Urusov Collection, box 20.

139 French foreign ministry, *Departmental memorandum*, 28.10.1903, DDF, IV: 70.

140 French foreign ministry, *Departmental memorandum*, 28.10.1903, DDF, IV: 71–2.

141 A.K. Benckendorff to Maria Feodorovna, 22.10/05.11.1903, GARF, f.642, ed.hr. 916, ll.59–61 ob.

142 S.P. Benckendorff to A.K. Benckendorff, [26.10]/09.11.1903, BC2, box 21.

> that in case we defeat Japan in a war, it will not be able to remain entirely uninvolved. The best for England would be to have the existing tension continue as long as possible, as it weakens us, and therefore its effective advice here is of moderation. America continues to insist on the inviolability of its treaty rights and refuses to be involved beyond that. At this point, China is placing its [hopes] only on Japan … I cannot answer the question which the Viceroy asked me, whether it is possible to resolve the Manchurian problem in a way that would favour us … There is no hope of restoring our good relations with the Chinese … The solution of the Manchurian issue is already out of our hands.[143]

Countess Benckendorff's letters confirm that all Russians in Paris at the time saw Benckendorff's endeavour above all as an attempt to avert a war, as it followed Russia's new proposals to Japan, authorized by Nicholas II from Mürzsteg. She wrote: 'I am very happy about what you say about Japan, for the moment we can breathe. I realize that England does not want to be drawn between us and Japan'.[144]

Benckendorff's first meeting with Lansdowne was on 7 November, the day after the he arrived and two days after Russian troops evacuated Mukden province of China. The count proposed to begin discussions with a view to removing all sources of misunderstanding between the two countries. He promised that in the meantime the Russian government would avoid all hostile action. They outlined the areas of discussions: Russian demands regarding direct relations with Afghanistan and the Far East. Benckendorff was confident that Russia would settle with Japan as soon as Lamsdorff recovered his full authority in foreign affairs. Lansdowne then told him that a commission would be sent to Tibet to demand reparations, but that no permanent occupation was envisaged.[145] From the ambassador's mild reaction, Lansdowne concluded that the Russian government's attitude to the Tibet issue had changed, and, to reciprocate, he telegraphed Spring Rice to abstain from communicating to Lamsdorff a note regarding Russian refusal to acknowledge the British role in Afghanistan political relations.[146]

But Benckendorff's reactions were not a good indicator of Lamsdorff's views. Their next meeting, ten days later, began in a very different mood because Russian consuls in Asia reported to Lamsdorff that Colonel Younghusband's actions looked like the first step towards a British protectorate over Tibet, especially considering that between 1885 and 1903 Britain had in a similar manner taken control over the frontier states lying between Tibet and India.[147] The foreign ministry held that British activity in the Tibet region was a reaction to the Russian occupation of

---

143 Lessar to Foreign Ministry (telegram), 19.11/02.12.1903, in V.V. Glushkov and K.E. Cherevko, *Russko-iaponska'ia voina 1904–1905*, 64.

144 S.P. Benckendorff to A.K. Benckendorff, 16/29.10.1903, BC2, box 21.

145 Lansdowne to Spring Rice, 07.11.1903. BD, 2: 222–4.

146 Memorandum on Russo-Afghan Relations, BD, 4: 519–20.

147 E.I. Alekseev to P.M. Lessar, 11.12.1903 *Rossi'ia i Tibet*, 52.

Manchuria, but the Far Eastern viceroy argued that the British forward policy in Tibet was part of the general strategy and that Britain could only be restrained by a symmetrical Russian move in Afghanistan or Persia.[148] Under the circumstances, Lamsdorff needed to have British explanations regarding Tibet or concede to the Russian military that a move against the British was in order. He ordered the reluctant Benckendorff to tell Lansdowne that a British force was heading for Lhassa[149] in violation of the status quo. Benckendorff asked Lansdowne if he could communicate to St Petersburg that the London cabinet had authorized the Younghusband expedition with reluctance and that its only goal was to obtain satisfaction from the Tibetans. Lansdowne consented to this, but did not confirm that Britain did not intend to alter the status quo in Tibet.[150] Benckendorff's account of the same conversation omitted all references to the status quo and reported that only an officer and a small escort were marching into Tibet 'to impose respect'. It was not an annexation or aggression, and the Foreign Secretary had intended to inform the Russian ambassador. Benckendorff had to add that, to his question about the date of the mission's departure, Lansdowne said it was imminent,[151] a *fait accompli* in the tradition of the Great Game. In Benckendorff's report, Lansdowne sounded almost apologetic, reversing their roles. Having made his point, Lansdowne invited the ambassador to outline the issues for discussion. Benckendorff named China, India and Persia. He said that he could not be more specific as he was only authorized to chat about the questions.[152] Lansdowne saw no point in further discussions.

But during the Windsor weekends, the king and his friend the counsellor of the British embassy at St Petersburg, Charles Hardinge, kept alive Benckendorff's hopes for a settlement. On Hardinge's invitation, Benckendorff listed all the concessions which he thought Russia could offer. It would open all treaty ports to international trade and hand the treaty port of Newchwang over to the Chinese, provided it had a privileged voice in the International Sanitary Commission and some concessions on tariffs and rates. As for the Manchurian question, the Bezobrazovtsy and the foreign ministry were fighting over it and rather than press for evacuation at this point it would be easier for Britain to seek compensation. Russia was ready to consider Afghanistan, Seistan, Tibet and countries coterminous with the Indian frontier an entirely British sphere of interest. The Russians wanted direct relations with local Afghan authorities and would guarantee the observance of the terms, even though Russia had never surrendered its right to have direct relations with Afghanistan. In Persia, Russia did not want a division of spheres, but needed a commercial outlet on the Persian Gulf, a railway terminus. The

148 Ibid.

149 Lamsdorff to A.K. Benckendorff, 30.10.1903, AVPRI, f.184, op.520, d.1005, l.21

150 Lansdowne to Spring Rice, 17.11.1903, BD, 4: 306–7.

151 A.K. Benckendorff to Lamsdorff, 05/18.11.1903, AVPRI, f.184, op.520, d.1005, ll.24–5.

152 Lansdowne to Spring Rice, 17.11.1903, BD, 4: 183–4.

main point of dissent was over Persia's integrity and independence, which the British wanted to be guaranteed and Russia did not. Hardinge also concluded that Benckendorff was allowed to present some of Lamsdorff's views to the British to see their reaction.[153]

The ambassador's authorization for overtures might be withdrawn at any moment. His wife, still in Paris, on Poklevsky's request asked the ambassador to telegraph whether he had news from St Petersburg: 'Have you had a counter-order from L or not?'[154] On 25 November Benckendorff induced Lansdowne to return to the subject of an understanding. Lansdowne spoke about an arrangement whereby Russia would acknowledge the fact of a British protectorate over Afghanistan, Tibet and Seistan in exchange for the British recognition of Russia's privileges in Manchuria, the right of direct non-political contacts with Afghan local officials and a commercial outlet in the south of Persia and on the Persian Gulf. Lansdowne was careful to point out that he doubted the practical value of this last concession since under Russian pressure Persia had declared a 10-year moratorium on railway construction.[155]

Then the conversations ceased. Hardinge explained to the king that 'we should not hurry or be eager until we see Lamsdorff is stable'. Besides, he added, Benckendorff was so impressed by the king's interest in an understanding that he would certainly report it to Nicholas II and so give another impetus to the talks.[156] Benckendorff, unable to control his impatience, and in view of Lamsdorff's continuing abeyance, tried to lure Lansdowne with a new idea: he would propose to the emperor an arbitration agreement with Britain, similar to the Anglo-French. This would pave the way for other agreements to follow. Lansdowne turned it down as pointless until Britain and Russia settled 'the other matters lately discussed'.[157] In December, Scott and Lamsdorff touched upon the London conversations. Scott told the Russian minister that Lansdowne wanted to have the Russian views. Lamsdorff vaguely promised to provide them, but refused to discuss specific questions with Scott. Nor did he allude to the subject later.[158]

Lamsdorff did not agree with Benckendorff that the moment offered unique opportunities to Russia. He felt that all the excitement and urgency had originated at Windsor, not in the Foreign Office. The minister explained to the Russian ambassador in Vienna, who insisted on a full and definite arrangement with Austria-Hungary, that a free hand was better for Russia: 'How can we declare beforehand what Russia will do when Austria occupies the Sanjak? They do not do it precisely because they do not know what our response will be'. Therefore,

153 Hardinge to Lansdowne, 22.11.1903, BD, 4:184–6.

154 S.P. Benckendorff to A.K. Benckendorff, 21.11.1903, BC2, box 21.

155 Lansdowne to Spring Rice, 25.11.1903, BD, 4: 186–8.

156 Hardinge to Knollys, 29.11.1903, RA VIC/MAIN/W/44/10.

157 Lansdowne to Scott, 09.12.1903, RA VIC/ADDC 7/2/Q, [printed for the use of the Cabinet as #353].

158 Scott to Lansdowne, 22.12.1903, BD, 2: 226.

Russia would always be open to exchanges of views, but she must not seek a full agreement. Compromises would not avoid an ultimate clash of opposing national interests. Lamsdorff cited the Anglo-Japanese treaty as a proof of the worthlessness of a settlement with Britain: Britain had first encouraged Japan's belligerence towards Russia and then declared its neutrality. He believed that, under the existing circumstances, even if Russia had compromised in order to get agreements on Afghanistan, Persia, Tibet or Manchuria, 'England, of course, would never cease to regard Russia as her most dangerous rival in Asia'. Nicholas II wrote on the margin: 'Absolutely true'.[159] But Benckendorff in London must have seen Lamsdorff's scepticism like a case of sour grapes: Japan was satisfied with its British alliance; France was nearing an amicable settlement with Britain. Russia would be lucky to join the group.

This episode is traditionally known as Lansdowne's overture to Russia,[160] but a closer look shows that it was a diplomatic sounding by Lamsdorff induced by the efforts of the French, Edward VII and Benckendorff. Important steps, like the one which Edward VII and Benckendorff attempted to force on Lamsdorff and Lansdowne, are not made on impulse. The foreign ministers on both sides foresaw that eventually they would try to settle the pending issues. The concern about the brewing Russo-Japanese conflict made it desirable for both sides to maintain communication. The Far Eastern conflict and Curzon's policy, along with German policy in Turkey and Persia and the budding Anglo-French entente, increased the interest in an eventual settlement.

---

159 Lamsdorff to P.A. Kapnist, 22.01/04.02.1904, AVPRI, f.151, op.482, ed.hr.63, ll.18–22 ob. Courtesy of Dr Irina Rybachonok.

160 Ian Nish, *The Origins of the Russo-Japanese War* (London, 1985), 143; *Korenn'ye interes'y Rossii*, 332.

Chapter 4
The Russo-Japanese War, 1904–1905

In January 1904 the Russo-Japanese war seemed unavoidable and Benckendorff postponed his regular winter visit to St Petersburg. His oldest son, a naval officer, was in the Far East and his younger son, a guardsman, wanted to go to the theatre of war as a volunteer. His wife and daughter were waiting in tense and gloomy Petersburg. On New Year's Eve the countess sent her husband a desperate telegram for which she apologized almost at once, explaining: 'Everybody was saying that everything was over and that it was war'.[1] Spring Rice explained to her what was happening behind the scenes at St Petersburg and the countess found the extent of his information frightening.[2] A week later Sofia Petrovna passed on a coded message to her husband. Pavel Benckendorff heard from the emperor that the departing Japanese ambassador told Lamsdorff: 'Japan wants peace but foreign advice [makes] war inevitable'.[3]

Lamsdorff blamed the emperor and his advisers for the crisis: 'No one thinks of adjusting one's desires to one's means and there is a tendency to hope for miracles and count largely on the unforeseeable fortune'. The amateur politicians at Port Arthur had trampled on other nations' rights and treaties, thinking them a diplomats' invention to block the actions of patriots. 'Such is the lovely doctrine which in the past four months has brought us to a situation not only threatening but also entirely at odds with all our former principles and great traditions'.[4]

A month earlier Lansdowne had been concerned that a Russian attack on Japan might draw Britain and France into the conflict[5] and even thought of intervening to help Russia and Japan come to a settlement.[6] Then the Foreign Secretary heard from the Japanese that they were ready and wanted war[7] and ceased to entertain the idea of mediation just when Lamsdorff persuaded Nicholas II that mediation was Russia's last chance. On 12 January Lamsdorff asked for France's good offices, if possible with Britain's approval, but Delcassé was reluctant to arrange for mediation because he knew Lamsdorff to be powerless and there seemed little chance that mediation would be effective if only the foreign ministry desired

1 S.P. Benckendorff to A.K. Benckendorff, 18/31.12.1903, BC2, box 21.
2 S.P. Benckendorff to A.K. Benckendorff, 21.01/03.02.1904, BC2, box 21.
3 S.P. Benckendorff to A.K. Benckendorff, 29.01/12.02.1904, BC2, box 21.
4 Lamsdorff to A.K. Benckendorff, 08/21.01.1904, BC2, box 13.
5 Paul Cambon to Delcassé, 11.12.1903, DDF, IV: 175–6.
6 Lansdowne to Monson, 11.12.1903, BD, 2: 224.
7 Lansdowne to MacDonald, 30.12.1903, BD, 2: 227–8.

it.[8] Lamsdorff's note to all powers stating the limits to Russia's expansion in the Far East was an attempt to avoid war or at least to establish Russia's position as non-aggressor. But, Cambon remarked, what the powers would have welcomed a month earlier, they now examined critically. Lansdowne and King Edward were not satisfied with the wording of the recognition of China's sovereignty in the note[9] and asked Benckendorff to get from Petersburg an explanation of the phrase. To Cambon's suggestion that Britain should moderate Japan's behaviour, Lansdowne retorted that he could not do it because Japan's demands were fair and because all the powers were interested in these issues.[10]

Britain's position in the issue of war was favourable to Japan. London did not make firm financial commitments to Japan, but did give it a loan which enabled it to buy warships in Italy.[11] Moreover, the Japanese minister in London had done an excellent job of creating sympathy for Japan by throwing his house open to London journalists and blaming the imminent conflict on Russia.[12] Under the circumstances, Benckendorff considered courting the press futile and beneath his dignity. Unfortunately for Russia, he believed in most of the classical diplomats' canons except for one: no adverse allegation or rumour, however absurd, should remain unanswered. In this he preferred to act with regard to attacks on his country's prestige as he would with regard to personal attacks. Early in January 1904 the French ambassador at St Petersburg mentioned 'a campaign of false rumours which the Anglo-Saxon press maintains with unique nastiness against Russia'.[13] The campaign was fuelled by the expulsion of *The Times'* correspondent from Russia[14] for reporting (wrongly) that the interior minister Plehve had incited Jewish pogroms in Bessarabia. The Russian government tried to refute the allegations but British papers refused to publish their official statement.[15] A publicity war against Russia raged, and *The Times* was winning'.[16] Recognizing his impotence in Britain, Benckendorff was concerned about allaying the general animosity towards Britain in Russian press and society. He made excuses for the British hostility and blamed Germany for the Anglo-Japanese alliance.[17]

Lamsdorff had got Far Eastern diplomacy back under his control on 24 January.[18] Diplomats still hoped that things could be resolved peacefully, once

8 Ian Nish, *The Origins of the Russo-Japanese War* (London: Longman, 1985), 230–33.

9 Lansdowne to Scott, 15.01.1904, BD, 2: 234–5.

10 Paul Cambon to Henri Cambon, 19.01.1904, *Correspondance*, 2: 109–110.

11 Ian Nish, *The Origins of the Russo-Japanese War* (London, 1985), 230–33.

12 Paul Cambon to Delcassé, 19.02.1904, DDF, IV: 382–4.

13 Bompard to Delcassé, 13.01.1904, DDF, IV: 246–7.

14 Sanderson to A.K. Benckendorff, 20.05.1903, BC2, box 14.

15 AVPRI, f.184, op.520, d.1086, ll.2–3.

16 Paul Cambon to Delcassé, 06.08.1903, DDF, 3: 520–23.

17 A.K. Benckendorff to V.N. Lamsdorff, 03/16.01.1904, GARF, f.568, op.1, d.326, l.82.

18 Paul Cambon to Delcassé, 24.01.1904, DDF, IV: 285–6.

diplomacy regained its place. Benckendorff believed that the British government's position was inherently peaceful.[19] Cambon more correctly assumed that Britain's refusal to mediate between Russia and Japan meant that the British and the United States had agreed to support Japan morally and financially. If Japan was defeated, they would intervene to save it,[20] and 'the terms which Russia might expect after a war would not be much better than those Japan offered today'.[21] Lamsdorff also used this argument on 1 February to pressure Nicholas II for more concessions, when he said that 'it follows from various historical examples that Russia's military victory will result in the Great Powers' interference on Japan's side and we will be faced with a dilemma of fighting a coalition or retreating'.[22] Nicholas II did not react then, but three months into the war he warned his uncle Edward VII that Russia would not tolerate another country mixing 'in this affair of ours and Japan's'.[23]

On 7 February Lansdowne told Benckendorff that the Japanese would desist from war if Russia signed a treaty with China pledging to abandon its claim to Manchuria.[24] But the Japanese told Lansdowne it was too late, and, when Benckendorff returned with a proposal of an official Russian declaration, Lansdowne told him that in the past the Russian government had frequently disregarded its declarations and therefore its mere assurances would not be sufficient. Benckendorff returned after a cabinet meeting to hear Lansdowne say once more that Britain would not intervene. Benckendorff was so distraught that Lansdowne could barely make out his words: that Russia had never thought of going to war with Japan.[25] Benckendorff hoped that it might work to Russia's advantage that England knew that Japan was the aggressor.[26]

The Outbreak of War

On 26 January/8 February 1904, without declaring war, the Japanese United Fleet attacked the Russian warships near Port Arthur. Benckendorff's invariable sympathy with all British actions did not impress Lamsdorff, but during the war this conciliatory attitude became useful. Lamsdorff needed to restrain the anti-British fury in Russia and settle the thorny issue of the neutral trade. Benckendorff's task

19 A.K. Benckendorff to Lamsdorff, 14/27.01.1904, GARF, f.568, op.1, d.326, l.83.

20 Paul Cambon to Henri Cambon, 19.01.1904, *Correspondence*, 2:110.

21 Ibid., 27.01.1904, 113.

22 V.N. Lamsdorff's memorandum, 18.01/01.02.1904, in V.V. Glushkov and K.E. Cherevko, *Russo-Japanese War 1904–1905*, 84.

23 Nicholas II to Edward VII, 04/17.04.1904, RA VIC/MAIN/X/37/58.

24 Lansdowne to MacDonald, 07.02.1904, BD, 2: 246.

25 Lansdowne to Scott, 08.02.1904, BD, 2: 247–8.

26 A.K. Benckendorff to Lamsdorff, 18/31.01.1904, GARF, f.568, op.1. d.326, ll.94–6 ob.

involved remaining on friendly terms with Lansdowne, using the Paul Cambon–Delcassé channel to pacify Nicholas II, trying to charm some of the London journalists away from their anti-Russian position and counteracting anti-British sentiment in Russia with positive reports.

In his letters the minister complained about his powerlessness against the Anglophobe 'military party' and 'the grand dukes'. Lamsdorff provided the ambassador with these excuses for the Russian actions which angered Britain and he counted on himself to defend Russia's interests from the fully expected British attempts to take advantage of Russia's difficulties.

Britain declared its neutrality on 11 February but Countess Benckendorff described the anti-British mood in Petersburg in such sinister tones that her husband was afraid that the Russian attitude would provoke the British. As usual, Benckendorff made it known in London, but not at St Petersburg that he did not share his government's attitude and behaviour. If he complained, it was to Count Metternich or Paul Cambon.

He told Cambon that his dispatches were ignored and that in order to make his government see some sense he would go to St Petersburg under the pretext of seeing his younger son off for war.[27] His son's departure was indeed a pretext for a visit to Russia but a pretext chosen by Lamsdorff who had urgently summoned the ambassador.[28] Benckendorff also took to Nicholas II the king's communication that Sir Charles Scott would be replaced by Sir Charles Hardinge. The ambitious Hardinge had intrigued to replace his former chief Scott and then he took care to let the king know that another candidate for the post, Sir Edward Goschen, was unsuitable for St Petersburg, because of his alleged Jewish origin, lack of drive and social talents.[29] Hardinge intended to be the author of an Anglo-Russian entente.

After an audience with the emperor, Benckendorff told Scott that Nicholas II could not control the anti-British press campaign because of his own unpopularity.[30] Scott and his staff were passing through unpleasant moments in Russia: after the war broke out they were boycotted by society.[31] The British diplomats also worried about the anti-Russian fury of the British newspapers. Young Viscount Cranley's father wrote from London that nothing could be done to moderate the British press, of which *The Times* was the most vicious and openly unfair.[32] But the British embassy was at one with Benckendorff and Lamsdorff in despising the media as cheap entertainment for the brutish masses.

Whatever their feelings about Britain, Lamsdorff and most of his colleagues called for restraint[33] so as not to give Britain grounds to enter the war; but Russian

27 Paul Cambon to Delcassé, 18.02.1904, DDF, IV: 377–9.
28 S.P. Benckendorff to A.K. Benckendorff, 29.01/11.02.1904, BC2, box 21.
29 Hardinge to Knollys, 17.12. [1903?], RA VIC/ADDC 7/2/Q.
30 Scott to Lansdowne, 23.04.1904, FO 800/140, 202–4.
31 Bompard to Delcassé, 13.01.1904, DDF, IV: 243–4.
32 4th Earl of Onslow to Cranley, 23.03.1904, OP, G 173/24/81a.
33 Lamsdorff to A.K. Benckendorff, 17.02/01.03.1904, BC2, box 13.

public opinion blamed Britain for the Japanese attack. Lamsdorff complained about the paper *Grazhdanin* [Citizen] which accused Russian diplomats of a lack of patriotic feeling and called for a more aggressive course. As he wrote, the paper was 'under the special protection of our August Master and the ideas it spreads are absolutely opposite of those you and I have heard from the mouth of His Imperial Majesty'.[34] As long as Nicholas II neither let his foreign minister resign nor defended him from attacks; told the minister to be conciliatory to Britain,[35] yet showed his favour to the Anglophobes, Lamsdorff was helpless.

Lamsdorff's letters to the ambassador show Nicholas II isolated from his own foreign ministry. The minister maintained correct diplomatic relations with other states while Nicholas II met with his back-door advisers and authorized reckless actions which cancelled or mocked the efforts of his own diplomacy. Seeing this, Witte attempted to overcome his sovereign's opposition and compensate for Lamsdorff's weakness by conducting his own policy in private meetings with the foreign diplomats at St Petersburg or through extra-diplomatic go-betweens, journalists or financial agents. It was little wonder that ambassadors also felt that obeying or disregarding the instructions from St Petersburg was a judgment call. When Benckendorff decided to ignore the minister's order to present protests to the British government regarding a loan to Japan, he asked for the advice of his Paris colleague Aleksandr I. Nelidov, but the ciphering clerk by mistake addressed Benckendorff's telegram to St Petersburg. The minister reprimanded Benckendorff[36] but the matter stopped there.

Under Lamsdorff's pressure, the emperor instructed Plehve to order the Russian press to abstain from attacks on foreign countries, especially Britain.[37] Sir Charles Scott attempted to resume receptions at the British embassy, but no Russians came.[38] Benckendorff was worried: 'We should not create around Scott a situation conducive to a break of relations'. He wrote that Scott's successor Hardinge was 'intelligent and reasonable' – which to Benckendorff could only mean a supporter of an Anglo-Russian rapprochement – and, indeed, the next thing he said was: 'Here they still dream, despite all, of a direct agreement with us, postponed for the moment'.[39] Benckendorff's 'they' was vague and while he wanted it to be interpreted as 'the government', he alluded to those people whose names constantly came up in his letters: Hardinge and King Edward, Cecil Spring Rice, Reginald Lister and Louis Mallet, all of them united by fear and suspicion of Germany.

34 Lamsdorff to A.K. Benckendorff, 13.02.1904, BC2, box 13.

35 Lamsdorff to A.K. Benckendorff, 16/29.02.1904, BC2, box 13.

36 D.I. Abrikossov, 113.

37 Spring Rice to Louis Mallet, 15/28.03.1904, FO 800/140, 207–8.

38 Lamsdorff to A.K. Benckendorff, 04/17.03.1904, BC2, box 13.

39 A.K. Benckendorff to Lamsdorff, 09.05.1904, GARF, f.568, op.1 ed.hr.326, ll.104–7.

When the war began, Lamsdorff ordered the ambassador to cease discussions. The Manchurian issue would be one of the first to settle in an Anglo-Russian understanding and there was no point in discussing it because it would depend on the issue of the war.[40] In April 1904 in Copenhagen, Edward VII, on his own initiative, told the Russian minister Iswolsky at length about his government's great desire for an entente with Russia.[41] He even allowed Iswolsky to put down their conversation in writing and initialled it,[42] raising false hopes on the Russian's side. Iswolsky reported the conversation to a sceptical Lamsdorff: it was too much like Benckendorff's initiative of 1903, a sample of the royal desire to go beyond his constitutional role. According to Cambon, it was his, Cambon's merit that after the visit to Denmark the king showered Benckendorff with attentions, warned him against German friendship and repeatedly spoke to him of an Anglo-Russian rapprochement.[43] All this encouraged Benckendorff to tell Lansdowne on 22 April that he was ready to report to St Petersburg the British government's views. To his disappointment, Lansdowne repeated that the outstanding questions could only be settled in the future.[44]

Lansdowne had suspended the talks partly out of consideration for Britain's ally Japan, but Russia's ally, France, entered the entente with Britain at the moment when their respective allies were fighting in the Far East.[45] The entente secured the safety of French Indochina[46] and at the same time ensured that France would be reluctant to come to Russia's aid against Japan. The large loans which Japan obtained in Britain between May 1904 and July 1905 were critical to its victory in the war. Still, the loans were raised without official involvement of the British government[47] and Benckendorff looked at this philosophically: the situation had to stimulate the Russian wish for a similar arrangement with Britain.

Lamsdorff found nothing objectionable in the text of the Anglo-French agreement[48] and, in the spring of 1904, hearing reports of King Edward's interest in an Anglo-Russian understanding, he even instructed Nelidov to discuss with Delcassé the possibility of opening conversations,[49] probably to mitigate the British hostility.

Benckendorff's counsellor, Graevenitz, reported from St Petersburg that although some ministry officials were angry because of Britain's infractions

40 Paul Cambon to Rouvier, 20.10.1905, DDF, VIII: 91–8.

41 Lord Newton, *Lord Lansdowne: A Biography* (London, 1929), 309.

42 Count Harry Kessler, *The Diaries of a Cosmopolitan* (ed. Ch. Kessler) (London, 1999), 258.

43 Paul Cambon to Henri Cambon, 09.04.1904, *Correspondance*, 2: 135–7.

44 Lord Lansdowne to Spring Rice, 22.04.1904, BD, 4: 188–9.

45 *The History of Anglo-Japanese Relations* (eds Ian Nish and Yoichi Kibata) (Basingstoke, 2000), 1: 205.

46 Paul Cambon to Henri Cambon, 19.08.1904, *Correspondance*, 2: 156.

47 *The History of Anglo-Japanese Relations*, 1: 205.

48 Russian Foreign Ministry, *Memorandum for Nicholas II*, 26.03/08.04.1904, AVPRI, f.151, op.482, ed.hr.63, l.106 ob.

49 Lamsdorff to Nelidov, 18.03.1904, AVPRI, f.151, op.482, ed.hr.63, ll.88–9 ob.

of neutrality, many 'understand the danger of this attitude and very reasonably believe that we have got enough trouble fighting a serious, difficult war against one power'.[50] When Hardinge arrived in May 1904, he found the foreign ministry conciliatory and interested in a partial agreement, which he opposed[51] because the Foreign Office wanted a general agreement with Russia, and because Lamsdorff's position still seemed shaky.

Central Asia and Tibet

The outbreak of the war delayed by several months the discussions of the Afghanistan and Tibet issues and presented Britain with an opportunity to move to more favourable positions. Lamsdorff's list of Britain's moves was long: Major MacMahon with 1,000 troops stayed for a year in the strategically important Seistan region, allegedly to finalize the work of the border delimitation commission. The Indian government encouraged Afghanistan to invade and seize parts of the Persian territory in the disputed Seistan. The caravan route, Quetta-Kuba, close to Seistan, was rebuilt into a railroad and the Indian telegraph system was linked to the British-built telegraph line from Teheran to Kuba.[52] In the spring, a Russian political agent in Bukhara reported that Afghan troops were moving towards the Russian border and the British into Kandahar. In September 1904 the British minister to Teheran, Arthur Hardinge, made a tour of Iranian Azerbaijan for the first time since his arrival in Persia.[53] All this undermined Russia's position because her passivity or retreat was seen by the Asian rulers as defeat.

Count Benckendorff opposed the suggestions of the military that Russia should advance in Turkestan (the region where traditionally Russia retaliated to any British advance elsewhere) or send agents to the Amir unless directly provoked by the British.[54] Lamsdorff already promised Lansdowne in December 1903 that Russia would not send agents to Kabul.[55] The minister reassured Benckendorff that the new Russian minister at Teheran, A.N. Speyer, would receive very precise instructions and would be 'frankly warned about the dangers which he must avert there'.[56] Speyer's instructions, nevertheless, prescribed following the line of his predecessors in order to ensure political and economic subordination of Persia.[57]

50 Graevenitz to A.K. Benckendorff, 25.03/07.04.1904, BC2, box 12.

51 Hardinge to Lansdowne, 25.05.1904. FO 800/140, 222–7.

52 Foreign ministry's instructions to A.N. Speyer, Russian minister at Teheran, 30.09/13.10.1904, *Korenny'ie interes'y Rossii*, 371.

53 A.F. Ostal'tseva, *Anglo-russkoe soglasheni'ie 1907* (Saratov, 1977), 72.

54 A.K. Benckendorff to Lamsdorff, 16.02.1904, GARF, f.568, d.326, l.98–100 ob.

55 Lansdowne to Scott, 19.12.1903, RA VIC/ADDC 7/2/Q.

56 Lamsdorff to A.K. Benckendorff, 24.06/07.07.1904, BC2, box 13.

57 Foreign ministry's instruction to A.N. Speyer, 360.

Rumours and reports about one or the other side being in secret negotiations with China or the Tibetans were incessant. Prince Louis Battenberg, the director of naval intelligence and the Russian emperor's brother-in-law, came to the baptism of Nicholas II's son in August 1904 with instructions to complain to the emperor about the Russian attitude to India. Lamsdorff assured him that Russia had no aggressive plans there.[58] Benckendorff informed the Foreign Office that a Russian division with artillery was sent to Central Asia as a response to the British amassing troops in India.[59]

Lord Onslow wrote in May 1904 that there were rumours about Russia having forestalled them in Tibet, adding, comfortably: 'I suppose we shall find out when we get to Lhassa'.[60] Early in 1904 Colonel Younghusband entered Lhassa, the Dalai Lama fled to Russia and his second-in-command signed the Lhassa convention which ensured British predominance in the country. Speaking to the Commons, Balfour referred to Tibet as a region in which Russia had no interests, which brought a reluctant protest from Benckendorff.[61] Lansdowne said it was Balfour's slip of the tongue and that there would be no occupation or permanent intervention in Tibet. At that moment Russia was in a position to do Britain a favour: following the Anglo-French entente, the new situation in Egypt had to be formalized by a Khedivial decree. Russia's adherence to the decree was necessary. Lamsdorff sought to exploit this to obtain British guarantees of the status quo in Tibet. Benckendorff, in his usual vein, wrote to St Petersburg that Russia should grant Britain's request in order to foster good sentiment. Lamsdorff answered:

> Earlier you tried to prove to us that if we did not give our immediate consent to the publication of the Khedivial decree we risked … compromising the attempts at a rapprochement made by the British and therefore obtaining nothing. As we could not accept Britain's demands without deriving some benefits we decided to limit ourselves at the moment to a memorandum and assurances given regarding the subject of Tibet … The memorandum is not a definitive answer, but the first step towards the issue and its further evolution, depending on the circumstances, might serve for a gradual improvement of our relations with England.[62]

Over Benckendorff's reluctance, Lamsdorff obtained in July the guarantees regarding Tibet in exchange for the Russian government's consent to the

58 A. Savinsky, *Recollections of a Russian Diplomat* (London, n.d.), 92.

59 A.K. Benckendorff to Lamsdorff, 25.08/7.09.1904, GARF, f.601, op.1, d.739–740, l.10 ob.

60 4th Earl of Onslow to Cranley, 18.05.1904, OP, G173/24/83.

61 A.K. Benckendorff to Lansdowne, 14.04.1904, AVPRI, f.184, op.520, d.1005, l.27.

62 Lamsdorff to A.K. Benckendorff, 24.05.1904, BC2, box 13.

publication of the Khedivial decree,[63] but in September 1904 the Lhassa convention was announced in the British newspapers. Once the British entered the hitherto inviolable Lhassa, Russia's prestige in the region, especially Mongolia and Siberia, was at risk[64] and the terms of the Lhassa treaty contradicted the British assurances given to Benckendorff.[65] The compensation which the British demanded and the terms of its payment infringed on the 'open door' principle[66] and made Tibet a British protectorate in disguise. In Benckendorff's absence, the chargé d'affaires, Sergei Sazonov, made a representation to Lansdowne. Embarrassed, Lansdowne assured Sazonov that the press version of the treaty went further than the official text and asked him to wait until it was published.[67] Benckendorff defended Lansdowne, blaming it all on Lord Curzon.[68] The Foreign Office and India Office were indeed opposed to Curzon's intention of securing Tibet for Britain and St John Brodrick, secretary of state for war, wrote: 'We are quite aware that it is necessary to adhere very closely to what was promised to Benckendorff', because the British did not want 'a second Kabul in Lhassa'.[69]

It mattered little to Lamsdorff, who was personally responsible for the British advance. He wanted to stop it. In October 1904 a British commercial mission departed from Bombay on a six-month expedition through Bender–Abbas–Kirman–Seistan– Bampour–Gwadar to stimulate commercial and political relations with Southern Persia. Some British voices expressed hope for an accident which would lead to a demand of compensation from Persia and might subsequently be followed by intervention.[70] Thanks to Benckendorff's explanations, the British realized that Russian movements in Central Asia were a bluff. Lord Onslow wrote: '[We] hear they have no transport and cannot leave the railway head'.[71] Nevertheless, the Indian government took precautionary steps against a potential mobilization in Turkestan. They wanted to show the Russians that they were no longer concerned about the Afghanistan border. Brodrick concluded with the cliché responsible for much of the Anglo-Russian hostility: '[T]he best way to have peace is by showing that we do not fear war'.[72]

Benckendorff reassured St Petersburg in regard to the new Anglo-Afghan treaty: he did not believe that British troops would ever enter Afghanistan, or that the treaty was an offensive-defensive alliance. In his opinion Russians

63 Hartwig to Lessar, 05.07.1904, *Rossi'ia i Tibet*, 57.

64 Geoffray to Delcassé, 22.10.1904, DDF, V: 459–60.

65 Bompard to Delcassé, 23.09.1904, DDF, V: 409–11.

66 Lamsdorff to A.K. Benckendorff, 16.09.1904, AVPRI, f.184, op.520, d.1005, l.41–3.

67 Georffray to Delcassé, 01.10.1904, DDF, V: 427–8.

68 A.K. Benckendorff to Lamsdorff, 22.09.1904, GARF, f.601, op.1, ed.hr.739–740, ll.11–12.

69 St John Brodrick to Cranley, 08.09.1904, OP, G 173/24/10.

70 Paul Cambon to Delcassé, 18.10.1904, DDF, V: 455.

71 4th Earl of Onslow to Cranley, 18.05.1905, OP, G173/24/86.

72 St John Brodrick to Cranley, 08.09.1904, OP, G 173/24/10.

worried overmuch about the treaty because they remembered Curzon's plans; but Curzon had lost support in the government. He pointed out that even though the announcement about the Russian government's intention to build the Orenburg–Tashkent railway alarmed the British, it changed nothing in the British policy: 'This line was necessary and it will be built … We simply must expect counter-measures. No diplomacy can prevent them'.[73] Still, Benckendorff realized that the arms race would endanger peace in the future. At the beginning of 1905 he spoke to Lansdowne about the British movements in Afghanistan: Curzon's programme of 'making Afghanistan a glacis for India' and the Anglo-Afghan negotiations would strengthen the British position.[74] The British saw a possibility of forcing Russia to accept a settlement by presenting her with a checkmate on all sides. Brodrick wrote in 1905 about the renewed Anglo-Japanese alliance: 'If anything will show the Russians the hopelessness of attacking us, this must'.[75]

Cambon wrote that Britain was doing everything to make Russia suspicious: a treaty with Tibet, an official mission to Kabul and another from Bombay to Persia, and Lord Curzon's announcement of a reorganization of the Anglo-Indian army. Cambon concluded ironically that it escaped British logic that England could not at the same time settle with Russia and profit from that country's difficulties.[76] Cambon still imagined that Russia would not accept any settlement unless it entailed her dominance.

The idea of settling with Russia, instead of embarking on Curzon's expensive program of forcing Russia's retreat, was gaining ground in the Conservative Cabinet. The Secretary for War, Brodrick, was of the opinion that India needed a rest rather than increased pressure of rivalry.[77] In 1904–5 he repeatedly wrote that the British government saw Russia as 'the pivot of interest' and, with an Anglo-Russian understanding in mind, he wanted Hardinge to know that 'people like Alfred Lyttelton[78] and myself rejoice that one of our generation has had the opportunity of proving what he can do at the most critical place in the most critical time'.[79]

Wartime Frictions

The critical issues 'in the most critical time' that strained Anglo-Russian relations were war contraband which British merchants supplied to Japan and which Russia wanted to stop, and the need for the Russian Black Sea fleet to pass through the

73 A.K. Benckendorff to Hartwig, 09.05.1906, GARF, f.1126, op.1 ed.hr.1, ll.1–2.
74 Von Bernstorff to Prince von Bülow, 27.02.1905, GD, III: 186–7.
75 St John Brodrick to Cranley, 31.08.1905, OP, G173/24.16.
76 Paul Cambon to Delcassé, 05.12.1904, DDF, V: 564–6.
77 St John Brodrick to Cranley, 31.08.1905, OP, G 173/24.16a.
78 Alfred Lyttelton – Colonial Secretary in Arthur Balfour's government.
79 St John Brodrick to Cranley, 22.02.1905, OP, G 173/24/13a.

Straits to join the Pacific Fleet in the Far East. As soon as war began, Benckendorff and Lansdowne agreed that 'we should nip in the bud mischievous allegations, and we certainly may count on each other's cooperation'.[80] The Russian navy did not have the resources to control the maritime traffic and Russian consuls in British-controlled ports with instructions to watch for infractions of British, American or German neutrality relied on second-hand or doubtful sources for their information and often could not prove their allegations. The ambassador demanded confirmation from the Russian officials before he presented complaints and so placed himself in a false position by making enquiries at the Foreign Office. The correspondence in the foreign ministry's file *Britain's Neutrality in Russo-Japanese War* bristles with telegrams from Russian consular officials in the Pacific rim reporting, for example, a British minesweeper *Handy* going to Hong Kong with five Japanese officers on board, to sabotage the Russian Baltic Fleet.[81] Lansdowne's answer is attached: the minesweeper *Handy* never left Hong Kong but a similar vessel, *Humber*, did leave Wei Hai Wei for Hong Kong with British officers, seamen and stores on board.[82] One of the letters from the embassy to St Petersburg in response to a report by the Russian consul in Hong Kong ended with an exasperated: 'Consul Bologovsky is at the very least mistaken'.[83]

To the embassy's inquiry about a British company that was raising sunken Russian warships in Port Arthur for the Japanese the Foreign Office answered that it was a purely commercial operation and did not warrant action on their part.[84] Countess Benckendorff was aware that her husband found it hard to defend the Russian navy's actions, and she wrote, with relief, after another ship had been seized and sunk: 'It is good that weapons were found on the *Malacca*'.[85]

When Russian accusations were irrefutable, the Foreign Office's stock answer was that during hostilities merchants carried contraband articles to any foreign part at their own risk, which was not contrary to international law.[86] But when the Russian navy began to capture or sink British merchant vessels carrying war contraband in the Indian and Pacific Oceans (taking the crews on board), the mood changed. Britain did not recognize the international convention on maritime contraband (Article 6 listed arms, coal, cotton and food as war contraband), so when the Russian navy seized British merchant vessels

80 Lansdowne to A.K. Benckendorff, 10.02.01904, AVPRI, f.184, op.520, d.1176, l.31–2.

81 A.K. Benckendorff to Lansdowne, 07/20.07.1904, AVPRI, f.184, op.520, d.1176, ll.64–5.

82 Lansdowne to A.K. Benckendorff, [n.d.], AVPRI, f.184, op.520, d.1176, ll.66–7.

83 Baron Ungern to Russian Foreign Ministry, 02/15.07.1904, AVPRI, f.184, op.520, d.1176, ll.61–2.

84 Foreign Office to Russian embassy, 10.04.1905, AVPRI, f.184, d.1176, l.91.

85 S.P. Benckendorff to A.K. Benckendorff, 26.07.1904, BC2, box 21.

86 Russian Foreign Ministry, *Memorandum*, [n.d.], AVPRI, f.184, op.520, d.1176, l.69.

carrying one or more of these items the British press stormed. Benckendorff energetically defended Britain, pointing to the US and Germany as the ringleaders in contraband who gained the most from it. After the Russians gave in to Britain on this issue he hastened to report that the British press had become less hostile to Russia.[87]

Benckendorff protested the seizures of merchant vessels on two accounts. First, since the British and the Russians disagreed on what constituted war contraband, the Foreign Office would never admit that the British side had been at fault. Second, when there was no close port to which the seized ship could be taken, the Russian navy sank British merchant vessels, which caused an even greater uproar in Britain. 'The view here is that they cannot sink our ships whether they have contraband or not', Lord Onslow explained to his son, adding that if the Russians persisted in this the British public would force the government to protect their merchantmen with men-of-war and then a conflict would be certain.[88] Benckendorff considered that these captures were not effective in turning around the war, but effectively damaged Anglo-Russian relations. He apologized to Lansdowne about the Russian navy's actions.[89] Lamsdorff shared his concern and Benckendorff's letters helped the minister to overcome the opposition in the question of war contraband from the heads of the navy and of the Volunteer Fleet. The seizures of British merchants ceased.[90]

Lamsdorff answered to Benckendorff's complaints about Russian hostility to Britain: 'I am against "snarling" at anyone, especially at the English. The English are wrong to think that we are aggressive'. But he reminded Benckendorff that his efforts should be directed towards dissipating Britain's suspicions, not Russia's. The Russian mood would not change unless the British demonstrated their alleged magnanimity:

> Their refusal to coal our ships, their smuggling, Yermoloff's report [about British assistance to Japan] ... All this is does not matter to us politically ... but it is no wonder that the imperial family and the government are so irritated ...[91]

In Search of Peace

At the beginning of the war Britain and France had expected a Japanese defeat,[92] but the Russians from the first were gloomy about their prospects. Countess

87 A.K. Benckendorff to Lamsdorff, 22.09.1904, GARF, f. 601, op.1, ed.hr. 739–40, ll.11–12.

88 4th Earl of Onslow to Cranley, 27.08.1904, OP, G173/24/86.

89 Lansdowne to Hardinge, 25.07.1904, FO 800/140, 237.

90 Poklevsky to A.K. Benckendorff, 27.08/9.09.1904, BC2, box 14.

91 Lamsdorff to A.K. Benckendorff, 05/18.08.1904, BC2, box 13.

92 Hardinge to Lansdowne, 30.06.1904, FO 800/140, 231–2.

Benckendorff reported to her husband in January 1904 that 'everyone says if there is a war Russia will do very poorly'.[93] Her 'everyone' included the foreign ministry, the war ministry and those in charge of Russia's finance. In April 1904 Lessar reported that China became aware of a possible Russian defeat.[94] The ambassador in the US reported a successful Japanese loan in the US following a Japan's victory.[95] In May 1904 the Korean emperor gave in to the pressure of the Japanese and British ministers, and declared all Korean treaties with Russia and all Russian concessions in Korea null and void.[96]

By August 1904 Lamsdorff had lost all hope[97] and complained about his inability to oppose the influence of Nicholas II's extra-official advisers: '*one* Russia ruled by *one* will is no more; there are only backstairs influences which paralyze systematic work of the legitimate authority'.[98] The split in Russian society resulted in a large part of it wishing defeat of the army, for patriotic reasons. Witte spoke to Hardinge of Russia's potential defeat as a mixed blessing, since military defeats usually spurred reforms in Russia and internal reforms were needed.[99] With every Russian military defeat irritation against Britain grew in Russia. Benckendorff, always with future rapprochement in mind, wrote to Lamsdorff in August 1904 about the need for more frankness in dealing with the British. He wrote that Russia's attempt to establish direct relations with the 'half-demented Amir' of Afghanistan would only allow the latter to play Russia against Britain and damage their fragile goodwill. He would repeat this Scott's argument[100] again and again about all Anglo-Russian frictions during his lifetime.

He suggested that an arrangement might be based on collaboration in Central Asia and quoted Lansdowne saying that 'such a set of interests at such a distance from the centre and aggravated by the passions which weak governments might exploit – this will become a source of danger between Russia and England, and it will grow, unless there is an entente'. Benckendorff assured Lamsdorff that Britain had ceased to be annexionist since the 1860s, so suspicions were absurd.[101] A month later he had to protest against the Lhassa convention.

---

93 S.P. Benckendorff to A.K. Benckendorff, 08/21.01.1904, BC2, box 21.

94 V.V. Glushkov and K.S. Cherevko, *Russko-Yaponska'ia voina, 1904–1905 gg*, 169.

95 A.P. Cassini to Foreign Ministry (telegram), 24.04.1904, in V.V. Glushkov and K.S. Cherevko, *Russko-Yaponska'ia voina*, 171.

96 A.I. Pavlov to Foreign Ministry, 14.05.1904 (telegram), in V.V. Glushkov and K.S. Cherevko, *Russko-Yaponska'ia voina*, 174.

97 Lamsdorff to A.K. Benckendorff, 05/18.08.1904, BC2, box 13.

98 Lamsdorff to A.K. Benckendorff, 10/23.06.1904, BC2, box 13.

99 Hardinge to Lansdowne, 30.06.1904, BD, 4: 2–4.

100 Scott to Lansdowne, 25.12.1902, FO 800/140, 121–41.

101 A.K. Benckendorff to Lamsdorff, 23.08/5.09.1904, GARF, f.601, op.1, d.739–40, ll.1–6.

The Embassy and the Revolution of 1905

The London embassy was torn by its own internal dissent. The first secretary, Petr Botkin, had spent years in the US and was happily married to an American. He retained very warm feelings for the country, and, infuriated by the intense anti-Russian campaign in the US and British press, he blamed American hostility to Russia on the British media, writing to the foreign ministry: 'This [British] press has played an ignoble role in the break of our relations with Japan. The egging-on came from here, from England, just as now the disinformation hostile to Russia is also coming from here'. Contradicting the ambassador's constant reminders of the dangers of angering Britain, Botkin assured his correspondent that Britain would not want to get involved in another war so soon after the Boer war, so 'Neither us, nor the Japanese should expect their arrival [at the seat of war]'.[102] He did not hide his feelings and quickly became persona non grata in the Benckendorffs' circle. The Foreign Office did not forget Botkin's attitude and ten years later opposed his appointment as Russian deputy foreign minister.

On a visit to St Petersburg in September Poklevsky was struck by the low spirits of the public and the general foreboding that the Baltic Fleet, which was about to sail to the Far East, would not get further than the Mediterranean.[103] The warships needed to reinforce the Fleet were locked in the Black Sea. For the first time since the Crimean war, Russia truly needed the passage through the Straits. Before the war started Lansdowne had warned Benckendorff that Britain would regard the passage of the Russian Black Sea fleet through the Straits as a *casus belli*. [104] He repeated it several times to different persons.[105] In August Lamsdorff began to negotiate with the Turkish government the passage of unarmed vessels of the Volunteer Fleet.[106] A month later the minister instructed Benckendorff to promise Russia's concessions in other areas in exchange for Britain closing her eyes to the passage of a few Russian warships through the Straits. Britain's example would help persuade Germany, France and the Sultan's government.[107] Benckendorff also was to plead with the British government to let the Baltic fleet pass without hindrance through the North Sea – which meant for the Russians letting them coal at a British port. But Benckendorff came up against Lansdowne's refusal.[108] In a burst of mortification he told his German colleague that the British

102 P.S. Botkin to Foreign Ministry, 04.03.1904, in V.V. Glushkov and K.E. Cherevko, *Russko-Yaponska'ia voina*, 163–4.

103 Poklevsky to A.K. Benckendorff, 27.08/9.09.1904, BC2, box 14.

104 Paul von Metternich to German Foreign Ministry, 18.08.04, GD, III: 180–82.

105 Lansdowne to Monson, 29.04.1904, BD IV: 50 and Paul von Metternich to German Foreign Ministry, 18.08.04 GD, III: 180–82.

106 O'Conor to Lansdowne, 04.08.1904, BD, IV: 52–3.

107 Lamsdorff to A.K. Benckendorff, 30.09.1904, BC2, box 13.

108 Lansdowne to A.K. Benckendorff, 16.08.1904, FO 800/140, 243–4.

decision was stupid because it was not even certain that the Baltic fleet would manage to sail from Libau.[109]

On 15 October 1904 Lamsdorff signed a treaty of neutrality with Austria-Hungary as a precaution against a possible armed conflict with Britain over the passage of the Volunteer Fleet through the Straits.[110] Realizing the enormous risk of such an enterprise, the minister did all he could to persuade the emperor to give up on the idea for it would become a precedent for the navies of other powers to enter the Black Sea.[111]

Seven unarmed Russian steamers were allowed by the Turkish government to pass through the Straits,[112] and the British did not object until the Russian press announced that two of them would be added as cruisers to the Baltic Fleet. As a compromise Lansdowne suggested that these ships be employed as tenders to the Russian fleet provided they did not interfere with neutral commerce.[113]

The Dogger Bank Incident

Poklevsky quoted Hardinge's words that Lamsdorff was so conciliatory that nothing could possibly spoil the bilateral relations;[114] but a fortnight later relations between Russia and Britain suddenly came to a critical point. The Baltic fleet, sailing at night through the North Sea on its way to the Far East, sank one British fishing boat and damaged four, mistaking them for Japanese torpedo-boats. As a result, two fishermen from Hull were killed and several more wounded.[115] The British were even more incensed because the Russian fleet sailed on, without trying to rescue the victims. The commander of the Russian fleet reported to St Petersburg that his vanguard had been attacked by two torpedo-boats and that in issuing the order to sail away he protected his ships from potential future attacks.[116]

The incident took place while Benckendorff was in Germany, celebrating his silver wedding. The chargé d'affaires Sazonov received the protest of the Foreign Office. In Petersburg, Lamsdorff came to the British embassy with condolences before Hardinge had presented the protest. The minister persuaded Nicholas II to

109 Paul von Metternich to German Foreign Ministry, 18.08.1904, GD, III: 180–82.

110 F. Roy Bridge, *From Sadowa to Saraevo: The Foreign Policy of Austria-Hungary 1866–1914* (London, 1972), 272.

111 E.G. Kostrikova, Bor'ba Rossii za peresmotr statusa Prolivov v nachale XX v., *Rossiia i Tchernomorskie proliv'y (XVIII – XX stolet'ia)* (Moscow, 1999), 256.

112 Townley to Lansdowne, 03.11.1904, BD, 4: 54.

113 Lansdowne to Hardinge, 03.11.1904, BD, 4: 55.

114 Poklevsky to A.K. Benckendorff, 27.08/9.09.1904, BC2, box 14.

115 V. Shatsillo and L.Shatsillo, *Russko-Yaponskaia voina 1904–1905* (Moscow, 2004), 228.

116 Admiral Z.P. Rozhestvensky to Admiral A.A. Birilev, 13/26.10.1904 (telegram), in V.V. Glushkov and K.E. Cherevko, *Russko-Yaponska'ia voina*, 247.

telegraph his regrets and an offer of compensation to the families of the victims, without waiting for a confirmation or disproval of the Russian version.[117]

Russian anger at the English providing cover for the Japanese was fanned by a series of press reports about witnesses arriving at Russian embassies and consulates in Europe to confirm that they had seen 'suspicious vessels' in the vicinity of Dogger Bank at the time of the incident. When an English pilot, a Captain Lucas, came to the Russian diplomatic mission in Brussels to testify that he had seen two 'strange' torpedo boats in the North Sea, five days prior to the incident,[118] chance would have it that he was received by Petr Botkin, who at once reported it to the foreign ministry. Confusion reigned in Russia.

Benckendorff returned to England the day after the incident and was booed by the mob during his short drive from Victoria Station to the embassy.[119] The fury of the London mob was so great that all European newspapers reported it. Benckendorff's wife read about it in Germany, his son in the Far East and his brother-in-law in Italy.[120] The countess wrote sympathetically. 'I can imagine the fury of England – and nothing to answer'.[121] The ambassador agreed with Lansdowne's demand for a full apology and disclaimer, reparations to the victims and an investigation.[122]

Lord Onslow wrote that he did not believe in a 'real jingo party' in Britain, but he was concerned that the press wanted to fan the war spark as *The Times'* editor Moberly Bell told him that Britain 'should never have so good a chance of giving Russia a blow which would keep her quiet for a century as now'.[123]

Delcassé, Cambon, his former Constantinople colleague and friend A.I. Nelidov, the Russian ambassador to France, and Benckendorff gathered in Paris to discuss how a compromise could be reached. Someone thought of the Hague tribunal as the institution which might conduct the inquest and Benckendorff telegraphed this to his minister.[124] On 15/28 October, after much pleading, Lamsdorff persuaded the emperor to accept the proposal.[125] He wrote to Benckendorff that William II was attempting to exploit the incident in order to quarrel Russia with Britain, and that any British attempt to stop the Russian fleet would be 'the last straw'[126] that would end in an Anglo-Russian conflagration.

117 A. Savinsky, 96.

118 Botkin to Foreign Ministry, 06.11.1904, in V.V. Glushkov and K.E. Cherevko, *Russko-Yaponska'ia voina*, 251.

119 S.P. Benckendorff to A.K. Benckendorff, 13/26.10.1904, BC2, box 21.

120 Alessandro Guiccioli, *Diario di un conservatore* (Milano, 1973), 299.

121 S.P. Benckendorff to A.K. Benckendorff, 12/25.10.1904, BC2, box 21.

122 Lansdowne to Hardinge, 25.10.1904, BD, 4: 10–11.

123 4th Earl of Onslow to Cranley, 29.11.1904, OP, G173/24/88.

124 Paul Cambon to Henri Cambon, *Correspondance*, 2: 166–7.

125 Lamsdorff to A.K. Benckendorff, 17/30.10.1904, BC2, box 13.

126 Lamsdorff to Benckendorff, 17/30.10.1904, BC2, box 13.

It could only add to everyone's desire to settle the issue. On the same day Benckendorff telegraphed to Petersburg the acceptance of the British government.[127]

But, without consulting his government, he accepted the British demand that the Russian officers responsible for the incident be landed and brought before the British court. Prime Minister Balfour embroidered on this in a public speech and British papers made the public believe that 'it had been definitely arranged that the whole Baltic fleet was to stay at Vigo [Spain] while the inquiry took place'.[128] Lamsdorff protested that he had not promised to detach officers before responsibility was apportioned by the investigation, and Hardinge found it reasonable. He realized that distraught Benckendorff misled Balfour by promising more than he was entitled to. Hardinge explained to Lamsdorff what happened and Lamsdorff promised not to disavow Benckendorff publicly,[129] thus letting the British public blame Russia for having failed to keep its promise.

To avert a break in diplomatic relations, the Russians, the British and the French worked in concert. The public feeling in Russia and in Britain, the insistence of the military on their innocence in the Russian case and on forcibly intercepting the Russian fleet on its way to the Far East in the British, were not allowed to influence the diplomats' discussions. The Russians, after initial hopes that the commander of the Baltic Fleet could present evidence of the presence of Japanese torpedo boats in the North Sea, tacitly accepted that the facts did not support the admiral's version, and, much as the emperor and his closest circle insisted that the British were covering up for the Japanese, the diplomats arranged for a calm discussion of compensations.

A hefty financial settlement for the victims' families settled the incident in the spring of 1905, with the Russian, French, American, Austrian and British admirals and legal experts from Russia and Britain agreeing on a formula which nearly exonerated the Russian fleet. The final document was issued in two versions. The one which the Russians took home stated that there had been no Japanese torpedo boats in the North Sea on the night of the incident; that the Russian vessels opened fire and killed and wounded several British fishermen, but nevertheless, there was no question of responsibility, guilt or mistake on the part of Admiral Rozhdestvensky or officers of his Fleet.[130] As Baron Taube, the Russian legal expert at the Paris Commission pointed out, such an innocuous outcome became possible only because neither Russia, nor Britain, nor France wanted an Anglo-Russian war. In this respect it was an encouraging sign. The British had heard worrying rumours of a Russo-German rapprochement and Cambon 'looked grave' as he confirmed to Lansdowne that William II was going out of his way to attract Russia. Britain had done a service to Japan by delaying

127 A.K. Benckendorff to Lansdowne, 28.10.1904, FO 800/141, 47–8.

128 D.O. Malcolm to Cranley, 09.12.1904, OP, G173/24/99.

129 Hardinge to Lansdowne, 02.11.1904, FO 800/141, 57–60.

130 M. de Taube, *La Politique russe d'avant-guerre et la fin de l' empire des tsars* (Paris, 1928), 41.

the departure of the Russian fleet from the Mediterranean and by denying it coaling facilities so that by the time the fleet reached the Far East it could hardly change the military situation.[131] Lansdowne and Cambon saw that ending the war was the best way to keep Russia out of Germany's embrace and were discussing mediation.[132] To Benckendorff, British behaviour during the incident proved their desire for a rapprochement. His enthusiastic references to Cambon's support met with Lamsdorff's scepticism:

> The activity of the French ambassador which supported yours has certainly been useful to us, but I do not think I am wrong in attributing it mainly to French self-interest. It seems to me that the French government wanted to avert the possibility of an Anglo-Russian conflict not for love, but because it would place France in an extremely difficult position.

The minister wrote tartly that he saw 'no reason to encourage the French foreign ministry's tendency to buzz around self-importantly' since without Russia's conciliatory steps a settlement would have been impossible. As for Benckendorff's complaint about the hostility he felt in Britain and the Russian hostility to Britain, Lamsdorff said that Russia's wish to achieve a 'rapprochement or even an entente' was frustrated by Britain's behaviour. Still he encouraged the ambassador to persevere 'insofar as it is reasonable'.[133]

Diplomatic Activity Around and After the Russo-Japanese War

In the winter of 1904–5 rumours of Benckendorff's pending recall from London appeared in the newspapers; it was a conclusion that the European press drew from the Russian press's periodic criticism of the London embassy.[134] They were wrong: with his connections at the Russian court and with the British and the French behind him, Benckendorff was firmly entrenched in London.[135] He went to Russia in December telling Lansdowne that he was going there in the hope of stopping the war.[136] Prior to leaving, he asked Lansdowne to allow Russian vessels to pass through the Dardanelles. Lansdowne asked Hardinge to warn Lamsdorff that it was out of the question, but Hardinge wrote that Lamsdorff had always said that the idea was absurd. The British assumed it was another of Benckendorff's initiatives because 'he was so nervous and diffident about it'[137]

131 Ian Nish, Yoichi Kibata, 205.
132 Lansdowne to Hardinge, 19.10.1904, FO 800/141, 28–30.
133 Lamsdorff to A.K. Benckendorff, 11/24.11.1904, BC2, box 13.
134 Alessandro Guiccioli, *Diario*, 302.
135 D.I. Abrikossov, 107.
136 Lansdowne to Hardinge, 22.12.1904, FO 800/141, 108–9.
137 Lansdowne to Hardinge, 20.12.1904, FO 800/141, 102–3.

In Petersburg the ambassador talked with Hardinge about the Russian government and the grand dukes in charge of the navy. He considered the ministers 'individually worthy' but too busy quarrelling with each other to wield any real power and he liked the grand dukes as little as the British. Hardinge was surprised to hear that Benckendorff did not fear Lamsdorff's rumoured resignation. Hardinge wrote what seems to have been the gist of Benckendorff's opinion of his chief: 'miserably weak' and afraid of committing himself without consulting the emperor. But Hardinge considered Lamsdorff 'an element of order' and well-disposed towards Britain, something which he did not think about the man whom Benckendorff said would succeed him, Aleksandr Petrovich Iswolsky.[138] Countess Benckendorff's letters may have an explanation of Benckendorff's low opinion of his chief: she was openly scornful of the minister's vacillations and failing nerves.[139]

Before leaving Petersburg the count told the British ambassador that he had attempted to organize a Russian press campaign in favour of immediate peace by opening a discussion of peace terms as an invitation to the Japanese. Lamsdorff told him it was not a good time to try to influence the press, but Benckendorff did it 'independently'. Hardinge concluded: 'You will be very interested if Benckendorff talks to you half as freely as he has talked to me here on the internal situation. I could hardly realize that he is a Russian'.[140] Alessandro Guiccioli recorded that his Benckendorff brothers-in-law were very pessimistic about the situation in Russia: 'Neither of them sees a way out, especially in the domestic situation. The main cause of the paralysis of the state is the emperor's absolute inability to stick to any decision'.[141]

Benckendorff returned to London depressed. His attempt to approach Suvorin[142] and to orchestrate a press campaign for peace had failed. The disorder in Russia was on the increase. His wife was furious because everyone in her circle was certain that the terrorists and striking workers in Russia were subsidized by the British. 'Pitt's gold', she scoffed, recounting a heated argument with her brother-in-law, the grand master of ceremonies. She declared that both she and her husband were ashamed of representing a government which was too weak to establish order and therefore blamed its disasters on foreign agents.[143] Her main comfort and confidant was Spring Rice, whose aversion for Russia the countess took for an aversion for the Russian autocracy, a feeling that she fully shared.

In early 1905 Hardinge informed the king that there was absolutely no government in Russia[144] and to a Foreign Office official Nicholas II reminded of

138 Hardinge to Lansdowne, 06.12.1905, FO 800/141, 95–8.
139 S.P. Benckendorff to A.K. Benckendorff, 12/25.01.1905, BC2, box 21.
140 Hardinge to Lansdowne, 08.02.1905, FO 800/141, 123–5.
141 Alessandro Guiccioli, *Diario*, 307.
142 Wesselitsky to A.K. Benckendorff, 23.12.1904, BC2, box 15.
143 S.P. Benckendorff to A.K. Benckendorff, 14/27.01.1905, BC2, box 21.
144 Hardinge to Knollys, 01.03.1905, RA VIC/MAIN/W/45/120.

Louis XVI.[145] The British observed the unrest in Russia with interest: 'Of course a revolution in Russia would suit us down to the ground', Lord Onslow replied to his son's reports of Russian events: 'We want to see her weakened but we do not want to fight her'.[146] *The Times* was attacking Russia more aggressively, concentrating on its pending bankruptcy. In a series of articles with titles like 'Is Russia Solvent?' an influential journalist Lucien Wolf called for a financial boycott of Russia.[147]

In April Lamsdorff wrote that the British press articles publicizing the itinerary and the whereabouts of the Baltic fleet en route to the Far East produced a storm of indignation in the imperial family. Nicholas II authorized Grand Duke Aleksandr to telegraph a protest to London newspapers 'as a private individual' and wanted Benckendorff to make a strong representation to Lord Lansdowne. Lamsdorff persuaded the Tsar to drop the issue because, according to Benckendorff, the British papers were reproducing the information originally published by the French press. But the imperial family and the Russian public were still ruffled.[148] In April 1905 Maria Feodorovna showed Pavel Benckendorff 'a pile of disgusting letters from England' and a no less disgusting book, *The Truth about the Tsar*.[149]

Benckendorff decided to quell the Romanovs' indignation by appealing to Maria Feodorovna. In a long letter, he quoted the New Testament and warned the empress against prejudice which 'leads us into wrong paths' and against blaming the British nation for the actions of individuals – his usual argument when faced with a manifestation of British Russophobia. He extolled the British magnanimity during the Russo-Japanese war: it had not done for Japan 'the tenth part of what France has done for us. And how do we respond?' Then he turned to his favourite subject, repeating what he had often heard at Windsor: 'King Edward came to the throne with a definite, clear programme: settle with Russia, then with France in the interests of the world peace which England needs. If he began with France it is because he never succeeded with Russia'. He continued: 'There is an excellent relation between the king and the emperor. Your son began [his reign] with the Hague programme, well received by the British public opinion' and he should culminate his work by accepting the British offer of friendship.[150] It needed all of Benckendorff's conviction to begin the letter by writing about the British hatred for Russia and end by reproaching Russia for ignoring Britain's offer of friendship. After a long silence Maria Feodorovna thanked him for his 'sincerity and good feelings' but refused to enter into a discussion.[151]

145 D.O. Malcolm to Cranley, 23.12.1904, OP, G 173/24/99.

146 4th Earl of Onslow to Cranley, 29.11.1904, OP, G 173/24/88.

147 Paul Cambon to Delcassé, 23.03.1905, DDF, VI: 232–4.

148 Lamsdorff to A.K. Benckendorff, 14/27.04.1905, BC2, box 13.

149 P.K. Benckendorff to A.K. Benckendorff, 27.04/10.05.1905, BC2, box 19.

150 A.K. Benckendorff to Empress Maria Feodorovna (draft), 06/19.04.1905, GARF, f.1126, op.1, d.4, l.9–12.

151 Empress Maria Feodorovna to A.K. Benckendorff, 21.04/04.05.1905, BC2, box 13.

The first rumours of the Japanese interest in peace reached Lamsdorff in early November of 1904; in early December the French informed a Russian foreign ministry official on a visit to The Hague that the Japanese minister thought it was the time to sign peace, 'for there are no victors and no defeated'[152] but Nicholas II would not accept peace talks without first having won a victory. But in December 1904, after several months of successfully resisting the Japanese attempts to storm Port Arthur, the commander of the fortress decided to surrender it, against the opinion of the majority of the officers.

Congratulatory telegrams poured into the Japanese embassy in London. In Benckendorff's absence, Poklevsky had to face the crowd of journalists who descended on Chesham House to see the Russians' reaction. He said that the disaster would unite all the Russians in their determination to continue the war.[153] Days later, the first Russian revolution broke out, with encouragement and financial support from the Japanese intelligence services.

Russia's military disasters in the Far East followed. In November–December 1904, the French attempted to bring about Russo-Japanese negotiations, but Japan wanted Russia to propose talks and Lamsdorff said that it was too early.[154] In March 1905, Hardinge wrote that Witte had persuaded Nicholas II to think of ending the war and outlined what Witte thought Russia's peace terms would be.[155] Witte suggested Edward VII's mediation between Russia and Japan, but Lansdowne preferred to wait until Russia was definitely beaten in the Far East. Unlike the Russians, whose great hopes hung on the 'last card', as Nelidov referred to the Baltic fleet,[156] Lansdowne foresaw that, unable to get either coal or supplies en route, the fleet would be useless when it arrived in the Far East.[157]

Nevertheless, Japan's resources were nearly exhausted and on 8 March 1905 the Japanese war minister, M. Terauchi officially asked the US ambassador to tell the president that the war had to end and that he was ready to stop the fighting.[158] In mid-March the French government made an attempt to force Russia to accept peace talks: French bankers refused to give Russia a new loan and at the same time Delcassé offered his mediation.[159] Hardinge passed to Lamsdorff King Edward's compliments and his confidence in Lamsdorff's love of peace. The beleaguered minister said: '… c'est mon culte et ma religion!' and promised to do all he could

152 F.F. Martens to Foreign Ministry, 06.12.1904, in V.V. Glushkov and K.E. Cherevko, *Russko-Yaponska'ia voina*, 257.

153 *New York Times*, 03.01.1905, 1.

154 Maurice Bompard, *Mon ambassade en Russie 1903–1908* (Paris, 1937), 94.

155 Hardinge to Lansdowne, 24.03.1905, FO 800/141, 138.

156 A.I. Nelidov to A.K. Benckendorff, 13.05.1905, BC2, box 13.

157 Lansdowne to Hardinge, 03.04.1905, FO 800/141, 143–6.

158 V.V. Glushkov and K.E. Cherevko, *Russko-Yaponska'ia voina*, 349.

159 Ibid., 353.

to frustrate the enemies' attempts to provoke a quarrel between Russia and Britain. He said he hoped for a settlement with Britain after the war.[160]

France and Britain wanted the war to end as soon as possible because the Morocco incident put France in need of Russia's support in Europe, while a continuing war would bring about a Russo-German rapprochement,[161] and, in Britain's case, because Japan was extremely strained financially. Tempting proposals flowed into the Russian embassy in London. Sir Marcus Samuel, one of the important City financiers and the former Lord Mayor of London, spoke first to Delcassé and then to Benckendorff about the Japanese desire for peace. Nelidov and Benckendorff agreed that Samuel's initiative showed the impatience of the British financial circles to see the war end. They hoped that the City would bring pressure on the Japanese to ease their peace terms.[162] Lord Revelstoke told Poklevsky that the London market would in all probability open to Russia after the end of the war, and if the domestic conditions in Russia and Anglo-Russian relations improved, Barings bank, the traditional partner of the Russian government, would undertake to organize a loan.[163] Lord Rothschild also spoke to the ambassador about the Japanese desire for peace. The financier suggested that if Russia found the Japanese demands of indemnity an obstacle, he might organize a loan in the City. Rothschild's proposal was in keeping with the interests of the Japanese who were gasping for money and already planned on the Rothschild's loan to Russia being subdivided, half of it remaining in London, a quarter going to Japan as cash and the last quarter also going to Japan in Russian bonds.[164]

Lamsdorff's reaction was that Russia needed peace but 'the more we desire it, the more cautiously and calmly we must proceed' to obtain it on acceptable terms.[165] Informed by Delcassé about the Japanese peace initiatives,[166] Lamsdorff instructed Nelidov to inquire through Delcassé about the terms on which direct negotiations might be opened. Then the soundings came to a stumbling block: Russia would not accept any terms humiliating to her dignity (namely: no territorial concessions, no contributions and freedom to keep a fleet in the Pacific). Delcassé suggested that he would personally ask Lansdowne to influence Japan. Lamsdorff told Benckendorff that although the emperor would never accept Britain's mediation, but if Delcassé, purely on his own, asked Lansdowne to encourage negotiations, that would be a different matter.[167] At this point, receiving the information about Japan's weakening and the assurances of his military advisers that Russia's strength was building up, Nicholas II became suspicious of the powers' motives in offering

160 Hardinge to Edward VII, 31.03.1905, RA VIC/MAIN/W/46/33.
161 Spring Rice to Lansdowne, 07.05.1905, BD, 4: 77–8.
162 A.I. Nelidov to Lamsdorff, 30.04/13.05.1905, BC2, box 13.
163 A.F. Ostal'tseva, 108.
164 Durand to Lansdowne, 05.06.1905, BD, 4: 79–80.
165 Lamsdorff to A.K. Benckendorff, 17/30.03.1905, BC 2, box 13.
166 Paul Cambon to Henri Cambon, 15.04.1905, *Correspondance*, 2: 184.
167 Lamsdorff to A.K. Benckendorff, 14/27.04.1905, BC2, box 13.

mediation and did not want to hear of peace talks. Neither would Lamsdorff, were it not for the worsening domestic situation, which the emperor did not want to consider. The minister cursed the Russian press which was 'doing its utmost to complicate the situation'. Lamsdorff wrote sarcastically: 'They are reproaching us [the ministry] for not exercising influence at Kabul, for not intervening in Tibet, for not threatening the British and other enemies everywhere. Are we not everywhere and always the strongest?'[168] However right the Russian press was in its assessment of Britain's efforts to capitalize on Russia's difficulties,[169] it complicated Lamsdorff's task.

Continuing imperial hopes for a naval victory in the Pacific led to the break-up of the spring Russo-Japanese *sondages* in Paris, but by stimulating diplomatic interaction between the British and the Russians they revived the idea of an Anglo-Russian understanding. At the same time, as Hardinge reported, Nicholas II's tendency for peace vanished, but as the Russians did not like William II's Moroccan exploit, Germany's image in Russia had suffered. The ambassador concluded: 'How well the German Emperor has been playing our cards …'[170] On 31 March 1905 the Kaiser visited Tangier and made a statement widely interpreted as a warning to France that Germany had interests in the region. Germany demanded an international conference to discuss the independence of Morocco and the French government, suddenly facing a possible war, went into a crisis over Delcassé's anti-German foreign policy; in June it ended with the foreign minister's resignation and a French concession to Germany aimed at repairing the relations. Britain and France hoped that Germany would be satisfied with this triumph and let the matter of a conference drop, but the Morocco crisis continued. It coincided with the Tsushima battle in May 1905, the greatest in a series of Russia's military defeats.

The Russian embassy learned of this new disaster during a Court reception and as the trickle of guests towards the Japanese diplomats, to congratulate them on the victory, kept growing, Benckendorff led his group out of the room and they drove away. The King sanctioned Benckendorff's request to be excused from attending the State Ball and the Opera.[171] Lansdowne's private secretary, Sir Eric Barrington and a few other government officials sent their condolences to the Russian embassy, emphasizing that they could understand the Russians' feelings because of their own bitter experiences of the Boer war.[172]

It was obvious to the diplomats that the war was nearing the end. The Russophobe mood so obvious in England at the beginning of the war, gave way to a calmer attitude now that Russia was defeated. Some, like Lord Esher, had mixed

168 Lamsdorff to A.K. Benckendorff, 28.05/11.05.1905, BC 2, box 13.

169 *Journals and Letters of Reginald Viscount Esher: Vol. 2 1903–1910*, (ed.) Maurice V. Brett (London, 1934), 77.

170 Hardinge to Knollys, 12.04.1905, RA VIC/MAIN/W/45/156.

171 Lord Clarendon to A.K. Benckendorff, 03.06.1905, BC2, box 12.

172 Barrington to A.K. Benckendorff, 30.05.1905, BC2, box 12.

feelings about the Japanese victories as they saw them in terms of the West being beaten by the East, which would not be 'a good thing for us *in the long run*'.[173] Others, like the *Westminster Gazette*, saw the Franco-German conflict in Morocco as a consequence of the disappearance of Russia's role in protecting the balance of powers.[174]

The Kaiser, worried by the spread of revolution in Russia, on 3 June, for the first time advised Nicholas II to open peace negotiations.[175] President Theodore Roosevelt offered to Russia US mediation on the request of the Japanese who wanted peace because they found that they had 'taken a bigger bite than they can chew'.[176] During an audience at Tsarskoe Selo on 7 June 1905 Lamsdorff used the verbal information from Benckendorff as one of his arguments to persuade Nicholas II to accept the mediation.[177] In the first days of June, Benckendorff had been anxious to get Lansdowne's reassurance regarding the modifications in the Anglo-Japanese treaty then under revision[178] and his verbal information must have been centred on the advantages of seizing the moment for ensuring Britain's goodwill before the Anglo-Japanese treaty was signed. Sazonov wrote: 'As for our relations with England, Ct. L. seemed to desire a rapprochement … and he told me that the best way to arrange it was a meeting of the monarchs, but that he did not believe it possible until after the peace was signed'. It was Lamsdorff's usual position, encouraging words, but no instructions. He expected Benckendorff to pass them on to the British and let them do the overtures, if they were as interested as Benckendorff believed they were.

Sazonov said Lamsdorff looked ill and was alarmed by Delcassé's resignation as a personal success of the German emperor. William II was extraordinarily assiduous, but Lamsdorff did not worry because, he said, Nicholas II allowed him to monitor the Willy-Nicky correspondence. Sazonov's appreciation of the domestic situation was gloomy: no promise of serious reform and Nicholas II's vacillation undermined all respect or confidence. Sazonov added an enthusiastic postscript to his letter on 8 June, when he heard that the emperor had accepted the US mediation, the first step towards ending the war.[179]

Following the Tsushima defeat, Lamsdorff for the first time spoke about a settlement with Britain in more than general terms, mentioning that Russia might agree to a division of spheres of interest in Persia.[180] It was also the first time that the idea of an agreement with Britain caught the imagination of some

173 06.09.1904, Journals *and Letters of Reginald Viscount Esher*, 2: 61.
174 A.F. Ostal'tseva, 93.
175 William II to Nicholas II, 03.06.1905, *Perepiska Vilgel'ma II s Nikolaem*, 376–80.
176 D. Mackenzie Wallace to Knollys, 10.09.1905, RA VIC/ADDC 7/2/Q.
177 Sazonov to A.K. Benckendorff, 08.07.1905, BC2, box 14.
178 Lansdowne to Hardinge, 02.06.1905, BD, 4: 79.
179 Sazonov to A.K. Benckendorff, 08.07.1905, BC2, box 14.
180 Ostal'tseva, 102.

of Nicholas II's military advisers.[181] At the same time, in every letter to London, Lamsdorff mentioned the emperor's anger against the British which manifested itself in his unwillingness to grant an audience to Hardinge.[182] Lamsdorff's pious hopes of a rapprochement with Britain do not seem more than a polite cliché throughout most of 1904–5, and only at the height of Russia's troubles they begin to ring somewhat truer. He preferred to placate Britain by small favours or promises at critical moments. For example, to allow Hardinge to report 'a small personal success', he managed to obtain the release of four British subjects arrested by the Russian military authorities for spying. He also sent Benckendorff copies of secret reports from the Russian ambassador to Turkey who had obtained information about alleged British intrigues in Constantinople directed against Russia.[183]

He assured Benckendorff (who was certain to tell Lansdowne) that Nicholas II would come round to more moderate views: 'The rapprochement with Germany will not pass beyond the limits of prudence; I can reassure you entirely on this account'.[184] But it did not mean that a general settlement with Britain became his goal. Lamsdorff's more pressing concern was that unless peace talks began soon Russia would be forced to ask for peace at any price: the revolution was spreading and the navy and the army were not reliable.[185] In July, on Lamsdorff's insistence and after some arm-twisting, the emperor reluctantly appointed Witte as the main negotiator in Portsmouth, New Hampshire. Lamsdorff wrote that he placed his hopes in God, as the emperor was apathetic.[186] Witte was of Lamsdorff's opinion: Russia needed peace. He also knew that Nicholas II wanted the negotiations to fail in order to proceed with the war. The emperor's interest was to demonstrate that he had tried to make peace but the Japanese did not respond. Therefore, to please the emperor Witte would have to fail Russia.

Lansdowne, who entertained the Russian ambassador at his Irish country house Derreen, noticed that he was nervous because things might go wrong at any moment.[187] The ambassador's personal worries had taken a toll of his health: in January 1905 his oldest son, naval Lieutenant Constantin Benckendorff, whose ship was sunk by the Japanese, was taken prisoner. The ambassador's nephew, a member of the German embassy in Tokyo, the Vatican, the Russian, French and British diplomatic networks ensured that Lieutenant Benckendorff's lot was immediately ascertained and that he received preferential treatment from the Japanese, but it was still a great shock. Petr Benckendorff volunteered for the Far Eastern front. Countess Benckendorff, in whose heart honour and duty were

181 A.F. Heyden, 'What Kind of Navy Does Russia Need?' 02/15.05.1905, *Korenny'ie interes'y Rossii*, 419.

182 Lamsdorff to A.K. Benckendorff, 26.05/8.06.1905, BC2, box 13.

183 Lamsdorff to A.K. Benckendorff, 07/20.07.1905, BC2, box 13.

184 Lamsdorff to A.K. Benckendorff, 09/22.06.1905, BC2, box 13.

185 Lamsdorff to A.K. Benckendorff, 23.06/6.07.1905, BC2, box 13.

186 Lamsdorff to A.K. Benckendorff, 07/20.07.1905, BC2, box 13.

187 Lansdowne to Hardinge, 21.08.1905, FO 800/141, 193–4.

foremost, wrote to her husband: 'Do not think that I am as much of a Spartan mother as I seem. I am frightened … but I know that some things just have to be done'.[188] Petr Benckendorff went missing while on a scouting mission and his parents lived through terrible moments until he reappeared, safe and sound. To crown it all, Russian revolution was gathering strength. Countess Benckendorff insisted on remaining in Sosnovka, while arsons and attacks by peasants on the landlords were taking place all around. When she left for a French resort in summer 1905, she was looking forward to great political changes in Russia.

Benckendorff shared his wife's delight in the rumours of a constitution in Russia,[189] but like her, he was not certain about the benefits of an urgent peace with Japan any more because 'while the war is continuing it reduces the chances of a war elsewhere in which we might be embroiled', that is, Russia's engagements towards France in case of a Franco-German war.[190] When Lansdowne told him of Lamsdorff's rumoured resignation, Benckendorff predicted that it would put an end to the Russo-Japanese peace negotiations.[191] But Witte carried off a diplomatic feat, achieving two goals: he signed the peace before Nicholas II recalled him in order to continue the hostilities, and managed to squeeze concessions out of the Japanese by showing that he was ready to break off the negotiations and leave at any time. He succeeded despite the hostility of the US, Britain and even Germany who all openly or secretly supported Japanese intransigence and in the process he managed to turn around US public opinion. In the history of late imperial Russia which abounds with doctrinaires trying to force their theories on the country, Witte stands out as a commonsensical man who instinctively felt where the danger for Russia lay and backed away without bothering about prestige, great power status or consistency, his own or his sovereign's. He was unsentimental about Russia's interests and other powers' altruism and friendship, which helped him to make good bargains. This was a talent that he shared with many British statesmen, but that Benckendorff lacked entirely.

Just as the ambassador feared, with the end of the war the conflicting pressures from the French, now buttressed by their entente with Britain and from Germany, drew Russia into the Morocco crisis, an outcome of the great powers' contest. Geoffrey Barraclough writes that in trying to establish her control of Morocco, France held to the principle of compensation which ruled the great powers' relations, and had bought off England, Spain and Italy, but did not make an effort to do so with Germany.[192] As a result, Germany stood up to France and since March 1905 the first Moroccan crisis had been gathering strength. France and Germany expected Russia's backing in their conflict.

188 S.P. Benckendorff to A.K. Benckendorff. 29.01/12.02.1904. BC2, box 21.

189 S.P. Benckendorff to A.K. Benckendorff, 21.06.1905, BC2, box 21.

190 S.P. Benckendorff to A.K. Benckendorff, 29.06.1905, BC2, box 21.

191 Lansdowne to Hardinge, 21.08.1905, FO 800/141, 193–4.

192 G. Barraclough, *From Agadir to Armageddon: Anatomy of a Crisis* (London, 1982), 78–80.

Britain and France had long worried about a Russo-German rapprochement. Cambon admitted that if he were Russian he would favour friendship with Germany, since German influence and support had been beneficial for Russia. From France's point of view, an Anglo-Russian entente was essential to avert this threat 'because the conflict of interests between Britain and Germany is a lasting one'.[193] William II, failing to achieve an arrangement with Britain, also saw the advantages of having Russia tied to Germany. In October 1904, at the height of the Dogger Bank passions, he had proposed to Nicholas II a defensive alliance of Russia-Germany-France against Britain.[194] Lamsdorff's opinion at that time was that a German alliance would be useful to Russia if it did not involve a quarrel with France.[195] He advised Nicholas II to prepare the grounds by explaining to the French ambassador that such a treaty would safeguard France from Germany and the old Triple Alliance. Then Nicholas II might ask if France would join. If it refused, Russia would have a free hand. William II objected to this course for fear of the British learning about it.[196]

The minister wrote that Germany intended to exploit Russia's difficulties in order to quarrel Russia with Britain and France. He could be certain that Benckendorff would pass on to Edward VII his confidences: 'William II incessantly writes and telegraphs touching warnings not to trust anyone except Germany and to form a *Continental* league of three great powers to bury British ambitions'. The minister warned Benckendorff (and, presumably, the British through him) that Nicholas II's anger with the British made him susceptible. He predicted: 'I am almost certain that there will be an attempt at this adventure …'.[197]

Indeed, unknown to Lamsdorff, the Björko meeting of the Russian and German emperors in July 1905 resulted in the signing of a preliminary Russo-German defensive treaty. It was a usual procedure for monarchs, and with a few adjustments it could have been harmonized with the Russo-French treaty.[198] Like Britain and Japan with their renewed alliance treaty, the emperors agreed to make the treaty public after the end of the Portsmouth talks. William II especially warned Nicholas II against disclosing the treaty to those whom he called the dupes of Edward VII: Benckendorff, Lamsdorff and the dowager empress.[199] He was right, because Edward VII sent for Benckendorff as soon as the Björko meeting was over,[200] but the ambassador had heard nothing. Soon after, Lamsdorff wrote to London that he, Lamsdorff, had angered the Kaiser by having 'neutralized three perfidious combinations which would involve us in a quarrel with England, with France and

193 Paul Cambon to Henri Cambon, 13.05.1904, *Correspondance*, 2:140.

194 Guillermo de Hohenzollern, *Mis Memorias* (Madrid, 1922), 62.

195 A. Savinsky, 97.

196 Ibid., 103.

197 Lamsdorff to A.K. Benckendorff, 17/30.10.1904, BC2, box 13.

198 M. de Taube, *La politique russe*, 63–5.

199 William II to Nicholas II, 22.08.1905, *Perepiska*, 388–9.

200 S.P. Benckendorff to A.K. Benckendorff, 02.08.1905, BC2, box 21.

even with Austria!' He agreed with Benckendorff that Germany's policy aimed at isolating and dominating Russia under the pretext of the traditional friendship of monarchs. Lamsdorff dismissed the rumour that he wanted to resign because he would resent answering the interpellations of the newly-legislated Russian parliament (Duma): he pointed out that he had participated in the elaboration of the Duma's statutes and knew that foreign policy was outside its prerogatives. If he left it would be because of the emperor's desire 'to see in my place someone new, less experienced and more eager to please'.[201] He foresaw that Nicholas II would continue attempts at directing foreign policy and he had no energy left to continue acting as a moderator: in the summer of 1905 Lamsdorff had two heart attacks and in Hardinge's prophetic opinion he would not last long.[202]

When the Portsmouth peace was signed on 23 August/5 September, the Björko treaty came into force. The Tsar gave Lamsdorff the text of the treaty on 30 August/13 September[203] and the next day heard his opinion that it gave Russia nothing in the East where she was under pressure while promising her help in Europe where Russia was in no danger, but Germany was. Lamsdorff criticized the details of the treaty.[204] It remained to be seen whether it could be made functional for Russia.

Following the Peace of Portsmouth Hardinge was also preparing to inform the Russian government about the new Anglo-Japanese treaty, which included the defence of India by Japan in case of an attack by a third country. To soften the impression from the anti-Russian clause of the text Hardinge obtained Lansdowne's authorization to stretch the truth by implying that the alliance had had a favourable influence on the Japanese demands in the peace talks. Nevertheless, Lansdowne did not authorize him to speak of a resumption of the discussions. Count Lamsdorff, after swallowing the bitter pill of the treaty, was the one to speak of his desire for an understanding when public opinion in Russia became more amenable to the idea.[205]

Lamsdorff persuaded Nicholas II to receive two supporters of an Anglo-Russian understanding in September 1905: Wesselitsky and the well-known British journalist and pacifist W.T. Stead.[206] At the same time he tried to hold back the eager ambassador in London. Lamsdorff offered his own behaviour with Hardinge as an example for Benckendorff to follow in his dealings with Lansdowne: 'The language I use to Hardinge is *of the most amiable kind* but I remain vague'. Lamsdorff explained his attitude: 'When the British clearly formulate acceptable terms for the questions of mutual interest, we shall accept

201 Lamsdorff to A.K. Benckendorff, 18/31.08.1905, BC2, box 13.

202 Hardinge to Lansdowne, 01.08.1905, FO 800/141, 184–6.

203 Lamsdorff's memorandum, 31.08/13.09.1905, AVPRI, f.138, op.467, d.236/237, ll.6–7 ob.

204 A. Savinsky, 115.

205 Hardinge to Lansdowne, 09.09.1905, BD, 4: 178–9.

206 A.F. Ostal'tseva, 125.

the discussions. But we cannot and must not provoke them, especially under the present circumstances'. The Tsar's Anglophobia was intense after the double shock of the Björko and the Anglo-Japanese treaty. Lamsdorff said: '[We] should see things as they are and not as they should be'. Initiating unauthorized talks would jeopardize them, because the British would immediately perceive Benckendorff's lack of authority. He preferred to wait until Berlin's perfidy became obvious, and 'then we shall be able to return to the great task of restoring the balance simply and purely in the interest of Russia, echewing false sentimentality and personal likes and dislikes which so terribly complicate things and never lead to anything good'.[207]

Lamsdorff, who had never lived in Britain, understood the British statesmen better than Benckendorff, for at the same time Lansdowne wrote to Hardinge: 'for the moment we must mark time and content ourselves with reminding the Russians here and at Petersburg that we are quite ready to talk to them whenever they feel inclined'.[208] But there was indirect encouragement from the British side: Lord Revelstoke applied his considerable influence to curbing the hostility of the British press to Russia.[209] *The Times*, the *Daily Telegraph* and the *Standard* became more moderate in their reporting of the Russian events and spoke of a future Anglo-Russian understanding as a certainty.[210] Benckendorff spent another week in Ireland with Lansdowne in September 1905 and a telegram from the dowager empress summoning him to Copenhagen came in his absence. His wife was all agog: 'Will you go? It is difficult to refuse'. Benckendorff must have related to his wife his conversations with Lansdowne because she echoed Lamsdorff's opinion: 'It seems to me that between us and England there can only be a diplomatic settlement without much fanfare, in order to achieve a détente and a *modus vivendi*'. She wrote this after Poklevsky returned from Paris where he had met Witte at the ambassador's request. Poklevsky reported to her that Witte felt very confident and encouraged Benckendorff to act. She wrote:

> [Witte] is of your opinion about this place here and being amiable in Berlin because we do not want to risk anything. He did not know about the A[nglo]-J[apanese] T[reaty] but when he read it he said: 'This means ten years [the term of the treaty] of abstention for us'.

She added that all Witte talked about was Britain and the finances:

> He is not overly enthusiastic about having the local market paired with the French one. He wants an international loan to avoid looking as if he acted against the

207 Lamsdorff to A.K. Benckendorff, 15/28.09.1905, BC2, box 13.

208 Lansdowne to Hardinge, 17.10.1905, FO 800/141, 217.

209 S.P. Benckendorff to A.K. Benckendorff, 22.09.1905, BC2, box 21.

210 Geoffray to Rouvier, 10.10.1905, DDF, VIII: 54–5.

others … I think W[itte] wants to be polite to everyone in order to retain his freedom of action'.[211]

Less than a week later, Benckendorff told Lansdowne that Lamsdorff was ready to discuss an understanding and they could begin discussions after his trip to Copenhagen and St Petersburg. Lansdowne replied that he would welcome discussions, provided they were kept secret. They agreed to discuss the outstanding questions one by one, and move on as they disposed of them.[212] The next day Benckendorff returned to warn Lord Lansdowne that nothing in the eventual understanding should be hostile to Germany.[213] At the same time Lansdowne heard that the French president after an interview with Witte considered that the chances for an Anglo-Russian settlement were poor.[214] So the Foreign Secretary could hardly have expected any great breakthrough.

William II told Nicholas II that Benckendorff had gone to Copenhagen in October 1905 on a secret mission from Edward VII to persuade Maria Feodorovna to use her influence in order to shift the Russian course to anti-German.[215] Despite the Tsar's protests that Benckendorff would never stoop to intrigues and that his visit was purely private,[216] the German foreign ministry believed that Benckendorff was working against Germany – presumably because he hoped that in an Anglo-German clash Russia would be the *tertia gaudens*.[217] Maria Feodorovna's invitation to the count was an answer to his letter after an audience with Edward VII. The ambassador opened his letter literally repeating Hardinge's complaint about the Björko meeting,[218] which in its turn echoed the words which William II ascribed to Edward VII: 'No one knows what took place [in Björko] – there is the danger'. Benckendorff predicted that keeping France in the dark at the time of the Franco-German crisis would lose Russia her ally's trust and lead to a Franco-British-Japanese alliance supported by the United States. 'They might come to dominate the world! That is what Germany is leading us into'. Russia's weakness would make her Germany's slave. The forward policy which Russia had pursued prior to the war was unsustainable because Russia had not yet 'achieved its maximum cohesion', that is, social and national peace, nor tapped her internal resources. An Anglo-Russian conflict would help Germany gain dominance in Asia or pave the way for an Anglo-German understanding and then Russia would be lost. Britain still wanted an arrangement with Russia and Russia should seize

211 S.P. Benckendorff to A.K. Benckendorff, 26.09.1905, BC2, box 21.

212 Lansdowne to Hardinge, 03.10.1905, BD, 4: 204–5.

213 Lansdowne to Hardinge, 05.10.1905, BD, 4: 207–8.

214 Lister to Bertie, 06.10.1905, FO 800/176, 224–5.

215 William II to Nicholas II. 02/15.10.1905, *Perepiska*, 402.

216 Nicholas II to William II, [n.d.], *Perepiska,* 403.

217 Bülow to William II, 15.06.1905, *Letters of Prince von Bülow* (London, n.d.), 57–65.

218 Hardinge to Lansdowne, 01.08.1905, BD, 4: 95.

the occasion as soon as peace with Japan was concluded. Unless, he repeated, it was too late, because he did not know what happened in Björko.[219] This last warning echoes Hardinge's conjecture that in Björko William II had encouraged Nicholas II to continue the war.[220] Benckendorff's arguments, even their wording in 1905, increasingly echoed the Foreign Office's assumptions and suspicions.

In Copenhagen, Benckendorff repeated these arguments to the empress and to Iswolsky who would soon take Lamsdorff's place. He mentioned to Iswolsky that a partition of zones in Persia and other regions would protect Russia's positions from Britain.[221] Considering that Benckendorff knew little about Asia and Russia's position there, this drastic opinion sounds like something he had heard from his friends in London. Iswolsky, who later openly admitted that he knew nothing about the Anglo-Russian issues,[222] was impressed, as shown by the admiring references to Benckendorff in his diary.

Russian diplomats were familiar with Benckendorff's views by this time because the foreign minister circulated his letters. Lamsdorff chose for lithographing and circulation parts of his correspondence with Russian envoys about the issues which he wanted the diplomats to know even if they were not directly relevant to their task. A month after learning about the Björko treaty, Lamsdorff made one of Benckendorff's letters the subject of a general discussion and one copy found its way to the private papers of the dowager empress. Benckendorff attacked the Björko treaty, no longer secret by then. He criticized the inappropriate moment and few benefits of the rapprochement with Germany and the fact that it would destroy Russia's alliance with France and lead to a triple Anglo-Franco-US alliance. Europe's 'truly exploitable' financial markets would be closed to Russia. Curzon's aggressive policy in Asia would receive a boost after Russia rejected Britain's offer of negotiations. He conceded that Lansdowne had not made a definite proposal, but pointed out that the Foreign Secretary had asked if Russia wanted to go back to negotiations.[223] Benckendorff's civic courage had a clear limit because he asked Lamsdorff not to show this letter to the Tsar.[224]

The echoes of the ensuing discussion are found in a letter from the counsellor of the Russian embassy in Constantinople, A.N. Svetchin, to the director of the minister's Chancellery A.A. Savinsky. Savinsky had written about the 'diametrically opposed political hypotheses' of the ambassador to the Ottoman empire, I. Zinoviev, and Benckendorff. Svetchin argued that their opinions were not as antagonistic as it seemed:

---

219 A.K. Benckendorff to Maria Feodorovna, 17/29.08.1905 (draft), GARF, f.1126, op.1, ed.hr.4, ll.1–4.

220 Hardinge to Lansdowne, 01.08.1905, BD, 4: 95.

221 A.P. Iswolsky, *Diary*, 22.03.1906, GARF, f.559, op.1, d.86, l.34.

222 Nicolson to Grey, 12.09.1906, FO 800/337, 103–5.

223 A.K. Benckendorff to Lamsdorff, 19.09/02.10.1905, GARF, f.642, op.1, ed.hr.917, ll.55–69 ob. (copy).

224 A.F. Ostal'tseva, 125.

> I think like Zinoviev that unless we achieve this necessary (in my opinion) arrangement England will continue to search for all possible guarantees against us. It is a sensible policy and that is why I do not agree that an arrangement with England will be unstable. On the contrary, as their goals are long-term, it increases the value of a serious, complete entente.

The Constantinople legation agreed with Benckendorff that a rapprochement with Britain was the best way to avoid a dependence on Germany.[225] Roman Rosen, the Russian minister in the US, wrote to Benckendorff in December 1905 that the cause of the war with Japan had been Russia's failure to conclude a general entente with Japan in 1898 or, failing that, an entente with Britain, because it would have been a guarantee against an anti-Russian Anglo-German alliance. Rosen called Russia's interest in the Persian Gulf and Tibet 'chimeras' which prevented a settlement with Britain and in 1905 had cost Russia her acquired position on the Pacific Ocean. Rosen's letter ended: 'But *no use crying over spilt milk*. Only don't let us spill any more'.[226]

In the meanwhile Lamsdorff, faced with his monarch's will and a signed declaration of intention to conclude a Russo-German treaty, made an attempt to follow it through. First he and then Witte,[227] asked the French ambassador about the possibility of France's joining the Björko treaty.[228] As a necessary counterpoise to the Anglo-Japanese alliance he suggested a quadruple combination of Russia, France, Germany and the US.[229] Lamsdorff said that the two blocs need not be hostile, since a Continental entente applying to the Far East would improve relations with the Anglo-Japanese bloc.[230] The French guessed that Lamsdorff was reluctant to ally Russia with Germany only; the French government countered the danger by rejecting Lamsdorff's proposal. Bompard promised Lamsdorff secrecy, and at once alerted Hardinge that the British should hasten to negotiate Russia's adherence to the Anglo-French entente.[231] From the British point of view an understanding with Germany would make sense for Russia[232] and the British were alarmed.[233]

On 5/18 October Lamsdorff proposed to Nicholas II that the Björko treaty text might be complemented by a declaration that it was not applicable to a Franco-

225 A.N. Svetchin to A.A. Savinsky, 18/31.01.1906, AVPRI, f. 340, op.706, ed. hr.11, ll.323–8 ob.

226 R.R. Rosen to A.K. Benckendorff, 11/24.12.1905, BC2, box 14.

227 Hardinge to Lansdowne, 04.10.1905, BD, 4: 205–6.

228 A. Savinsky, 98–102.

229 Hardinge to Lord Lansdowne, 14.10.1905, BD, 4: 211–2.

230 Bompard to Rouvier, 14.10.1905, DDF, VIII: 62–5.

231 Hardinge to Lansdowne, 04.10.1905, BD, 4: 205–6.

232 Hardinge to Lansdowne, 13.06.1905, BD, 4: 196–7.

233 Spring Rice to Mallet, 05.01.1906, FO 800/72, 25–8; Lister to Bertie, 06.10.1905, FO 800/176, 224–5.

German war. The treaty might still be viable in this form as a secret guarantee against either Russia or Germany entering a hostile agreement with Britain.[234] When the German side refused to compromise, Lamsdorff understood that for Germany the Björko treaty was a means of undermining either the Franco-Russian or the Anglo-French arrangements. Witte and Lamsdorff persuaded Nicholas II that futile efforts to draw France into a Continental league would end in Russia's isolation. The emperor wrote to William II on 13(26) November 1905 that the treaty would only be valid after France joined.[235] It was the end of Lamsdorff's active efforts to make the Björko treaty terms acceptable for Russia.

Benckendorff, Nelidov and Cambon had been discussing an Anglo-Russian rapprochement for years. In the autumn of 1905 they agreed that a rapprochement with Britain was the best way of avoiding Russia's semi-subjugation to Germany and buttressing France's European position.[236] Benckendorff thanked Nelidov for supporting his views with Lamsdorff. He summarized for Nelidov's sake the main points of view which he must have formed during years of discussions with the British: until Russia achieved national cohesion and prosperity, a forward policy was unrealistic. The Anglo-Japanese alliance need not concern Russia if it achieved an Anglo-Russian rapprochement. The area where frictions had to be settled urgently was Persia and Constantinople, where Russia and Britain could find a mutually satisfactory position as the 'Turkish issue' had passed from Britain to Germany. German expansionism augured ill for Russia while if England felt confident of Russia's friendship it would make concessions. The Far Eastern region also presented possibilities for an understanding but Britain would not make concessions unless all the issues were discussed together. He agreed with the British on this point, while Lamsdorff did not want a general agreement with Britain.[237]

Benckendorff had another letter from the minister, reminding him that it was not a good moment to begin serious talks and warning that William II was aware of Benckendorff's and Poklevsky's efforts to prevent a rapprochement with Germany. The minister repeated that to maintain good relations with Germany and to make her amenable, Russia needed the French alliance and complained about William II's continuing efforts to prevent an improvement in Anglo-Russian relations.[238]

Benckendorff and Nelidov ignored Lamsdorff's warnings of caution and the ambassador went as far as discussing specific Russian interests with Lansdowne. On 8 October Lansdowne wrote to the British ambassador to France, Sir Francis Bertie:

---

234 Ignatiev, 97.

235 O. Airapetov, *Vneshna'ia politika Rossiiskoi imperii 1801–1914* (Moscow, 2006), 517.

236 Paul Cambon to Henri Cambon, 08.07.1905, *Correspondance*, 2:148.

237 A.K. Benckendorff to Nelidov. 07/19.09.1905, GARF, f.1126, op.1, ed.hr.5, ll.1–2.

238 Lamsdorff to A.K. Benckendorff, 29.09/12.10.1905, BC2, box 13.

> Benckendorff … thinks that we ought, though not immediately, to be able to come to an understanding with Russia, but he explained to me that he meant a comparatively modest arrangement, and that he did not expect us to offer them Constantinople.[239]

In Paris, where the French government was doing its utmost to ensure Russia's unconditional support for France in the brewing Morocco crisis, Nelidov discussed with Paul Cambon ways to bind Russia to Britain through joint guarantees of China's integrity and independence, but Lansdowne rejected the idea as a weak pretext since the principle had already been stated in earlier documents.[240] In October Bompard wrote to his minister: 'Do you realize that owing to the circumstances the Anglo-Russian rapprochement now would be anti-German? So the Russians will not negotiate unless the British talk to them directly'.[241] Hardinge still believed that it was too early for the negotiations.[242]

Only in late October 1905 did Nicholas II grant an audience to Hardinge, who brought him a personal letter from Edward VII. The emperor spoke about an Anglo-Russian understanding. Hardinge told Nicholas II that an Anglo-Russian agreement would be easy to make as it would not be against any other power. The British did not seek allies in Europe and only sought peace with all powers.[243]

Nelidov advised Benckendorff to precipitate the negotiations by asking Lansdowne to explain them in more detail a letter in which the Foreign Secretary expressed his wish for an understanding. 'Only then it will be clear whether we can reach an understanding and get an arrangement, and not, as the minister's letter says, that during the negotiations for an entente we shall see whether there are grounds for explanations … I sent my ideas to Witte. Pomogi Vam Bog [God be with you]'.[244]

Rosen's reference to the minister's excessive caution, Nelidov's advice to disregard Lamsdorff's instructions to wait and see, and Benckendorff's words about missed opportunities cited in Rosen's letter, spoke about the general impatience for an immediate improvement in Russia's international position. Lamsdorff was too timid in their eyes.

Despite all this pressure, a month later Lamsdorff's and Nicholas II's position remained unchanged. On 8/21 November 1905 Lamsdorff telegraphed to London: 'We do not need any agreement'.[245]

239 Lansdowne to Bertie, 08.10.1905, FO 800/176, 227.
240 Lansdowne to Bertie, 25.10.1905, BD, 4: 217–8.
241 Bompard to Rouvier, 08.10.1905, DDF, VIII: 48.
242 Hardinge to Edward VII, 10.10.1905, RA VIC/ADDC 7/2/Q.
243 Hardinge to Edward VII, 24.10.1905, RA VIC/ADDC 7/2/Q.
244 Nelidov to A.K. Benckendorff, 01.11.1905, BC2, box 13.
245 A.F. Ostal'tseva, 143.

Chapter 5
The Anglo-Russian Rapprochement, 1905–1907

Internal turmoil in 1905–6 imposed on the Russian government the need to look for remedies at home and abroad. The measures ranged from unprecedented concessions to the liberal opposition to attempts to stabilize Russia's international position and the London embassy actively participated in bringing about the long-sought rapprochement with Britain.

Countess Benckendorff spent much of 1904–6 in Russia and sent her husband daily issues of the newspaper *Russkie vedomosti* [Russian Bulletin] with detailed instructions as to how to read them:

> Skim the leading article and patiently read all the telegrams and telephone reports from Petersburg. After a few days you will see the point and will be up to date – I will not say on Russian opinion, but, rather, the mood in Russia.[1]

Lamsdorff's letters were more straightforward: in July 1905, he piled one metaphor on another: 'We are sitting on a volcano and the revolutionary whirlwind is dragging us towards an abyss at a dizzying speed'.[2] Pavel Benckendorff echoed him: 'We have never witnessed such horrors in this country. The dynasty is losing more ground every day'.[3]

To understand the Russian events, the ambassador suggested that Edward VII read Maurice Baring's article in the *Morning Post*.[4] Despite his initial enthusiasm for the awakening of the Russian nation, Baring came to the conclusion that at the moment Russia was not suffering so much from want of liberty as from want of law[5] and the Benckendorffs, sharing his opinion, welcomed Witte's appointment, hoping that he would soon restore order.[6]

The London embassy staff argued about the extent of reforms which, all agreed, were necessary in Russia.[7] Benckendorff imposed limits on disputes,

---

1 S.P. Benckendorff to A.K. Benckendorff, 23.10/06.11.1906, BC 2, box 21.

2 Lamsdorff to A.K. Benckendorff, 07/20.07.1905, BC2, box 13.

3 P.K. Benckendorff to A.K. Benckendorff, 27.04/10.05.1905, BC 2, box 19.

4 A.K. Benckendorff to Knollys, 25.06.1906, RA VIC/MAIN/W/49/63.

5 Maurice Baring, *Russian Essays and Stories* (London, 1909), 93.

6 S.P. Benckendorff to A.K. Benckendorff,10/23.10.1905, BC 2, box 21.

7 A.K. Benckendorff to A.P. Iswolsky, 29.05/11.06.1906, *Au service de la Russie*, 1: 303–5.

saying that as the emperor's representative he could not listen to or express certain opinions.[8] But he did not observe the rule too strictly, complaining to Jusserand, who was passing through London, about the emperor's 'lack of forcefulness' and the empress's pedantic attachment to the imperial status which made Nicholas II resist all attempt at change.[9] He criticized the October Manifesto for its ambiguity and vague promises which would be easy to ignore or modify later.[10]

On the eve of the manifesto's appearance, with the strikes and violence in Russia spreading, Benckendorff telegraphed to Maria Feodorovna advice for the emperor to concede a 'widely and clearly liberal constitution' and appoint a responsible cabinet of ministers chosen from outside the existing administration. Benckendorff reminded his correspondent that unless a constitution were conceded expressly by the Tsar's will before he appointed a prime minister, the latter would become a dictator and the assembly he convoked would produce its own constitution, stripping the monarch of all authority.[11] The next day he telegraphed: 'Must add to my yesterday's telegram to your majesty that I believe Witte the only man capable and suitable to be the president of the ministers. Any other but him would lack authority'.[12]

Benckendorff was, probably, one of many people who at the time offered Maria Feodorovna advice hoping that it would reach her son, and Witte was the man that friends and foes alike believed to be able to deal with the crisis. Still, it so happened that the day after receiving Benckendorff's telegrams Maria Feodorovna sent an urgent message for Nicholas II: 'I am sure that the only man who can help you now and be useful is Witte'.[13] Also, a day later the first two sentences of the manifesto were changed so as to show that it was granted by Nicholas II.[14]

Having asked Witte for help, the Tsar complained to his mother about the man's authoritarian behaviour. Benckendorff protested through the dowager empress, that Witte 'has his defects but each day that he stays is a day gained. I see no one else but him'.[15] The next week, Maria Feodorovna advised her son to support Witte as the only capable man he had.[16] Throughout the autumn and winter of 1905 she repeatedly telegraphed Benckendorff to tell him that she agreed with his opinions and to thank him for advice. Apparently answering Maria Feodorovna's opinion

8 D.I. Abrikossov, 114.

9 J.J. Jusserand, 306.

10 D.I. Abrikossov, 121.

11 A.K. Benckendorff to Empress Maria Feodorovna, 14/27.10.1905, GARF, f.642, op.1, ed.hr.918, ll.74–6.

12 A.K. Benckendorff to Empress Maria Feodorovna, 15/28.10.1905, GARF, f.642, op.1, ed. hr.918, l.77.

13 Empress Maria Feodorovna to Nicholas II, 16/29.10.1905, *The Letters of Tsar Nicholas and Empress Marie*, ed. E. Bing (London, 1937), 183–4.

14 Hardinge to Lansdowne, 30.10.1905, FO 800/141, 222–7.

15 A.K. Benckendorff to Empress Maria Feodorovna (draft), 25.11/8.12.1905,GARF, f.1126, op.1, ed. hr.4, ll.5–8.

16 Empress Maria Feodorovna to Nicholas II, 02/15.12.1905, *The Letters,* 193.

that the Jewish pogroms in Poland, Byelorussia and Ukraine were a reaction to Jewish terrorism, Benckendorff wrote in one of his letters:

> As for ... the Jews one should ask not whether they are innocent or guilty [of terrorism]. That is not the question, nor is it important. They should not be massacred ... It cannot continue. First of all, because it shows that we have no authority any more ...[17]

Control and authority was the pivot of Benckendorff's reasoning, and he deplored disorder as a clear manifestation of the Russian state's weakness. He would welcome reforms only if introduced by a stable government from a position of strength. Although he deplored the October Manifesto, he insisted on the need to keep its promises.[18] His wife, obviously referring to his advice to Copenhagen, exclaimed: 'Only you, remaining absolutely loyal are at the same time truly liberal ... Only you have the courage to say all you think'.[19]

In 1906–7 the ambassador kept reminding his minister of the obvious: the pogroms and mutinies were a symptom of government's weakness and the disclosure of weakness would be followed by a drop in value of Russian bonds on the financial markets and increasing political pressure from the powers.[20] But he drew impracticable conclusions from these general truths: concessions were not to be made unless from a position of strength, after order had been restored, but order ought not to be restored either by concessions or by force, as both were a symptom of weakness. Still, when Stolypin's government cut the Gordian knot by a violent suppression of terrorism in the country in 1906–7, everyone was relieved, including Russian and British diplomats of liberal views.[21] It is one thing to applaud freedom fighters from a distance and another to live in the midst of bomb explosions and electricity blackouts caused by workers' strikes.

Debates around the Anglo-Russian Rapprochement

In December there was a rumour that Witte had switched from his earlier pro-German stance to a pro- British one.[22] In Britain Balfour's Conservative government resigned and the Liberals, led by Sir Henry Campbell-Bannerman, took office and won the general election. Also in December, Lamsdorff gave to

---

17 A.K. Benckendorff to Empress Maria Feodorovna (draft), 25.11/8.12.1905, GARF, f.1126, op.1, ed.hr.1, d.4, ll.5–8.

18 A.K. Benckendorff to A.P. Iswolsky, 16/29.05.1906, *Au service de la Russie*, 1: 297–301.

19 S.P. Benckendorff to A.K. Benckendorff, 18/31.03.1906, BC2, box 21.

20 A.K. Benckendorff to Iswolsky, 14/27.06.1906, *Au service de la Russie*, 1: 311–6.

21 Nicolson to Hardinge, 24.09.1906, FO 800/337, 108–10.

22 Spring Rice to Grey, 03.01.1906, BD, 4: 219–20.

the Tsar, Benckendorff's letters reporting that the Liberals were looking forward to the discussions, and the king personally received even second rank diplomatic agents posted to Asia and told them to avoid conflicts with Russia.[23] The new Foreign Secretary, Sir Edward Grey, told Benckendorff that to demonstrate his sincere wish for a rapprochement he would abstain from disturbing the status quo in Asia. Benckendorff told him that Russia preferred to postpone the conversations because of domestic unrest. No one could guarantee that the concessions which the actual Russian government made would be respected by the next one or that they would not be used in order to attack those who agreed to them.[24] Benckendorff pressed Lamsdorff to hurry or the British would attempt an Anglo-German understanding.[25] As usual, he put an excessive price on Grey's friendly gesture for the latter wrote:

> As a matter of fact I don't want to do anything on the Indian frontier or in Persia and in Turkish affairs we no longer pursue an anti-Russian policy anyway – so it is no sacrifice on our part.[26]

When Benckendorff came to St Petersburg for a routine visit in January 1906, Lamsdorff several times invited him to his house to meet Witte and discuss in private the government's immediate goals. Witte had liked the idea of the Continental league until he returned to Russia and read the text of the Björko treaty.[27] He agreed with Lamsdorff that it was not acceptable to Russia in its original form and that futile efforts to create a Continental league would end in Russia's isolation. He also considered Nelidov's argument that if France distanced herself from Russia, then it would join Britain against Russia in the Eastern Question, a danger that had to be averted. Witte's and Lamsdorff's decision to abandon the Björko treaty and the decision to pursue a rapprochement with Britain were taken nearly simultaneously.[28] Witte expressed his approval of an agreement with Britain, while preserving Germany's friendship. A settlement with Britain, apart from other advantages, would help to restore Russia‘s equilibrium between Germany and the Entente. In his New Year letter, Lamsdorff wrote that he was prepared to welcome Hardinge's overtures, but a serious and practical discussion of a settlement would only be possible when the British government had presented its terms.[29]

Lamsdorff's policy in 1905 revolved around three axioms: first, Russia had to maintain an independent political course between the Triple Alliance and the entente

23 A.K. Benckendorff to Lamsdorff, 12/25.12.1905, GARF, f.601, op.1, d.741, l.49.

24 Grey to Spring Rice, 13.12.1905, BD, 4: 218.

25 A.K. Benckendorff to Lamsdorff, 29.11/12.12.1905, GARF, f.1126, op.1, ed. hr.10, ll.20–22 ob.

26 Grey to Spring Rice, 22.12.1905, FO 800/72, 13.

27 S. Yu Witte, *Vospominani'ia*, 2: 455.

28 I. Astaf'iev, 25–7.

29 Lamsdorff to A.K. Benckendorff, 22.12.1905/04.01.1906, BC2, box 13.

because of their antagonistic character.[30] Second, an arrangement with Britain was desirable but Russia's and Britain's national interests remained incompatible;[31] therefore an arrangement was not worth the sacrifice of the positions which Russia already held or of her freedom of action. Third, Russia could not seek deals at the time of weakness.[32] It was classic diplomatic logic, which the British had also followed in 1902–3 when they were in the weaker position.[33] Lamsdorff thought of an understanding similar to the Mürzsteg entente, about the maintenance of the status quo in various areas of contact. Until the situation improved, he hoped to placate the British by gestures of goodwill, such as tacitly recognizing the Anglo-Tibetan Lhassa convention and the Anglo-Chinese convention relating to Tibet[34] and mentioning his willingness to consider the partition of Persia. As he offered friendly gestures to Berlin, the minister asked Benckendorff to allay Anglo-French suspicions:

> … our August Master deigned to confer St Andrew's order with diamonds to Prince Bülow … Considering the bad impression produced in Paris and London by Bülow's last speech, we should take precautions that this sign of special favour should not be interpreted by the hostile elements and press as a hostile demonstration in regard to France and Britain.

He explained that the order was conferred to mark the conclusion of a new Russo-German commercial treaty and that the same courtesy had been extended to the German and Austro-Hungarian foreign ministers in the past under the same circumstances. In 1905, besides, it was a sign of Russia's gratitude for Germany's support in the recent war, but it carried no anti-Entente connotation whatsoever.[35]

British, French and Russian Interests

Anglo-German antagonism was a widely accepted fact and Clemenceau reminded the British at every opportunity that an Anglo-German war was a question of time only.[36] At least since the Boer war the British had been alarmed by the prospect of Germany's growing strength one day turning against them.[37] The Entente cordiale

30 M.A. Taube, *Zarnitsy: Vospominani'ia o tragicheskoi sud'be predrevolutsionnoi Rossii (1900–1917)* (Moscow, 2007), 83–4.

31 Minister's instructions to A.K. Benckendorff, *Korennye interesy*, 332–8.

32 Lamsdorff to A.K. Benckendorff, 15/28.09.1905, BC2, box 14.

33 Hardinge of Penshurst, *Old Diplomacy: The Reminiscences of Lord Hardinge of Penshurst* (London, 1947), 84.

34 Boutiron to Bourgeois, 05.05.1906, DDF, X: 52–4.

35 Lamsdorff to A.K. Benckendorff, 04/17.12.1905. BC2, box 28.

36 Louis Mallet, *Memorandum*, 13.07.1905, FO 800/145, 259–61.

37 Keith Hamilton, *Bertie of Thame: Edwardian Ambassador* (London, 1989), 65.

was a corollary to this situation: France gave up her long-standing interests, such as Egypt, counting on British backing in their colonial contest with Germany in Morocco. The Morocco crisis was the result of the new grouping: France attempted to capitalize on the British recognition of Morocco as a French sphere of interest. Germany opposed France in order to test the entente.[38] Averting a Russo-German alliance was Britain's main concern in 1905. Lord Esher as early as September 1904 had written of Russo-German friendship being an immediate threat to Britain,[39] and this thought recurred in the British diplomats' dispatches.[40] The Morocco crisis converted this concern into a pressing need for bringing Russia to the Entente side.

Russia's position between France and Germany was precarious. By the winter of 1905–6 the aborted Björko treaty had damaged Russo-German relations: when the French and British wanted Nicholas II to make a personal appeal to William II, Lamsdorff opposed it because the Russian ambassador in Berlin reported that William II would not heed it.[41] At the same time, the French alliance was to Lamsdorff 'a card in the game of Russian policy he would not part with',[42] because Russia's weakness would have made her a sad follower in a coalition with Germany and Austria-Hungary. Lamsdorff tried to assuage William II's disappointment by the prospect of a political agreement. As revolutionary disorders were spreading in January 1906, Lamsdorff suggested to Nicholas II to seek support in a league of conservative states of Europe,[43] Germany and the Vatican being the foremost (and Britain the one which fostered sedition in Russia, as he stated in his last memorandum to Nicholas II).[44] Germany did not answer this proposal.

Lamsdorff accepted the need for a settlement with Britain after Nicholas II's personal diplomacy and the Russian revolution had tipped the balance too close to Germany. In Bompard's judgment, 'the little count was not ambitious': his only aim was peace and his method of ensuring it was to settle, as amicably as possible, every thorny issue which came up in Russia's relations with other states.[45] But in moving away from Germany after Björko Lamsdorff inevitably came closer to the Entente, for there was no room for more sophisticated manoeuvring. With Russia's 1905 defeat it was a common opinion in Europe that now the remaining European

38 Keith Wilson, *Problems and Possibilities. Exercises in Statesmanship, 1814–1918* (The Mill, Brimscombe Port, 2003), 173.

39 *Journals and Letters of Reginald Viscount Esher. vol. 2 1903–1910* (London, 1934), 62.

40 Spring Rice to Mallet, 05.01.1906, FO 800/72, 25–8; Lister to Bertie, 06.10.1905, FO 800/176, 224–5.

41 I.I. Astaf'iev, *Russko-Germanskie diplomaticheskie otnosheni'ia 1905–1914 gg. (Ot portsmutskogo mira do potsdamskogo soglasheni'ia.)* (Moscow, 1972), 36.

42 Freiherr von Schoen, *The Memoirs of an Ambassador: A Contribution to the Political History of Modern Times* (New York, 1923), 50.

43 M.A. Taube, *Zarnitsy*, 91.

44 M.A. Taube, *Zarnitsy*, 101.

45 Maurice Bompard, 3.

giants, Britain and Germany, were facing each other and their rivalry would shape the new coalitions.[46] As for Witte, from whom everybody demanded miracles, he needed to produce a quick success which would silence his enemies, relieve Russia's financial situation and give him the authority he needed for implementing his domestic policy.[47]

When three people confer as often as Cambon, Benckendorff and Nelidov did in late 1905, it is difficult to judge who inspired whom, but Paul Cambon reported to his minister three German attempts to promote in British public opinion the idea of an Anglo-German rapprochement in December 1905,[48] and Benckendorff also used this threat to prod his chief.

By January 1906, with the Moroccan issue unresolved and with Witte and Lamsdorff refusing to share the French and the British concern, the Foreign Office began to get anxious about Russia's position regarding Germany.[49] They needed Russia's commitment and Benckendorff's energetic efforts in this respect must have been most welcome. Answering Benckendorff's question, which was of great interest to France and Britain, Lamsdorff wrote that Nicholas II might appeal to William II to help France, but if Germany disregarded Nicholas II's request, then Russia's long-term relations with Berlin would seriously suffer.[50] Russo-German relations were so fraught with difficulties that Nicholas II did not write to the Kaiser.

In January 1906 Nicholas II received Benckendorff in his suburban seclusion. After the first audience Benckendorff told the British Chargé d'Affaires, Cecil Spring Rice that the Tsar feared that after the disastrous war and forced peace with Japan, a purely negative arrangement with Britain would be seen as weakness. Then the ambassador obviously passed from quoting the Tsar to speaking his mind. He pronounced the fateful words, 'Bosporus' and 'Dardanelles': if Russia and Britain could make a dual arrangement regarding these and if the agreement contained 'some provision for "publication" which would appear to give Russia the … commercial access to the Persian Gulf', then Russian society would welcome an arrangement with Britain.[51] Benckendorff emphasized that negotiations could begin in secret and then be 'clinched' by a personal meeting of Nicholas II and Edward VII.[52] N.G. Hartwig, Director of the Asiatic department of the foreign ministry, also spoke to Spring Rice about an arrangement including the Straits.[53] Hartwig and Benckendorff flouted Lamsdorff's ban on making proposals to the British,

46 Alessandro Guiccioli, *Diario di un conservatore*, 308.
47 Marina Soroka, 'Debating Russia's Choice', 16.
48 P. Cambon to Rouvier, 05.12.1905, DDF, VIII: 261–5.
49 C. Spring Rice to Lord Knollys, 31.01/13.02.1906. RA VIC/MAIN/W/48/26.
50 Lamsdorff to Benckendorff, 14/27.01.1906, BC2, box 13.
51 Spring Rice to Grey, 26.01.1906, FO 800/72, 42–8.
52 Spring Rice to Grey, 26.01.1906, BD, 4: 222–4.
53 Spring Rice to Grey, 01.03.1906, BD, 4: 226–7.

in particular regarding the Straits,[54] and their indiscretion immediately produced Spring Rice's recommendation to the Foreign Office to use the Straits' issue as a bargaining chip and tell the Russians that it was impossible.[55] Benckendorff did not get instructions in January, although Lamsdorff agreed to discuss with the British a Persian loan and the Afghan-Persian border status quo.[56]

Russia's Looming Financial Collapse

In February 1906 the deadlock at Algeciras conference threatened Russia's chances to obtain a loan in foreseeable future. Witte wrote a letter to the Kaiser, through an intermediary, while Lamsdorff wrote to the Russian ambassador in Berlin on the same day. Both letters spoke of Russia's urgent need to have the Moroccan issue resolved in order to obtain a loan. Both held out to Germany hope of a continental alliance in case of an amicable Franco-German settlement.[57] The attempt failed.

At the beginning of March Cecil Spring Rice officially told Lamsdorff that Britain would support France at the Algeciras conference.[58] Russia's financial situation was desperate; Bülow decided to apply pressure on France through Russia and promised Witte a loan as soon as the French accepted German terms for a settlement. Witte and Lamsdorff appealed to France and it made some concessions, but when Britain's declaration of full support made France unyielding and the conference stalled, Russia sided with France and Britain, partly to put an end to the conference and get the loan.[59] The French were pushing Lamsdorff away from Germany and towards Britain; Benckendorff and Nelidov helped them to the extent of provoking Germany's resentment, as occurred when Nelidov leaked to the French press Lamsdorff's confidential despatch with instructions for the Russian representative at the Algeciras conference Arthur Cassini to support France.[60]

At the same time Benckendorff made another unauthorized friendly gesture toward the British: he told them that the Russian ambassador in Constantinople had obtained copies of documents relating to alleged Anglo-Turkish-Japanese secret alliance negotiations. Lansdowne denied the truth of the rumour. Lamsdorff reacted with an angry letter:

---

54 A.V. Ignatiev, *Vneshnaia politika Rossii*, 104.

55 Spring Rice to Mallet, 31.01.06, *Letters and Friendships of Sir Cecil Spring Rice. A Record.* (ed. Stephen Gwynn) (London, 1929), 2: 61.

56 A.F. Ostal'tseva, 157.

57 J.A. White, *Transition to Global Rivalry: Alliance Diplomacy and the Quadruple Entente, 1895–1907* (Cambridge, 1985), 196.

58 Viscount Grey of Fallodon, *Twenty-Five Years, 1892–1916* (New York, 1925), 1: 107.

59 I.I. Astaf'iev, *Russko-Germanskie diplomaticheskie otnosheni'ia*, 52–3.

60 S.P. Benckendorff to A.K. Benckendorff, 03/16.04.1906, BC2, box 21.

As you were leaving Petersburg I did not omit to emphasize to you that prior to communicating to the London cabinet the documents about Anglo-Japanese negotiations with Turkey, you were to wait for the opinion of our Ambassador at Constantinople … Yet, without waiting for his verdict, you found it opportune to give Hardinge the most important of these documents as soon as you arrived in London ….

… In any case now you will have to find a way … to avert the unpleasant consequences feared by our ambassador in Constantinople.[61]

Witte's hope for obtaining an international loan after several months of negotiations between the British, French, Dutch, German and US financiers was frustrated. First, the French financiers followed their government's instructions not to enter combinations with German banks,[62] then, in March 1906 German finance, also obeying its government, refused to participate in the loan.[63] Lamsdorff discussed with Nicholas II Russia's need for specific agreements with Britain on 21 February/5 March,[64] following his last futile appeal to Berlin.

After another long conversation with Benckendorff on 25 February/11 March 1906, Nicholas II swallowed his resentment of the British and authorized him to inform the British government that he was ready to hear their proposals[65] and ordered Lamsdorff to prepare Benckendorff's instructions.[66] Until his last day in office, Lamsdorff was trying to repair Russo-German relations and assuage William II's mortification about Björko and Algeciras by the prospect of a political agreement.[67] His reasoning was very typical:

Personally I, am anti 'anti-groups' of all sorts, and, of course, so is our sovereign, so far. It may not be a very exciting political course … this balancing between France, our ally, and Germany, to which we are attached by millennial historical, dynastic, cultural and economic bonds. So, as long as I am the foreign minister of Russia, no … [French cajoling] will move me from sitting on two chairs to one of them … so that my other neighbour could pull at the other chair and then I would hit the floor … with all the unpleasant consequences. Let one of my successors enter new, more effective combinations and new wars … which will end in a revolution …[68]

61 Lamsdorff to A.K. Benckendorff, 10/23.03.1906, BC2, box 28.
62 A.V. Ignatiev, *Vneshniaia politika Rossii v 1905–1907 gg.* (Moscow, 1986), 70.
63 A.V. Ignatiev, *Vneshniaia politika Rossii*, 73.
64 A.F. Ostal'tseva, 158.
65 A.K. Benckendorff to Lamsdorff, 25.02.1906, GARF, f.568, op.1, d.326, l.119.
66 Lamsdorff to A.K. Benckendorff, 28.02.1906, BC2, box 13.
67 M.A. Taube, *Zarnitsy*, 91.
68 M.A. Taube, *Zarnitsy*, 84.

The minister refused to present Russia's proposals to Britain, hoping that the British would show their hand.[69] But Grey also decided to hold on to the papers about British interests on the Indian frontier because Lamsdorff was leaving 'and the next man will use them against us'.[70] The eagerly-awaited elections to the first Duma were to take place in April, and a new 'constitutional' government would come to power. This expectant mood partly explains the delay in the official opening of the Anglo-Russian negotiations. Campbell-Bannerman's cabinet did not want to be associated in the public eyes with the unpopular and weak autocracy when a new Russian government would soon be in place. The French and the British held up the loan until the meeting of the Russian Duma was close and the Algeciras conference was over: they did not want to lose a means of pressuring Russia nor anger their own electorate by seeming to support the Russian autocracy.[71]

The loan of £89,325,000 which Lord Revelstoke negotiated for Russia was the first Russian loan encouraged by the Foreign Office.[72] It was the largest in European history[73] and for Russia politically the most important: it allowed the government certain independence in dealing with the first Duma. In April 1906 the loan went through despite protests both in Russia and abroad that it would enable Nicholas II to strangle the democratic movement in the country.[74] London alone took £13 million of the Russian bonds, causing anger among the Rothschilds and the Russian radicals who hoped to see the Russian government toppled.[75] It was a show of the Anglo-French support for the Russian government to offset Germany's distancing. The official explanation given by the British embassy at St Petersburg to the press emphasized it: Britain was helping Russia out of the financial difficulty which Russia had incurred by standing by her ally France [against Germany] at Algeciras.[76] Lord Lansdowne congratulated Benckendorff on the success of the loan[77] although some British newspapers spread the false rumour that Barings was in trouble because of large amounts of unsold Russian stock.[78]

A.P. Iswolsky and Count Benckendorff

Witte and Lamsdorff had played their part, as far as Nicholas II was concerned, and resigned. Tradition has it that Iswolsky (Fig. 5.1) was appointed foreign

69 Boutiron to Bourgeois, 05.05.1906, DDF, X: 54–5.

70 Grey to Spring Rice, 16.04.1906, *The Letters and Friendships*, 2: 72.

71 Hardinge to Lansdowne, 08.10.1905, BD, 14: 208–10; Spring Rice to Grey, 03.01.1906, BD, 14: 219–20.

72 Philip Ziegler, *The Sixth Great Power: Barings 1762–1929* (London, 1988), 312.

73 S.Yu.Witte, *Vospominani'ia* (Tallinn, 1993), 3: 237.

74 *British Documents on Foreign Affairs – Reports and Papers*, 4: 53.

75 Philip Ziegler, 312–3.

76 Spring Rice to A.K. Benckendorff, 05/18.04.1906, BC2, box 14.

77 Lansdowne to A.K. Benckendorff, 30.04.1906, BC2, box 13.

78 Philip Ziegler, 314.

Fig. 5.1 Aleksandr P. Iswolsky
Source: By kind permission of the Archive of Russian Imperial Foreign Policy.

minister on Maria Fedorovna's advice.[79] [80] But in early 1906 he was not certain of his appointment[81] as the Tsar was hesitating between him and Benckendorff. As Iswolsky weighed his chances to become minister he compared himself to Benckendorff:

> Count Benckendorff is undoubtedly an intelligent man, who is far superior to his reputation, but his education, his reasoning and his appearance are entirely

79 M.A. Taube, *La politique russe d'avant-guerre*, 90.
80 M.A. Taube, *Zarnitsy*, 95.
81 A.P. Iswolsky, *1906 Diary*, 26.12.1905/8.01.1906, GARF, f.559, op.1, ed.hr.86, l.5.

> un-Russian, and his position regarding the Duma would be very difficult. I doubt that he will accept such an ungrateful task. As for myself, I am, of course, rather popular with Russian society ...[82]

Benckendorff must have turned down the proposed ministry, for his sister Olga Guiccioli wrote in November 1905: 'My dear old man, forget about getting a position at home. You are useful, super-useful where you are ... I do not know, really if your nerves can resist this other job, and as for our family ... I believe that it is enough that Paul is there'.[83]

Iswolsky was apprehensive about accepting because after 30 years of life abroad he was westernized,[84] used to an easy life and, though flattered by the promotion, later he found the minister's duties 'exacting and excessive' and without promise of quick success.[85] The French conceded that Iswolsky was a man of cultivation and a sincere liberal.[86] All parties that dealt with him agreed that he was intelligent but very vain and the statesman in him often gave way to the courtier and snob. No other Russian minister gave rise to persistent rumours of being financially (and, it was implied, politically) dependent on his wealthier friends, one of them being his and later Benckendorff's subordinate Poklevsky.[87] Spring Rice contrasted Iswolsky to Lamsdorff; now that Lamsdorff had left, Spring Rice referred to him almost affectionately as a man with a great knowledge of European politics and a clear and impartial judgement,[88] all of which his successor lacked.

In mid-March, when Iswolsky's appointment was certain, he visited Paris and London to consult the most important Russian ambassadors in the coming diplomatic course, Nelidov and Benckendorff. The omission of the ambassadors to Germany and Austria-Hungary was an early indication of what his priorities were. In London Iswolsky had meetings with Haldane and Asquith arranged by Benckendorff and the British support for the Russian loan gave him hope for successful negotiations.[89]

As witnessed by his correspondence, throughout Iswolsky's ministerial appointment London occupied the central place in his mind and consequently in Russia's foreign policy. There were right and wrong reasons for that. The need for an arrangement with Britain was universally acknowledged and this alone

82 Ibid., 02/15.03.1906.,GARF, f.559, op.1, ed.hr.86, l.26 ob.

83 Olga Guiccioli to A K. Benckendorff, 07.11.1905, BC2, box 25.

84 Nicolson to Hardinge, 26.10.1906, FO 800/337, 116–7.

85 Nicolson to Hardinge, 06.12.1906, FO 800/337, 137–8.

86 *Les Carnets de Georges Louis*, 1: 58.

87 *Les Carnets de Georges Louis*, 2: 63.

88 Spring Rice to Mallet, 31.01.06, *Letters and Friendships of Sir Cecil Spring Rice*, 2: 61.

89 A.P. Iswolsky, *1906 Diary*, 19–22.03.1906, GARF, f.559, op.1, ed.hr.86, ll.34–35 ob.

made the ambassador to Britain an important source of information and channel of influence, especially at the time of the negotiations. There were also Iswolsky's liberal political views which made him welcome a rapprochement with Britain. As Iswolsky explained to the British minister in Denmark in 1904, he belonged to a group in Russia that favoured an Anglo-Russian understanding 'and in fact sees salvation in such a policy' because closeness to the stable monarchic Britain would serve Russia's 'real progress and development'. Iswolsky's understanding of the usefulness of a rapprochement with Britain was, thus, identical to Benckendorff's. Unsurprisingly, they had been in contact, bypassing Lamsdorff, long before Iswolsky became minister[90] and they would continue to meet and correspond till the end of their days.

For the ambitious Iswolsky the Anglo-Russian settlement was also personally important as a centerpiece of his diplomacy. Benckendorff's much-touted intimacy with the king of Britain added to the ambassador's prestige. Benckendorff repeatedly assured Iswolsky that with the advent of the 'naïve' Grey and the novice Liberal government, the British government, and in particular Grey, were guided by Edward VII. He said he recognized the king's words in Grey's speeches,[91] when it, probably, was the opposite. The king did his best to create the impression of being the great influence behind the scenes but in fact he was 'credited with much more opportunity of initiative and power than he really possessed', as a British diplomat said.[92] As subjects of an absolute monarch, neither Iswolsky nor Benckendorff could entirely believe that a monarch might have less influence on the national foreign policy than a minister, and Iswolsky tended to rely on Benckendorff's exaggerated estimations of Edward VII's personal contribution to British foreign policy.

Iswolsky could not resist the lure of being, through Benckendorff, a 'personal friend' of the British sovereign. Sir Arthur Nicolson, the ambassador to Russia in 1906–10, only slightly exaggerated for the sake of a good story when he told his son that in 1908 'Iswolsky, who had arrived in London to discuss the Dardanelles, was so thoroughly softsoaped by the King that he utterly forgot ever to mention the Straits'.[93] It is very noticeable that the king and his 'special relationship' with Benckendorff became a staple of the ambassador's letters after Lamsdorff's resignation. Whether it was because Benckendorff became particularly welcome at the court after the Anglo-Russian rapprochement or because Benckendorff felt that Lamsdorff did not attach much importance to his social success, but allusions to the king's words, smiles and gestures became very prominent after Iswolsky's advent. It is also characteristic of his vision of the British political world that he nearly does not mention Sir Charles Hardinge or Sir Arthur Nicolson. His ears

---

90 Goschen to Lansdowne, 16.04.1904, FO 800/122, 40–45.

91 A.K. Benckendorff to Iswolsky, 24.6/07.07.1906, *Au service*, 1: 311–6.

92 Bertie to Ponsonby, 27.11.1912, FO 800/174, 148.

93 Count Harry Kessler, *The Diaries of a Cosmopolitan 1918–1937* (London, 1999 [1971]), 374.

were only open to several persons in London: Edward VII, the Cecils, Grey and Lord Lansdowne – probably mostly because of his informal friendly ties to them.

Benckendorff's spell over his chief was reinforced by their shared liberal convictions, their critical view of the earlier Russian policies and the pride in being trailblazers. The minister deferred to the ambassador's worldly experience and sought his approval. Iswolsky found Benckendorff's personality congenial and their private correspondence conducted on the terms of 'dear friend' became the minister's source of comfort. Phrases like 'I will only mention it if you approve'[94] and 'I am putting together the arguments in support of your (and my) opinion',[95] are sprinkled throughout the letters. Benckendorff, for his part, mentioned to his wife that he found in Iswolsky 'an echo, and an excellent editor' of his ideas.[96]

Finally, Iswolsky and Benckendorff appreciated each other's erudition; both flourished quotations and historical anecdotes in company and delighted in correcting each other's misquotations in any of the four languages they spoke.[97] They had the kind of mildly pedantic personality greatly admired in the nineteenth century when Latin Scrabble was a popular salon game.

A nervous, insecure man prone to accumulating chips on his shoulder, Iswolsky became minister at a time when Russia's internal and external situation required making difficult choices. The new terms on which politics would be conducted were unclear. Iswolsky had to navigate unknown waters – the United Government and the Duma – at the same time as trying to adapt to a coalition policy abroad. The factions within the government were fighting because the survival of the empire was at stake. It was hard to remain impartial or to maintain a balanced view of the situation and Iswolsky developed a persecution mania. He sought approval and praise with an unbecoming eagerness and if he did not find it he would retreat, but on later occasions he would make vindictive gestures which provoked his opponents and led him, repeatedly, into situations incompatible with his or his government's dignity. He was overly sensitive to press opinion and on many occasions was indiscreet in interviews through which he tried to influence public opinion. His attempts to be clever did not deceive anyone. Sir Arthur Nicolson considered that 'Iswolsky never lies … but he can never be completely frank. He always conceals something of the truth. When he begins to twist his monocle in the corner of his eye as he speaks, I know that all of a sudden he became frightened of having said too much'.[98] Diplomats are not known for their openness and frankness, and Nicolson really pointed out that Iswolsky was a bad actor. His fear of saying too much was justified but belated, for every move he

94 Iswolsky to A.K. Benckendorff, 02/14.07.1906, BC2, box 13.

95 Iswolsky to A.K. Benckendorff, 08/21.07.1906, BC2, box 13.

96 A.K. Benckendorff to S.P. Benckendorff, 12.10.1908, (copied by S.P. Benckendorff), BC2, box 28.

97 *Les Carnets de Georges Louis*, 1: 58.

98 *Les Carnets de Georges Louis*, 1: 57.

made was immediately and correctly interpreted by Europe in the light of one or another of his earlier ideas which he had failed to keep to himself.

If Benckendorff had had a level-headed, confident minister, his attempts to guide Russia's political course would have been neutralized or balanced by the reports from the ambassadors to other great powers. But Nelidov in Paris and Osten-Sacken in Berlin were old, ill and, in Osten-Sacken's case, never too mentally agile. They became increasingly passive while the energetic Benckendorff held Iswolsky's confidence. The count's reports were a sympathetic and favourable exposition of the views and thinking of his British acquaintances. By the same token, whenever the Russian position diverged from the British, he found the former unreasonable, and, in response to the British protests or questions, he, as Spender said, 'threw up his hands in a comic despair'.[99]

Iswolsky believed himself to be a constitutional minister and at first spent more time in the State Council than at the ministry[100] which he antagonized by his open contempt for its old-fashioned views and inefficiency. Benckendorff shared and encouraged the new minister's attitude. Benckendorff and his minister referred to the opponents and critics of the Anglo-Russian convention as enemies of peace, progress and transparency in Russia.[101] Russian liberals saw the Anglo-Russian rapprochement as a guarantee of Russia's pursuit of gradual modernization which 'will heal the internal ulcers, which will purge us of internal corruption, which will give us a chance of standing side by side with the other nations' as one of the early Russian liberals formulated the goals of liberalism, explicitly tying the internal reform to a possibility of achieving an equal status with other nations which had chosen a similar path.[102] Benckendorff's repeated praise of Iswolsky's fresh approach and reminders of his great task of cleaning out the Augean stables reinforced the minister's vision of himself as a great reformer uncommitted to the mistakes of his predecessors.[103]

Anglo-Russian Negotiations

Nicholas II accepted Witte's and Lamsdorff's resignations on 1/13 May 1906, shortly before the opening of the Duma. The persistent notion that Lamsdorff's resignation opened the road to an Anglo-Russian rapprochement was born out of the face-saving lie accepted on both sides that a pro-German foreign minister stood in the way of Nicholas II's loyal friendship for Britain. Lamsdorff, as the

99 J.A. Spender, 1: 176.

100 A.A. Savinsky, 136.

101 A.K. Benckendorff to Iswolsky, 05/18.09.1906, *Au service de la Russie*, 1: 374–6.

102 *Rossiiskie liberal'y*, eds. B.Itenberg and V. Shelohaev (Moscow, 2001), 3.

103 A.K. Benckendorff to A.P. Iswolsky, 08/21.08.1906, *Au service de la Russie*, 1: 352–6.

British well knew,[104] had paved the road to the rapprochement even though the terms and the outcomes of the final achievement would have dismayed him.

The press hailed these resignations as a victory for the progressive new forces which were preparing to exercise an active role in domestic and foreign policy. While Lamsdorff was still minister, Cecil Spring Rice was pessimistic about the coming talks because Lamsdorff would do his utmost to reduce to the minimum Russia's concessions.[105] Spring Rice wrote that Lamsdorff was too timid 'to come to any agreement with England in which Russia does not come off very much better than England'.[106] Iswolsky's appointment inspired optimism in the Foreign Office. Since August 1905 the Persian shah had been seeking a loan which first Russia and then Britain refused to give him. As a goodwill gesture, the British and Russian governments sent new ministers, Nikolay Hartwig and Cecil Spring Rice, to Teheran with instructions to cooperate with each other.[107]

On 11 May Sir Edward Grey, alarmed by the reports from Persia and Constantinople about the interest of the German financiers in a loan to the shah, asked Benckendorff to press his government to begin Anglo-Russian discussions before the status quo was disturbed by 'third persons'. Britain was expecting Germany's proposal to participate in the Baghdad railway and since Russia was interested in having a commercial outlet on the Persian Gulf, Grey asked if Russia might want to reconsider her position and get a share in the project.[108]

The news of the coming discussions of a settlement in Turkey, Persia, Afghanistan and Tibet was published on 24 May/6 June. The new ambassador, Sir Arthur Nicolson, of recent Algeciras fame, the man who had outwitted the Germans, came to Russia with Grey's instruction not to rush into discussions while the domestic situation in Russia was unstable. The French ambassador, in his role as a midwife to the Anglo-Russian rapprochement, hovered over Nicolson, reassuring him that in Russia the domestic situation had nothing to do with foreign policy[109] and that British inaction would let Germany take the initiative in talking to Iswolsky, already suspected of pro-German tendencies. Prior to the opening of the Anglo-Russian talks, Iswolsky spoke to his good acquaintance the German ambassador von Schoen: he explained that there would be 'no general rapprochement' with Britain, only a series of settlements, because Russia's weakness precluded even the maintenance of the status quo in Asia. He mentioned that Russia needed access to the Persian Gulf even more than before because it was now cut off from the Far East and that he needed a parallel arrangement with Germany regarding the railway construction in Persia, also suggesting to von

104 Lansdowne to A.K. Benckendorff, 30.04.1906, BC2, box 13.

105 Spring Rice to Grey, 16.02.1906, *The Letters and Friendships*, 2: 63.

106 Spring Rice to Grey, 29.03.1906, *The Letters and Friendships*, 2: 70.

107 A.K. Benckendorff to Iswolsky, 30.05/12.06.1906, *Au service de la Russie*, 1: 307–8.

108 Grey to Spring Rice, 11.05.1906, BD, 4: 382–3.

109 Bompard to Bourgeois, 31.05.1906, DDF, X: 128–30.

Schoen an agreement regarding the Baltic status quo. The issues which an Anglo-Russian understanding would solve were outside Germany's sphere of influence or interest and therefore she could offer nothing to Russia to counter British offers. So, von Schoen wrote, Germany blessed the discussions.[110] His only provision was that if participation in the Baghdad railway was part of the talks, Iswolsky should consult Germany as an interested party.[111]

In his first private letter to Benckendorff from the ministerial chair, Iswolsky formulated his intentions. He wanted a firm base for his relations with England and Germany in Asia: Germany's recognition and acceptance of the Anglo-Russian entente would leave his hands free to negotiate with Britain. He was ready to guarantee to Germany the rights which she had already acquired and expected that Britain would agree, as according to Benckendorff, Britain wanted to decrease the tension surrounding the Baghdad railway affair. He hoped that his openness would reassure London and erase the 'shameful impression' of Björko in Berlin.[112]

Iswolsky wanted to settle each issue as a separate agreement, which seemed to be Lamsdorff's idea. But Nicolson told him he did not want an incomplete agreement.[113] The settlement of each issue would depend on whether the parties achieved a general understanding. Iswolsky agreed that they would follow the procedure which had served Lansdowne well in the talks with France: discuss one question after another until they were all settled and then sign a general agreement. Iswolsky asked Benckendorff to support him by extra-official advice. 'The idea of a direct exchange of ideas with you eliminates a good part of my concerns', Benckendorff wrote immediately. He promised: 'I will tell you all I think and you can do whatever you like with it ...'[114] The count wrote lengthy weekly letters, sometimes two on the same day. He confessed: 'I have no time to edit or copy my official reports and yet here I am writing a private letter'.[115] The number of private letters between Iswolsky and Benckendorff in 1906–10 is quadruple that between the minister and the rest of the Russian ambassadors.

In Benckendorff's view, Britain's friendship was key to Russia's relations with the rest of the world. In the Balkans and even in Persia, Russia had to account for Austro-Hungarian and German interests; without the British support, this would lead Russia into a dead end. If Russia went along with the French obsessive fear of German aggression, she might find herself in a conflict with Germany; if she refused to follow the French lead, she might lose the French alliance. An Anglo-Russian understanding would reassure France and in good time allow Russia to become the arbiter of peace and conciliation in Europe. Otherwise, Germany

110 Freiherr von Schoen, 38–42.

111 Spring Rice to Grey, 24.05.1906, BD, 4: 232–4.

112 Iswolsky to A.K. Benckendorff, 10.05.1906, BC2, box 13.

113 Nicolson to Grey, 07.06.1906, BD, 4: 239–40.

114 A.K. Benckendorff to Iswolsky, 16/29.05.1906, *Au service de la Russie*, 1: 297.

115 A.K. Benckendorff to Iswolsky, 14/27.06.1906, *Au service de la Russie*, 1: 316–19.

could not help Russia in preventing Britain's take-over of the Persian Gulf and all of Persia.[116]

Benckendorff assured that the British were so eager for an understanding that they would not let anything stand in the way.[117] The King's interest in the rapprochement he described as 'passionate'. He found sympathy for the rapprochement in both Liberal and Conservative parties: even when members of parliament condemned the pogroms they would next speak of their hope for a friendship with Russia. Benckendorff took at face value the traditional rhetoric of British statesmen that Britain was perfectly satisfied with her international position and assured Iswolsky that Britain did not feel that she needed Russia. From this he derived his argument that the British interest in the Anglo-Russian settlement was not dictated by self-interest alone but partly arose from a genuine sympathy for Russia.[118] He cited several examples of British determination to achieve an understanding: after the Byelostock pogroms King Edward warned Lord Rothschild, the leader of British Jewry, that the Foreign Office would ignore Jewish complaints. The Liberal cabinet, after debates, decided that a naval squadron would visit Russia no matter what happened,[119] that is, despite the protests of British public.

Even the dismissal of the 'red' Duma in July 1906 and the resulting public outcry did not discourage the British government. Rather, it slowed down the Russian side. Grey wrote to several public figures advising them to withhold their signatures from the address to the Duma and telling them that the Russian ambassador explained that at the moment there was no Duma in Russia and a visit would make no sense.[120]

Benckendorff wanted to begin a new era in Anglo-Russian relations by sweeping the negotiating table of all petty irritants, asking Iswolsky, for example, to put an end to the secret police's stealing or copying British embassy files. He complained that it was clumsily performed, useless and extremely embarrassing for him.[121] Iswolsky complied. The ambassador insisted that the king's amiability to him should be reciprocated by equal or greater friendliness towards the British diplomats and visitors to St Petersburg.[122]

Benckendorff strongly supported the visit to Russia by a British naval squadron in the summer of 1906. The visit had been proposed by the British as a symbolic gesture, but, with disorders in St Petersburg, the near-war between the government and the first Duma, and the loud protests in the British parliament and press against gestures of friendship towards Russian despotism, it was attracting too much attention for the

116 A.K. Benckendorff to Iswolsky, 23.08/05.09.1906, *Au service de la Russie,* 1: 358–63.

117 A.K. Benckendorff to Iswolsky, 14/27.06.1906, *Au service*, 1: 311–16.

118 A.K. Benckendorff to Iswolsky, 24.06/07.07.1906, *Au service*, 1: 322–6.

119 A.K. Benckendorff to Iswolsky, 28.06/11.07.1906, *Au service*, 1: 326–30.

120 Grey to Archbishop Randall Cantuar, 11.09.1906, RA VIC/ADDC 7/2/Q.

121 A.K. Benckendorff to Iswolsky, 3/16.05.1906, *Au service de la Russie*, 1: 295–7.

122 A.K. Benckendorff to Iswolsky, 17/30.05.1906, *Au service de la Russie*, 1: 302–3.

Russian government's taste. The military and the foreign ministry pointed out the embarrassing fact that the British could not be met and escorted by a proper convoy of warships, because the Baltic fleet no longer existed. To the last, Benckendorff, who gave the highest importance to public relations, kept assuring Iswolsky that a postponement of the visit would be a success for the enemies of the Anglo-Russian settlement.[123] Still, on Nicholas II's request the visit was postponed.

The visit of the Russian Duma delegation and of the members of the State Council to the Mother of Parliaments became an event because it coincided with the news of the dissolution of the Duma. The much-mentioned speech of Sir Henry Campbell-Bannerman welcoming the Russian guests and ending with the 'Duma is dead. Long live the Duma!' paraphrased the traditional public proclamation of the death of a king and the accession of the next one. It was quite correct because the date was set in Russia for the elections to the next Duma and Benckendorff attended the formal inter-parliamentary lunch at Westminster Hall, because Russia had not ceased to be a 'parliamentary monarchy'.

But the newspapers chose to interpret it as the prime minister's challenge to the Russian emperor or, from the point of view of the Conservatives, a gauche blunder. The British court and the Conservative opposition were more indignant than the Russians. The count was less concerned about a phrase pronounced in London than about the damage to Russia's financial and moral standing from the dissolution of the Duma. His twin nightmares, which he often discussed with the Foreign Office, were Russia's bankruptcy and a financial rescue by Germany, followed by military assistance.[124] Iswolsky's and Benckendorff's discussions constantly referred to this. 'I do not mention our domestic political situation, but I cannot help thinking of it, because ultimately everything depends on it', Benckendorff wrote in March 1907.[125]

When the talks began, Benckendorff's advice flowed. He was dealing with a man who openly confessed to Nicolson that he knew nothing about the issues which they would discuss and would have to rely on 'expert advice'.[126] Iswolsky could not hold out against the barrage of advice from London, so in dealing with Japan, with Germany and with Austria-Hungary, as well as with France, Persia or Turkey, Iswolsky made a mental reference to Anglo-Russian relations as the pivot of his policy.

The Baghdad Railway

Russia was powerless to block the construction of the Baghdad railway and her finances did not allow her to participate in it. The way of neutralizing its effects was

123 Ibid.
124 A.K. Benckendorff to Iswolsky, 12/25.07.1906, *Au service*, 1: 335–8.
125 A.K. Benckendorff to Iswolsky, 28.2/13.03.1907, *Au service*, 2: 16–20.
126 Nicolson to Grey, 06.06.1906, FO 800/337, 58.

by building a line to connect the Russian and Indian railway systems, but Britain did not accept it. So, Russia had to resign herself to the tripartite consortium of Germany, France and Britain and to seek guarantees from Germany that there would be no branches built towards the Persian border. Iswolsky hoped to make Persia extend beyond 1910 the provision of no railroad construction in the north and have the existing treaty with Turkey about railway concessions in Asia Minor extended in Russia's favour.[127]

Paris and London wanted to involve Russia in negotiating 'three against one' in the Baghdad railway issue with Germany after agreeing on a joint policy.[128] Cambon pushed Benckendorff in that direction, while Bompard did the same to Iswolsky.[129] On the eve of the negotiations, Benckendorff, who previously believed that it was preferable for Russia to remain outside these talks as an arbiter, told Iswolsky that he agreed with the British that the Baghdad railway was an opportunity for Russia and Britain to settle Persia in order keep Germany out.[130] Learning that Russia could not participate in the project for lack of finances, he argued that Britain and France wanted Russia to participate so much that an ad hoc loan could be arranged.[131] In 1907 Grey told Benckendorff that he was expecting German proposals about the railway and would stipulate that any proposal would have to include Russia's interests.[132]

Tibet

Benckendorff's reports led Iswolsky to believe that Nicolson wanted to begin discussions of the Baghdad railway and the Persian loan. But, fearing Iswolsky's alleged intimacy with the German ambassador von Schoen, Nicolson said that he wanted to discuss Tibet first, and treat the Baghdad railway separately. He wanted to establish a clear separation between the Anglo-Russian interests and those which would also concern Germany.[133]

From Benckendorff's point of view, the Tibet issue was of a purely symbolic value to Russia. Russia had to prove to Britain that she had no intention of encroaching on Tibet, otherwise frictions with Britain and China would make impossible Iswolsky's policy of 'concentration, calm and peace'. He wrote: 'Higher interests and prudence require that we renounce it'. Benckendorff persuaded Iswolsky that Russia's aim in Tibet, preventing its annexation by

127 Russian Foreign Ministry, *Ministerial Council meeting*, 01.02.1907, BD 4: 270–71.

128 A.K. Benckendorff to Iswolsky, 16/29.05.1906, *Au service*, 1: 297–301.

129 Paul Cambon to Bourgeois, 24.09.1906, DDF, 10: 320–1.

130 A.K. Benckendorff to Iswolsky, 03/16.05.1906, *Au service*, 1: 294.

131 A.K. Benckendorff to Iswolsky, 29.05/11.06.1906, *Au service*, 1: 303–6

132 Grey – Nicolson, 07.03.1907, BD, 4: 277–8.

133 Nicolson to Grey, 29.05.1906, BD 4: 237–8.

Britain, was already achieved and it only remained to consolidate the status quo of 1905–6. The best for Iswolsky would be to accept the British draft.[134] Rather than worry about the Tibet issue, Iswolsky should seek British recognition of Russia's interests in Mongolia. The ambassador had already asked Grey about it[135] and Grey was ready to discuss the idea if Iswolsky told Nicolson what Russia's interests were.[136] These ideas were echoed in Iswolsky's memorandum for Nicholas II regarding Tibet.[137]

Afghanistan

Benckendorff had last discussed the Afghan issue with Lansdowne in March 1905. Lansdowne wanted Russia's recognition that Afghanistan was wholly outside of the Russian sphere of influence. Benckendorff replied that Russia would accept this if Britain recognized the right of Russian authorities to settle local non-political issues with the Afghan local officials and the British guaranteed that their policy towards Afghanistan would remain unchanged. Afghanistan would remain a 'buffer state', as Lamsdorff put it.

To Iswolsky's question about Russia's interests in Afghanistan Benckendorff answered unhesitatingly that they were negligible and that the Amir played Russia and Britain against each other and 'all these people tremble at the idea that we might settle: the Dalai Lama, the Amir, the Shah, the Sultan … [and] Germany, to emphasize the danger'.[138] He recommended more concessions to Britain even before the British had formulated their requests, pointing out to Iswolsky that in order to avert possible parliamentary criticism of British concessions on the Afghanistan issue, Iswolsky should offer the British more military guarantees without waiting for them to ask.[139]

When they first tackled Afghanistan, Nicolson asked for Grey's authorization to acquaint Iswolsky and Benckendorff with the British proposals so as to give them ammunition for defending their position in the 'inter-departmental committee' which would oversee the negotiations.[140] Grey replied that the proposals should be withheld at least until the Amir's visit to India was over: no one knew what concessions the Government of India might still obtain.[141] In March 1907 Benckendorff told Grey that Russia would be satisfied with a clause

134 A.K. Benckendorff to Iswolsky, 07/20.06.1906, *Au service*, 1: 308–11.

135 A.K. Benckendorff to Iswolsky, 07/20.06.1906, *Au service*; 1: 308–11.

136 A.K. Benckendorff to Iswolsky, 14/27.06.1906, *Au service*, 1: 316–19.

137 A.P. Iswolsky, *Memorandum regarding the proposals of the British government for the Tibet issue*, 0.05/13.06.1906, Rossi'ia *i Tibet*, 85–9.

138 A.K. Benckendorff to Iswolsky, 14/27.06.1906, *Au service,* 1: 311–16.

139 A.K. Benckendorff to Iswolsky, 16/29.05.1907, *Au service*, 2: 46–8.

140 Nicolson to Grey, 30.01.1907, BD, 4: 522.

141 Grey to Nicolson, 06.02.1907, BD, 4: 522.

saying that neither side would do anything unless the Amir took action which rendered action necessary on Russia's part.[142] Poklevsky brought to the minister Benckendorff's letters and oral advice to call an inter-ministerial conference to deal once and for all with the Afghan issue but Iswolsky was nervous about fighting the 18 generals of the Defence Committee.[143] On 29 March/11 April Poklevsky wrote that there was no counter-proposal for Afghanistan because of the inordinate claims of the ministries of finance and commerce. Poklevsky in the meantime prepared a draft of the Afghahistan convention and sent a copy for Benckendorff's approval. He wrote: 'I begin with your preamble, then with paragraphs I and IV containing the essence of the British demands'. The British demands were formulated on the basis of a 1905 letter from Lansdowne to Benckendorff and paragraph III (H.M. Government's engagement not to encourage Afghanistan to take military measures which Russia could see as a threat to her security) was Iswolsky's maximum concession to the Russian military.[144] The minister approved of Poklevsky's draft with Benckendorff's corrections and at the end of April he prepared for the debate with the military regarding Afghanistan. The preparations included a consultation with Sir Donald Mackenzie Wallace about Anglo-Afghan relations. Poklevsky reported: 'The conversation was very interesting but unfortunately Sir Donald's information is *not quite up to date*'.[145] In 1906–7 the king on several occasions used Wallace, long known and well-liked at the Russian court as his personal messenger to Nicholas II. Benckendorff strongly recommended that Iswolsky talk to Wallace and help him meet the Tsar.[146] In 1907, as the negotiations came to a standstill, Poklevsky wrote to the ambassador: 'Wallace is going to Petersburg on 14 February to take up his mission of last year'.[147] On every visit Wallace was received by Nicholas II and also visited Iswolsky, so the latter used the British journalist as an additional way of influencing the emperor, explaining to Wallace his ideas and the difficulties of his situation.[148]

Persia

One of the most difficult issues to settle was Persia. In the period between 1900 and 1905, Britain had made her political presence felt in Persia to an unprecedented degree: the legation dominated the Persian government as much as Russians did; the British Imperial Bank of Persia controlled the revenues of the Gulf ports

142 Grey to Nicolson, 07.03.1907, BD, 4: 277–8.
143 Poklevsky to A.K. Benckendorff, 15/28.03.1907, BC2, box 14.
144 Poklevsky to A.K. Benckendorff, 29.03.1907, BC2, box 14.
145 Poklevsky to A.K. Benckendorff, 12/25.04.1907, BC2, box 14.
146 A.K. Benckendorff to Iswolsky, 25.07/07.08.1906, *Au service*, 1: 339–42.
147 Poklevsky to A.K. Benckendorff, 21.1/06.02.1907, BC2, box 14.
148 Iswolsky to A.K. Benckendorff, 08/21.11.1906, *Au service*, 1: 394–5.

and Curzon successfully established a British presence in Seistan.[149] The issue for Russia in 1905 was maintaining her position in the northern part of Persia. At the height of the Russo-Japanese war and domestic troubles in 1905, the finance minister, V. Kokovtsev, stated that Russia was in no position to extend her control over Persia and some of the military agreed. When the shah asked for a loan, he was not turned down only for fear he would sell his benevolence to some other power. The government had no money and it also realized that the shah was not credit-worthy and was so unpopular among his subjects that a power which supported him would share his unpopularity.[150] Since January 1906 there had been what the French called an *entente verbale* between Russia and Britain in Persia.[151] Nevertheless, by the end of 1906 Russia had begun to recover her position, sending a consul to a Persian Gulf port and representatives to Seistan. The ministers praised each other's conciliatory attitude, but the British minister, Spring Rice, complained that the Russians were stalling the negotiations because they realised that the British were not as strong in Teheran as they had feared.[152]

Benckendorff knew that German penetration in Persia worried the British,[153] but he did not see any relation between this and a greater flexibility which Britain might show at the talks. He encouraged Iswolsky to see German penetration, (through the Baghdad railway and the Deutsche Bank) as Russia's greatest concern in Persia.[154] He strongly disagreed with Hartwig, the new Russian minister in Teheran, who considered German encroachments trifling matters compared to the British ambitions.[155] Benckendorff accused Hartwig of adopting the Persian views and supporting them against the British: 'I cannot come here [to the Foreign Office] with the Persian declarations and Hartwig's conclusions … The only reply I would get would be that as long as we believed the Persians more than we did the British, there was nothing to discuss'.[156]

A conflict between the Russian and the British legations arose when the British legation gave asylum to 14,000 anti-government rebels,[157] which the Russian minister considered contrary to the pledge of non-intervention in Persian internal politics. Benckendorff wrote that even if Hartwig were right, the British minister was only a small cog in the big diplomatic machine,[158] and his mistaken attitude could be corrected by the Foreign Office. No matter what the British legation did

---

149 D. McLean, *Britain and Her Buffer State: The Collapse of the Persian Empire, 1890–1914* (London, 1979), 71–2.

150 A.F. Ostal'tseva, 175.

151 Bompard to Pichon, 25.01.1907, DDF, X: 635–6.

152 Descos to Pichon, 26.01.1907, DDF, X: 637–8.

153 Geoffray to Bourgeois, 09.10.1906, DDF, X: 342–4.

154 A.K. Benckendorff to Iswolsky, 16/29.05.1906, *Au service*, 1: 297–301.

155 Descos to Bourgeois, 10.08.1906, DDF, X: 276–7.

156 A.K. Benckendorff to Iswolsky, 08/21.08.1906, *Au service*, 1: 352–6.

157 I.A. Zinoviev, *Rossi'ia, Angli'ia i Persi'ia* (St Petersburg, 1912), 18.

158 A.K. Benckendorff to Iswolsky, 26.07/08.08.1906, *Au service*, 1: 342–4.

or seemed to do in Persia, Iswolsky had to remember that the best policy would be to ignore the tug-of-war between the legations and petty local issues. The minister had better show the British that he was the master of Russian foreign policy by putting an end to Hartwig's cries of alarm against the British.[159] Iswolsky agreed, and, to Hartwig's requests to support the new pro-Russian shah, the minister replied by orders to maintain neutrality which in three years unseated the shah and resulted in civil strife in the Persian Empire.[160]

In July, Nicolson asked permission to discuss Persia with Iswolsky instead of Afghanistan because Germany might become established in Persia if the negotiations dragged for a long time.[161] Hardinge authorized this, and when Benckendorff learnt of it from someone at the Foreign Office[162] he sent Poklevsky to Petersburg to talk to Iswolsky.[163] A week later Poklevsky visited Nicolson, 'anxious to know about our views as to the future of Persia'. Trying to get information out of the prudent British ambassador Poklevsky used Nicolson's own words to Hardinge a month earlier: now it was Iswolsky who thought that Britain and Russia had to come to an agreement before Germany had gained a footing in Persia.[164] It is difficult to say who was more suggestible, Benckendorff or Iswolsky.

Grey and Benckendorff agreed that an entente regarding Persia should be based on non-intervention which would not exclude prudent and salutary reforms but would oppose violent and illegitimate movements. As always, Benckendorff was at his best in his defence of British diplomacy by means of general truths: 'Back home people do not understand that Britain sees her interests in her own way, not in the way we see them. She is infinitely more anxious to promote her interests than to thwart those of others'.[165] After the convention was signed the British would take care of their own interests and in the process would promote the Russian ones.

Benckendorff recommended that Hartwig should do what he did in London: take his concerns to the British and ask for explanations. He guaranteed that the British either would explain that the Russians misunderstood them or would apologize and desist from what they had been doing. During the Teheran riots, he told Grey that Russia did not care where the rebels found asylum, but the fact that they were at the British legation was symptomatic of the situation between the legations; it would be useful if a common point of view were formulated and the two ministers cooperated on its basis. As a result, Grey hurried Spring Rice's departure for Teheran.[166] Iswolsky optimistically wrote: 'Spring Rice will put

159 A.K. Benckendorff to Iswolsky, 08/21.08.1906, *Au service*, 1: 352–6.
160 I.A. Zinoviev, 44.
161 Nicolson to Hardinge, 29.07.1906, FO 800/337, 85–7.
162 A.K. Benckendorff to Iswolsky, 09/22.08.1906, *Au service*, 1: 357–8.
163 A.K. Benckendorff to Iswolsky, 09/22.08.1906, *Au service*, 1: 357–8.
164 Nicolson to Hardinge, 29.08.1906, FO 800/337, 98–100.
165 A.K. Benckendorff to Iswolsky, 27.07/9.08.1906, *Au service*, 1: 345–9.
166 A.K. Benckendorff to Iswolsky, 29.07/11.08.1906, *Au service*, 1: 350–51.

Hartwig at ease'.[167] At first, cooperation in Persia seemed to function,[168] but Spring Rice and Hartwig were suspicious of each other. A French observer concluded that both exhibited the classic Anglo-Russian diplomatic attitudes: the Englishman considered that Russia had to pay for her defeat in the war by concessions to Britain in Persia. The Russian was obstinate and dragged his feet on joint actions which, in his opinion, would favour Britain.[169]

Spring Rice understood that Persia was a means not the goal[170] in the Anglo-Russian convention but he kept warning Grey of Britain's imminent loss of prestige and positions in Persia because of the Anglo-Russian arrangement.[171] As negotiations were progressing, Grey put an end to Spring Rice's prophesies of Russia's absorption of Persia. He wrote that settling with Russia would help avoid a situation in which Britain would have to assist Persia by force or at least would make a clear case for doing so if Russia violated the terms of the arrangement.[172]

The London Embassy's Role

Poklevsky and Benckendorff shuttled between London and St Petersburg, taking turns at Iswolsky's side. The ambassador had fought against Lamsdorff's decision to transfer Poklevsky, insisting that without him Benckendorff's own task would become nearly impossible.[173] After Iswolsky became minister, he at once had Poklevsky return to London. Poklevsky shared Benckendorff's conviction that a weak Russia's only protection from Japan was an entente with England and good relations with the US.[174] His letters convey the atmosphere at the foreign ministry and the London embassy's role in Iswolsky's campaign for pro-British orientation:

> Iswolsky is very grateful for your letters; he says that you are the only ambassador who keeps him informed … They are sending you in the same bag the 'vsepoddaneishaia zapiska' [memorandum submitted to the emperor] and the draft of the telegram to Hartwig based on the conclusions reached at the conference [regarding Persian affairs]. You will be, I am sure, very content with the result which is in perfect accord with the ideas which you kindly communicated to me at the time of my departure.

Poklevsky saw the minister almost every day, and used the occasions to carry out Benckendorff's instructions. This seemed to be bringing results: the minister

167 Iswolsky to A.K. Benckendorff, 03/16.08.1906, BC2, box 13.
168 Paul Cambon to Pichon, 08.03.1907, DDF, X: 681–2.
169 Boutiron – Bourgeois, 20.11.1906, DDF, X: 464–6.
170 Descos to Bourgeois, 15.10.1906, DDF, X: 351–2.
171 Spring Rice to Grey, 21.12.1906, BD, 4: 420–21.
172 Grey to Spring Rice, 12.06.1907, BD, 4: 470–71.
173 S.P. Benckendorff to A.K. Benckendorff, 29.03/11.04.1906, BC2, box 21.
174 Poklevsky to A.K. Benckendorff, 10/23.01.1907, BC2, box 14.

referred to a settlement with Britain as 'the policy of the future', established excellent relations with Nicolson and rejected Hartwig's urgent requests for a loan to Persia. Poklevsky also reported that Iswolsky had suspected an intrigue against him at the Asiatic Department because, until he asked, they had not informed him about an important conversation between Lamsdorff and Spring Rice in February 1906.[175] Nor was Iswolsky tempted by the Persian proposal of a military alliance which Hartwig reported. Benckendorff at once attacked Hartwig's reasoning with his usual argument: Russia's influence in Persia did not depend on the shah or his government, but on acting jointly with Britain. Conciliation of the British was the best policy, not Hartwig's policy of stand-off.[176]

Hartwig, like his British counterparts, wanted to give away as little as possible of the advantages which Russia had or hoped to get in the region but agreed that a compromise was necessary for the sake of the agreement. His proposed corrections to the terms of the partition were based on the existing Russian trade and strategic interests,[177] but to Benckendorff this was a petty and blind policy: Russian interests in Persia did not matter. If Iswolsky did not immediately follow Benckendorff's demands of replacing Hartwig in order to restore the ease of his relations with Grey, it was because Hartwig enjoyed Nicholas II's sympathy.[178]

New Japanese demands slowed down the Russo-Japanese talks to finalize the Portsmouth treaty. Several times they were on the verge of a breakdown, which Russia feared, and Iswolsky asked his friend Benckendorff to find out if the British would exercise unofficial pressure on their ally. At first, Iswolsky even wished for a secret clause in the Anglo-Russian arrangement about the British support of the status quo in the Far East, but Benckendorff disabused him, saying that the British would not accept a secret clause, and particularly one with an anti-Japanese character.[179] After Iswolsky had complained that the negotiations arrived at a critical point, at Benckendorff's request, Grey reminded the Japanese ambassador about Britain's great interest in the success of the Russo-Japanese negotiations.[180] Benckendorff sympathized with Iswolsky's difficulties and predictably offered his solution for the talks: give the Japanese what they ask because Russia had no need of those Far Eastern rivers and valleys.[181]

The Balkans

In the autumn of 1906 Iswolsky made his first tour of Europe as a minister. Poklevsky, Hardinge, Grey and Iswolsky exchanged a dozen anxious messages to

175 Poklevsky to A.K. Benckendorff, 17/30.08.1906, BC2, box 14.
176 A.K. Benckendorff to Iswolsky, 23.08/05.09.1906, *Au service*, 1: 358–63.
177 N.G. Hartwig to Iswolsky, 02/15.03.1907, AVPRI, f.559, op.1, ed.hr.32, ll.6–7.
178 Iswolsky to A.K. Benckendorff, 01/14.1908, BC2, box 13.
179 A.K. Benckendorff to Iswolsky, 07/20.06.1906, *Au service*, 1: 308–11.
180 A.K. Benckendorff to Iswolsky, 27.12.1906/09.01.1907, *Au service*, 1: 418–19.
181 A.K. Benckendorff to Iswolsky, 12/25.12.1906, *Au service*, 1: 411–14.

reassure each other that Iswolsky's failure to accept a last-minute invitation from King Edward would not be allowed to influence the rapprochement. Iswolsky went to Paris where he had meetings with the French president. As the only railroad to Russia lay through Berlin he was going to take the opportunity to reassure Bülow and William II about Russia's disposition and get their reassurances regarding the favourable attitude to the Anglo-Russian settlement in Persia. Benckendorff, who had gone to Paris to talk to Iswolsky, 'explained his explanations' to the British: Russia could not afford to be on bad terms with Germany and the minister had to go to Berlin for the sake of the Anglo-Russian convention.[182] Iswolsky assured the British through Benckendorff that he was aware of their impatience, but could do little: the resentments outside Russia were allayed but the resentments brewing internally needed a strong argument in favour of a settlement with Britain.[183] These words about the need for a quid pro quo he had recently told Nicolson, who at once knew that Iswolsky meant 'a deal over the near East', more precisely, 'some modification of certain Treaty clauses which hamper and restrict his liberty of action'.[184]

Before his departure for Paris and Berlin, Iswolsky had also written to the chief of the general staff, Fyodor Palytsin. He justified the retreat from Russia's traditional refusal to give guarantees to Britain in any of the areas of friction by the possibility of getting British support in the Straits issue.[185] He must have discussed it with Benckendorff at their Paris meeting in October 1906, for there are no prior mentions of it in their correspondence.

Benckendorff and Iswolsky felt encouraged by the current Balkan situation. In the past decade, the Cretan, Armenian and Balkan Slav problems had greatly undermined the support which British public opinion had once offered to the Turks. After Britain had lost her dominant position in Turkey to Germany, the British and Russians largely shared a view of the Near Eastern situation. Benckendorff considered that Russia's friendship with a pro-German Ottoman Empire could only favour Austria-Hungary and make Britain despair of Russia's desire for a settlement and take over the whole of Persia. Conversely, Britain's goodwill obtained through cooperation in the Balkans might bring about a solution to the Straits issue for Russia.[186] This agreed entirely with Iswolsky's ideas: he considered Lamsdorff's entente with Austria a mistake and talked about the Mürzsteg agreement as 'a cannonball on his leg'[187] to various persons in and out of Russia. He dreamed of Anglo-Russian cooperation in the Balkans.[188] The minister's repeated proclamations of a policy of equidistance between the Entente

182 Bertie to Grey, 22.10.1906, BD, 4: 244–5.

183 Iswolsky to A.K. Benckendorff. 08/21.11.1906, *Au service*, 1: 394–5.

184 Nicolson to Grey, 07.11.1906, FO 800/337, 126–9.

185 A.F. Ostal'tseva, 179.

186 A.K. Benckendorff to Iswolsky, 23.08/05.09.1906, *Au service*, 1: 358–63.

187 Wesselitsky to A.K. Benckendorff, 09.12.1907, box 15, BC2.

188 *The Diary of Edward Goschen 1900–1914*, 03.10.1903 (London, 1980), 82.

and the Triple Alliance do not agree well with this early intention. His argument that he should end the entente with Austria in order to please public opinion seems atypical, but, also atypically, Benckendorff agreed with him that in this case the government should heed it.[189]

Benckendorff thought that if the minister presented his military opponents with the British status quo guarantee in Mongolia and the consent to the change of the Straits' regime, they would agree to guarantee to the British the security of 'this useless India where we will never go'. (He asked rhetorically: 'What do we need Seistan for, when all is said and done?'[190] He never alluded to the reasons why Britain needed Seistan. In his eyes Britain's fears of Russia were legitimate, unlike Russia's fears of Britain.)

On Benckendorff's instructions, Poklevsky told Hardinge on 27 November that Russia would like an article recognizing the status quo in the Far East as a 'moral guarantee' against Japanese encroachments in the region and also mentioned the Straits issue. Hardinge said Britain did not have direct interests in the two regions and therefore could not initiate discussions, but it would receive favourably any Russian proposals.[191] The British had been prepared since Spring Rice's conversations with Benckendorff and Hartwig. In 1903 the Committee of Imperial Defence took the view that the right of passage for the Russian navy would not significantly change the balance of power in the Mediterranean, and in 1904 Hardinge and King Edward agreed that the Straits might be a useful *quid pro quo* in the eventual negotiations.[192]

When the ambassador came to St Petersburg in January 1907, Nicolson was enthusiastic because Benckendorff would stimulate the talks by 'lobbying' influential courtiers and the military.[193] Benckendorff considered that his main contribution would be obtaining Russia's quid pro quo. He confided to Nicolson that the Tsar[194] and the officers of the general staff had doubts about the wisdom of having the talks so soon after a bad war when Britain might capitalize on Russia's weakness and mentioned their interest in a political concession in exchange for Seistan.[195]

He was present at the meeting between Nicolson and Iswolsky on 6/19 February, where Iswolsky in principle accepted the British draft of the Tibet settlement and presented the Russian draft proposal on Persia, including the line between the zones of influence and maintaining existing concessions in respective zones.[196] When Benckendorff returned to London,[197] Poklevsky

189 A.K. Benckendorff to Iswolsky, 23.08/05.09.1906, *Au service*, 1: 358–63.
190 A.K. Benckendorff to Iswolsky, 12/25.12.1906, *Au service*, 1: 410–14.
191 Poklevsky to Iswolsky, 05/18.11.1906, *Au service*, 1: 400–402.
192 Hardinge, *Memorandum*, 16.11.1906, BD, 4: 236–7.
193 Nicolson to Grey, 25.01.1907, BD, 4: 269–70.
194 Nicolson to Grey, 27.01.1907, BD, 4: 272.
195 Nicolson to Grey, 10.02.1907, BD, 4: 272–3.
196 Nicolson to Grey, 19.02.1907, BD, 4: 275.
197 S.P. Benckendorff to A.K. Benckendorff, 01/14.03.1907, BC 2, box 16.

replaced him at Iswolsky's side, bringing Grey's memorandum with a promise to view favourably Russia's attempts to change the Straits' issue at some point in the future. Nicholas II and Iswolsky were delighted with the document, but noticed that it did not say clearly that Britain would recognize Russia's exclusive right of passage through the Straits. Poklevsky reassured the minister that Benckendorff and Grey had never discussed anything else, and that 'the English will recognize the principle after they receive from us an equivalent concession'. Iswolsky agreed with Grey that including an international question in the negotiations would be awkward.[198] If Iswolsky, nevertheless, decided to act on this, Grey wanted him to think of an equivalent concession to the British in the Baghdad railway or Egypt (where the British needed formal consent of the great powers for Egyptian treasury operations).[199] Benckendorff advised Iswolsky to emphasize the connection between the Straits and the Egyptian issue by sending Grey a memorandum: '[Our] point of view on Egypt will be modified if we arrive at an arrangement'. Otherwise, Iswolsky could take up Grey's idea of summing up Anglo-Russian conflicts and the way they were settled in the text of the convention. It would allow introducing the subject of the British concession in the Straits and tie them down for the future.[200] The minister told Poklevsky to write a letter for Benckendorff to use as an answer to Grey's memorandum relating to the Straits. A copy would be sent to Nicolson.[201] Nicolson was not eager to have a written answer because Grey explained to him how risky it would be to bring the issue into the agreement. France would have to be consulted; the discussion of Russia's reciprocal concessions would slow down the negotiations; and a British concession about the Straits might arouse opposition in Parliament. An anti-Russian campaign might lead Russia to break off the negotiations.[202] Hardinge also became apprehensive after a report from Constantinople that the 'exchange of ideas regarding the Straits' was leaked to the Turkish government and that it might incline the Turks towards an alliance with Germany,[203] a possibility which could not be discounted under Abdul-Hamid.

Benckendorff's insistence that the exchange with Grey should be fixed in writing came up against Nicholas II's resolution not to send a memorandum to Nicolson.[204] Benckendorff suggested that Iswolsky might at least tell Nicolson the essence of the memorandum,[205] but the affair was closed without Grey's pledging anything but creating an impression that he did. Benckendorff's raptures over

198 Poklevsky to A.K. Benckendorff, 15/28.03.1907, BC2, box 14.

199 A.K. Benckendorff to Iswolsky, 08/21.03.1907, *Au service*, 2: 21–3.

200 A.K. Benckendorff to Iswolsky, 01/14.04.1907, *Au service*, 2: 25–7.

201 Poklevsky to A.K. Benckendorff, 29.03.1907, BC2, box 14.

202 Grey to Nicolson, 01.04.1907, *The Mirage of Power*, 3: 460.

203 A.K. Benckendorff to A.P. Iswolsky, 26.04/09.05.1907, *Au service*, 2: 37–8.

204 Iswolsky to A.K. Benckendorff, 25.04/08.05.1907, BC2, box 13.

205 A.K. Benckendorff to Iswolsky, 30.05/12.06.1907, Au *service,* 2: 52–4.

the great step forward in the Straits' issue contributed to Iswolsky's feeling of achievement.

Anglo-Russian Negotiations and Russo-German Relations

During the negotiations, Iswolsky attempted to placate Germany by keeping her informed about the Anglo-Russian discussions. He explained to the mortified Poklevsky that, just as the Foreign Office had communicated to the French the formula which they proposed to Russia for China, he would confide in the German government 'to the degree and extent which he will previously discuss with the British government'. Poklevsky found it risky in case Germany protested against a clause in the Anglo-Russian arrangement which was not yet signed:

> I also doubt that it is in our interest to show the British what exaggerated considerations we have for the Germans … the only mistake the British made was in not warning us they were going to give the formula to the French … I told this to Iswolsky, but I think that these arguments would have much more weight if you thought it possible to reiterate them.[206]

Benckendorff warned Iswolsky against analogies between Anglo-French openness and Russian disclosures to Germany. He persuaded Iswolsky that Berlin was making much of The Hague conference issues and the foreign tours of King Edward VII in order to create a rift between Russia and Britain and that Iswolsky's friendliness with Germany would alarm the British: 'We will at once abandon the system of confidence and frankness which has so uniquely characterized these negotiations'.[207]

Iswolsky was concerned about the opposition of the Russian general staff which considered that there was no need for a general settlement with Britain. In the Far East Britain allied to Japan would be useless to Russia; Russia could only obtain Britain's favours in Asia by considerable concessions; an agreement regarding Persia would lead to Russia becoming Germany's rival. The chief of the general staff, Palytsin, thought that Iswolsky should limit himself to a treaty with Japan and a specific agreement with Britain, excluding anything of interest to Germany.[208] Benckendorff dismissed Iswolsky's fears of the military opposition. Yermolov, according to Iswolsky, had been one of the most determined opponents of accepting the British terms for Afghanistan and Persia. Yet, in London Benckendorff found that Yermolov and his colleagues were resigned to giving in to Iswolsky.[209] Benckendorff was right: the military, after a two-week delay, accepted Iswolsky's Afghanistan convention and the other ministers were forced to edit the parts of the

206 Poklevsky to A.K. Benckendorff, 12/25.04.1907, BC2, box 14.
207 A.K. Benckendorff to Iswolsky, 16/29.04.1907, *Au service*, 2: 31–4.
208 A.F. Ostal'tseva, 198.
209 A.K. Benckendorff to Iswolsky, 16/29.04.1907, *Au service*, 2: 31–4.

draft relating to trade. Poklevsky wrote: 'It seems to me that our counter-draft should not displease the English because it gives them satisfaction in the main questions and recognizes Afghanistan as the sphere of exclusive British influence'.[210] Only commercial issues remained to be settled and Benckendorff recommended signing the rest of the agreements and settling the Afghanistan tariff rates later.[211]

The talks still lagging, Iswolsky tried to push Nicolson to sign by July 15. Benckendorff, approving of Iswolsky's determination, wrote that the British wondered whether Iswolsky's haste was encouraging or if it meant he was under pressure from his opponents. He also asked about the meaning of 15 July.[212] It was the day when Nicholas II was going to meet William II at Swinemünde, which was kept secret for fear of terrorist attacks. Iswolsky accompanied the emperor and gave Bülow his draft of a secret Russo-German protocol regarding the Baltic Sea. It was an element of Iswolsky's balanced relations with Britain and Germany. On the eve of the meeting, he had asked Benckendorff to reassure the Foreign Office about the meeting: his presence should guarantee to Grey that nothing untoward (like another Björko treaty) would happen. He had signed the treaty with Japan the day before and wished that the treaty with Britain had also been concluded prior to the emperors' meeting: 'I would be going with a wholly different sense of freedom and independence'.[213] Benckendorff replied that Iswolsky's letter, which he read to the king and Grey, dissipated all doubts, if there ever had been any.[214] But he commented to Cambon that the king did not like his explanations,[215] probably reflecting the Foreign Office's suspicions. The British and French were coming to the opinion that Iswolsky, for all his good intentions, was not reliable: in May the notoriously indiscreet Elim Demidov, a member of the Russian embassy at Vienna, had told the British ambassador Goschen about the Austrian foreign minister Aehrenthal's secret suggestion to Iswolsky to form an Austro-Russo-Franco-German group for settling the Macedonian reforms issue.[216] When the leak became known, Iswolsky assured Grey, through Benckendorff, that he would never have agreed to anything but one-on-one cooperation with Austria-Hungary; but it left a bad impression.

The Persian Gulf

The Anglo-Russian negotiations stalled when the British introduced the statement about the status quo in the Persian Gulf in the preamble to the Persian convention.

210 Poklevsky to A.K. Benckendorff, 26.04/09.5.1907, BC2, box 14.
211 A.K. Benckendorff to Iswolsky, 02/15.05.1907, *Au service*, 2: 38–40.
212 Ibid.
213 Iswolsky to A.K. Benckendorff, 18/31.07.1907, BC2, box 13.
214 A.K. Benckendorff to Iswolsky, 23.07/05.08.1907, *Au service*, 2: 78–9.
215 Paul Cambon to Pichon, 08.08.1907, DDF, XI: 208–10.
216 Hardinge of Penshurst, 141.

It was an unpleasant surprise for Iswolsky. A year before, Grey was disposed to give Russia access to the Persian Gulf, though retaining the control of the estuary of the Tigris and Euphrates.[217] In September 1906 Iswolsky said that the Russian sphere of influence would need access to the Gulf and Nicolson saw no difficulty in it.[218] Now the British declared that they could not afford to annoy British public opinion by seeming to abandon their positions in the Gulf.[219] The haggling went on for a long time, and Hardinge and Grey agreed privately that in the last instance they would authorize Nicolson to take out the mention of the Gulf. Iswolsky insisted that the Persian Gulf was, like the Baghdad railway and Kuwait, an issue of international interest and its appearance in the Anglo-Russian convention would provoke Germany. He said that he might discuss it later but not at the moment when it might create a crisis on the Russian side.[220] He realized that if he accepted the British amendment it would favour the British without any compensation for Russia. As could be expected, Benckendorff responded with a warning that Iswolsky should focus on the Anglo-Russian rapprochement and not be distracted by details:

> [We] are not in a position to obtain a brilliant settlement, the main points, the brilliant ones, will only become obvious with time. But we can get a good bargain. An *all round* arrangement which would guarantee, inasmuch as it is humanely possible, all our immense borders … would, I believe, strongly impress our public opinion …[221]

He prodded Iswolsky by writing that the delays made the British wonder whether the negotiations would succeed. He advised Iswolsky to hurry:

> As for the word in the preamble about the Persian Gulf, I believe that under the circumstances something should be done. And, after all, what is so terrible about it? In itself this subject has become absolutely of no interest to us. I believe that back home no one thinks any more about the possibility or need for a Russian port in this area. It is a matter of wording, to exclude the application of the principle to Germany.

He ended the letter with the usual reminder:

> Should our negotiations fail, an Anglo-German agreement, no matter what we are told or promised, would materialize in no time.[222]

---

217 Grey to Nicolson, 10.08.1906, BD, 4: 241–2.
218 Nicolson to Grey, 17.90.1906, BD, 4: 392–3.
219 Nicolson to Grey, 14.06.1907, BD, 4: 475–6.
220 Iswolsky to A.K. Benckendorff, 20.06/03.07.1907, BC2, box 13.
221 A.K. Benckendorff to Iswolsky, 13/26.05.1907, *Au service*, 2: 44–5.
222 A.K. Benckendorff to Iswolsky, 13/24.06.1907, *Au service*, 2: 57–60.

The Afghanistan and Persia parts would be settled as soon as Nicolson and Iswolsky agreed on the wording of the texts. After the concessions the British made on the issue of Mongolia and the Dardanelles, Nicolson received instructions to be firm on the Afghanistan proposals.[223] After Benckendorff's return from St Petersburg, Grey explained to him that Britain was making a great concession to Russia in allowing Teheran to be in the Russian zone. Benckendorff naively asked how Teheran could have not been in it, being in the north. Grey insisted that still it was a great advantage and therefore Russia should give in on another issue: British special interests in Afghanistan did not allow them to put a piece of Perso-Afghan border into the Russian zone. The line had to be re-drawn. Benckendorff agreed at once,[224] but the Russian military were reluctant: a short-lived convention would be followed by a renewed conflict in which every concession would be regretted. General Palitsyn's opposition was based on the fears of a British attack through Afghanistan. The British military attaché feared that the Russians' direct relations to the Afghanis would only remain harmless as long as Anglo-Russian relations remained cordial.[225] Benckendorff never tired of repeating that Russia had to be generous to the British in Afghanistan because 'Britain gave us Teheran'. The British interest in the country was real since Afghanistan's attitude, the ambassador thought, might endanger India. Could it ever be a danger to the Russian Empire? Benckendorff answered with an emphatic 'No'. Therefore, Russian concessions were in order. Benckendorff drew a frightening picture:

> Where would we be today if the negotiations had not begun, and what will happen if, God forbid, they break up? We will have our hands full of problems for the next twenty five years. The elements which we have obtained, of the Bosporus and the Åland Isles, these last reminders of the Crimean war, will be lost. We will find ourselves facing a shut door at Tokyo, Peking, Constantinople and probably at Paris … At the end there will be a war for which we will pay, one way or another, and war means revolution …[226]

The Signing of the Convention

The final text of the Afghanistan convention contained all the British desiderata, with a provision advised by Benckendorff. It mentioned the Amir as the sovereign ruler of the country. Otherwise, the ambassador said, it would look as if Russia recognized Britain's absolute rights in the country. This rare surge of caution is explained by the ambassador's next words that the British would welcome the mention of the Amir, because they did not want to annoy him at a difficult moment

223 Grey to Nicolson, 20.03.1907, BD, 4: 525–7.

224 Grey to Nicolson, 07.03.1907, BD, 4: 277–8.

225 Lieutenant-Colonel Napier to Nicolson, 27.04.1907, BD, 4: 530–32.

226 A.K. Benckendorff to Iswolsky, 27.06/10.07.1907, *Au service*, 2: 60–63.

Fig. 5.2 Map of Persia with the Russian and British Zones
Source: By kind permission of O. Gopanchuk.

in Anglo-Afghan relations.[227] Only in the matter of the Persian Gulf status quo did the Russian military prevail to a degree and the British provision was attached to the convention as a special declaration (Fig. 5.2).

The discussions of the Afghanistan and Persian conventions continued till Grey, in Benckendorff's words, made a serious attempt at reconciling the proposals. Benckendorff emphasized the great concessions which the British made in taking out of the convention the phrases about Russia's unconditional guarantees to Britain and about the Persian Gulf status quo. Now Russia's position respecting Afghanistan was almost equal to that of Britain, he thought. 'And do not forget that they have given up on the Persian Gulf, another difficult issue … It is amazing what a long way you have come since you became minister, I believe all this and more would have been lost [without you]'. Rarely has a misjudgement been so dramatically offset by a comment from the other side. He warned Iswolsky not to push the British further for they might break off the negotiations: '[They] feel that their concessions have gone well beyond their intentions'.[228] When the details of the Russian proposal arrived in London, it turned out that the Russian sphere of influence was even less than Lord Curzon had assigned them and there was no question of access to the Persian Gulf for Russia.[229] Hardinge sent Grey's

227 A.K. Benckendorff to Iswolsky, 11/24.07.1907, *Au service*, 2: 70–74.
228 A.K. Benckendorff to Iswolsky, 08/21.08.1907, *Au service*, 2: 82–4.
229 Keith Neilson, *Britain and the Last Tsar* (Oxford, 1995), 283.

Gulf memorandum to the king with an explanation that it was written to show the Russians that the Foreign Office was making great concessions to obtain other, more essential points. 'It is not the way in which we would put our case before an impartial Englishman', he concluded, and reiterated: 'we have not sacrificed any principle and all we have done is to try to save the Russian face'.[230]

Iswolsky sent the final text to London and asked Benckendorff to support Nicolson's plea to Grey not to make last-minute changes in the texts. He complained about the hostility of the Russian press to the Anglo-Russian convention and hoped that Benckendorff's contact at the *Novoye Vremya,* G. Wesselitsky, would help to assuage the fully-expected editorial fury at the arrangement.[231] As soon as he signed the convention, Iswolsky left for Marienbad to meet with King Edward, then with Franz Joseph II and with Aehrenthal. He invited Benckendorff to meet him in Carlsbad and then in St Petersburg because 'after the signature it will become particularly important for us to discuss all the consequences'.[232]

J.A. Spender recalled that, in 1906–7, Spring Rice wrote to him constantly about the importance of preventing a deal between Russia and Germany. He hailed the Anglo-Russian convention as a victory over German hegemonic aspirations. When Spender repeated this to Benckendorff, to his surprise, the latter told him that there was nothing that Russia could do with Britain or for Britain that would be worth the cost of a rupture with Germany.[233] For Britain the convention was useful in itself, but for Russia it was an instrument to be used in establishing a balanced relationship with Germany.

Russia came to the rapprochement in a state of extreme weakness and it showed during the negotiations. The course was adopted in an atmosphere, described by a contemporary as 'a total confusion in external and internal policies'.[234] Russian diplomacy was not experienced in working out compromises on such a large scale. A settlement with Britain had never been seriously contemplated in the previous decade[235] and its terms had not been discussed under calmer circumstances. What Russia could concede and what she could expect in return, was decided among factional quarrels and under a barrage of advice from the London embassy. As a result on the Russian side some of the promises were later impossible to keep and wishful thinking and unspoken assumptions were allowed to take precedence over the stated terms of the convention.

Benckendorff's main contribution to the negotiations was in emphasizing the great concessions which the British made and demanding more concessions on Russia's side.[236]

---

230 Hardinge to Lord Knollys, 06.08.1907, RA VIC/ADDC7/2/Q.
231 Iswolsky to A.K. Benckendorff, 11/24/08.1907, BC2, box 13.
232 Iswolsky to A.K. Benckendorff, 15/28.08.1907, BC2, box 13.
233 J.A. Spender, 1: 215.
234 M.A. Taube, *Zarnitsy*, 87.
235 R.R. Rosen to A.K.Benckendorff, 11/24.12.1905, BC2, box 14.
236 Marina Soroka, 'Debating Russia's Choice', 17.

Throughout the negotiations, Iswolsky and Benckendorff collaborated with the British much better than they did with their Russian colleagues. Iswolsky had to listen to or read the considerations of the military and the finance minister, but from the outset he was determined to reject them, while Benckendorff treated others' ideas dismissively. The result reflected Benckendorff's Eurocentric vision and Iswolsky's and Poklevsky's manifold fears.

The Russian government saw the Anglo-Russian settlement as part of a policy of equilibrium and disengagement from foreign entanglements, but the new foreign minister also viewed it as a way for Russia to recover her great power status in Europe. Iswolsky readily admitted that the terms of the Persian settlement were not beneficial to Russia, but implied that Persia was more of a pretext for an agreement with Britain than a reason for it.[237] The reason was Britain's expected support of Russia in the Near East. Such a view, tacitly supported by Nicholas II, encouraged the minister to pursue the solution of the Straits question, precipitating the Bosnian crisis of 1908.[238]

Count Benckendorff, Iswolsky's friend and confidant, shares the responsibility; he had preached since 1905 that the main value of an Asiatic settlement between Britain and Russia was in its European implications, which materialized in 1907 as a vague British promise to be favourable to Russia's efforts to obtain a change of the Straits regime.

Paul Schroeder writes that the British: 'did drop repeated hints to Russia about how cooperation in Asia would eventually help her in Turkey and the Straits'.[239] This thinking was not the least of reasons why Russian diplomacy in the wake of the Anglo-Russian convention attempted to activate its European policy in a series of injudicious and unsuccessful steps. By 1914, various Russian diplomats and statesmen associated the Anglo-Russian rapprochement with the pursuit of the 'Straits' mirage' and a looming clash with Germany in the Balkans.[240]

237 M. de Taube, *La politique russe d'avant-guerre*, 140.

238 A.F. Ostal'tseva, 241.

239 Paul W. Schroeder, 'World War I as Galloping Gertie: A Reply to Joachim Remak' in *Systems, Stability, and Statecraft* (New York, 2004), 151.

240 P.N. Durnovo's Memorandum, February 1914 in *Imperial Russia: A Source Book, 1700–1917* (ed. B.Dmytryshin) (New York, 1990), 495; Yu. Soloviov, *Vospominaniia diplomata, 1893–1922* [Memoirs of a Diplomat, 1893–1922] (Minsk, [1928] 2003), 198.

Chapter 6
The School of Compromise, 1907–1908

In Britain and Russia the opposite reactions to the convention were rooted in shared assumptions. British liberal and radical circles condemned the 'entente' (as it became known by association with the *Entente cordiale*) because a rapprochement with a despotic regime tarnished Britain's moral prestige, while officials feared it might result in losses to the wily and unscrupulous enemy.[1] Russian liberals rejoiced that a rapprochement with the constitutional Britain would help them wrestle political power from the autocracy[2] by tying its hands; the conservatives and the military opposed it for the same reason.[3]

The Foreign Office was pleased because, among other things, the convention succeeded in 'bringing [Russia] back to Europe'[4] and harnessing her into the Entente's course of resistance to German expansion[5] while previously Russia had managed to steer a midway course between the Triple Alliance and France. It is no accident that all the Foreign Office officials whom Benckendorff described as friends of Russia are known for their fear of Germany's ambitions: from Charles Hardinge to Louis Mallet[6] and Eyre Crowe. Britain now had two continental powers on its side to face the German menace. But more acquisitions bring more concerns. If British foreign policy's predicament throughout the 1900s was 'how to hold France to the entente and yet at the same time not to give it sufficient support to encourage it' to lead an intransigent course,[7] after August 1907 the predicament more or less doubled with the inclusion of Russia.

Overall, the Foreign Office officials felt pleased because, as they told *The Times'* foreign editor Valentine Chirol, in Persia and elsewhere, by the terms of the convention 'we have got the substance ... and merely give away the shadow'.[8] This last was the reason why the Russian military and the officials of the Asiatic Department were suspicious of the convention.[9] They considered that

1 O'Beirne to Bertie, 28.05.1907, FO 800/174, 10–11.

2 Nicolson to Hardinge, 10.10.1906, FO 800/337, 114–6.

3 Yu. Solov'ev, *Vospominaniia diplomata 1893–1922* (Minsk, 2003), 198.

4 Spring Rice to Bertie, 19.10.1907, FO 800/173, 12–13.

5 J.A. White, *Transition to Global Rivalry*, 290.

6 Keith Robbins, *Sir Edward Grey: A Biography of Lord Grey of Fallodon* (London, 1971), 139.

7 Geoffrey Barraclough, *From Agadir to Armageddon*, 115.

8 *The History of The Times: The Twentieth Century Test, 1884–1912* (London, 1947), 502–4.

9 M. de Taube, *La politique russe d'avant-guerre et la fin de l'empire des tsars*, 139.

Russia gave up her long-maintained position that Afghanistan was a sovereign country and a chance to establish relations with it under different conditions. Tibet was proclaimed as outside the spheres of influence of both empires, but with Britain having a favourable ruler in Lhassa. In Persia, Russia's zone was limited to the north which had been dominated by Russia anyway. Witte, with the wisdom of hindsight, wrote that the Anglo-Russian settlement in Persia opened the door to German pressure on Russia for a similar settlement, thus leading to the 1910 Potsdam convention and Russia's promise of joining her railway network with the Baghdad railway.[10] The terms of the 1907 convention regarding non-interference in Persian internal political struggles, later prevented Russia from exercising full political control over its sphere of influence in Persia after 1907 and led to the collapse of the central government.[11] Witte was capable of stating his case against Iswolsky's policy. Less articulate opponents in the exclusive St Petersburg Yacht Club expressed their resentment by blackballing Poklevsky when he attempted to join.[12]

Benckendorff, Iswolsky, and, initially, their colleagues, considered that Russia gave up what she could not hold anyway. Benckendorff did not consider that in the foreseeable future Russia would require more of a stake in Central Asia than the convention allowed. Russia needed to tap her internal resources first, and these would be sufficient for a long time. Overcoming political dissent by prudent and consistent reforms which would allow Russia to become a constitutional monarchy, achieve economic recovery and domestic peace, was a greater priority than spheres of influence in Asia.[13] Peaceful coexistence with Britain was compatible with this long-term goal and favourable to Russia's modernization.

Iswolsky's Policy and Benckendorff's Advice

Iswolsky's views in 1906 were less set than Benckendorff's, which meant that the ambassador had to apply himself all the more to the task of keeping his chief on the straight and narrow path, by preaching to him that the focus of Russian policy was to side with Britain in checking Germany.

Contemporaries were excessively impressed by Iswolsky's declaration that he had a policy, while Lamsdorff had been merely 'groping'.[14] But his policy's outline varied according to his audience. The foreign ministry legal expert Baron Mikhail A. Taube heard from the minister that the new conventions would allow Russia 'to turn to her historical interests in Europe', where she would henceforth

10 S.Yu. Witte, *Vospominani'ia ...*, 3: 442–3.

11 I.A. Zinoviev, *Rossi'ia, Angli'ia i Persi'ia*, 158.

12 Iswolsky to A.K. Benckendorff, 27.02/11.03.1908, BC2, box 13.

13 A.K. Benckendorff to Empress Maria Feodorovna, 15/28.08.1905, GARF, f.1126, op.1, ed.hr.4, ll.1–4 ob.

14 M. de Taube, *La politique russe d'avant-guerre*, 100.

be able to count on Britain's support.[15] Wallace recorded that Iswolsky planned to restrict the understanding with Britain to the subjects in the convention, to conciliate Germany and make a rapprochement with Austria, focusing on South-Eastern Europe.[16] At the same time, Iswolsky explained to A.S. Suvorin that his agreements would incorporate Russia into a network joining Britain, Japan, France and Russia and help defend Russia's interests from German attempts at dictate and, in this way, guarantee a decade of peace. Then Iswolsky blurted out: 'We will only rise through a victorious war with someone, anyone'. Suvorin asked him about the Straits, and Iswolsky assured him that Britain would support Russia. He added: 'Our next goal is Austria's inheritance. In the Balkans, [we will partition it] with Bulgaria'.[17] To the Defence Budget Committee of the Duma, Iswolsky explained that the Anglo-German struggle for world supremacy was bound to end in an armed conflict. Germany's victory over Britain would close the Baltic Sea to Russia just like the Black Sea, and Russia would become an economic tributary to Germany. Therefore, Russia had to side with Britain.[18]

Five years later, after several disappointing ventures, Iswolsky began to emphasize that 'his policy' was imposed on him by the situation in 1906 when the only staple of Russian foreign policy was the French alliance. Iswolsky said that he had his reservations about this brainchild of the military, but by abandoning France, Russia would have lost at the same time her honour, her alliance-worthiness and her independence of Germany. The decision to steer away from Germany imposed the need to consolidate the ties with France through conventions with the powers which already were in the latter's orbit, Britain and Japan. Tellingly, he described his course as 'perhaps less secure but worthier of Russia's past and of her greatness'.[19]

Iswolsky's arguments for the rapprochement with Britain were underpinned by his pessimistic conviction that a European war was unavoidable and that Russia could not hope to stay out of it. This conviction dictated his day-to-day policy choices and made for a course which ultimately doomed his 'balancing'. He tried to follow the course which he and Benckendorff favoured,[20] while engaging in gestures of outward compliance to the discordant demands of Russia's United Government, the Tsar and public opinion. All the while he spoke of moderation, meaning insecurity, and succeeded only in leaving behind a distinct impression that he feared the Entente's displeasure more than Germany's.

His concessions in the convention, like most of his initiatives developed out of the ideas that Lamsdorff had been contemplating at one time or another. Lamsdorff recognized that Russia in 1905 was too weak to continue the stand-off in Asia and

15 Ibid:, 100–1.

16 *The History of The Times*, 836.

17 A.S. Suvorin, *Dnevnik Alekseia Sergeevicha Suvorina* (London, 2000), 537–8, 532.

18 N.V. Savich, *Vospominani'ia* (St Petersburg, 1993), 101–2.

19 Iswolsky to Stolypin, 21.07/03.08.1911, *Au service*, 2: 299–304.

20 A.P. Iswolsky, *Vospominaniia* (Minsk, 2003), 62.

in early 1906 was considering the old British desire to partition of Persia.[21] But he was biding his time. If he had conducted the negotiations he would have been very thrifty with promises and would have insisted on specific agreements which could have left him with at least a partial achievement even if a general understanding proved impossible.[22] That was exactly what the Foreign Office was determined to avoid, and Benckendorff persuaded Iswolsky that his goal was a rapprochement, which reduced the discussions to removing one Russian objection after another.

Iswolsky readily admitted to Taube that the terms of the Persian settlement were not beneficial to Russia, but implied that the convention allowed Russia freedom of action,[23] which he was going to employ in the Near East. The desirability of a change of the Straits' regime had also been discussed under Lamsdorff. But for Benckendorff, the Straits' question became the core of the convention for Russia. He mistakenly believed that he had brought Lansdowne around to the idea, and in 1907 he crowed delightedly about Grey's memorandum as the result of his own efforts.[24] Yet, the way in which he and Iswolsky handled the issue – letting the Foreign Office see their interest and then accepting a vague promise as a quid pro quo for a real concession – made their 'achievement' valueless.

As for the freedom of action for Russia, Iswolsky and Benckendorff seem to be alone among European statesmen who believed in it after 1907.

The Entente Chain

It is natural that William II interpreted the convention as the final step towards a 'military coalition à trois'.[25] Neither Britain nor Russia in 1907 had such a thing in mind, but because of the Anglo-French entente the convention became a pact of adhesion to a coalition facing the Triple Alliance.[26] As long as France's differences with Germany and Britain made her dependent on the Russian alliance, Russia retained a considerable freedom of action.[27] After 1904, Russia's diplomatic manoeuvrability gradually shrank, for both France's reliance on Russia diminished and Russia's dependence on France increased. If Russian memoirists, beginning with Witte, frequently state that in 1907 Russia surrendered her freedom of hand, they do not mean that Russia lost her freedom of hand to Britain, but *vis-à-vis* France backed by Britain, Russia had to follow or risk isolation. That was why the deterioration of Russo-German relations was seen as a consequence of the 1907 convention.

---

21 A.F. Ostal'tseva, 103.

22 Hardinge to Lansdowne, 04.10.1905, BD, 14: 205–6.

23 M. de Taube, *La politique russe d'avant-guerre*, 140.

24 A.K. Benckendorff to Iswolsky, 15/28.11.1906, *Au service*, 1: 402–5.

25 William II to Bülow, 26.11.1905, *Letters of Prince von Bülow*, 187–9.

26 S.Yu.Witte, 3: 438.

27 I.S. Rybachonok, *Soyuz s Frantsi'ei vo vneshnei politike Rossii v kontse XIX v.* (Moscow, 1993), 313.

Oddly, Iswolsky had not foreseen from the outset that in Berlin his policy would be associated with the anti-German aspect of the Entente. Benckendorff encouraged him in thinking that he could reap the advantages of the Anglo-French backing without incurring Germany's rancour for repeatedly siding with her opponents. Indeed, at first the Germans sympathized with Iswolsky, believing that the Anglo-Russian talks had been Lamsdorff's inheritance rather than Iswolsky's idea.[28] The latter was glad to maintain this impression in Berlin. Already during the negotiations of 1906–7, he was troubled by the Anglo-French initiatives to press Germany out everywhere. In January 1907 the Entente diplomats began secret negotiations with Spain for a treaty which would close Spanish ports in the Canary and Balearic Isles to the German navy.[29] When Iswolsky was presented with the fait accompli in the summer of 1907, he was alarmed: the treaty emphasized the split of Europe into two coalitions just as he was bringing Russia to the Entente's side. The secrecy of the Anglo-Franco-Spanish negotiations belied Benckendorff's promises of the Entente's open and trusting friendship. Very clear-sighted when it did not concern his own political moves, Iswolsky criticized this flurry of international agreements for making it difficult to localize even the smallest conflict because all the powers formed part of one network or another.[30] He complained to Benckendorff that the agreement would needlessly annoy Germany and lead to more tensions.[31]

Benckendorff's brother-in-law, the Italian ambassador in Japan, summed up the situation: 'Russia, England, France and Japan would form a quadrangular *bloc* difficult to oppose in Asia and in the Pacific'.[32] Iswolsky feared that Germany saw it in exactly the same way and that a weak Russia would pay for the others' ambitions. Cambon discussed with Hardinge and Grey the idea of an Anglo-Russo-Franco-Japanese agreement in March 1907. To keep Germany out, Grey suggested that France sign an agreement with Japan and after the Anglo-Russian and Russo-Japanese conventions the bilateral arrangements between the four powers would form a chain into which Germany could not enter. Benckendorff told Grey that Iswolsky and Nicholas II would certainly approve.[33] Iswolsky protested that he did not want to create an impression of contributing to the isolation of Germany. Grey's suggestion to sign simultaneously the Anglo-Russian and the Russo-Japanese conventions[34] would make them look in Germany's eyes as if Russia

28 I. Astaf'iev, 87.

29 Paul Cambon to Pichon, 10.01.1907, DDF, X: 617–8.

30 Bompard to Pichon, 15.06.1907, DDF, XI: 50–3.

31 Iswolsky to A.K. Benckendorff, 26.06/09.07.1907, AVPRI, f.184, op.520, ed.hr. 1243, ll.10–11 ob.

32 Alessandro Guiccioli to A.K. Benckendorff, 28.06.1909, BC2, box 12.

33 Paul Cambon to Pichon, 13.03.1907, DDF, X: 690–2.

34 Hardinge to Nicolson, 19.03.1907, in J.A. White, *Transition to Global Rivalry*, 252.

had joined the Anglo-Japanese alliance without giving Russia the guarantees of an alliance. Iswolsky declared that he did not want the Anglo-Russian convention to extend beyond the three regions already under discussion.[35]

To Iswolsky's fears of going beyond the initial rapprochement, Benckendorff replied that an Anglo-Franco-Russo-Japanese accord would 'ease things and offer us another guarantee'. The French initiative may have been risky but in British hands it was perfectly safe for Russia to accept. The only danger he saw was the opposite: creating in the Entente an impression of Russia's closeness to Germany.[36] He strongly advised Iswolsky against making a clean breast to Germany about the proposed 'entente chain' on two grounds: formally it had nothing to do with the Anglo-Russian convention to which Iswolsky's promise of consulting with Germany applied. Also, Grey would take such a disclosure very badly from the 'moral point of view rather than politically'.[37] Benckendorff's absolute principles only applied where Grey's susceptibility was concerned.

Iswolsky's nervousness increased as the scale of Anglo-French strategy was becoming clearer to him. He asked the French at least to delay the signature of their agreement with Japan until after his negotiations were concluded.[38] When the French settled with Japan ahead of him and did not even warn him well in advance; he was left with 24 hours to attempt to influence the press comments by playing down the significance of the arrangement.[39] This lack of consideration rankled with him for a long time.[40]

The idea was abandoned at Cambon's suggestion, but even so 'the three treaties which ultimately emerged were coordinated in ways which suggested … the original unitary concept'.[41]

Benckendorff had to impose his views on Iswolsky: he always denied that a pro-British policy might eventually force Russia to choose between Germany and Britain as two warring sides. He insisted that if only the unfounded German fear of Britain disappeared, the two countries would come to an agreement, because their rivalry was purely economic.[42] But influenced by the company he kept in London, Benckendorff saw Germany's sinister plans everywhere and emphasized that Britain's rapprochement with Russia rested on Russia's readiness to support Britain against Germany. Iswolsky was not convinced about the German threat – or not until he had accumulated enough personal grudges.

---

35 Bompard to Pichon, 22.03.1907, DDF, X: 714–6.

36 A.K. Benckendorff to Iswolsky, 19.03/03.03.1908, *Au service*, 2: 132–6.

37 A.K. Benckendorff to Iswolsky, 16/29.04.1907, *Au service*, 2: 31–4.

38 Paul Cambon to Pichon, 03.05.1907, DDF, X: 788–9.

39 Bompard to Pichon, 11.06.1907, DDF, XI: 37–8.

40 Nicolson to Grey, 04.12.1907, BD, 8: 138–9.

41 J.A. White, *Transition to Global Rivalry*, 256–7.

42 A.K. Benckendorff to Iswolsky, 14/27.11.1906, *Au service*, 1: 399–400.

The Godfather of the Convention

After August 1907, Benckendorff became a regular visitor to the Foreign Office but his name is rarely mentioned in the *British Documents on the Origins of the War* relating to 1907–14. If he did not contribute much to the Cambon-Grey discussions, in his regular private letters to Iswolsky, Grey's and Cambon's silent partner became extremely loquacious. Just as the count got a dose of British and French political analysis at his meetings with Grey and Cambon, so did Iswolsky get a weekly ration of it in his confidential letters.

The ambassador saw himself as the godfather of the convention and thus Iswolsky's guide and Grey's chief champion in St Petersburg. He went out of his way to remind Grey and Iswolsky that their roles in history were inextricably tied to the Anglo-Russian understanding. Iswolsky's continued presence at the foreign ministry should be as much the Foreign Office's concern as the Liberal government's survival should be of prime interest to Iswolsky and the Russian government.[43]

In the ambassador's eyes, Grey was managing his side well, but Iswolsky needed regular catechism lessons. Benckendorff wrote numerous private letters to the minister, saying that often his official letters were out of date by the time they were posted,[44] so the private ones gave a better idea of the situation. 'I will do nothing without reaching a consensus with you',[45] Iswolsky wrote to Benckendorff during the convention talks. It remained so during his ministry. The tactful ambassador made his disapproval obvious by withholding flattery but gushed about Iswolsky's actions of which he approved: 'What a great job you have accomplished in Berlin and in other places … I wish you the same success in St Petersburg, in this nest of prejudice and childish misconceptions!'[46]

Iswolsky complained about the reactionaries who prepared the dissolution of the Duma and the United Government; but the new representative assembly did not inspire much confidence. Fedor F. Martens, the eminent legal expert of the Russian foreign ministry, wrote in *The Times* that the Second Duma failed because it refused to condemn terrorism and violence in Russia and instead indulged in rhetoric of 'discontent and unlimited hate'. The illiterate and uneducated deputies, who were a considerable proportion of the Duma, were unfit to discuss the laws submitted to them.[47] When the letter appeared Benckendorff gently reproached Iswolsky for his inability to control his subordinates' public statements.[48] Iswolsky accepted the criticism: 'What a stupid letter Martens wrote to *The Times*. I disclaimed [in the Duma] its

43 A.K. Benckendorff to Iswolsky, 6/19.02.1908, *Au service*, 2: 125–8.
44 A.K. Benckendorff to Iswolsky, 18.04/01.05.1907, *Au service*, 2: 35–7.
45 Iswolsky to A.K. Benckendorff, 25.04/08.05.1907, BC2, box 13.
46 A.K. Benckendorff to Iswolsky, November 1906, *Au service*, 1: 396–8.
47 F. de Martens, 'The Duma and the Nation' in *The Times*, 15.04.1907, 4.
48 A.K. Benckendorff to Iswolsky, 03/16.04.1907, *Au service*, 2: 27–31.

official character'.[49] Like most liberals the two friends were at a loss to decide what the right attitude was: the Duma was a zoo,[50] but its dissolution would be a reactionary measure, and Martens' frankness gave ammunition to the reactionaries. Benckendorff, Iswolsky and Poklevsky limited themselves to ridiculing the Duma in private.[51]

Smoothing the Difficulties in London

Benckendorff meanwhile put to rest a long-standing feud between *The Times* and the Russian government which had begun with the expulsion of their correspondent Dudley Disraeli Braham from St Petersburg in 1903, when the paper declared that it would have to be either Braham or no one for Russia. During the convention talks Lord Revelstoke helped Poklevsky begin his negotiations with the newspaper.[52] It took six months for the embassy and the paper to reach a compromise:[53] Robert Wilton, already at St Petersburg, became *The Times'* next correspondent.

Benckendorff dealt with the British press with tact and consideration, but in his opinion Russian papers had no business discussing the actions of the foreign ministry or its officials.[54] This arrogance was very much the reaction of a St Petersburg bureaucrat, the side of his personality which he would have said did not exist. Wesselitsky loyally supported the count for 15 years, but unlike Russian ambassadors in Paris and Vienna, Benckendorff never deigned to invite the journalist to the embassy when he entertained important Russian visitors[55] like Iswolsky or Sazonov.

In the 1905–7, Benckendorff spent considerable time on discussions and correspondence with Russian and British authorities regarding Russian political emigrants wanted by the Russian government or arrested upon their return from Britain, as was the case with a veteran member of the terrorist organization *People's Will*, Nikolai Tchaikovsky. In 1874 he escaped from Russia, where a warrant for his arrest was issued, and spent many years in Britain, married an Englishwoman and, as Benckendorff wrote to Iswolsky, 'led a normal existence' though continuing to profess 'very advanced views'. Benckendorff emphasized that he did not know nor was he interested in learning any facts

49 Iswolsky to A.K. Benckendorff, 12/25.04.1907, BC2, box 13.

50 Grand Duke Nikolai Mikhailovich to F. Masson, 25.02/10.03.1907, *Au temps de l'alliance franco-russe* (Paris, 2005), 417–18.

51 Poklevsky to A.K. Benckendorff, 29.03.1907, BC2, box 14.

52 Poklevsky to Iswolsky, 01/14.11.1906, AVPRI, f.340, op.835, d.26, ll.108–11.

53 *The History of The Times*, 490–91.

54 A.K. Benckendorff to S.P. Benckendorff, 29.09/12.10.1912, GARF, f.1126, op.1, ed.hr.153, ll.133–6 ob.

55 G. Wesselitsky to A.K. Benckendorff, 11.10.1908, BC2, box 15.

about Tchaikovsky: he could have easily learned that in Britain the man worked for Russian opposition groups, violent and otherwise. Since 1904 he had been a member of the Central Committee of the Socialist-Revolutionary party, organizers of terrorist acts in Russia, and after 1905 he organized the smuggling of arms into Russia, travelling on a false passport. In 1907 he was arrested during an illegal crossing of the border.[56] The British press demanded that the Foreign Office intervene, pleading the man's respectable reputation in Britain and the fact that the government of Russia had offered amnesty for political crimes. The ambassador defended Russia's position in very effective letters to the editors of those newspapers which were Tchaikovsky's champions. He suggested that the amnesty did not cover the use of a false passport to enter Russia; that the secrecy surrounding Tchaikovsky's stay in Russia may have implied he was involved in anti-governmental activities; and that he did not see how the law-abiding life of a Russian subject in England made him immune to prosecution for the crimes committed in Russia. Benckendorff noted with satisfaction that the tone of the papers switched from demands of justice to clamours for 'clemency'. But at the same time, the count pleaded with Iswolsky to save the Foreign Office from the wrath of radical groups which would blame the Anglo-Russian understanding for the British government's passivity in the affair.[57] He advised Iswolsky to obtain the veteran terrorist's freedom for the sake of the convention. In October 1908, on Iswolsky's insistence, Tchaikovsky was freed on bail. In 1910 he received a token sentence. In this way the foreign ministry placated British public opinion irritated by Russian troops' presence in Persia.

Benckendorff dismissed the effect of Russian emigrants' activities or propaganda in Britain and considered such petty affairs a waste of his time,[58] but he succeeded in having the finance ministry abolish the surtax on Indian tea sold in Russia, so as to please London merchants.[59] He also insisted that the claim of the owners of a British vessel, *Knight Commander*, sunk by the Russian navy during the Russo-Japanese war should be satisfied as a goodwill gesture to British society.[60] Iswolsky tried in vain to use Benckendorff's usual argument about the insignificance of the issue compared to the survival of the Anglo-Russian understanding: getting his way, he wrote, might provoke a press campaign against him and his policy of friendship with Britain.[61] But Benckendorff refused to see any similarity between Iswolsky's and Grey's domestic liabilities.

---

56 P.A. Stolypin, *Perepiska* (Moscow, 2004), 129.

57 A.K. Benckendorff to Iswolsky, 28.12/10.01.1907/8, *Au service*, 2: 110–13.

58 A.K. Benckendorff to Iswolsky, 02/15.05.1907, *Au service*, 2: 38–42.

59 Iswolsky to A.K. Benckendorff, 09/22.04.1908, BC2, box 13.

60 Iswolsky to AK. Benckendorff, 14/17.02.1908, BC2, box 13.

61 Iswolsky to A.K. Benckendorff, 14/27.02.1908, BC2, box 13.

Benckendorff as His Minister's Mentor

Iswolsky's letters railed against the barbarous Russian 'bureaucracy', a euphemism for Nicholas II's monarchy; he dissociated himself from the unsatisfactory replies he had to give to the concerned British public. 'I asked the minister of interior to expand on the meagre press communiqués [regarding the anti-Jewish riots in Poland] but received no answer'.[62] (Stolypin replied to him four days after this letter, adding that he had delayed responding in order to verify the information.[63]) Iswolsky wanted London to know that he was engaged in a struggle with the forces of reaction; hence, his frequent complaints about his colleagues' lack of understanding and his desire to resign.

Benckendorff warned his chief against easing his enemies' job and marvelled at the obtuseness of Russian conservatives who did not see that Iswolsky was carrying out a diplomatic revolution: 'But can anyone [in Russia] seriously contemplate the idea of going back into the dark of the night? Don't they realize what impression your resignation … would make? I know that it would be an extremely bad one'. He ended by saying that he had written on the subject in another letter which Iswolsky was free to use as he saw fit.[64] Presumably, he meant that Iswolsky might want to show it to Nicholas II and the members of the government. Referring to a persistent rumour about Iswolsky's pending resignation, he exclaimed: '*[For] Heaven's sake*, or rather, for *ours*, think well'. He ended with a reprimand: 'Autocracy or not, the times when a minister was no more than a servant of a monarch and this latter assumed responsibility are gone … Besides, you are still winning'.[65]

On another occasion, when Iswolsky complained about his exhaustion and his enemies' intrigues,[66] Benckendorff answered sharply that, domestic troubles apart, Iswolsky was lucky because since he had become minister he had not faced any serious external crises thanks to the détente produced by the Anglo-Russian talks.[67] He encouraged Iswolsky's initiative in speaking to the Duma and the press:

> Now that foreign policy everywhere has transcended the walls of Cabinets, our silence … would create confusion, doubts and mistrust in Russia and abroad and lead to all sorts of intrigues and flights of fancy in the press, and, given the lack of discipline which characterizes our press, it would become more and more dangerous. You have filled in this gap.[68]

62 Iswolsky to A.K. Benckendorff, 08/21.06.1906, BC2, box 13.
63 Stolypin to Iswolsky, 12.06.1906, P.A. Stolypin, *Perepiska*, 99.
64 A.K. Benckendorff to Iswolsky, 05/18.03.1908, *Au service*, 2: 144–5.
65 A.K. Benckendorff to Iswolsky, 09/22.01.1908, *Au service*, 2: 117–20.
66 Iswolsky to A.K. Benckendorff, 14/27.09.1906, *Au service*, 1: 377–9.
67 A.K. Benckendorff to Iswolsky, 27.06/10.07.1907, *Au service*, 2: 62.
68 A.K. Benckendorff to Iswolsky, 03/16.03.1908, *Au service*, 2: 136–40.

Benckendorff made sure that the minister had his opinion on every political issue, as well as was given general guidelines on how to conduct Russian foreign policy and recommendations on the posting of diplomats. The prestige of Russia was low in the eyes of Europe: 'some accuse us all of treachery … others, of organized indiscipline, chaos'.[69] Attempts to cover up problems would not repair Russia's reputation.[70] Openness and frankness were the only way for a diplomat. He commended British diplomacy for its straightforward character and assured Iswolsky that Russia's interests required that its diplomats have absolutely clean hands. Only on this condition would Russian diplomacy have the moral right to sit in judgment on others.[71] The count meant mostly that diplomats should not be caught red-handed. He did not go to the extreme of rejecting the common practices of the diplomats. He did not refuse to buy secret documents, though he despised those who sold them; he cultivated his 'confidential sources' and understood the occasional need for bribery, for example when it was necessary to make Russian newspapers' tone more favourable to Britain.[72]

In preaching a new ethical conduct in the relations with Britain, he insisted that 'to return to discussing a subject after a promise had been made, is not correct'. Iswolsky ought to feel bound by a promise which Lamsdorff had made a year before in a conversation with Spring Rice. He praised Iswolsky for having found out about this verbal engagement by his predecessor: 'Were it not for your political instinct we would have been drawn into a dishonest action which would have built an insurmountable wall between us and England or any other Power'. Had he, Benckendorff, been forced to explain to the Foreign Office that the Russian Tsar and his foreign minister did not know about this promise, no one would have believed him.[73] Benckendorff was right that the British would not give the benefit of the doubt to the Russians in a case like this first of all because of their low opinion of Russians, and secondly, by that time European diplomats had talked themselves into a state of mind where they saw sinister calculation in every move of their opponents and allies. Yet Russian actions which the British regarded as devious or sinister often were the result of incompetence or disorganization in the system where few officials had full knowledge of the contents of the Chancellery's files, documents got lost, instructions were forgotten, and only gossiping tongues worked tirelessly to produce false rumours and leaks of secret information.

Benckendorff shared Iswolsky's low opinion of the diplomatic agents posted in Asia and of the ministry's First Department. Referring to Hartwig's inquiry, he wrote haughtily: 'Despite all my appreciation of Hartwig's qualities, he is taking a line … which is far from *sound.* … he wants to make me, or worse, Russia, a

69 A.K. Benckendorff to Iswolsky, 08/21.08.1906, *Au service*, 1: 352–6.

70 A.K. Benckendorff to Iswolsky, 08/21.08.1906, *Au service*, 1: 352–6.

71 A.K. Benckendorff to Iswolsky, 08/21.08.1906, *Au service*, 1: 352–6.

72 A.K. Benckendorff to Sazonov, 19.12.1915/01.01.1916, AVPRI, f.134, op.473, d.103, l.26.

73 A.K. Benckendorff to Iswolsky, 23.08/05.09.1906, *Au service*, 1: 358–63.

laughing stock'.[74] The leading lights of the department, the two friends agreed, had to be transferred away from St Petersburg; otherwise, their criticism of Iswolsky's concessions might endanger the cooperation with Britain.[75] Benckendorff sympathized when the minister complained about the opposition he met among the officials familiar with Asia: 'These so-called experts are a pest'. He advised the minister to deal with the First department in the British way: send the Oriental experts to the West and those from Western Europe to the East. He suggested that the troublesome Hartwig could be posted to Switzerland and a 'young, honest and unprejudiced man' – the reverse of Hartwig? – could replace him in Teheran.[76] He watched out for those who did not toe his line and asked Iswolsky to look closer at the activity of the Russian minister in China: 'It seems to me that Korostovetz has strayed off the path. The tone of his letters is exactly like that of the good old times when we [and Britain] were adversaries'.[77]

Steering the Middle Course

Iswolsky's regular references to the need for Russia to be on good terms with Germany, vexed his Entente colleagues and annoyed Benckendorff.[78] To reassure Germany, the Russian minister kept the British military at arm's length. When Sir John French, inspector-general of the army, and Winston Churchill, president of the Board of Trade, in 1907[79] and 1908[80] respectively, expressed interest in attending the Russian manoeuvres, both requests were politely declined. In a more positive spirit, Iswolsky planned a rapprochement with Germany on the basis of a Baltic Sea agreement which he had discussed with von Schoen in 1904–5. It seemed natural because Germany and Russia were favourable to the imminent dissolution of the Swedish-Norwegian Union[81] in 1905. Russia was the first European state to recognize Norwegian territorial integrity and her next planned step was to obtain the abrogation of the 1855 Canrobert convention, guaranteeing Swedish-Norwegian territorial integrity against Russia. Iswolsky needed to get France and Britain, the signatories of the 1856 Peace of Paris, to agree to the abrogation.

Since the summer of 1905, Lamsdorff had been preparing the grounds for the abolition of this post-Crimean war document which perpetuated the climate

74 A.K. Benckendorff to Iswolsky, 26.07/08.08.1906, *Au service de la Russie*, 1: 342.

75 Iswolsky to A.K. Benckendorff, 31.08/13.09.1906, *Au service*, 1: 366.

76 A.K. Benckendorff to Iswolsky, 08/21.08.1907, *Au service*, 2: 82–4.

77 A.K. Benckendorff to Iswolsky, 07/20.01.1909, *Au service*, 2: 191–3.

78 Barrère to Pichon, 20.04.1907, DDF, X: 765–6.

79 Iswolsky to A.K. Benckendorff, 14/27.03.1907, BC2, box 13.

80 Iswolsky to A.K. Benckendorff, 18.06/01.07.1908, BC2, box 13.

81 Freiherr von Schoen, 15.

of hostility to Russia. Iswolsky took up the idea but gave it a character which Lamsdorff had opposed.[82]

He suggested to Schoen to replicate the Anglo-Russian convention by a similar Russo-German one about the Baghdad railway and a Baltic accord whereby the Baltic states adhered to the *status quo* in the region.[83] The sleeping dog which Iswolsky woke by his first step was the question of the Åland Isles, situated at the entrance of the three gulfs. A naval station there would have allowed the Russian government to control the maritime traffic near the Russian coastline, which was why after the Crimean war Russia was forbidden to fortify them. As the Baltic accord would recognize the principle of the status quo of all the actual possessions of the coastal states, it was necessary to exclude the Åland Isles or the ban on building fortifications there would become perpetual.

Iswolsky began negotiations with Sweden and Germany in Berlin and in St Petersburg, at the same time as he made enquiries in Paris and London. In January 1907 Iswolsky sent to London the Russian counter-draft regarding the Norwegian draft treaty and Grey told Benckendoff that, with small modifications, it was acceptable. He wanted to please Iswolsky and in doing so stimulate the ongoing Anglo-Russian talks.[84] But, unsuspected by Benckendorff, Norwegian neutrality which was stipulated in the Russian counter-draft, was the subject of much debate among the French and the British. France pointed out that if Sweden and Denmark also became permanently neutral, it might mean the closure of the Baltic straits to France and Britain.[85] Norwegian neutrality was unacceptable to the Foreign Office and the CID, for it would allow Germany to use Danish ports during a war while Britain could not use the Norwegian ones. Grey wanted 'neutrality' omitted in the draft, but he was afraid to arouse suspicions in the Scandinavian countries. When, against his hopes, in June France, Germany and Norway accepted the second Russian counter-draft with the 'absolute neutrality' clause, his position became difficult. If he rejected it, Britain would be guilty of undermining an agreement.[86] A week later, Benckendorff presented to Grey a memorandum regarding the abolition of the Åland Isles' servitudes. Iswolsky argued that the recent war with Japan had destroyed the equilibrium in the Baltic Sea, where Russia no longer had a navy, leaving Germany in control of the Baltic. The fortification of the islands would restore the equilibrium. This gave Grey a pretext for refusing to adhere to the Norwegian neutrality. He refused to raise the restrictions on the Åland Isles until Sweden agreed. Otherwise, he said, it would push Sweden into Germany's arms.[87]

82 Paul Cambon to Pichon, 08.11.1907, DDF, XI: 324–5.

83 Freiherr von Schoen, 30.

84 Foreign Office, *Minutes*, 22.01.1907, BD, VIII: 103.

85 David W. Sweet, 'The Baltic in British Diplomacy before 1914', in *Historical Journal*, 13, 3 (September 1970), 461.

86 Ibid., 464.

87 A.K. Benckendorff to Iswolsky, 27.06/10.07.1907, *Au service de la Russie*, 2: 63.

Benckendorff did not see Grey's motives and assured Iswolsky that the Foreign Secretary did not want to make concessions until he signed the Anglo-Russian convention because it would give Russia all her desires: 'It is somewhat like the Bosporus [issue]'.[88] His conclusion was that, by promptly signing the convention, Iswolsky would solve this problem and he repeated Grey's complaint that the Åland issue complicated a very simple matter. Grey suggested to have all the old treaties replaced by one, which meant that the issues would have to be considered by a conference.

Iswolsky dropped the subject of the Islands because his priority was to sign a convention with Norway, but the British still informed Sweden about Iswolsky's confidential request to Grey regarding the Islands, and blamed Russia for the delay in the signing. Iswolsky complained to the ambassador about the British indiscretion. He was ready to accept Grey's proposal, even though he did not see why Grey was so anxious to replace Norwegian 'neutrality' with 'integrity'.[89] Benckendorff did not see it either, and replied that Grey would have agreed if it were not for the risk of pushing Sweden towards Germany.[90] Iswolsky's third proposal had no 'neutrality' in it.

During the emperors' meeting at Swinemünde in July 1907, Iswolsky proposed to Bülow a secret agreement to exclude all but the coastal states from participation in the Baltic affairs. He also suggested special agreements with Sweden and Denmark to recognize their territorial integrity and guarantee the status quo in the Baltic region. The meeting made all European diplomats dig in their memory for Iswolsky's earlier revelations and soon Spring Rice wrote from Teheran that, according to Hartwig, the foreign minister had long cherished a dream of a Baltic accord with Germany and Sweden to close the straits into the Baltic Sea.[91] Benckendorff's explanation, that Iswolsky went to Swinemünde largely to make sure that the Russian political course did not swerve towards reaction, did not convince either Cambon or King Edward,[92] who at once let Iswolsky know through Benckendorff that he wanted to meet him.[93] In August, Iswolsky not only met the king but also Clemenceau who found him gloomy and nervous about the Entente's insistence on involving Russia in a coalition against Germany.[94] And no wonder, for Clemenceau talked to the king mostly about the inevitability of an Anglo-German war and the need for Britain to begin building a land army.[95]

Benckendorff contributed to Iswolsky's doubts about the efficacy of balancing. In every personal letter he wrote about the German plots against Britain (which

88 A.K. Benckendoff to Iswolsky, 10/23.07.1907, *Au service de la Russie*, 2: 66–69.
89 Iswolsky to A.K. Benckendorff, 04/17.07.1907, BC2, box 13.
90 A.K. Benckendorff to Iswolsky, 10/27.07.1907, *Au service*, 2: 66–9.
91 Grey to F. Bertie, 07.11.1907, BD, 8: 135–6.
92 Paul Cambon to Pichon, 08.08.1907, DDF, XI: 208–10.
93 A.K. Benckendorff to Iswolsky, 23.07/05.08.1907, *Au service*, 2: 77–8.
94 Clemenceau to Pichon, 02.09.1908, DDF, XI: 760–3.
95 Joseph Caillaux, *Mes memoires, 1863–1909* (Paris, 1942), 1: 269.

now involved Russia): 'the relations between England and Germany are the pivot of all the difficulties'.[96]

When Germany proposed modifications to Iswolsky's draft, finding it too anti-British,[97] Iswolsky agreed, but pressed Germany to accept his plan for a secret treaty.[98] On 16/29 October 1907 at St Petersburg, von Schoen and Iswolsky's deputy minister Konstantin Goubastov signed a secret treaty whereby Germany and Russia promised to support each other during the discussions of the Baltic agreement and Germany confirmed that it would not oppose an eventual abrogation of the Åland servitude.[99] The agreement was to remain secret until they agreed to make it public.[100] Forty-eight hours later Britain's ambassador to France informed Grey that the French were worried about Iswolsky's secret agreement with Germany.[101] Soon Benckendorff warned Iswolsky that Germany was trying to create a rift between Russia and Britain by approaching first one and then the other and advised him to hold fast to the British friendship or else he would lose everything.[102]

Two weeks later, the German ambassador in London and Iswolsky in Petersburg informed Grey and Nicolson respectively about the Russo-German-Swedish negotiations. They described their goal as being similar to the Anglo-Franco-Spanish agreement about the Mediterranean status quo, with Sweden's position being identical to that of Spain. The German government wanted to supplement it with an identical North Sea agreement to which Britain would be a party but Russia would not.[103] Grey agreed to discuss it, provided that France was also invited. The identical timing and the wording of the explanations indicates that Russia and Germany had agreed to reveal their negotiations, but the North Sea agreement was a German improvization and Iswolsky was mortified. He saw his secret talks as a reassurance to Germany and a lesson to France. It turned out that Germany did not appreciate the reassurance, but used it for approaching Britain, while leaving him behind. He complained: 'It is one of the disadvantages of our present weakness and of the need to cater to both sides'. He repeated that he did not see any difference between his secret talks with Germany and Sweden and Franco-British-Spanish secret talks in May:

> … if the Anglo-Franco-Spanish agreement has not produced protests from us, why would a document, or rather two documents which are its exact copies, arouse England's protests? Certainly, Paris will not be too happy, but it will be a

96 A.K. Benckendorff to Iswolsky, 03/16.03.1908, *Au service*, 2: 136–40.
97 A.V. Ignatiev, *Vneshna'ia politika Rossii v 1905–1907 gg.* (Moscow, 1986), 208.
98 Ibid., 209.
99 M. Taube, *Zarnitsy*, 100.
100 A.V. Ignatiev, 210.
101 M. de Taube, *La politique russe*, 158.
102 A.K. Benckendorff to Iswolsky, 08/21.11.1907, *Au service*, 2: 92–94.
103 Grey to Count de Salis, 04.12.1907, BD, 8: 137–8.

> good lesson to the French government, to teach them that they cannot treat us as a negligible quantity, as they have done on many occasions lately.[104]

The British and the French thought that Iswolsky was forced into this situation by Germany to break up the Anglo-Russian convention and force France to follow a German policy.[105] Benckendorff warned Iswolsky that Grey was concerned about Russo-French frictions caused by the French suspicions, and praised Grey for trying to calm the French. In his efforts, Grey went as far as to tell the French government that he found their ambassador to Russia 'insuffisant'.[106]

Poklevsky was not convinced by Iswolsky's arguments in favour of the Baltic accord and suspected that it was the minister's retribution for Britain's attitude in the Norwegian question.[107] Benckendorff warned Iswolsky that the British were suspicious of his explanations because of 'certain damaging indiscretions', which he blamed on the Germans. He pointed to the risk of Russia turning to Germany: 'The [Franco-Russian] alliance is not endangered, they need it too much, but it has been depreciated since our war and since the rapprochement with Britain on which they count very much'.[108] Benckendorff, nervous by his own admission, approved of Iswolsky's 'little lesson' to France, but repeated that the minister should keep in touch with Grey on all issues for the sake of Anglo-Russian and Franco-Russian relations. He emphasized that '[A] secret Russo-German negotiation concerning an affair in which Grey had been involved from the beginning, has produced distaste here…' and, besides, it had been unnecessary. Grey understood Russia's interests and the fewer secrets there were between him and Iswolsky, the better it would be for Russo-German relations; but secrets shared with Germany, on the contrary, would be a weapon in Germany's hands against Russia.[109]

Next Poklevsky reported that the Baltic accord met with Swedish opposition. Sweden and Germany were trying to push Iswolsky further than his loyalty to the Entente permitted, but the minister promised to remain loyal to his commitment. Poklevsky and Iswolsky realized that if negotiations with Sweden about the Åland Isles failed, Russia would be open to blackmail by the secret treaty with Germany:

> [There] still remains the document which you saw and whose existence itself is in a flagrant contradiction with our new political orientation. It is true that the document is secret, but can we be certain of Germany? What a pity that these negotiations were initiated at all. The existence of this document is also

104 Iswolsky to A.K. Benckendorff, 22.11/05.12.1907, BC2, box 13.
105 R. Lister to Grey, 11.12.1907, BD, 8: 145.
106 A.K. Benckendorff to Iswolsky, 12/25.12.1907, *Au service*, 2: 100–4.
107 Poklevsky to A.K. Benckendorff, 08/21.12.1907, BC2, box 14.
108 A.K. Benckendorff to Iswolsky, 20.11/11.12.1907, *Au service*, 2: 95–9.
109 A.K. Benckendorff to Iswolsky, 12/25.12. 1907, *Au service*, 100–4.

> an insurmountable obstacle to the acceptance of Grey's proposal regarding the Åland Isles.[110]

When Benckendorff wrote on a different occasion that 'shallow and slippery machiavellism' usually brought paltry political results,[111] he may have been describing Iswolsky's Baltic accord. It gained nothing for Russia and undermined the minister's reputation. It also left Benckendorff's reputation under a cloud in Petersburg. Years later, Taube wrote: '[Although] there is no positive proof which would allow accusing Count Benckendorff, of… giving away M. Iswolsky's secret [treaty] to London, the minister never hesitated in pinpointing him'. Taube said that the deputy minister Goubastov was dismissed for having leaked the secret to his old friend Benckendorff.[112]

In his reply to Poklevsky, written for Iswolsky's benefit, Benckendorff made a point: the negotiations with Germany had demonstrated that Russia could not maintain the same relations with Germany in the Baltic region as she had with Britain in Asia, because Germany intended to separate Russia from the Entente. Russia could establish neighbourly relations with Germany only after restoring French and English confidence in her loyalty by being firm in her opposition to Germany. After November 1907 he thought it was safe to do so, because the Germans could not seriously think of war unless they achieved Russia's isolation:

> Then there would have been a danger, even a certainty of war. That is why I believe we can and must strengthen our international ties and at least temporarily suspend our attempts at direct negotiations with the Berlin cabinet. I am speaking purely *from the point of view of Russia's interests* … The sad truth, after all, is that the French army and the English navy ensure the security of the Russo-German frontier; the Baltic Sea is mostly our interest, because England has only secondary interests there … In Persia England is almost in retreat, how shall we protect our gains without the Franco-English combination …? At the same time England almost does not need us to protect the only place which interests her, the Persian Gulf. Berlin knows that and that is why they are trying to isolate us. Ignoring the German onslaught has not been too profitable to us and might even cost us in the future.[113]

Iswolsky extricated himself from this situation by transforming the secret agreement into an open one signed by four powers instead of two, just as Grey proposed. On 23 April 1908 the Baltic agreement was signed in St Petersburg

---

110 Poklevsky to A.K. Benckendorff, 20.12.1907/02.01.1908, BC2, box 14.

111 A.K. Benckendorff to Empress Maria Feodorovna, 05./[18].10.1906, GARF, f.642, op.1, ed.hr.917, ll.72–7 ob.

112 M. de Taube, *La politique russe*, 161.

113 A.K. Benckendorff to Poklevsky, 25.12.1907/07.01.1908, GARF, 1126, op.1, ed.hr.10, ll.10–15 ob.

and the North Sea agreement, in Berlin. Hardinge wrote to Nicolson that the agreements were worthless because if Germany tried to close the Danish Straits, Britain would ignore the neutrality of Norway.[114] Hardinge found – and time showed him to be right – that German policy was inevitably driving Iswolsky into Britain's arms.[115] Taube also believed that the scandalous revelation of Iswolsky's secret dealings with Germany made the minister even more pliable and docile with the British.[116]

The Baghdad Railway

Despite the failure of his first attempt at a 'balancing policy', Iswolsky would not rest. He had other issues to settle with Germany. He explained to Nicolson early on that for Russia, the Baghdad railway was a Persian issue. He hoped to get German guarantees that no lines would cut across Russia's commercial routes. Russia had never negotiated the terms of her participation in the Baghdad railway and only promised in exchange to cease the opposition to the project. Iswolsky believed that the negotiations were likely to fail anyway and counted on Britain's support to oppose German penetration of Persia. In the case of four-party discussions, Russia would be free from commitments but the British should not be surprised if at times Russia would side with Germany.[117] During Iswolsky's first visit to Berlin, in 1906, he gave Bülow a memorandum regarding Russia's interests in the railway project and Russian and German interests in Persia. The German side delayed its reply. A year later, in November 1907, Benckendorff reported that Grey agreed to discuss the Baghdad railway with Germany, provided Russia and France participated. The new German foreign minister and former ambassador in Russia, Schoen told Grey that prior to the negotiations he would have to consult Iswolsky because only Iswolsky's illness had prevented Russia and Germany from achieving an agreement.[118] Benckendorff at once reassured Grey that Russo-German negotiations were only about Russia's favourable attitude to the project and moreover, they had stalled. He also asked Iswolsky to calm Britain and France, or else they would turn to Germany.[119] In December 1907, amidst the uneasiness produced in the Entente by the Baltic affair, Poklevsky informed Benckendorff that the German reply to Iswolsky's 1906 Baghdad railway memorandum contained practically the opposite of Russia's wishes. Germany agreed not to seek concessions in Persia, but failed to recognize Russia's political and strategic interests there and demanded Russia's engagement to build a line in Persia, which would connect to a branch

114 Hardinge to Nicolson, 05.02.1908, BD, 8: 164–5.
115 Hardinge to Nicolson, 21.01.1908, BD, 8: 160–1.
116 M.de Taube, *La politique russe*, 159.
117 Iswolsky to A.K.Benckendorff, 22.11/05.12, 1907, BC2, box 13.
118 A.K. Benckendorff to Iswolsky, 05/18.11.1907, GARF, f.559, op.1, d.43, ll.3–4.
119 A.K. Benckendorff to Iswolsky, 29.11/11.12.1907, *Au service*, 2: 95–9.

of the projected German Baghdad–Sadidje–Khanekin railway. Poklevsky advised the minister to drop the negotiations with Germany and side with Britain. Iswolsky agreed in principle to break negotiations with Germany and keep England up-to-date concerning Russia's position, but not before seeing what new instructions the German ambassador, Count von Pourtalès, brought to Petersburg. Poklevsky insisted that if Russia accepted the German proposals then it would not be able to discuss the political side of the enterprise at the time of the envisaged four-party discussions, and '… considering the bad impression produced in France and England by our Baltic accord, it would be a good policy to march with these two powers at least in the Baghdad question'.[120] This letter shows why Taube believed that the backhanded dealings in the Baltic accord led to Iswolsky's solicitous behaviour towards Britain – not without pressure from the London embassy.

When Count von Pourtalès said that the Windsor talks were a formality and that there would be no four-party negotiations any time soon, Iswolsky lost the main reason to take a position similar to that of England and France. Poklevsky explained:

> He decided to drag out his separate talks in the hope that the break would come from the German side. He even instructed me to compose our counter-proposals which had to 1) reiterate our initial demands, and 2) include everything that he said on the subject in the last letter he wrote to you. It was all to be communicated to London and Paris in confidence.
>
> Before taking up this ungrateful task I implored Iswolsky to wait for your answer. He agreed, and in the meanwhile the German attitude in Persia took such an anti-Russian turn that yesterday Iswolsky told me not to hurry with the writing and the sending of our counter-proposals.[121]

Benckendorff's long reply discussed the Baltic affair, the Baghdad railway and Persia, but the main point was the need for Iswolsky to break away from Germany:

> You say that Aleksandr Petrovich [Iswolsky], influenced by Germany's behaviour in Teheran decided to change his decisions about the talks in Berlin. This was inevitable. Why should we postpone the presentation of our counter-proposals regarding Baghdad? It might be better to take advantage of their confirmed underhanded actions in order to present them with counter-proposals which are unacceptable to them. I believe we should not change a single line. If we modify them even a little the atmosphere will be like it was during the Baltic Sea talks. What then?

120 Poklevsky to A.K. Benckendorff, 08/21.12.1907, BC2, box 14.
121 Poklevsky to A.K. Benckendorff, 20.12.1907/02.01.1908, BC2, box 14.

> … The Baghdad railway and England: on the one side what Pourtalès told Iswolsky is true. Grey also believes that the discussions were 'academic'… Grey is ready to discuss anything with Germany for the sake of a détente. But he counts on us after our declarations.[122]

Iswolsky decided to stop the negotiations under the pretext advised by Benckendorff, of being angered by German activity in Persia; the German side did not insist, fearing a conflict.[123] Benckendorff explained to Iswolsky that Germany's goal had been to demonstrate to Grey that Russo-German negotiations were of a general character while the Anglo-Russian convention was only local.[124]

The Convention in Persia

Poklevsky shuttled between Benckendorff and Iswolsky, but in December 1907 he wrote: 'There are rumours in society about my pending departure from London, but Iswolsky has not returned to this subject and, I confess, I am very pleased'.[125] Iswolsky and Benckendorff indeed had other plans for their friend: he was the man to tackle the greatest test of the Anglo-Russian convention, Persia.

Persian events were gathering momentum. The shah confirmed the constitution in January 1907 and died soon after. In June 1908 the new, pro-Russian shah successfully used his personal guard, the misnamed 'Cossack brigade' (Persian soldiers commanded by a dozen Russian officers) to crush nationalist opposition. But in July 1908, the Young Turks' coup, the Anglo-Russian convention (which implied to them a pending partition of their country) and the absence of Russian support for the shah encouraged the nationalists to stage another uprising. After a year of growing disorder, the nationalists took Teheran in July 1909 and the shah abdicated. His son became a constitutional ruler in an unruly empire under an ineffective parliament.

British policy in Persia followed several imperatives: to keep Russian influence contained in the northern sphere; to prevent the collapse of Persia which would lead to the disappearance of the buffer between Russia and British territories; to promote closer economic and strategic ties between India and the adjacent Persian territories; and to protect the British position in the Gulf. Direct military intervention in Persia was too costly and politically undesirable as it would put an end to any appearance of Persian integrity and thus defeat the purpose of the Anglo-Russian convention. It would also jeopardize any support which the Entente might require from the Russian army in Europe. British diplomats, besides sharing

122 A.K. Benckendorff to Poklevsky, 25.12.1907/07.01.1908, GARF, f.1126, op.1, ed.hr.10, ll.10–15 ob.

123 I. Astaf'iev, 105.

124 A.K. Benckendorff to Iswolsky, 08/21.11.1907, *Au service*, 2: 92.

125 Poklevsky to A.K. Benckendorff, 08/21.12.1907, BC2, box 14.

with their countrymen a sympathetic view of a 'reform movement' and dislike for the shah's despotism, realized that a nationalist triumph would work to Britain's advantage, as Russian influence in Persia was based on ties to the Qadjar dynasty. For the same reasons separatists were easier for the British to manipulate than the central government in Teheran.

Russia's security required the control of the areas contiguous to the restless Caucasian border. It imposed the need for controlling the roads leading into the northern region and preventing railway construction in the area for as long as Russia could not afford to build them. Railways would bring in foreign commerce and allow third powers to claim that they needed to defend their interests in Persia. The Far Eastern situation would re-play itself in Central Asia. Russia had obtained a guarantee of no railroad construction in Persia till 1910; but beyond that she could only fight off the competition from other powers by supporting a central authority weak enough to give in to Russia's pressure and only strong enough to keep the country in economic and political limbo.[126] Russian society, including Nicholas II, resented being the policeman of Persia[127] and agreed that reforms were necessary and that standing in their way was futile. But among the Russian officials, only Benckendorff and Poklevsky believed that these abstract ideas constituted a workable policy. The Russian consuls in Persia were dealing with present-day realities and their duty was to prevent political sedition from spreading to Russia, to protect Russian commercial interests in Persia, to stem the flow of contraband into Russia and to assert Russia's prestige in the eyes of the local population. As a result, British ministers at Teheran complained of the Russian ministers' abetting and assisting the 'reactionary' government.[128] The Russian minister, Hartwig, complained about Britain encouraging the anti-government 'revolutionaries', despite the Anglo-Russian agreement to keep out of Persia's domestic affairs.[129] As early as March 1907 Iswolsky planned to get rid of Hartwig after the convention was signed,[130] because the man was complicating Anglo-Russian relations with his efforts to consolidate Russia's position in Teheran.

Hartwig sent reports of the connections between Persian 'agitators' and extremist groups in the Russian Caucasus. He warned that disorders were threatening the whole country if they spread, so he asked for Britain's support on the Seistan-Gulf border; but, Spring Rice refused, saying that the disorders were close to the Russian zone and thus not a British concern.[131] Nevertheless, after the murder of a Russian subject during riots, in December 1907, Iswolsky was compelled to ask the war minister to station two Russian army detachments on the

126 Nicolson to Grey, 14.11.1907, BD, 4: 607–9.

127 Poklevsky to A.K. Benckendorff, 15/28.07.1909, BC2, box 14.

128 Keith Robbins, *Sir Edward Grey*, 195.

129 De la Martinière to Pichon, 03.02.1908, DDF XI, 465–6.

130 Poklevsky to A.K. Benckendorff, 15/28.03.1907, BC2, box 14.

131 Hartwig to Iswolsky, 31.1/13.2.1907, GARF, f.1126, op.1, ed.hr.32, 1.

border. The war minister refused, saying that it would be the first step to an armed intervention which would draw Russia into a new adventure.[132] Iswolsky was placed between a rock and a hard place: Benckendorff described the damaging consequences of an intervention to his pro-Entente course, while Hartwig warned that if nothing was done Russia's security would suffer. Benckendorff's position had not changed since 1906 when his heartfelt advice was:

> When Somov [a Russian consul] says that he defends Russian interests as well as Persian ones, he opens the door to an accusation of interference in Persian domestic affairs. He should look after Anglo-Russian interests which would be quite a handful, and as for Persian interests, who knows what they are.[133]

Benckendorff told Grey that Iswolsky did not want military intervention, but if it became unavoidable, he would do nothing without previous consultation.[134] Grey did not deny Russia's right or need to police the northern zone and tried to go along with it insofar as compliance with Russian actions did not threaten the Liberal government's position. Nicolson's representations and Grey's complaints to Benckendorff transmitted to St Petersburg as the ambassador's advice, delayed the entry of the Russian troops into Persia by half a year, until April 1909.[135]

In a conflict between the two Teheran legations, Poklevsky and Benckendorff sided with the British unreservedly.[136] Iswolsky tried to keep the middle line, insisting that at the moment of crisis both ministers in Teheran proved their inability to rise above local issues.[137] Benckendorff blamed Hartwig for endangering the convention. If the convention failed, then anarchy would reign in Persia, which would be fatal for Russia's interests anyway.[138] Benckendorff insisted on Hartwig's recall and on personally discussing the latter's replacement with the Foreign Office prior to any appointment by Iswolsky.[139]

When Spring Rice came from Persia Benckendorff told this trusted friend, in secret, that Hartwig would be recalled and sought his opinion about the situation. Spring Rice naturally suggested that in order not to push the Persian constitutionalists into Germany's embrace Russia and Britain should avoid getting embroiled in Persian affairs:

---

132 A. Rediger, *Istori'ia moei zhizni: Vospominani'ia voennogo ministra* (Moscow, 1999), vol.2, 195.

133 A.K. Benckendorff to Iswolsky, 27.07/09.08.1906, *Au service*, vol.1, 347.

134 Paul Cambon to Pichon, 08.03.1907, DDF, X: 681–2.

135 David McLean, *Britain and Her Buffer State: The Collapse of the Persian Empire, 1890–1914* (London,1979), 81.

136 Poklevsky to A.K. Benckendorff, 02.07.1908, BC2, box 14.

137 Iswolsky to A.K. Benckendorff, 18.06/01.07.1908, BC2, box 13.

138 A.K. Benckendorff to Iswolsky, 19.06/02.07. 1908, *Au service*, 2: 172–7.

139 A.K. Benckendorff to Iswolsky, 09/22.07.1908, *Au service*, 2: 182–5.

> I would think the best course is to leave Persia alone as much as possible … I cannot imagine any true friend of Russia desiring to encourage her to raise the Persian question at present. Hartwig and I were agreed on that. My advice is 'Do nothing whatever'.[140]

If Russia did nothing, the nationalists and the constitutional regime would be strengthened, which would work for the British interests. So this friendly advice, which Benckendorff supported, was not popular in the Russian legation in Persia. They saw what David McLean described as 'a flexible interpretation of non-interference' by the British: the pro-British nationalists received help but when the shah asked for financial assistance, non-interference was invoked.[141] All the while, Benckendorff assured Iswolsky: 'The British government wants to maintain the dynasty'.[142]

Benckendorff wrote that the best choice for Teheran would be a man who understood that 'Anglo-Russian cooperation in Persia was not a means [for Russia to improve her position], but the goal', to which everything was to be sacrificed. Poklevsky would be the best choice because he was intelligent and energetic, with a deep knowledge of the political situation (that is, the priorities of the Entente). His second advantage was that he was known to the British and they would not suspect him of foul play.[143] Most importantly for Benckendorff, Edward VII approved of Poklevsky's candidature.[144]

As the situation deteriorated Iswolsky came to see that if the two powers continued to deny the shah financial support to consolidate his authority, an armed intervention in northern Persia would become the only way to protect Russia's interests in the country.[145] He complained about the London cabinet's pedantic attachment to the magic word 'constitution':

> Well, the constitution alone cannot restore order in Persia, and money and reforms are needed, accompanied by a necessary amount of control. If we keep beating about the bush instead of dealing with the question, we risk letting Persia collapse into anarchy and dissolution, and then armed intervention will become unavoidable. Things are complicated by the fact that here Persian policy has become practically a domestic issue and I am attacked on these grounds.[146]

Benckendorff replied that the British would not agree to a loan to the shah without guarantees of reforms[147] and cited the opinions of veteran British colonial

140 Spring Rice to A.K. Benckendorff, 06.12.1907, BC2, box 14.

141 David McLean, 90.

142 A.K. Benckendorff to Iswolsky (draft), 10/23.06.1908, GARF, f.1126, op.1, d.10. l.1.

143 A. K. Benckendorff to Iswolsky, 23.06/06.07.1908, *Au service*, 2: 177–82.

144 A.K. Benckendorff to Iswolsky, 21.07/03.08.1908, *Au service*, 2: 186–8.

145 A. Rediger, *Istori'ia moei zhizni*, 2: 263.

146 Iswolsky to A.K. Benckendorff, 15/28.01.1909, BC2, box 13.

147 A.K. Benckendorff to Iswolsky, 21.12.1908/03.01.1909, *Au service*, 2: 188–9.

administrators about the benefits of a constitution for an Asian empire, conveniently forgetting that these statesmen had not granted constitutions to Britain's Asian colonies. On Benckendorff's insistence, Hartwig, whom the British considered 'the brains of the Foreign Ministry',[148] was sacrificed to the Anglo-Russian convention by the minister who was unable to control him. The British minister remained in Teheran.

The new Russian first secretary in Teheran, Evgueni Sablin, arrived with instructions to support the Anglo-Russian convention above all. He remained in charge of the legation until mid-1909. He complained that while he was trying to improve relations with the British diplomats and the Persian nationalists, his colleagues in other posts warned him: 'The motherland will curse you but Count Benckendorff and Sir Edward Grey will approve of you for selling Persia to the English'.[149] This is how for some Russian diplomats Benckendorff's name by 1909 had become a synonym for betrayal.

Chaos reigned in Persia, but Iswolsky's and Grey's representatives continued to insist that order would ensue as soon as the impotent and bankrupt government implemented reforms. When the situation in Persia worsened, Grey agreed to Russian troops advancing to Tabriz against the shah's army which besieged the city. Iswolsky's deputy minister wrote to London that he expected the Foreign Office was pleased with the fact that Russian troops were ordered to march on Tabriz only after Nicolson had asked for it, in the same spirit of cooperation which had caused St Petersburg to cancel the advance of the troops into Persia in the autumn of 1908 'on a simple hint from Sir Edward Grey'.[150] The Russian army entered Tabriz in April 1909 when the siege endangered Russian subjects' lives and properties and brought the inhabitants to the verge of starvation. By 1914 Russian military force in Persia had reached 20,000 soldiers, putting at risk the existence of the convention.[151]

The Russian occupation force neither supported the shah nor tried to stop the nationalists from taking Teheran, thus complying with the convention. The chaos continued. Poklevsky wrote to London prior to his departure for Persia:

> … the last actions of our troops were not authorized and we are trying to have their number reduced, but Iswolsky is very much afraid that the Cabinet will oppose him, because of the prestige and vanity. Iswolsky is sincerely upset because the good effect created by despatching our troops to Tabriz will be considerably diminished.[152]

A partial withdrawal of the Russian army brought some relief to Benckendorff, but he did not stop reminding Iswolsky of the Indian party in Britain which was

148 5th Earl of Onslow, 107.

149 E. Sablin to Savinsky, 05/18.12.1908, AVPRI, f.340, op.806, d.14, ll.172–7 ob.

150 Tcharykow to A.K. Benckendorff, 09/22.04.1909, BC2, box 12.

151 David McLean, *Britain and Her Buffer State*, 81.

152 Poklevsky to A.K. Benckendorff, 21.05/03.06.1909, BC2, box 14.

predicting that Russia's next step would be the annexation of Persia and the disappearance of the buffer state. He hastened to say that the Indian party in itself was of no consequence but the Germans might take advantage of this mood to harm Russia's image in Britain.[153]

Poklevsky's appointment was settled between Nicholas II and Edward VII at Cowes. Prior to leaving for Persia he was confident that he would be able to serve Anglo-Russian relations by doing everything in agreement with Sir Edward Grey. He would have no meetings with the deposed shah, show no sympathy for his followers and would cooperate with the new constitutional government of Persia:

> The Emperor, the government and public opinion are delighted that our troops did not advance beyond Kasvin. The Emperor told me … that he did not want to be the policeman in Persia … provided they respected our interests and the life and property of our countrymen … My difficulty will be in pulling back our troops without a guarantee that the new government in Persia will maintain order. Iswolsky fears that internal struggle in Persia will continue and that without money or troops the Persians will not be able to control the anarchy … In any case, I hope that I will manage to convince the Persian government of the absolute need to take serious military measures in Tabriz and on the Engali–Teheran road, and also to maintain the Cossack brigade as a guarantee of security in Teheran. After this I will be able to insist on the withdrawal of troops.[154]

Benckendorff, inspired by Grey, saw Persia only as a battlefield where German and entente interests clashed. He wrote to Iswolsky: 'You know that I have always favoured the idea of consolidating our position in Persia by direct negotiations with Germany, certainly not over Britain's head, but keeping her informed about everything …' But Grey told him that Germany's purpose was to split Russia and Britain. When Benckendorff informed him that Iswolsky and the German ambassador Pourtalès were discussing a joint demarche to the Persian government, Grey demanded collective negotiations. Benckendorff wrote: 'Going it alone means betraying him [Grey], depriving him of our support'.[155] Iswolsky agreed that he would propose three-party negotiations. It would show Berlin that Anglo-Russian understanding was not hostile to Germany. If Berlin turned the proposal down, the British would not be able to abandon Russia and settle separately with Germany.[156]

Anarchy spread to the south of Persia in 1910: the Indo-European telegraph line in Seistan was destroyed and the roads had become unsafe, but Grey did not want to follow the Russian example and instead had a Persian gendarmerie organized under Swedish officers. The force mainly served as a British bulwark

---

153 A.K. Benckendorff to Iswolsky, 08/21.07.1909, *Au service*, 2: 237–9.
154 Poklevsky to A.K. Benckendorff, 15/28.07.1909, BC2, box 14.
155 A.K. Benckendorff to Iswolsky, 12/25.05.1910, *Au service*, 2: 268–71.
156 Iswolsky to A.K. Benckendorff, 19.05/01.06.1910, BC2, box 13.

against Russian consular agents in the neutral zone, but it was not otherwise very successful, and the Russians refused to let it operate in their zone.[157]

Poklevsky asked for Benckendorff's advice. He did not see how he could harmonize the measures required to protect Russian subjects in the spreading chaos and the support of the Anglo-Russian convention:

> You may recall that the main goal which I hoped to achieve at Teheran was to maintain our entente with England despite the Persian imbroglio. I have never lost sight of this goal and there has never been disagreement between me and my British colleagues. Even on the questions of loans and especially now, when our troops are in Persia, Marling [the British minister] seems to share my opinion entirely. But does Grey also share it? It often seems to me that he must suspect me of having crossed over to the other side, and yet my opinion is only influenced by the events which are taking place here.

He complained that the Persians could not form a viable constitutional government and that the only course for Britain and Russia was to 'put this country under friendly supervision'. He added in a postscript: 'You cannot imagine how miserable my existence is here, especially compared to the happy times in London …'.[158]

Benckendorff's and Grey's hand-picked candidate soon disappointed them. During a crisis, Poklevsky told the Persian government that Russian troops would withdraw if the government offered safety guarantees to the Russian subjects. Benckendorff, alive to Grey's difficulties in justifying the Russian occupation to the public opinion, wrote to Iswolsky that Poklevsky's action placed Russia's policy at the mercy of the Persian government: 'What if the Persians resist despite Marling's energetic actions?' He concluded: 'Poklevsky has two excellent qualities: interest in politics and interest in business. But sometimes it happens that the second outweighs the first'.[159]

The flow of confidential letters from London ensured that Iswolsky's ideas for a national policy were strongly infused with Anglo-French opinions.

157 David McLean, 107–8.

158 Poklevsky to A.K. Benckendorff, 1910, BC2, box 14.

159 A.K. Benckendorff to Iswolsky, 23.06/06.07.1910, *Au service*, 2: 282–4.

Chapter 7
Balance Abandoned, 1908–1910

Benckendorff believed, like many of his London friends, that Germany's every move was calculated to destroy the Entente; and as Russia was an informal but recognized member of the coalition, he estimated every initiative planned at St Petersburg by its potential to thwart Germany's purpose. He assured St Petersburg that British statesmen's wariness of a powerful Germany also meant that they wanted Russia to be strong. He used this assumption, rather unexpectedly, to deny the truth of Russian conservatives' complaints that Britain undermined the Russian Empire by providing refuge to Russian radicals and terrorists.[1] He refused to dwell on the idea that, as in Persia, Britain would be pleased to see the regime which he represented replaced by a parliamentary system[2] and that British tradition did, in fact, make it convenient for the enemies of the existing Russian government to work against it from the British territory and to enjoy the sympathy of the British public. He refused to see the difference between Russia's and Britain's political traditions as a barrier to cooperation, because he imagined that the Anglo-Russian convention was working toward a liberal and constitutional Russia.

He kept repeating to Iswolsky that the friendship of a wealthy and stable Britain was the basis for Russia's future and, when necessary, it would provide a fulcrum for the Russian lever – a wrong conclusion which Iswolsky tried to put into practice. Iswolsky meanwhile wavered between trying to impress the Tsar and the government with his achievements and catering to the interests of the future liberal westernized Russia.

To remain on friendly terms with Britain, Benckendorff taught his minister, Russia had to reject firmly any semblance of closeness with Germany and Austria-Hungary. Iswolsky had thought of ending the Mürzsteg entente since the early 1900s. Benckendorff approved – because he assumed that the Austrian foreign minister was a German puppet and also because it would entail a more positive cooperation with Britain in the Balkans.[3] As a sop to a policy of caution, the two friends agreed that a shift in Balkan policies towards Britain should be gradual and that, until it was accomplished, Russia should maintain the entente with Austria-Hungary, provided it did not mean acting with Germany.[4] Practically from the moment the Anglo-Russian convention was signed, such an intention became an obstacle to joint action with the Dual Empire.

1 A.K. Benckendorff to Iswolsky, 02/15.05.1907, *Au service*, 2: 38.
2 Descos to Bourgeois, 14.08.1906, DDF, X: 281–3.
3 Paul Cambon to Pichon, 20.06.1907, DDF, XI: 92–4.
4 A.K. Benckendorff to Iswolsky, 26.05/08.06.1907, *Au service*, 2: 49–52.

By the standards of old diplomacy which ruled that a statesman's quality was measured by his ability to keep silent and never commit himself in writing, Iswolsky was a poor specimen. When he made concessions they were real; when he refused to make them, he failed to create the impression that he had made them. The minister was indiscreet; he had neither ability nor resources to maintain a convincing fiction of cooperation either with Germany or Austria-Hungary while in reality helping the Entente to counter their every move. Benckendorff pinned him to his privately expressed opinions by disclosing to the Foreign Office the extent of concessions Iswolsky would be prepared to make on issues under discussion. While Iswolsky told Nicolson during the negotiations that he approved of the British proposal of a demarcation line in Persia, he always added that it was only his personal view, intending to try for compensation. He was taken aback when he learnt from Nicolson that Benckendorff had already told Grey that the minister had decided to accept the line.[5]

Moving Away from the Austrian Entente

Iswolsky especially wanted to reassure the Entente after the suspicions awakened by his Baltic Sea negotiations and having been late in reporting to London, Austria's suggestion of Austro-Russian-Franco-German cooperation in the Macedonian reforms. London interpreted the latter episode as an Austrian attempt to restore the Three Emperors' League which during the 1880s had unnerved the French and the British, and it inspired several indignant letters from Benckendorff to Iswolsky who justified himself by saying: 'An entente *à deux* is the only possible one for me with Austria. Aehrenthal abandoned it but very soon circumstances brought him back. I expect he has learnt his lesson'.[6] The lesson which Aehrenthal learned was that Grey wanted to seize the initiative in the Macedonian question and that Iswolsky's pro-British position made him an unreliable partner for Austria. He accepted that the Mürzsteg entente's days were numbered and decided to forge ahead and protect Austrian interests. On 27 January 1908 he announced the Austrian project of building a railway in the Bosnian Sanjak Novi Bazar.[7] This was a unilateral breach of the Austro-Russian agreement of 1903, whereby both powers had promised to maintain the *status quo* in the Balkan Peninsula. Iswolsky was caught unprepared.[8] He was also nervous because the chief of the general staff, General Fyodor F. Palytsin, in January persuaded him and the emperor that Turkey was preparing for war and insisted

5 Nicolson to Hardinge, 26.10.1906, FO 800/337, 116–17.

6 Iswolsky to A.K. Benckendorff, 25.05/05.06.1907, BC2, box 13.

7 F.R. Bridge, *From Sadowa to Saraevo: The Foreign Policy of Austria-Hungary 1866–1914* (London, 1972), 296–7.

8 Iswolsky to A.K. Benckendorff, 01/14.01.1908, BC2, box 13.

on mobilization in the Caucasus.[9] Benckendorff poured fuel on the fire by writing that Grey was disappointed by Iswolsky's earlier rejection of the British proposal for Macedonia and was inclined to ignore the Austro-Russian leadership in the region and act independently, since Vienna was following Berlin. Benckendorff heard from Grey that the British were so determined to get results in Macedonia that they would not oppose coercive measures to make the Ottoman government accept the reforms. Grey also promised him Britain's full support if Turkish pressure on Persia brought about a Russo-Turkish war. Benckendorff added that, since Grey's promise was not formal, he had not mentioned it in his official report, but that Grey's attitude was symptomatic of his general belief that all paths might ultimately lead to war. This new situation, he wrote, presented Iswolsky with three tasks: to avert war, to resist Austria and to distance himself from the Berlin-inspired Austrian policy: 'We must be ready for extreme measures: think of the army and avoid complications in Finland'.[10] He neglected to point out that British 'full support' did not include a promise of Britain's direct participation in any coercive measures against Turkey.[11]

The Russian government eventually realized that Turkish war preparations were a hoax.[12] Nevertheless, following the Austrian move and the war rumours in February 1908, Iswolsky declared to the senior members of the government that the changes in the Balkans called for a new policy. He intended to abandon the Mürzsteg programme and reopen the Eastern Question. The conference warned Iswolsky that Russia's military and financial state precluded an active policy and in his Balkan initiatives he could only count on his own diplomatic skills.[13]

As a result, the minister replied to Benckendorff's letter about Grey's promise of support to Russia: 'The easiest and the most logical thing would be to abandon the *entente à deux* [with Austria-Hungary] and join England. I would do it unhesitatingly if Russia were in a normal state', but Russia's military and naval weakness and internal instability precluded it: '... *no mobilization, even on the smallest scale, is possible*. This consideration prevails in the situation and must determine all our decisions'. He wrote that he was looking for a peaceful way to end the entente with Vienna and regain Russia's freedom of action in the Balkan Peninsula which, he hoped, would please England. He hinted at a plan which was still too vague to describe.[14] He also puzzled Nicolson by telling him that

9 A. Rediger, *Istori'ia moei zhizni*, 2: 208.

10 A.K. Benckendorff to Iswolsky, 23/01/05.02.1908, *Au service de la Russie*, 2: 120–4.

11 Memorandum by Sir E. Grey on Turkey, January 1908, (eds) *The Mirage of Power: British Foreign Policy 1902–22* (ed. C.J. Lowe and M.L. Dockrill) (London, 1972), 3: 461–3.

12 A. Rediger, 2: 206–7.

13 E.G. Kostrikova, 'Bor'ba Rossii za peresmotr statusa Prolivov v nachale XX v', in *Rossi'ia i Chernomorskie prolivy (XVIII– XX stoleti'ia)*, (eds L.N. Nezhinskii and A.V. Ignat'iev) (Moscow, 1999), 260.

14 Iswolsky to A.K. Benckendorff, 14/27.02.1908, BC2, box 13.

he was glad that the convention enabled Russia and England to work together in questions outside its scope, that is, in Europe.[15] In April, the Foreign Office considered the Mürzsteg programme dead[16] and Iswolsky was eagerly discussing Macedonian issues with Grey and incorporating Benckendorff's suggestions in his memoranda. He thought of creating at Constantinople and Salonica 'a group of powers sincerely desirous of implementing the reforms'. He hoped to persuade Grey to support Russia in the question of a Balkan railroad concession for Serbia and even join in the enterprise. [17] Grey promised to talk to the Turkish government about parity of concessions for Austria and for Serbia-Russia if he and Iswolsky reached a consensus about the reforms. Benckendorff pointed out to the minister that Germany had become particularly obliging to Russia and to Britain after the end of the Austro-Russian entente.[18] He described in detail his conversations with the king about a closer Anglo-Russian cooperation in three questions: Macedonian, the Baltic Sea and the Congo. The ambassador believed that the king revealed to him the innermost thinking of the Foreign Office.[19]

Nicholas II's wish for a visit from Edward VII had been turned down in 1906, so the Foreign Office thought that it would be useful to consolidate the Anglo-Russian rapprochement by a meeting of the two monarchs in June 1908. The British insisted on the greatest secrecy in the preparations because of fears of a terrorist act and hostile British public opinion. They stipulated that the king would arrive in a Russian port on his yacht and remain on board. At Edward VII's request, the port had to be sufficiently far from the German border, to avoid William II descending on the two monarchs,[20] so Reval was the place of choice. To placate the Labour MPs and emphasize the meeting's family character, the permanent under-secretary of the Foreign Office, Hardinge was to accompany the king instead of Grey.[21] The king wished to meet Prime Minister P.A. Stolypin: this would make a good impression in London.[22] Asquith and Grey told the ambassador that many of the Radical MPs' questions and protests were inspired by the propaganda of the Russian political exiles and it would help if the statesmen could oppose to it their own first-hand knowledge of Russian realities.[23]

During the French president's visit to Britain, Benckendorff got a good idea of the questions which would be discussed in Reval: 'I believe the theme is the following: "To secure the peace we need Russia to be stronger than she is". I

15 Nicolson to Grey, 12.02.1908, FO 800/337, 218–9.
16 F.R. Bridge, 299.
17 Iswolsky to A.K. Benckendorff, 09/22.04.1908, BC2, box 13.
18 A.K. Benckendorff to Iswolsky, 16/29.04. 1908, *Au service*, 1: 155–8.
19 A.K. Benckendorff to Iswolsky, 16/29.02.1908, *Au service*, 2: 130–31.
20 A.K. Benckendorff to Iswolsky, 03/16.03.1908, *Au service*, 2: 136–40.
21 13.06.1908, *Journals and Letters of Reginald Viscount Esher*, 2: 298.
22 A.K. Benckendorff to Iswolsky, 26.04/09.05.1908, *Au service*, 2: 158–60.
23 A.K. Benckendorff to Iswolsky, 14/27.05.1908, *Au service*, 2: 163–6.

would not be surprised if Hardinge expanded on this subject'. The corollary would be that France and Britain would willingly lend Russia money to rebuild the Baltic fleet but not to build a Manchurian railroad which would anger the Japanese and distract Russia from the European interests of the Entente. Hardinge would also discuss the Balkan, Persian and perhaps even Far Eastern affairs.[24]

Besides the official agenda, the king came to Reval with a wish list from his friends. The Foreign Office would have preferred to avoid all subjects which might spoil the mood at Reval, such as Lord Rothschild's request to the king to speak to the Russian side about the Jewish issue or Sir Ernest Cassel's request to promote his business interests in Russia. But much as Hardinge and Nicolson tried, they failed to dissuade their sovereign from his intention 'to grind other people's axes'. Still, the Russians' mood did not seem to be affected.[25] Nicholas II made King Edward admiral of the Russian navy and the king reciprocated by making Nicholas II admiral of the British navy. The king had consulted Benckendorff, but not his own government about this step. The radicals and the British court blamed Grey for he had sent the king on the visit without a responsible minister at his side.[26]

The general tenor of the Reval meeting corresponded to what Benckendorff had promised the minister, and Iswolsky interpreted what he heard from the British in the way prompted by Benckendorff: they wanted Russia stronger, they would support Russia in Europe and an Anglo-Russian alliance was not a mirage. The Russian press reflected this general impression in referring to the Anglo-Franco-Russian bloc as the 'New Triple Alliance' and publishing cartoons with humorous allusions to Germany's alarm.[27] The British Conservatives, who were Benckendorff's preferred company, some officials at the Foreign Office and some of the military, like Admiral Sir John Fisher, believed that Britain should have made an alliance with Russia and fortified her for the expected Anglo-German conflagration.[28] Benckendorff usually dismissed the existence of the Cabinet and presented the views of this group as the prevailing British opinion. Rumours of King Edward's generous promises to Nicholas II were rife at St Petersburg after the Reval meeting. Taube cited them as proof that the British had, directly or indirectly, encouraged Iswolsky to take up his bold course of 1908,[29] but the effect of Benckendorff's encouragement cannot be discounted.

Another event in the first half of 1908 to push Iswolsky into action was the Young Turks' coup at Constantinople. Grey decided to postpone presenting

24 A.K. Benckendorff to Iswolsky, 14/27.05.1908, *Au service*, 2: 163–6.

25 Hardinge to Knollys, 04.06.1908, RA VIC/MAIN/W/53/101.

26 13.06.1908, *Journals and Letters of Reginald Viscount Esher*, 2: 298.

27 A clipping from *Peterburgska'ia gazeta*, 15/28.05.1908, AVPRI, 340, op.706, d.58 (1908), l.142.

28 Sir John Fisher's memorandum, 14.03.1908, RA VIC/MAIN/W/59/14.

29 M. de Taube, *La politique russe*, 186.

demands of reforms to the new Ottoman government, hoping that the new rulers would dispense with German friendship and look for advice and direction from Britain.[30] Iswolsky was content to follow Grey's lead and give the new Turkish institutions an opportunity to carry out reforms of their own free will.

In the summer, he assured Nicolson of his intention 'to go hand-in-hand with Her Majesty's Government through the many episodes and adventures which, quite possibly, the future has in store for us in the Middle and Near East'.[31] Iswolsky's hints referred not only to Macedonian reforms but also to the plan which had been brewing since the previous autumn but now was forced to the forefront by Aehrenthal's activity. Aehrenthal planned to pull Austrian garrisons out of the Sanjak in order to avoid being drawn into conflict between the Serbs and the new Turkish rulers. But, as compensation he wanted to annex the Serb-populated Bosnia and Herzegovina, which Austria-Hungary had administered since the Berlin Congress. Aehrenthal had to hurry because the Young Turks were planning to reassert Turkish influence there by summoning Bosnian deputies to parliament and perhaps granting autonomy to the provinces. Iswolsky wanted to be ahead of Aehrenthal's next move in the Balkans by proposing cooperation in the Austrian plans in exchange for Austrian help in securing Russia's regional interests.[32] Tentative discussions between Iswolsky and the Austrian minister had taken place in September 1907. On 2 July 1908 Iswolsky proposed to Aehrenthal Russia's benevolent attitude in the event of the annexation in exchange for Austria's benevolent attitude in altering the rule of Straits in Russia's favour.[33] Iswolsky incautiously committed himself by this memorandum,[34] so Aehrenthal delayed answering to it; when he announced the coming annexation to his colleagues he assured them that they need not fear opposition of the great powers, for he had settled the issue with them and was about to reach a settlement with Russia.[35]

An inter-ministerial conference at St Petersburg discussed the Balkan situation on 21 July/3 August and told Iswolsky once again that Russia was not ready for independent action. Still, the general staff was instructed to prepare a plan of peaceful occupation of the Bosporus. The secret was leaked almost at once, naturally angering the rulers at Constantinople.[36] At the beginning of August, as European newspapers were discussing the effects of the Constantinople coup on the Balkan situation, Iswolsky discussed the imminent annexation with his deputy minister Nikolai V. Tcharykow and the Tsar. In 1877, on the eve of the Russo-Turkish war, Russia's secret consent to the annexation bought Austria-Hungary's

30 Hardinge to G. Barclay, 30.06.1908, *The Mirage of Power*, 3: 464.
31 Nicolson to Grey, 13.08.1908, FO 800/337, 247–9.
32 M. de Taube, *La politique russe*, 176.
33 F.R. Bridge, 301–2.
34 E.G. Kostrikova, 262.
35 F. Roy Bridge, 303.
36 E.G. Kostrikova, 263.

neutrality. So, in 1908 Russia could not claim compensation for a right conceded 30 years earlier; but Iswolsky thought he could qualify this earlier consent by six conditions relating to compensation for the Balkan states and one which stipulated that the Bosporus and the Dardanelles would be open to the egress of Russia's men-of-war. Nicholas II approved.[37]

In August the minister left for his annual spa cure. He would meet Benckendorff at Carlsbad and King Edward at Marienbad; then he would visit Buchlau, a nearby country seat of the Austrian ambassador to Russia, Count Berchtold. Aerenthal would also be there for a discussion. Iswolsky was planning a tour of European capitals in the autumn and wanted to come to London in late October[38] to discuss Persian affairs with Grey.[39] Benckendorff planned to take most of August and September to settle his private affairs, leaving the embassy in the charge of Sevastopoulo and Poklevsky,[40] but he would cut his leave by two weeks in order to be in London when Iswolsky came. Benckendorff promised him a delightful stay because the meeting with Grey would be 'a perfect case of *plain sailing*' a meeting of kindred minds.

> The king will be, I believe, at Balmoral, but since, I believe, you will see him at Marienbad, you will be able to arrange it with him. Grey … will come to London for a few days to meet with you. And I hope to arrange for you several meetings with Asquith and other ministers.[41]

In the summer of 1908 there was a growing expectation on the continent and in Britain regarding Balkan events. Austrian agents were spreading the idea that Austria-Hungary had replaced Russia as the traditional protector of the Slavs, and they presented the imminent annexation of Bosnia-Herzegovina as proof.[42] All of this made Benckendorff advise the minister to abandon the consultations with Germany and Austro-Hungary regarding Macedonian reforms. By doing so, Iswolsky would win over the new Turkish cabinet: 'The English sympathy for the new regime does not surprise anyone, ours is more unexpected and it would increase its value in the eyes of the Turkish government …'.[43] As usual, Benckendorff's advice harmonized with Grey's need to establish good relations with Turkey without antagonizing Russia.

Iswolsky read in the newspapers about the Austrian preparations at the same time as he received Aehrenthal's belated answer to his July memorandum. He was indignant, because Austria-Hungary had agreed not to take any steps in the Balkans

---

37 N.V. Tcharykow, *Glimpses of High Politics* (London, 1931), 269.
38 Iswolsky to A.K. Benckendorff, 17/30.07.1908, BC2, box 13.
39 A.P. Iswolsky to A.K. Benckendorff, 18.06/01.07.1908, BC2, box 13.
40 A.K. Benckendorff to Iswolsky, 23.06/06.07.1908, *Au service*, 2: 177–82.
41 A.K. Benckendorff to Iswolsky, 09/22.07.1908, *Au service*, 2: 182–5.
42 G. Wesselitsky to A.K. Benckendorff, 21.07.1908, BC2, box 15.
43 A.K. Benckendorff to Iswolsky, 21.07/03.08.1908, *Au service*, 2: 186–8.

without prior consultation with Russia, but he found it encouraging that Vienna still considered the annexation tied to the Straits issue.[44] He was certain that the annexation was inevitable, but he did not think it would affect Russia's interests. His concern was that Austria would incite Bulgaria to proclaim independence simultaneously and in this case Bulgaria – and her protector Russia – would share Turkey's wrath.[45] On 25 August Iswolsky told *The Times*' reporter at Carlsbad that he and Aehrenthal were estranged over the issue of the Sanjak railway. To prepare public opinion for his subsequent call for a conference, he added that the annexation of Bosnia-Herzegovina would be an infraction of the Berlin treaty and therefore a European issue.[46]

The Meeting at Buchlau and the Aftermath

On 15/28 September Iswolsky, accompanied by his former subordinate and friend, now posted in Vienna, Elim Demidov, arrived at Buchlau. Benckendorff wrote in March, he did not see any reason to conceal from Grey what Poklevsky had told him of Iswolsky's plans.[47] Iswolsky had many ideas, so it is impossible to assert that the 'plans' referred to the Straits, but the subject of Buchlau discussions in the autumn of 1908 was easy to guess: the pending annexation. Iswolsky presented his terms, among them the right for Russian and other coastal states' warships to pass the Straits singly with the maintenance of the closure of the Straits to warships of other powers. The status of Constantinople would remain intact. According to Iswolsky, Aehrenthal accepted his terms; according to Aehrenthal he did not.[48] They agreed that all this would culminate in a European conference. Only Aehrenthal insisted later that the conference was to ratify the annexation, while Iswolsky said he meant the conference to authorize the annexation. Aehrenthal had not informed the Russian minister about the imminence of the annexation and Iswolsky went on a tour to organise support for his programme of a conference.[49] As no memoranda were exchanged, Iswolsky exposed himself once again. Gentlemen's agreements only work between gentlemen and it was Iswolsky's mistake to take Aehrenthal for one. Besides, Iswolsky's choice of Elim Demidov as his companion for the Buchlau meeting meant that the subject of Iswolsky-Aehrenthal talks had ceased to be a mystery to Paris and London long before Iswolsky arrived there.[50]

44 E.G. Kostrikova, 263.
45 E.G. Kostrikova, 264.
46 *The History of The Times*, 613.
47 A.K. Benckendorff to Iswolsky, 19.02/03.03.1908, *Au service* 2: 132.
48 E.G. Kostrikova, 264.
49 F.R. Bridge, 303.
50 M. Taube, *Zarnitsy*, 115.

Iswolsky sent a triumphant telegram to St Petersburg, saying that Aehrenthal had accepted his terms; Tcharykow prepared a draft of a memorandum to the Austro-Hungarian government, formulating Iswolsky's six conditions of Russia's consent to the annexation. Nicholas II approved it and Tcharykow at last informed the government of Iswolsky's achievement. But an indignant Stolypin and most of the ministers declared that secret conniving with Austria-Hungary to violate the Berlin treaty was unacceptable. Nicholas II, recognizing the strength of the argument, at once retreated. Tcharykow improvised another idea: Russia should instead negotiate with Constantinople[51] and offer to waive Russia's claim to the payments of 1877–78 war indemnity in exchange for the acceptance of modifications to the Straits treaty.[52]

But on 23 September/5 October, leaving Iswolsky no time for more manoeuvring, Bulgaria declared independence. The Austrian declaration of the annexation of Bosnia-Herzegovina followed on 25/7 October. Russian society was indignant because the annexation dashed the hopes of the Serbs in the two provinces of eventually joining their mother country; the British press condemned the violation of the Berlin treaty which undermined the Turkish position.

Iswolsky was surprised by the news in Paris. The French and the British did not take seriously his shocked reaction because they reasoned that Austria-Hungary would not have risked the adventure without his consent.[53] Iswolsky failed to obtain a firm promise of French support in demanding a conference to revise the Berlin treaty and continued his scheduled tour of Europe.[54] Wesselitsky, like most European journalists and statesmen was spending August and September between Baden-Baden, Marienbad and Karlsbad. On 4 October he wrote to Benckendorff about the imminent annexation, asking him for instructions.[55] Benckendorff ordered him to meet Iswolsky on the way from Paris and interview him for the *Novoye Vremya*, so as to give the minister a chance to defend his actions. After the annexation news broke out Wesselitsky refused:

> It was painful for me to realize that a minister whose patriotic, clear, firm, sincere policy I had admired grossly lacked cleverness, prudence and even dignity in his relations with Austria.

He mentioned the bad impression which Iswolsky's conduct and his interview to a French newspaper had produced, and added: 'I am appalled that someone wants a [European] Congress to ratify a theft (from the Turks) and a murder (of B-H and of the Serbian nation)'.[56] It was the public reaction in Russia, too.

51 N.V. Tcharykow, 269–70.
52 Nicolson to Grey, 08.10.1908, FO 800/337, 257–9.
53 Bertie to Grey, 04.10.1908, BD V: 382–4.
54 E.G. Kostrikova, 266–7.
55 G. Wesselitsky to A.K. Benckendorff, 04.10.1908, BC2, box 15.
56 G. Wesselitsky to A.K. Benckendorff, 11.10.1908, BC2, box 15.

Iswolsky in London

Poklevsky met the minister on the way to London to warn that Grey would not support Russia's Straits claim, although he was angry about the annexation.[57] Indeed, Aehrenthal dealt a blow to the Ottoman Empire whose friendship Britain was seeking. As for the Russian hopes, the British ambassador to Constantinople reported that Turkey would oppose the opening of the Straits to the coastal states only, and would rather the question were not discussed at the conference.[58] Grey was also angry with Austria because when the Russian press became excited about the Slavs every European foreign minister recalled 1877 and feared that the Russian government might be pushed into another war. When Nicolson reported that the Russians did not clamour for compensation and simply sympathized with the Slavs,[59] Grey was confirmed in his opposition to reopening the Straits issue and all Iswolsky got from him was a memorandum with a proposal to neutralize the Straits.[60]

The Entente partners were largely anxious about retaining the Turks' goodwill and preventing the German influence at Constantinople. Cambon took it for granted that Iswolsky would next go to ask for support in Germany, but he was sure that Berlin would not oblige, as it had not forgiven Iswolsky the Anglo-Russian convention. The only hypothetical risk of the situation was that Iswolsky's resignation might push Russia back into the 'German embrace'. It was the main reason why the British and the French supported Iswolsky's call for a European conference.[61] But that concern was assuaged by Nicolson's next report: the Dardanelles were of little interest to the Russians and Iswolsky's resignation would not necessarily lead to the fall of the Stolypin government.[62]

Benckendorff wrote a dozen letters to his wife about Iswolsky's London stay. Years later, the countess copied fragments from the letters into a booklet that was filed at Bakhmetev archives as an anonymous diary relating to 1910 events in Europe. The excerpts give a good idea of how Iswolsky was received at the Russian embassy: his friends and subordinates ranged themselves on the side of the Foreign Office. During the first dinner at the embassy, with Poklevsky, Iswolsky, Etter and Benckendorff present, Iswolsky floated his ideas regarding the talks with Grey. Benckendorff qualified them as 'sensible' but more appropriate for the future. The following morning, on the eve of his first meeting with Grey, the minister gave Benckendorff a rough copy of new proposals, saying, 'My brain

57 M. de Taube, *La politique russe*, 192–3.

58 Sir George Lowther to Grey, 12.10.1908, BD V: 426.

59 Nicolson to Grey, 13.10.1908, BD V: 431–2.

60 Memorandum, 14.10.1908, BC2, box 12.

61 Paul Cambon to his son, 11.10.1908, *Correspondance, 1870–1924* (Paris, 1940), 2: 245.

62 Nicolson to Hardinge, 21.10.1908, FO 800/337, 261–4.

has been working'.[63] Iswolsky's evenings were occupied by receptions: on the 11th he attended an official dinner with 30 guests offered by the king. On the twelfth Grey invited Benckendorff, Iswolsky and Morley – to discuss Central Asia. The day after there was a grand official dinner at the embassy with 20 guests. Lansdowne could not come but Benckendorff invited two Barings, Lord Cromer (the former viceroy) and Lord Revelstoke. During the London discussions, on Benckendorff's advice, Iswolsky agreed to most that Grey suggested for Persia, including Hartwig's recall, the removal of the Russian officers from the command of the shah's 'Cossack' brigade and limiting their duties to instruction and drilling of the force.[64] As for his programme of a European conference, Iswolsky also dropped the demands for territorial compensation for Serbia and Montenegro, to which Austria would never agree, and replaced them with a vague claim for 'advantages'. He, Benckendorff and Grey discussed Persia and Afghanistan, where Iswolsky accepted that the Anglo-Russian convention would remain binding even though the Amir of Afghanistan did not recognize it.[65] Benckendorff found Iswolsky 'remarkably flexible' and a quick learner, and added: 'I find in [Iswolsky] an excellent echo and interpreter of my ideas'.[66] Iswolsky made another desperate attempt to get a private reassurance from the British regarding Russia's interests in the Straits. He wanted the Foreign Office to support his proposal that in peacetime only the coastal states' warships could pass through the Straits but that in wartime all belligerents would have equal rights. This last idea was Iswolsky's attempt to get something he could present at St Petersburg as his achievement. Hardinge wrote to Nicolson that the cabinet and the Foreign Office successfully opposed the inclusion of the issue in the conference programme because Russia could offer nothing in exchange 'as shop-window ware for the [British] public'.[67] Grey suggested that if Russia and England cooperated to pull Turkey through the crisis, it would prepare the ground for dealing with the Straits issue and prepare British public opinion.[68]

Wherever Benckendorff and Iswolsky turned for sympathy, they heard the same gently worded refusal. Even Admiral Fisher, whose support the two friends tried to enlist, reiterated Grey's arguments against raising the Straits issue.[69] Benckendorff drafted a reply to Fisher in which he agreed that it was too early to raise the issue and promised that the Straits' question would find a

63 10.10.1908, Selections from Benckendorff's letters to his wife, BC2, box 28.

64 Grey to Edward VII, 13.10.1908, RA VIC/MAIN/W/54/107.

65 D.W. Sweet, 'The Bosnian Crisis', in *British Foreign Policy Under Sir Edward Grey*, (ed. F.H. Hinsley) (Cambridge: Cambridge University Press, 1977), 181.

66 12.10.1908, Selections from Benckendorff's letters, BC2, box 28.

67 Hardinge to Nicolson, 13.10.1908, BD V: 434–6.

68 Grey to Iswolsky, 15.10.1908, BC2, box 12.

69 Sir John Fisher to Iswolsky, 15.10.1908, *The Correspondence of Admiral of the Fleet Lord Fisher of Kilverstone* (ed. Arthur J. Marder) (London: Jonathan Cape, 1952–1959), 2: 197–9.

solution in a new relationship of trust between Russia and Turkey.[70] He echoed the opinions of his British friends, writing to his wife that as soon as Iswolsky spoke to him of the Straits '*I made up my mind* that it was nonsense' because the new Turkish regime might become friendly to Russia and then the issue would be solved without forcing Turkey's hand. 'We should improve the relations between "the new Russia" and "the new Turkey"', he concluded.[71] Iswolsky left London having made concessions in Persia and having obtained nothing in exchange. To bolster his spirit, Grey wrote to Nicolson that he had advised the Turks that eventually some opening of the Straits would be inevitable. He did not exclude the possibility that he would later advise them to sign an agreement with Russia.[72]

Lord Esher summed up the results of Iswolsky's conversations with Grey as follows: England, Russia and France had agreed on the terms on which the two coups, the Austrian and the Bulgarian, were to be accepted and Germany was going to be shut out of Asiatic enterprises.[73] Iswolsky, seconded by Benckendorff, was making concessions on all issues in order to maintain the appearance of Anglo-Russian cooperation and friendship at a time when he needed to show to his critics at home and abroad that the Entente was behind him.

London Campaign to Save Iswolsky

After four days in Berlin, Iswolsky returned to Russia empty-handed and humiliated. He offered to resign but the government decided that his resignation at the moment would reflect badly on Russia's prestige. Russia could not expect to gain anything from a conference any more and the government decided to drag on the affair[74] until it died a natural death.

Benckendorff sent Iswolsky a comforting letter which ended up in the hands of the French ambassador in Rome and must have pleased the Quai d'Orsay. Benckendorff reiterated Grey's explanations of why he could not support Russia in the Straits issue: the British public opinion, the Liberals' great regard for the treaties and sympathy with the Young Turks. He drew Iswolsky's attention to the main points that were all very positive: he agreed with Grey that Germany's efforts to encircle Britain were behind all the Austrian actions of 1908. Also, Iswolsky's visit to London sealed the trust which the Russian policy inspired there; now Russia needed to come out openly on the side of the Entente to which she already

70 A.K. Benckendorff to Sir John Fisher, 16.10.1908, GARF 1126, op.1, d.10, ll.7–8 ob.

71 16.10.1908, Selections from Benckendorff's letters, BC2, box 28.

72 Grey to Nicolson, 19.10.1908, BD, V: 456.

73 14.10.1908, *Journals and Letters of Reginald Viscount Esher*, 2: 351.

74 E.G. Kostrikova, 270.

belonged and whose support she had. It was not a risk: there was a possibility of war whatever political orientation Russia chose.[75]

Poklevsky and Benckendorff, trying to summon support for the minister, presented Iswolsky to everybody in London as a victim of a pro-German cabal at St Petersburg. As a result Hardinge asked the king to intervene with Nicholas II on Iswolsky's behalf. He pointed to Iswolsky's efforts to support the Anglo-Russian convention: he had just obtained the withdrawal of Russian troops from Tabriz by threatening his own resignation.[76] Accordingly, Edward VII wrote to Nicholas II praising the results of Iswolsky's conversations with Grey and making a clear connection between Iswolsky's ministry and British support of Russia, 'not only in Asia but also in Europe'.[77] Iswolsky drafted Nicholas II's reply in the spirit of Benckendorff's advice of openly siding with the Entente. The Tsar invited Britain to form a 'still closer understanding upon other political questions' besides Asia and mentioned the Balkans. Informing Benckendorff about the essence of the letter, Iswolsky added that the Austrian-Serbian tensions were mounting dangerously.[78]

The Casablanca Crisis

Two events heightened the inter-bloc tensions in Europe and seemed to confirm Grey's suspicion of Germany. First, the *Daily Telegraph* published William II's words that during the Boer war, France and Russia proposed to him a joint attack on Britain. Feelings were running high in Britain, Germany and Russia. An angry Nicholas II showed Nicolson a letter from the Kaiser suggesting that Russia should attack India. A week later, Iswolsky informed the government that Germany presented an ultimatum to France regarding the Casablanca incident[79] and that Paris decided to reject it. If France was attacked, Russia would have to enter the war.[80] Iswolsky wrote to Benckendorff that he was more worried about the Franco-German crisis than the Balkan one. If William II provoked a war, Russia would be in a tragic situation: the army all but collapsed and the public mood remained half-seditious. Stolypin said that mobilization would cause rioting in the interior of Russia. Iswolsky wrote:

> I have just talked to Nicolson … In the course of the conversation I asked him, what will England do? He replied after a moment of reflection: 'I believe we

75 A.K. Benckendorff to Iswolsky, 12/25.10.1908, DDF, XI: 949–53.

76 Hardinge to Edward VII, 22.10.1908, RA VIC/MAIN/W/54/116.

77 Edward VII to Nicholas II, 27.10.1908, GARF 601, op.1, d.1388, ll. 37–8 ob.

78 Iswolsky to A.K. Benckendorff, 06/19.11.1908, BC2, box 13.

79 In September 1908 three deserters from the French Légion Etrangère in Morocco were given asylum by the German consulate in Casablanca. It gave rise to the second Franco-German Moroccan crisis.

80 A. Rediger, 2: 229.

> will march. We were ready to do so before Algeciras. It was France that did not have the determination. Now it seems to me there is even more reason to do so, because public opinion in England is excited against Germany by Emperor William's latest prank'.... If there is war between Germany and France, that is, a European war, and if England remains neutral, it would put paid to our future relations, because it would be said that again it has fooled and abandoned us ... The question which I asked Nicolson, can you ask it of Asquith and Grey?[81]

Benckendorff asked Grey a different question. Convinced that Anglo-Russian solidarity in Europe needed to be brought out into the open,[82] he tried to make Grey promise Britain's support for Russia in the Balkans in the event of a conflict. He blamed the existing Russo-German tensions on Germany's rancour for Russia's rapprochement with Britain. Benckendorff then said that he believed that the Austro-German alliance had been extended to cover the Balkans and asked what Britain would do if Germany intervened in a Russo-Austrian conflict there. Grey answered that it would all depend on who was the aggressor; for example, the English press had rallied to France's side over the Casablanca ultimatum because it was clear to the British nation that France was attacked because of her friendship with Britain.

Benckendorff understood it as an indication that the British government would also support Russia against Austria-Hungary if public opinion was favourable. He explained to Iswolsky that Grey's emphatic statements of support to France in the Casablanca incident were equivalent to Britain's commitment to support Russia in the Balkan question.[83] To Grey's counter-question of what France would do if Germany intervened in an Austro-Russian war in the Balkans, Benckendorff replied that France would side with Russia, immediately adding the mantra of the Russian foreign ministry that in the event of a Balkan conflagration 'sharp, decisive action on [the British] part would keep the peace' by giving an effective warning to the aggressor. Grey replied that a decision on such a question would be made under the pressure of a crisis. Once again, Benckendorff emphasized to Grey the similarity between Russia's and France's conflict with the Triple Alliance, repeating that Berlin was hostile to Russia on account of the Anglo-Russian rapprochement.[84]

As Benckendorff asked about support for Russia, Grey's answer seemed to apply to Russia, were it in the same situation as France. It was not a promise, but it gave Benckendorff hope, especially since Iswolsky was sincerely determined to avert a Balkan war[85] and Benckendorff's claim about the cause of German

81 Iswolsky to A.K. Benckendorff, 23.10/05.11.1908, BC2, box 13.

82 A.K. Benckendorff to Iswolsky, 12/25.10.1908, DDF, XI: 949–53.

83 A.K. Benckendorff to Iswolsky, 21.01/03.02.1909, *Au service*, 2: 195–200.

84 Grey to Nicolson, 10.11.1908, FO 800/73, 136–7.

85 Iswolsky to A.K. Benckendorff, 06/19.11.1908, BC2, box 13.

hostility was generally correct.[86] On the British side, there were people who shared Benckendorff's opinion: Hardinge wrote to Nicolson in November 1908 that Britain would be unable to avoid participating on the Russian side in any war that the Balkan situation produced.[87] On another occasion Hardinge said that the Russians must realize that if they were involved as France's allies it was not likely that Britain would not participate.[88] After the French entente, the events gradually reduced the odds of Britain's staying out of a European conflict, despite remaining formally uncommitted – as was conclusively demonstrated in August 1914.

The Bosnian Crisis Intensifies

In late 1908 Benckendorff wrote to his wife that Austrian-Hungarian expansion in the Balkans (supported by Germany) could be contained without a direct Entente involvement by a Balkan League, described as 'a Slav-Turkish combination which will emerge quite on its own or even with European [the Entente?] backing, and which will give Austria a lot more trouble than it has ever expected'.[89] As often happened, Benckendorff's idea followed the thinking of his acquaintances at the Foreign Office: on 1 December Hardinge outlined to the ambassador at Constantinople his view of a course which Turkey should follow. After Aehrenthal refused to take over part of the Turkish debt in order to settle with Turkey, Turkey should settle with Bulgaria and then the conference would not be necessary. If Turkey also signed ententes with Serbia and Montenegro, the four Balkan powers would be in a strong position and could checkmate Austria's moves.[90]

Poklevsky was at Iswolsky's side throughout this time. He reported to London that the minister was depressed by the right-wing campaign against him and feared that Austria would reject his proposal for the judiciary reform in Macedonia and formally put an end to the Mürzsteg entente. Nevertheless, Iswolsky was prepared to risk it, if Britain would openly support him. Poklevsky still believed that the present crisis was caused by Russia's 'fear of angering Germany or of going too far with England'. His next statement illustrated the considerations which a pro-Entente course imposed on Russia: 'Iswolsky is not overly content with the new English proposal for Macedonia. It seems we cannot accept it, but his refusal might reflect unfavourably on the activity of the Entente powers'.[91]

86 William II to Nicholas II, 09.01.1909, *Perepiska Vilgel'ma II s Nikolaem II*, 423–6.

87 K.M. Wilson, 'Isolating the Isolator: Cartwright, Grey and the Seduction of Austria-Hungary, 1908–12', in *Empire and Continent*, 85.

88 K.M. Wilson, 'The Fiction of the Free Hand', in *The Policy of the Entente: Essays on the Determinants of British Foreign Policy, 1904–1914* (Cambridge: Cambridge University Press, 1985), 92.

89 A.K. Benckendorff to S.P. Benckendorff, 20.12.1908/03.01.1909, BC2, box 16.

90 Hardinge to Lowther. 01.12.1908, *The Mirage of Power*, 3: 465.

91 Poklevsky to A.K. Benckendorff, 3/16.12.1908, BC2, box 14.

Aehrenthal's 8/23 December circular to the powers made references to his secret negotiations with Russia prior to the annexation. Austro-Russian relations deteriorated even more.[92] On 12/27 December Iswolsky defended his policy in the Duma. He said that the government wanted an international conference in order to ask for a revision of the articles of the Berlin treaty which were not beneficial to Russia, Turkey and Balkan states and endorsed a Balkan league with Turkey in order to seek national and economic sovereignty of the Balkan states.[93] Benckendorff's last letter of 1908 spoke of the excellent impression produced in London by Iswolsky's speech, of the Foreign Office's mistrust of Aehrenthal and of the king's reluctance to visit William II. This last he presented in a way apt to console a sulking child: King Edward was going to Berlin because the Foreign Office wanted to annoy Austria.[94]

Instead of replying on Nicholas II's desire for an alliance with Britain, the royal family sent him warm Christmas wishes,[95] but Grey felt that the emperor's obliging behaviour had to be rewarded by an invitation to visit Cowes in August 1909.[96] The Kaiser tried to move Nicholas II in the opposite direction by a promise of support on the Straits issue and suggesting Russia should ask France to press London.[97] Nicholas II replied that it was untimely because of the more pressing threat of an Austro-Serbian war and asked William II to moderate Austria's conduct.[98]

William II refused to comply with the request, reproaching Russia for having since 1907 joined a coalition hostile to Germany.[99] Iswolsky drafted Nicholas II's answer. He blamed Austria for having caused the crisis and the division of European powers and once again appealed to Germany to restrain Austria. Nicholas II, on his own impulse, also addressed the main source of Germany's hostility:

> I state once again that we have not signed and have not intended to sign a general agreement with England. We are quite satisfied with the existing agreements because they spare us all the troubles and concerns on our Asian border. I quite agree with you that Russia and Germany must be as united as possible.[100]

While the terms of an Ottoman-Austrian-Bulgarian settlement were discussed, Iswolsky offered that Turkey accept Bulgarian independence in return for money

---

92 Harold Nicolson, *Sir Arthur Nicolson*, 292.

93 A.V. Ignatiev, *Vneshn'aia politika Rossii, 1907–1914: Tendentsii, Sobyti'ia, Liudi* (Moscow: Nauka, 2000), 87.

94 A.K. Benckendorff to Iswolsky, 21.12/03.01.1908/9, *Au service*, 2: 188–9.

95 George V to Nicholas II, 29.12.1908, GARF, 601, op.1, d.1219, ll.22–3.

96 Grey to Knollys, 26.11.1908, RA VIC/ADDC 7/2/Q.

97 Harold Nicolson, 292.

98 Nicholas II to William II, 15/28.12.1908, *Perepiska Vilgel'ma II s Nikolaem II*, 421–3.

99 William II to Nicholas II, 09.01.1909, *Perepiska Vilgel'ma II s Nikolaem II*, 423–6.

100 Nicholas II to William II, 12/25.01.1909, *Perepiska*, 427–33.

which it owed in indemnities to Russia since the 1878 war.[101] Benckendorff congratulated the minister on his wise decision: '… it has certainly been a victory for Russian policy and, therefore, for your personal position, here in London, and I believe, in Paris'. He explained that the Foreign Office as good as promised to support Russia in the Balkans even though '[when] Turkey settles with Austria and Bulgaria, it will not be possible to count on [Britain's] military support for the sake of Serbian and Montenegrin affairs'.[102] Referring to the German chancellor's recent suggestion that France should mediate between Russia and Austria, Benckendorff emphasized that it was a devious attempt to start a quarrel between Russia and France which France had frustrated by replying that she could only side with Russia.[103] This lesson in ethics was undercut the next day when Benckendorff learned that, on the contrary, the French had replied that they would not refuse to talk to Russia if Germany wanted to talk to Austria. He had to tell Cambon that a French offer of mediation would not be welcome in St Petersburg.[104]

Edward VII's visit to Berlin produced a communiqué declaring a complete understanding between Germany and Great Britain in regard to affairs in the Balkans.[105] France also settled with Germany and Iswolsky saw that Russia remained isolated in her standoff with Austria-Hungary for the sake of compensations to Serbia. When Austria had reached an agreement with Turkey and could focus on subduing Serbia, Prince von Bülow told the British ambassador that the Eastern question was over:[106] Germany would not support a conference about the Balkan issues for Russia's benefit.

In February, Iswolsky made two unsuccessful attempts to organize joint demarches of the Entente and Russia to Vienna to prevent an Austrian attack on Serbia and demand explanations of Austria's intentions. Neither the British nor the French intended to support Russia if it meant joining the conflict in which they had nothing to gain. Iswolsky's plight inspired more derision than sympathy. The French ambassador at Constantinople told his German colleague that the Russians were naïve to expect support from the Entente, and William II scribbled on this report: 'We think so too. That is the basis of our policy!'[107]

Benckendorff fell ill in December and left for Egypt early in 1909 for a long rest cure, but the German naval attaché at St Petersburg reported to William II a rumour that '… in London they so snubbed Benckendorff over the Straits that he even began to think of withdrawal'.[108] The countess provided her husband with news: according to Hardinge, Benckendorff's early return to London would be

101 Iswolsky to A.K. Benckendorff, 15/28.01.1909, BC2, box 13.
102 A.K. Benckendorff to Iswolsky, 21.01/03.02.1909, *Au service*, 2: 195–200.
103 A.K. Benckendorff to Iswolsky, 07/20.01.1908, *Au service*, 2: 193–5.
104 Pichon to Jules Cambon, 21.01.1909, DDF, XI: 1036–7.
105 Harold Nicolson, *Sir Arthur Nicolson*, 296.
106 Jules Cambon to Pichon, 22.01.1909, DDF, XI: 1040–41.
107 I. Astaf'iev, *Russko-germanskie otnosheni'ia*, 180.
108 William II to Bülow, 13.12.1908, Prince *Bülow's Letters*, 278–81.

pointless because all outstanding political issues would be settled in a few days.[109] Her next letter said: 'I have not written because things were getting gloomier. I believe Pokel [Poklevsky] is doing well here, you do not need to worry on that account'.[110]

Poklevsky wrote to Iswolsky that the British hesitated to support Russia at Constantinople since more pressure would result in Turkey's shift to 'another Power', but that Grey categorically denied any change in Britain's Near Eastern policy. Even if there were an entente with Germany, Britain would maintain the same course in the issues for which 'she has already found firm support among other friendly powers'.[111]

As passions were heating in Serbia and Montenegro, France and Britain insisted in February 1909 that Iswolsky had to think of the European repercussions and join them in advising Serbia to put her fate in the hands of the Entente to speak on her behalf to Austria.[112] Iswolsky obeyed, incurring indignation at Belgrade and in Russia, but Grey praised him for a 'statesmanlike courageous action'.[113] The Russian embassy was still under Countess Benckendorff's supervision. She reported to her husband that at a ball the king asked Poklevsky to let the ambassador know that Russia 'had everything going for peace and ... would receive support'.[114]

Austria's behaviour towards Serbia was becoming more threatening, and Iswolsky asked the French what their position would be in case of a Russo-Austrian war. They answered that Serbian interests did not constitute a vital interest to Russia and an Austro-Russian war over these would not be a *casus foederis*, an answer indicative of Russia's low standing with her ally: France was telling Russia what her vital interests were.[115] Nicholas II once again asked William II to intervene with Austria.[116] As it was obvious to Germany that Russia was determined to avoid war,[117] William II did not answer. Instead, on 9/22 March, Bülow demanded from Iswolsky a clear answer to the question: would Russia accept the annexation and make Serbia accept it? If Russia quibbled, Germany would let Austria invade Serbia. Iswolsky feared that in the latter case public opinion in Russia might force the government enter on Serbia's side.[118] Austrian military measures on the border

109 S.P. Benckendorff to A.K. Benckendorff, 16.02.1909, BC2, box 22.

110 S.P. Benckendorff to A.K. Benckendorff, 22.02.1909. BC2, box 22.

111 Poklevsky to Iswolsky, 04/17.02.1909 (1), *Au service*, 2: 201–6.

112 P. Cambon to Xavier Charmes, 26.02.1909, *Correspondance*, 2: 276–7.

113 Poklevsky to Iswolsky, 18.02/03.03.1909, *Au service*, 2: 206–8.

114 S.P. Benckendorff to A.K. Benckendorff, 04.03.1909(1), BC2, box 22.

115 A.V. Ignatiev, *Vneshnai'ia politika Rossii*, 91.

116 Nicholas II to William II, 09.03.1909, *Perepiska Vilgel'ma II s Nikolaem II*, 433–4.

117 Freiherr von Schoen, 82.

118 30.06.1909, *Les carnets de Georges Louis*, 1: 28.

with Russia and Germany's high preparedness for war made him fear that the Triple Alliance was decided on a war against Russia.[119] He capitulated.

The Consequences of the Crisis

Now the Foreign Office's task was to prevent Iswolsky's resignation and Russia's shift towards Germany. A barrage of consolations and advice followed from London. Poklevsky defended Britain's position to his Russian colleagues: the Liberal government did not consider the annexation of Bosnia-Herzegovina a *casus belli,* and Germany's policy did not affect Britain's interests.[120] Poklevsky's letter to Iswolsky, 24 hours after Russia had accepted the ultimatum, referred to the main lesson of the Bosnian crisis for Russian diplomacy, that of the danger and humiliation of weakness. He spoke of a day in the future when 'Russia, having recovered her strength, will be able to resist German pretensions of spreading her hegemony over Europe'. Most importantly, from his point of view, German and Austrian conduct awakened (!) in the Foreign Office a fear of German hegemony in Europe and therefore worked for Russian interests. Cambon told him that from this moment Britain would not be able to stay neutral if France or Russia was drawn into a war against Germany.[121] In the next letter Poklevsky reported that 'those responsible for the British policy *are not angry with us at all*, although, like us, they are concerned about the future' and more aware of the Germanic danger.[122] The words he chose to argue against Iswolsky's intention to resign[123] echoed the arguments of the dowager empress who was visiting her sister Alexandra. Maria Feodorovna wrote to Nicholas II that Iswolsky was irreplaceable and his resignation 'would be another satisfaction for our enemies'. She enclosed for the Tsar's consideration 'the notes which Benckendorff wrote *for me*; he is writing precisely about this'. She told her son that in England – that is, in the royal family – everyone blamed Germany for having masterminded the crisis in order to destroy Iswolsky.[124]

Through Maria Feodorovna, a shallow thinker at all times, Benckendorff advised her son (a vindictive and shallow man in his own right) of the worst possible reason for keeping an unreliable minister: to spite Germany. A French minister to Copenhagen in the 1890s was shocked by the Danish king's 'implacable memory' of the German annexation of Schleswig-Holstein in the 1860s.[125] The king's

119 Nicolson to Grey, 24.03.1909, FO 800/337, 310–12.

120 A. Nekludoff, *Diplomatic Reminiscences Before and During the World War, 1911–1917* (New York: E.P. Dutton & Company, 1920), 311.

121 Poklevsky to Iswolsky, 12/25.03.1909, *Au service*, 2: 212–5.

122 Poklevsky to Iswolsky, 18/31.03.1909, *Au service*, 2: 215–7.

123 Poklevsky to Savinsky, 31.03/13.04.1909, AVPRI, 340 op.806, ed.hr.14, l.107 ob.

124 I. Astaf'iev, *Russo-germanskie otnosheni'ia*, 192–4.

125 J.J. Jusserand, 182.

daughters, Maria and Alexandra, inherited his vendetta which court memoirists in the inter-war decades raised to the rank of 'pro-Entente political views'. In 1909 Maria Feodorovna's vindictiveness made it easy for her to side with those who prompted that Iswolsky had to be retained.

Iswolsky justified his capitulation to Germany in a letter to his friend the ambassador:

> I am accused of having acted too brusquely, without having informed the Cabinets … With documents in hand I proved to Nicolson and Touchard that their governments were aware of every detail … but their diplomats at Vienna strongly pressed for us to accept …

Nicolson had told him that the British might send a squadron to the Adriatic Sea, but this would not have saved Russia from an invasion. He finished by saying: 'London's displeasure offends and upsets me'.[126] The ambassador, following his usual logic, presented Russia's humiliation as Iswolsky's finest hour: 'I am not sure, *in re*, that we have not gained. The main point for us was peace, I do not see how it could have been assured if it were not for the reservations of London, Paris and Rome'. England's desire to cooperate with Russia had never been stronger than after the crisis. He implored the minister to forget about resignation, because it would be interpreted as Russia's shift towards Germany, a move which would bring the dynasty and the country to an impasse.[127]

Bulgarian independence was settled by the Russian financial transactions in the beginning of April and Iswolsky left for Bavaria to undergo surgery. Benckendorff felt the blow which Iswolsky's (and his) policy had suffered, for in April he most unusually agreed with Wesselitsky that Grey's attitude in the crisis had been a mistake, although still insisting that an Entente course remained the only possible one for Russia. He instructed the journalist to insert in his *Novoye Vremya* articles the following arguments: because of a close correlation between Russian domestic and foreign policies, Iswolsky's dismissal would bring about the resignation of Stolypin's government to be replaced by the reactionary Goremykin, Durnovo and Witte 'who are backed by the [*illegible*: foreign?] state which represents and maintains the monarchic order, it is a throwback to the 1884 combination … that … led to the Double [Russo-German] Alliance'.[128] Nicolson, probably influenced by Iswolsky himself, also predicted a pro-German cabinet if Stolypin and Iswolsky fell,[129] so Edward VII pleaded Iswolsky's case again in May:

> Reports have reached me that there is a possibility of M. Stolypine and M. Iswolsky retiring from the important posts which they now occupy but I sincerely

126 Iswolsky to A.K. Benckendorff, 25.03/04.04.1909, BC2, box 13.

127 A.K. Benckendorff to Iswolsky, 26.03/08.04.1909, *Au service*, 2: 217–9.

128 Wesselitsky to A.K. Benckendorff, 09.04.1909, BC2, box 15.

129 Nicolson to Hardinge, 06.05.1909, FO 800/337, 324–7.

> trust that you will be able to retain their valuable services which are so important for your country and the 'entente' between our two countries! Other names have been mentioned which I will not mention but I feel their views are very different to those of M. Stolypine and M. Iswolsky and if appointed the 'entente' between our two countries would *greatly* suffer![130]

Iswolsky remained in his post for a year and a half longer, owing mostly to the support of the British government and the scarcity of candidates. Tcharykow was sacrificed to the public wrath after the annexation crisis and replaced by Sazonov. Iswolsky told him from the beginning that he would be understudying for the ministry. Half of the time in 1909–10 Iswolsky was on leaves of absence. Sazonov's preparation consisted of following Iswolsky's negotiations with foreign states and reading on the most relevant political issues of the previous decade. Of those Sazonov later recalled only two: Russia's relations with Japan and with Britain which Iswolsky cherished as his personal achievements, attributing the Anglo-Russian convention to his 1904 conversation with Edward VII.[131]

Russians Visit Britain

The representatives of the Russian Duma and State Council were received 'warmly but tactfully', without anti-government outbursts, in the summer of 1909. Benckendorff hoped this visit would smooth the path to Nicholas II's arrival;[132] but the announcement of his visit in September 1909 drew protests from British Socialists and Russian political emigrants, though the Labour party officially withdrew from the anti-Russian campaign because of the outbursts of violence.[133] The 'Cowes' file in the embassy files is full of letters and telegrams from British political activists, some, like the Social Democratic Federation, cursing the 'inhuman scoundrel Nicholas the Bloody of Russia',[134] others assuring the ambassador that the Wolverhampton protest meeting, attended by 500 people, did not represent the feeling of the 100,000 inhabitants of the borough.[135] Grey dismissed the protests of Labour and radical Liberal MPs against the visit, saying that he welcomed Nicholas II to Britain as the head of a great and friendly state.[136]

---

130 Edward VII to Nicholas II, 03.05.1909, GARF, 601, op.1, d.1388, ll.39–40 ob.

131 S.D. Sazonov, *Vospominani'ia* (Minsk: Harvest, 2002), 18–22.

132 A.K. Benckendorff to Iswolsky, 10/23.06.1909, *Au service*, 235–8.

133 A.K. Benckendorff to Iswolsky, 08/21.07.1909, *Au service*, 238–9.

134 'Chas. Bayliss to the Secretary of the Russian Embassy', AVPRI, 184, op. 520 (1909) d.1349, l.165.

135 A ratepayer of Wolverhampton to A.K.Benckendorff, 26.07.1909, AVPRI, 184, op. 520 (1909), d.1349, ll.166–7.

136 Telegram to Edward VII. AVPRI, 184, op.520 (1909), d.1349, ll.156–64.

Throughout July Benckendorff and Lord Knollys exchanged lists of guests, of attendants, of the persons to be given awards, programmes and suggestions regarding the British officials whom Nicholas II should meet. A week before Nicholas II's arrival, Knollys sent Benckendorff the headings of the king's dinner speech, asking if Benckendorff or Iswolsky would wish the king to touch upon any other subjects. Edward VII was going to emphasize that Nicholas II was escorted by two fleets which protected Britain's coasts. He would speak of his pleasure in receiving the Duma delegates and of the growing good feeling between Russia and Britain,[137] thus reminding to the readers of the press about Britain's preparedness for war, the success of the convention and Russia's continued liberalization.

Nicholas II sailed into Cowes escorted by the British ships, the *Indomitable*, the *Inflexible* and the *Invincible*.[138] The names aptly describe Grey's conduct during the conversations with the Russian guests. On 3 August he had a discussion with Nicholas II and then with Benckendorff and Iswolsky, mostly about Persian affairs. Grey insisted that Russian troops had to withdraw from Persia in Russia's best interests; he assured the emperor that obvious British successes in Teheran (a new pro-British shah) did not undermine Russia's position. He noted with relief that Nicholas II did not repeat his request for a more binding agreement with Britain,[139] but Nicholas II left a petitioner's role to Iswolsky.

Grey repeated much the same to Iswolsky, cutting through the latter's explanations of the Persian situation. Neither violent disorders nor Turkish encroachments on Persian territory mattered to Grey: Russian troops had to withdraw. Iswolsky tried to turn the conversations to an Anglo-Russian entente when he spoke of his fears of a new Balkan crisis, which, as he correctly foresaw, might arise from Turkey's instability. He told Grey that he had turned down an Italian proposal of a Russo-Italo-Austrian agreement about the Balkans because it would look as if Russia had joined the Triple Alliance. As a reward, he hoped to get Britain's guarantees for the eventuality of a joint Austrian-Bulgarian attack on Turkey and occupation of Salonica and Macedonia which would bring them closer to Constantinople. He asked what Britain would do in this case. Grey answered that in order to avoid it, Russia and Britain should support Turkey.[140] Iswolsky failed to extract any promises or guarantees from Grey. The Tsar sailed away, leaving in his wake a snowfall of requests for donations and thanks from The Widows' Friend Society, The British and Foreign Sailors' Society, the Urban District Council of Cowes and others.

To avoid speculation, Nicholas II warned Grey that he would have a second meeting with William II on the return voyage. Both meetings had been proposed by Nicholas II in an attempt to return to the 'balanced course', but nothing happened

137 Knollys to A.K. Benckendorff, 26.07.1909, AVPRI, 184, op.520 (1909), d.1349, ll.199–200.

138 Sir John Fisher to A.K. Benckendorff, AVPRI, 184, op.520 (1909), d.1349, l.83.

139 Sir Edward Grey's memorandum, 06.08.1909, RA VIC/ADDC/7/2/Q.

140 Ibid.

during the meeting because Germany, confident of Russia's weakness, would not make offers and Stolypin and Iswolsky dissuaded the emperor from showing any initiative.[141]

Benckendorff and King Edward VII

Iswolsky continued to seek protection against new Austrian expansion: in October 1909 he signed a secret accord with Italy to preserve the status quo in the Balkans. He continued working on a Balkan League and in November asked for France's assistance in mending relations with Austria.[142] But the French foreign minister had already rejected the same suggestion by his own ambassador to Vienna, explaining that if Russia and Austria-Hungary made up their quarrel it would culminate in a new Three Emperors' Alliance.[143]

Grey informed Russia and France about a German proposal of a general naval and political agreement in September, assuring them of Britain's loyalty to the existing ones. Unlike previous years, Iswolsky welcomed the news, hoping that Russia would be able to participate 'morally' in an Anglo-German understanding, proving wrong those in Russia who still feared the consequences of a pro-British course (Fig. 7.1). He looked forward to a détente between the two groups of European powers.[144] Benckendorff wrote that he did not know anything of the Anglo-German talks, and could only offer Iswolsky his impressions from a stay at Balmoral where he understood that the king and Grey wished for a rapprochement with Germany but were sceptical about its feasibility. Haldane, who had been one of the Balmoral party, told Benckendorff that Germany's overtures need not worry Russia because the security of the British frontier in Asia was a necessary factor in the European balance.[145] Benckendorff described the stay in Balmoral to his wife: McKenna, Haldane, Rosebery, Lord Cawdor and a mass of others guests, and all the conversation conducted, encouraged, made natural and amusing by His skill, His tact, His aptitude to avoid quite effortlessly saying a foolish thing … Telegrams are pouring in and He is reading them aloud, with aside comments, as if alone in the room … And all of this in my presence. And then to compare – that is what hurts.[146]

The ambassador's letters became animated as soon as it came to the things which he understood and to which he tended to reduce politics and policies – catching and interpreting the moods and shades of meaning in after-dinner

141 I. Astaf'iev, *Russko-germanski'ie otnosheni'ia …*, 210–14.

142 *Les carnets de Georges Louis*, 1: 64.

143 *Les carnets de Georges Louis*, 1: 27.

144 Iswolsky to A.K. Benckendorff, 09/21.09.1909, BC2, box 13.

145 A.K. Benckendorff to Iswolsky, 19.09/02.10.1909, *Au service*, 2: 247–9.

146 A.K. Benckendorff to S.P. Benckendorff, 23.09/06.10.1909, GARF, 1126, op.1, d.152, ll.76–7 ob.

Fig. 7.1 'Russia in England', Count Benckendorff by the Spy

conversations between statesmen. He admired Edward VII and believed that the king inspired and guided British statesmen. He would have been shocked to hear Sir Francis Bertie's condescending acknowledgment that 'when he was put in possession of the requisite information there could be no better ambassador' than the king because he knew what to say[147] and did not allow himself major improvizations. Benckendorff could not help comparing Edward VII and Nicholas II. He drily mentioned that Nicholas II impressed the British statesmen as an 'entirely unaffected but well-informed' country gentleman.[148] Coming from the British, it might have been construed as a compliment, but not in the eyes of a Russian or European aristocrat.

The Baghdad Railway after 1908

In 1909, after years of warning Iswolsky about the dangers for Russia of an Anglo-German rapprochement, Benckendorff caught the London mood of wanting to talk to Germany and began to write of the advantages for Russia. It would mean European peace for a good many years and Russia's role gradually growing. But as to its feasibility, he echoed Nicolson's doubts.[149] Sir Ernest Cassel, whom the ambassador had asked to help Russia in the Baghdad railway affair, was negotiating 'things which are rather embarrassing and difficult for us', as Benckendorff wrote to his wife.[150] When Cassel returned with empty hands, Benckendorff wrote to Iswolsky that the British would be content if the affair remained where it was but realized that the opposition to the Baghdad railway was futile and so they were thinking again about connecting the Russian and the Indian railroad networks to diminish the significance of the Baghdad railroad.[151]

It was a Russian idea which the Foreign Office did not reject but did not actively support either. In 1908 Tcharykow told Nicolson that to forestall German railway construction in Persia after 1910 their governments should get concessions from the Persian government. While Iswolsky spoke of a line running parallel to the Afghan frontier on the Persian side, which Kitchener considered dangerous for India,[152] Tcharykow thought that Russia could build a line Julfa–Teheran–Kerman with her wider gauge, and Britain would build a Nushki–Kerman–Shiraz–Ahwaz line with the European gauge, thus creating a railway Calais–Calcutta which could

147 Bertie to F.M. Ponsonby, 27.11.1912, FO 800/174, 148.

148 A.K. Benckendorff to S.P. Benckendorff, 14.09.1909, GARF, 1126, op.1, d.152, ll.70–71 ob.

149 A.K. Benckendorff to Iswolsky, 21.09/04.10.1909, *Au service*, 2: 250–55.

150 A.K. Benckendorff to S.P. Benckendorff, 05/18.12.1909, GARF, 1126, op.1, d.152, ll.107–12 ob.

151 A.K. Benckendorff to Iswolsky, 08/22.12.1909, *Au service*, 2: 256–9.

152 Spring Rice to Bertie, 23.11.1902, FO 800/176, 153–9.

well compete with the Baghdad railway.[153] When Hardinge became the viceroy of India, he did not oppose the idea of connecting the railway networks, but the Foreign Office preferred to delay a Russian decision to build a railroad in the north. At the end of 1910 a joint Anglo-Franco-Russian Societé d'Études was created. The Foreign Office's attitude was 'favourable in principle but so hedged about with qualifications as to route and timing as to be almost meaningless'.[154] In the meanwhile, Anglo-German negotiations went on. Late in 1909 when a British company applied for railroad concessions in Constantinople, Iswolsky became worried that Germany had persuaded Britain to abandon the idea of four-party negotiations.[155] The ambassador replied that Grey suggested that Russia could also negotiate with Germany independently, but with a reservation that prior to concluding the negotiations they would discuss them among the four. Benckendorff reminded Iswolsky to make it clear to Germany that Russia wanted only an economic arrangement. 'As long as in Berlin there is hope of making a political arrangement with us or with England, the German cabinet will continue its game, which, apart from everything, makes an economic agreement impossible'.[156] To arrest a German advance into Persia, Russian and British ministers had tried to obtain control over the Persian government in the question of concessions of political or strategic importance to foreign countries, and Poklevsky frankly told the German minister that in Persia all concessions were political,[157] provoking a protest of the German government.[158] Talks with Germany were imminent.

Britain, Russia and Germany in 1910–1914

On 5 May 1910, Goschen, the British ambassador to Germany, wrote in his diary that Grey decided that an entente with Germany was only possible on the basis of reducing naval budgets. Otherwise, he preferred to remain free to support France or Russia.[159] Germany suggested that the naval issue would be treated in a general political arrangement with Britain, but in July, giving a summary of the conversations to the cabinet, Grey explained that any engagements with Germany which might lead to misunderstanding or loss of friendship with France and Germany [Russia?] would be inexpedient.[160] Grey promised to Benckendorff that he would not settle with Germany without France and Russia and would not treat

153 Nicolson to Hardinge, 10.03.1908, FO 800/337, 229–30.
154 Philip Ziegler, *The Sixth Great Power: Barings*, 317–8.
155 Nicolson to Grey, 19.11.1909, BD, VI: 390–1.
156 A.K. Benckendorff to Iswolsky, 26.05/08.06.1910, *Au service*, 2: 272–3.
157 I. Astaf'iev, 235.
158 Grey to Nicolson, 11.05.1910, BD VI: 480–81.
159 05.05.1910, *The Diary of Edward Goschen*, 245–6.
160 Keith Robbins, *Sir Edward Grey*, 221–2.

separately the Persian and the Baghdad issues.[161] Iswolsky was worried by the simultaneous German overtures to Russia and Britain in May 1910. He wondered whether he should insist on three-party negotiations or deal with Germany directly, asking Benckendorff to ensure the British and French backing for his proposal to Germany. But he was inclined to agree with Benckendorff that Russia should insist on a three-party negotiation, to show her perfect loyalty to Britain.[162]

Wesselitsky travelled to St Petersburg via Vienna in early 1910 and reported from Vienna the preparations for an attack against Russia, Serbia and Italy, but also spoke of Aehrenthal's desire for a new, better entente with Russia to prevent the collapse of the Ottoman Empire and to agree beforehand on the terms of its partition. At St Petersburg he ascertained that Iswolsky wanted no entente with Austria, but rather 'a general entente'. Wesselitsky found more hostility to the Anglo-Russian convention at St Petersburg than in London. The *Novoye Vremya* staff organized a dinner in his honour and during the celebration Wesselitsky's colleagues reproached him for having promoted the Anglo-Russian convention: 'The old Suvorin shouted: "He has put us all under England's heel, we do not want it"'. Even at the foreign ministry he found opposition to the pro-British orientation. In the service of the cause, Wesselitsky delivered a lecture on Anglo-Russian relations at the Club of Public Activists and met Stolypin. He established good relations with *The Times*' and the Reuter's correspondents and believed that it would allow him to influence the tone of their reports to London.[163]

A New Reign in Britain and a New Minister in Russia

In May 1910 Benckendorff was so distraught by the death of Edward VII that he asked for a leave. He wrote: 'He was a real and sincere link between Russia and England, besides, during the time I have known him we have formed a very strong personal bond'. Indeed, as Max Beerbohm's sketch of the king's three favourite ambassadors[164] implies, Benckendorff was one of the trio that entertained the easily bored Edward VII on weekends. Mensdorff was known for his unparalleled knowledge of seating etiquette at dinners, Soveral was a ladies' man and a teller of risqué jokes. Benckendorff endeared himself to everyone by his good humour and absent-mindedness. The Austrian, Portuguese and Russian ambassadors enjoyed a much greater standing in society than among their colleagues.

Benckendorff referred to the new king as '[v]ery straightforward, very conscientious and not at all weak'; not too friendly to William II, but no more than that. Predictably, he found the new king lacking on one account: 'There is one thing

161 A.K. Benckendorff to Iswolsky, 06/19.05.1910, *Au service*, 2: 264–7.

162 Iswolsky to A.K. Benckendorff, 19.05/01.06.1910, BC2, box 13.

163 Wesselitsky to A.K. Benckendorff, 26.01.1910, BC2, box 15.

164 'Three ambassadors', Max Beerbohm papers, Harry Ransome Centre Art Collection, University of Texas at Austin, 65.224.8.

a sovereign cannot bequeath to his successor – his personal prestige'.[165] For eight years the greatest satisfaction of his career and his life had been his relations with Edward VII. He fell under the spell of the king's opinions. Benckendorff's hostility to Germany, completely absent from his letters prior to his posting in Britain, to a great degree reflected Edward VII's known dislike for his nephew and his policies, which his intimate friends either shared or imitated.[166] What in Edward VII was an expression of personal feelings and could be subdued or disguised for the sake of political interests, in Benckendorff became a rigid political doctrine, further strengthened by the general British mood of suspicion regarding Germany.

Iswolsky's decision to resign was another blow to Benckendorff. The Bosnian crisis left a cloud over their relations, which Iswolsky tried to dispel during their meeting in late 1909, in St Petersburg,[167] telling Benckendorff his version of the Buchlau incident. The ambassador described Iswolsky's initial tone during the conversation as 'bombastic and a little nervous'. He confided to his wife:

> First of all, I take back some suspicions I had about certain documents previously unknown and recently divulged as to their alleged content [Aehrenthal's press interviews about the Buchlau]. What astonishes me and what I did not expect is the Danube [Aehrenthal]. I could have cleared it up with Albert [Mensdorff] at the earliest occasion. He [Iswolsky] is pure as driven snow and the lie is on the Danube. This makes me happy.

His confidence in Iswolsky's honour restored, Benckendorff sympathized with his difficult position. He saw himself and Iswolsky as the only champions of peace and progress in the Russian government: '… one has to realize that … he is alone at the Pont de Chantres [the foreign ministry] with his ideas … and mine'.[168]

In July 1910 Iswolsky wrote that he had parted ways with Stolypin over the latter's policies in Finland. Besides, the elderly Nelidov would soon retire and Iswolsky wanted to take over the Paris embassy. He wrote:

> I will frankly confess that the only embassy which really attracts me is the one which you occupy with such distinction, and in which I wholeheartedly wish you to stay for many years to come, because I am certain that no one can do as much as you in the position. Nevertheless, if for any reason you would prefer to swap London for Paris, I could suggest this combination to H.M. I implore you, dear friend, not to take this letter for an imposition. I would follow through with this idea only if *it would be convenient to you from all points of view*, Please

165 A.K. Benckendorff to Iswolsky, 28.04/11.05.1910, *Au service*, 2: 262–4.

166 Prince von Bülow, Memoirs 1903–1909 (London: Putnam, [1931–2]), 35.

167 Iswolsky to A.K. Benckendorff, 07/20.11.1909, BC2, box 13.

168 A.K. Benckendorff to S.P. Benckendorff, 26.11/09.12.1909, GARF, 1126, op.1, d.152, ll.116–19 ob.

> reply with the next courier, if possible. As for the thorny and important issue of my successor, I do not see any possible candidate but Sazonov.

Sazonov's appointment would ensure that the policy continued. Stolypin was not too favourable to his brother-in-law's appointment, fearing accusations of nepotism, but the emperor liked him.[169] Benckendorff tried flattery to dissuade Iswolsky: 'Sazonov will be considered a good choice. But he is not a force'. He advised Iswolsky to lay open his soul to Nicholas II and to let the Tsar persuade him to stay. He firmly turned down Iswolsky's offer of the Paris embassy:

> Religion, old attachments, everything there would work against me. It is so with Paris, it is also so with other important positions, except for London. If I managed to be of some use here, it is because circumstances have placed me in the only post where I could be useful, for only here I can be Ambassador of Russia and nothing else. I am so convinced of this that I decided, if God gives me a longer life and if the Emperor still wants my services, I can only be of use to him in London.

A Shift in the British Attitude to Russia

The ambassador spoke of his despair at seeing the future of the Russian policy suddenly uncertain,[170] but the entente seemed to be thriving. Even the British attitude to Russia was improving thanks to the slowly developing Anglo-Russian cultural and economic relations. When Sergei Diaghilev began to bring his yearly *Saisons Russes* and Russian opera to Central and Western Europe, the fashion for all things Russian had trickled into London. Russian fiction was translated; Russian musicians toured England, achieving a turnaround in the attitude to Russia among the educated British. When the fashion for Russia spread into the popular culture, Russian protagonists appeared in romance fiction. One such popular novel, Baroness von Hutten's 1907 *What Became of Pam,* even featured a dashing secretary of the Russian embassy who courted and conquered an English spinster. The author must have taken inspiration in the incipient vogue for Russia and, to be fair to Poklevsky's efforts, in the reputation of splendour and elegance which surrounded the Russian embassy in London. And yet, Benckendorff was no different from other Russian bureaucrats in seeing the increased numbers of common Russians travelling to Europe as a source of concern. Benckendorff preferred to see a Prince Obolensky and a Princess Wiazemsky represent Russia in Britain. They were certain to mix with the right sort of the British and to benefit from their stay in Britain.

169 Iswolsky to A.K. Benckendorff, 15/28. 07.1910, BC2, box 13.
170 A.K. Benckendorff to Iswolsky, 20.07/02.08.1910, *Au service*, 2: 287–9.

The ambassador, with his own exclusively Western tastes in arts and literature, does not seem to have been enthusiastic about attending Russian artistic performances. He did not expect to enjoy them and he worried about possible outbursts of Russophobia in the audience. He'd rather not know about them. But his subordinates pressed him to attend the last performance of a Russian balalaika orchestra at the Colosseum theatre. He went with Etter and Sevastopoulo. At the end he lived through anxious moments:

> … a balalaika plays *Rule Britannia* – the audience ecstatic. *God Save the King* … I am wondering what the devil is going to happen next. I am sitting very much in the public view. I am getting worried. The orchestra strikes up *God Save the Tsar*.

There was applause, but Benckendorff was only half reassured by this demonstration of goodwill, he wrote to his wife,[171] though in a letter to his minister he described it as an example of friendliness to Russia among the right sort of British.[172] A right-wing deputy, making a criticism of the Russian diplomatic service, told the Duma that the Russian ambassador at London had advised the musicians not to perform the Russian anthem for fear of an anti-Russian demonstration. The incident was picked up by the *Novoye Vremya* and Benckendorff was sufficiently concerned about their attack to explain to Sazonov that the conductor of the orchestra asked him about the etiquette and the ambassador had explained that either both British and Russian anthems should be performed or neither.[173] He must have thought that he had been right in not wishing to attend the performance in the first place.

Wesselitsky commented on an article in the *Novoye Vremya* which Benckendorff had recommended to him. The article dealt with the Anglo-German antagonism, alleging that Russia's position allowed her to balance between the two rivals. Wesselitsky dismissed the idea as a dream but denied that England would be able to stay out of a Russo-German conflict:

> In England very few even among the most extreme pacifists believe in English neutrality in case of a Russo-German conflict. Baron Reuter rightly summarized the opinion of all serious English politicians when he told me, 'The health of each of the Three can be guaranteed provided none of them has separate meals'.[174]

References to the eventuality of a general European war in the correspondence and conversations between Nicolson, Iswolsky, Benckendorff, Grey and Benckendorff

171 A.K. Benckendorff to S.P. Benckendorff, 05/18.12.1909, GARF, 1126, op.1, d.152, ll.107–12 ob.

172 A.K. Benckendorff to S.P. Benckendorff, 06/19.12.1909, GARF, 1126, op.1, d.152, ll.113–14 ob.

173 A.K. Benckendorff to Sazonov, n.d., AVPRI, 340. op.812, d.10, l.89.

174 Wesselitsky to A.K. Benckendorff, 10.08.1910, BC2, box 15.

and Hardinge and Nicolson, as well as Wesselitsky's assessment of British public opinion, reflect the fact that there were quite a few people, some of them in the Foreign Office, who believed that Britain would not be able to stay out of a continental war. Following the Bosnian crisis, everything seemed to indicate it would be fought around the Ottoman inheritance when Russia recovered her strength. Sir Edward Goschen asked the German state secretary Kiderlen-Wächter if he believed that a Balkan war could be localised, and the German replied in the affirmative on the condition that Britain kept Russia back.[175] And yet Britain avoided a commitment to Russia. Grey thought it quite sufficient to get his way at St Petersburg through Benckendorff who put forward Grey's considerations as his own and defended Grey's refusals to comply with Russian desires. The undemonstrative and reserved Grey encouraged Benckendorff's inclination to play the devil's advocate with the Russian government. At a large dinner party at Mrs Keppel's house, the Foreign Secretary complimented the Russian ambassador on the attitude which he would have never tolerated in a British one. Benckendorff reported to his wife: '[He] said that whatever the Russian government's or his government's opinion, I always have one of my own: "He sticks to it and usually wins. He is a really independent Ambassador". Benckendorff added modestly: "I have never seen myself in that light"'.[176]

He saw Anglo-Russian friendship after 1907 as a reality and his vision of Russia's interests stemmed from this assumption: to him, Russia was part of the Entente and everything that would benefit the coalition would be to Russia's benefit. His regular reminders to Iswolsky of Britain's promised support in the Straits issue as the great achievement of the convention encouraged Iswolsky to compensate for Russia's difficulties in Persia and for the lost positions in the Far East by pursuing the Balkan dreams. The 1908–9 events in Europe and Asia showed that Benckendorff's judgment was unreliable. His professional reputation in Russia suffered, but Empress Maria Feodorovna's and Iswolsky's friendship made him impervious to criticism.

175 *The Diary of Edward Goschen*, 09.08.1910, 217.

176 Marina Soroka, 'Debating Russia's Choice', 6.

Chapter 8
Waiting for an August War, 1910–1913

After facing a possibility of a European war in 1908–9, the great powers attempted to move away from the brink. Since the 'balance of power' game continued, the only thing to do was to replace the actors. New initiatives required from those who would implement them reasonable optimism and another rare commodity among politicians: freedom from rancour and suspicion. This could be best done by new men. And, indeed, the cast of actors considerably changed in 1909–10, sometimes without human intervention. Edward VII passed away, fulfilling the fervent wish of the German government for this 'element of unrest to be removed from the English clockwork'.[1] William II and Nicholas II temporarily desisted from personal diplomatic initiatives. Bülow and Iswolsky were replaced respectively by Bethmann-Hollweg and Sazonov.

Sir Arthur Nicolson left St Petersburg to replace Hardinge as permanent under-secretary of the Foreign Office, while Hardinge became viceroy of India.

The Foreign Office remembered Benckendorff's grief in 1905, at the news of Hardinge being replaced by Nicolson at the Petersburg embassy: it had required a personal letter from Hardinge to reassure the ambassador[2] that his transfer did not signal an about-face in the British political course. So, the news was preceded by a letter from King George V to Nicholas II, promising that the two moves (Hardinge's and Nicolson's) would guarantee the continuity of the British policy towards Russia and the Anglo-Russian entente.[3] 'From a ship off Aden' Hardinge sent a farewell letter to Benckendorff, pledging to do his best in India to remove the atmosphere of suspicion between England and Russia which still acted as a 'malarial fog obscuring the vision of all weather'.[4] Concerning Nicolson's successor, Sir George Buchanan, Benckendorff wrote:

> I would not say he has Nicolson's calibre, but I have known him for a very long time as a sympathizer of Russia since the days of his youth, a true gentleman. I know that he has very sound opinions regarding Turkey and the Balkans.[5]

1 Bülow to William II, 15.07.1908, *Letters of Prince Bülow*, 248–51.

2 A.K. Benckendorff to Hardinge, 22.11.1905, Cambridge University, Hardinge Archives, 9/53/7.

3 George V to Nicholas II, 03.07.1910, GARF, f.601, op.1, ed.hr.1219, ll.31–2 ob.

4 Hardinge to A.K. Benckendorff, 10.11.1910, BC2, box 13.

5 A.K. Benckendorff to Iswolsky, 21.07/03.08.1910, *Au service*, 2: 289–92.

Buchanan, who was to stay in Russia until 1918, to the end of his days never cleared himself from the persistent rumour that he had been conspiring with or encouraging Russian opposition in their efforts to unseat Nicholas II during the war. He was a conscientious diplomat who to the best of his ability carried out his instructions – not a trait to impress Benckendorff, of course. As for his ideas, in diplomatic memoirs and correspondence 'sound' was a synonym for 'Machiavellian'. A sample of Buchanan's sound views was recorded in late 1916 by a Russian diarist. Deploring Bulgaria's entry in the war on Germany's side, Grand Duke Andrey Vladimirovich said that the action proved that Bulgarian statesmen cared little about their mother country. Buchanan replied: 'That should not be a surprise: we have all been corrupting them through bribes'. And he explained to his host that in Britain the attitude to bribery was simple: if a politician made it known that he would perform certain services for money, common sense required that he should be paid.[6] No doubt, Buchanan had many sound ideas, but, as with his colleagues from other powers, they were tidily compartmentalized: one set for dealing with one's equals and another, for the Balkan politicians.

Not for the first time, a rumour originating in St Petersburg had it that Benckendorff would also be replaced; there was an opinion, ignored by Nicholas II, that the ambassador had outlived his usefulness in London. Benckendorff was concerned enough that he asked Iswolsky to make the emperor promise to leave him in London. After a meeting with Iswolsky in Frankfurt, Benckendorff telegraphed to his chargé d'Affaires: '*The Times* is wrong in sending me to Berlin. It is absurd' and asked St Petersburg for an official disclaimer of the rumour.[7]

Iswolsky resigned on the eve of the Potsdam meeting of the Russian and German emperors in the autumn of 1910. Russo-German relations were too fragile to leave Nicholas II unchaperoned in Potsdam,[8] so, on Stolypin's recommendation, the Tsar summoned the deputy foreign minister Sazonov to Germany and appointed him 'the director of the foreign ministry'. The interim rank was due to Russian concern about the Entente's sensitivities if the new foreign minister made his debut in the Russo-German talks.[9]

The New Foreign Minister

Sergei D. Sazonov (Fig. 8.1) was the third in a series of Nicholas II's foreign ministers chosen among relatively junior members of the diplomatic service, who lacked prestige in and out of Russia. A contemporary Russian politician described him as 'a puny, physically weak man with a low voice devoid of firm commanding

6 Grand Duke Andrey's Diary, [11/24.09.1916] in *Gibel' imperii* (Moscow, 2000), 301.

7 N. Etter to S.D. Sazonov, 1/14.09.1910, AVPRI, f. 340, op.812, d. 141, ll–2 ob.

8 Stolypin to Iswolsky, 21.10.1910, P.A. Stolypin, *Perepiska*, 376–7.

9 S.D. Sazonov, *Vospominani'ia* (Minsk: Harvest, [1928] 2002), 36.

Fig. 8.1 Sergei D. Sazonov
Source: By kind permission of the Archive of Russian Imperial Foreign Policy.

tones, a man who carefully chose his words and presented his ideas in a deliberately vague, nebulous form … his opinions were the same as his predecessor's, but his speech lacked confidence …'.[10] The appointment illustrates the Tsar's conviction that a foreign minister was no more than his secretary. Taube, never kind to his chiefs, described the pious and honest Sazonov as the worst foreign minister in Russian history, blaming his appointment on British influence. He considered Sazonov inconsistent, ignorant and prone to self-delusions. To him, Sazonov was the opposite of Iswolsky in everything except his political views: he was also

10 N.V. Savitch, *Vospominani'ia* (St Petersburg: Logos, 1993), 106.

pro-Entente and even more of an Anglophile.[11] By this time in Russia the Entente meant Britain. Sazonov's nervousness and hesitations were easily understandable to most well-informed Russians. He realized that his task was not the maintenance of the national prestige or attempts to resolve great historical tasks of Russia, but protecting peace at all costs, so as to gain time to restore the army and settle domestic affairs.[12]

But public opinion and the emperor expected him to combine all of the above and no wonder Sazonov wore himself out under the stress.

Benckendorff continued to be important because of the ascendancy which Anglo-Russian relations had acquired over Russian policies in the previous period. Most of Sazonov's moves aroused exasperation and suspicions among British and French diplomats, and Benckendorff's task became to take to Grey requests for support from Sazonov and transmit to the minister Grey's refusals and Cambon's reproaches in a much softened version. Sazonov's compliance was not as easy to obtain as Iswolsky's. He worked under the supervision of the head of the government, so Benckendorff's pressure came up against Stolypin's and, later, Ivan Goremykin's will, even if Sazonov might have wanted to give satisfaction to Grey.

Sazonov's letters to Benckendorff are curt, their content restricted to the current political matters directly related to Anglo-Russian relations. There was also a marked difference between Benckendorff's guarded letters to Sazonov and his effusions to Iswolsky. The count pleaded the British case in a more circumlocutory way, appealing to Russia's interests rather than to her chivalrous obligations. Iswolsky and Benckendorff tried to restrain their natural desire to dictate to their former subordinate, but both wanted to continue steering Russian foreign policy.

In his postwar memoir, Sazonov wrote that Iswolsky's European inheritance was satisfactory, though he qualified this generous statement by saying that the situation on the borders with Austria, Persia, Turkey and China caused concerns,[13] meaning that in 1910 Russia had no secure borders either in Europe or in Asia. He omitted to mention the extended border with Germany, Russia's most worrisome neighbour, because in 1910 he still hoped to repair relations there. Indeed, his optimism was not unfounded: some in the German foreign ministry still thought that the Anglo-Russian convention did not make Russia a greater threat to Germany's security although it did make Britain more dangerous.[14]

Russo-German Potsdam Agreement

When, in October 1910, Sazonov took up with Bethmann-Hollweg the Baghdad railway question, dormant since 1907, Anglo-German informal talks were still

11 M. Taube, *Zarnitsy*, 165.
12 N.V. Savitch, 106.
13 S.D. Sazonov, 31.
14 I. Astaf'iev, 255.

dragging on. The Foreign Office suspected that the talks were mostly a bait to detach Britain from France and Russia[15] and lead to her isolation and Germany's supremacy on the continent. Neither Russia nor Britain would accept an agreement with Germany unless they could dictate the terms in order to preserve their free hand. The Foreign Office decided that no agreement was possible unless Germany decreased naval expenditure and made concessions on the Baghdad railway.[16]

Germany did not demand concessions in the Russian zone of Persia, but in exchange expected Russia to accept the joining of railroads of Asia Minor with the future Russian network which would connect the Caucasus with Teheran. Sazonov promised to build it by 1920. He hoped to bring Britain into the affair by that time and so avert a German monopoly. The only new point in the Potsdam agreement was that Russia promised not to oppose Germany in the construction of the Baghdad railroad,[17] and he insisted that he did not contravene the terms of the Anglo-Russian convention as Russia was not admitting Germany into Persia.[18] Like Grey in 1909, Sazonov in 1910 received a German proposal for a general agreement. Germany would not support Austro-Hungarian expansion in the Balkans (with an aside that Austria had given assurances of having no expansionist plans) and Russia would not support Britain's anti-German policy. Both parties would guarantee the safety of the Balkan states and of the Ottoman Empire. They would jointly oppose the expansion in Persia of any other nation, including Turkey.[19] Sazonov was tempted, but he was committed to the Entente and tried to soften his refusal, saying that Nicholas II had already promised all of that during the Potsdam meeting and monarchs' promises were worth more than treaties.[20] Nevertheless, on 4 December, Bethmann-Hollweg spoke in parliament about the Russo-German understanding which guaranteed that Russia and Germany would not enter combinations against each other.

The alarmed and irritated Entente asked to know the content of the Potsdam talks.[21] Cambon complained to Benckendorff that Sazonov's draft of the agreement did not emphasize strongly enough Russia's solidarity with the Entente. Benckendorff agreed that if Sazonov's had indeed requested to Germany to make Austria-Hungary respect the Balkan status quo, he was in the wrong.[22] He joined Buchanan, Nicolson and George V in criticizing the wording of the Russo-German draft treaty and warned Sazonov that British alarm might lead to a change in Anglo-

---

15 18.08.1908. Minute by Eyre Crowe, *The Mirage of Power*, 430–31.

16 Hardinge to Goschen, 26.04.1910, *The Mirage of Power*, 431–2.

17 S.D. Sazonov, 34.

18 I.V. Bestuzhev, *Bor'ba v Rossii po voprosam vneshnei politiki 1909–1910 gg* (Moscow, 1961), 328.

19 Ibid., 331.

20 I. Astaf'iev, 252–4.

21 *The Diary of Edward Goschen*, 227.

22 Paul Cambon to Pichon, 07.12.1910, DDF, XIII: 121–5.

Russian relations as they, too, were expecting to receive proposals from Germany.[23] Sazonov replied that he had given the draft text to the Entente ambassadors, and had announced he would visit London and Paris in the following spring. He could do no more. He had told Buchanan that 'the Baghdad railway' in the document meant only the Konia-Baghdad section, under construction at the moment. He did not discuss the sections in the Persian Gulf basin or on the Mediterranean, of interest to Britain and France respectively, because these would be discussed at a later stage by the four parties, as Britain proposed. Besides, he had told Bethmann categorically that Russia would not give financial or economic assistance to the enterprise.[24]

But the Foreign Office and the Quai d'Orsay thought that there was nothing economic or financial in the Baghdad railway and by the treaty with Germany, Goschen concluded, Russia detached itself from the Entente.[25]

Persia: Morgan Shuster

Benckendorff wrote to Sazonov that although in principle the Entente accepted Russia's right to direct talks with Germany, he had conducted the Potsdam talks as if the neutral zone of Persia and the British zone were none of his concern and so he had gone against the spirit of the convention. He risked losing British support against the Persians in the north. Benckendorff reminded him of Grey's sacrifice: in order to keep German ministry advisers out of Persia, Grey had opposed the French ones too; the British note to the Persian government and Russo-German negotiations caused unrest in Turkey, so Grey had to increase the security force on the southern roads and in the neutral zone.[26] (Benckendorff did not notice that Grey's 'sacrifice' gave Britain considerable advantage over Russia in the neutral zone). He praised Sazonov's decision not to finance the restoration of the pro-Russian dethroned shah: 'We should be neutral in this issue, right down to the withdrawal from Kazvin and the issue of our officers in the Brigade'.[27]

In Persia, the centrepiece of the convention, Russia and Britain managed to keep Germany out, although the construction of the Baghdad railway would affect their interests. Due to the Russian policy of push and pull, where every push advised by the Teheran legation or by the Caucasian administration was followed by a pull imposed by the fear of destroying the convention, Russia was haemorrhaging millions of roubles without ensuring peace on the 2,000 km border

23 A.K. Benckendorff to Sazonov, 06/19.12.1910, AVPRI, f.340, op.812, d.10, ll.96–9.

24 Sazonov to A.K. Benckendorff, 01/14.12.1910, BC2, box 14.

25 *The Diary of Edward Goschen*, 231.

26 A.K. Benckendorff to Sazonov, 04/17.01.1911, AVPRI, f.340, op.812, d.10, ll.4–5.

27 A.K. Benckendorff to S.D. Sazonov, 17.11.1910, AVPRI, f.340, op.812, d.10, ll.90–91.

or significant advances in trade. When a gradual Russian withdrawal began in June 1909 despite robbery and pillaging in the region,[28] the ambassador asked Iswolsky to ignore the Russian press which spoke of Russia's loss of prestige in Persia: 'True prestige demands that a great country's policy remain faithful to the engagements taken in full awareness of the cause and in the name of Russia's most important interests'.[29]

'Persian independence' became a card in the two powers' game. In the form in which it was, it worked for Britain better than for Russia. Even those diplomats who arrived in Teheran imbued with Benckendorff's ideas sooner or later realized that London embassy's opinions were not always applicable to Persian difficulties. Buchanan was embarrassed by the flow of British complaints about Persia which he had to take to Sazonov. The minister finally retorted that though the entente with Britain was the cornerstone of his policy, he had had enough:

> Do whatever you wish [in your zone] and let me act in mine, because ultimately I will remain loyal to the principles of our understanding. And I have given in on so many issues! You have wished us to abandon the old Shah, I have abandoned him. You have wanted us to give a joint loan to Persia, we have accepted, etc. Here I am reproached for all the concessions which are termed 'weaknesses'. I have received – I am telling you in confidence – three letters accusing me of treason and threatening death. And on top of this you keep coming to complain. It's truly inadmissible![30]

Throughout 1911 Russian and British foreign ministries argued about Morgan Shuster, an American financial expert invited by the Persian government with the blessing of the Russian and British authorities, to put Persian finance in order. His actions would reduce Russia's control over northern Persia, and St Petersburg opposed them with increasing energy.

Shuster appointed two British subjects as representatives in Isphahan and Shiraz and planned to do the same in other cities, both in the neutral zone and in the north. Russia thought it was a shift in the *status quo*; the Foreign Office insisted that it was not. After an incident between a Russian consular official and Shuster's subordinates, the Persian government officially demanded the recall of the Russian consul general in Teheran. Poklevsky presented an ultimatum to the Persian government threatening a break of diplomatic relations unless they presented apologies. Neratov asked for Britain's support:

> What we are hoping for from England at this moment is that it would offer a tangible proof obvious to everyone here [in Russia] that England does not play a

28 Nicolson to Grey, 14.06.1909, RA VIC/ADDC7/2/Q.

29 A.K. Benckendorff to Iswolsky, 27.05/09.06.1909, *Au service*, 2: 232–4.

30 *Les carnets de Georges Louis*, 20.04.1912, 2: 1–2.

> double game in the north of Persia and that it gives us freedom of action, always respecting Persian independence.[31]

Shuster also appealed to Britain – through the press – giving rise to a campaign to save Persian independence from Russia. Benckendorff argued that Russia's prestige and influence would be strengthened if she supported Shuster's reforms. He compared Shuster with Lord Cromer in Egypt who brought peace and prosperity to the country and created favourable conditions for foreign investments.[32] Neratov retorted: 'Prior to developing Egypt the English occupied it'. Shuster intended to appoint a British officer as the head of the Treasury gendarmerie; to make a new appointment at the postal and telegraph service and to engage the services of the Seligman bank (a private US bank with ties to the British Rothschilds).[33] Seligman and the treasurer were guaranteeing each other's permanence in Persia: without Seligman's permission Shuster could not be dismissed, the loan would be guaranteed by Seligman's right to take over the control of any Persian state's sources of revenue, except the customs; he would also control spending. Neratov wrote: 'The three projects, if implemented, would give England an exceptional position in all of Persia because Shuster means to stay in his post for a long time and become a dictator'.[34] The Russian finance minister was not opposed to Persia's loan from the Seligman bank, but the terms of the loan would allow Seligman to control Persia's financial policy and would create British political interests in the Russian zone.[35] Benckendorff insisted that Seligman and Shuster gave no cause for Russian concern,[36] as they were not British. Finally, the Russians managed to consolidate the Persian debts, and the loan went through in January 1912.[37]

Whether he did not know and relied on the Foreign Office's or his City friends' assurances, or he knew and did not care, Benckendorff misinformed Neratov in defending Shuster as a straightforward businessman who was simply trying to do his duty by the unfortunate Persians and had nothing to do with British commercial interests. Morgan Shuster, despite his official position as an adviser to the Persian government, worked for the New York banking firm of Kuhn, Loeb and Co, closely involved with the British and Dutch oil interests (Cassel, Marcus Samuel and Deterding). In 1911 he was helping a British oil company founded by William D'Arcy and Lord Strathcona to spread their operation into the Russian

---

31 Neratov to A.K. Benckendorff, 28.07/10.08.1911, BC2, box 14.

32 A.K. Benckendorff to A.A. Neratov, 14/27.09.1911, AVPRI, f.340, op.812, d.10, ll.45–7.

33 David McLean, *Britain and Her Buffer State: The Collapse of the Persian Empire, 1890–1914* (London, 1979), 98.

34 Neratov to A.K. Benckendorff, 22.09/05.10.1911, BC2, box 14.

35 Neratov to A.K. Benckendorff, 22.09/05.10.1911, BC2, box 14.

36 A.K. Benckendorff to Neratov, 27.09/10.10.1911, AVPRI, f.340, op.812, d.10, ll.48–50.

37 Keith Robbins, *Sir Edward Grey*, 225.

zone. When he met Russian opposition there,[38] Shuster presented it to the Persian nationalists as an attempt against Persian sovereignty,[39] setting them against the Russians and so provoking violent unrest in the north.

In October 1911, after repeated Russian complaints, the Foreign Office agreed that Shuster became a threat to the Anglo-Russian understanding.[40] Grey used parliamentary criticism to call Benckendorff's attention to the danger to the Anglo-Russian convention.[41] Benckendorff reported to Neratov at once that opposition to Grey was growing and asked to provide Grey with arguments to defend his policy in Persia. The British needed to pacify the indignation of the Shi'ia masses in India after Russia had occupied a region in Persia which was a part of the Muslim world. British public opinion was also excited against Russia: 'We need England's absolute trust'. Then he repeated Nicolson's words to Lord Stamfordham:[42] 'If the Anglo-Russian convention survives this crisis it will be justified in the eyes of its opponents and they will fall silent'. He also asked the ministry to explain Britain's policy through the Russian press and 'put an end to the hysterical shouting in then] press which excites the masses'.[43] He disapproved of Poklevsky's ultimatum to the Persian government: 'Our behaviour is the result of our public opinion whose hasty and extremist campaign will complicate the situation if the Persians do not give in'. He unfavourably compared Poklevsky's actions with the British: The British were consistent and did not become distracted by unimportant details. Benckendorff blamed the foreign ministry for not keeping Grey abreast of their intentions and allowing the opposition to attack Grey in parliament.[44] The Persian situation alarmed him so much that he went to Paris to talk to Sazonov, who stopped there.

With the blessing of the Foreign Office, Benckendorff tried to buttress Grey's policy by preventing Russian troops from entering Teheran. Nicolson informed the king that Benckendorff had sent 'two exceedingly strong telegrams' to St Petersburg. The British knew that 'he has gone so far as to say that such a step might possibly create a cabinet crisis here and seriously affect the stability of our understanding with Russia'.[45] In February Sazonov promised unconditional withdrawal from the occupied city. Benckendorff hurried to assure him that Russia's cooperative attitude staved off the threat of an Anglo-German rapprochement

---

38 Geoffrey Barraclough, *From Agadir to Armageddon: Anatomy of a Crisis* (London, 1982), 9.

39 A.K. Benckendorff to Neratov, 07/20.10.1911 in *Entente Diplomacy and the World Matrix of the History of Europe, 1909–1914* (ed. G.A. Schreiner) (New York, 1921), 109.

40 Nicolson to Barclay, 24.10.1911, *The Mirage of Power*, 470–72.

41 Keith Robbins, *Sir Edward Grey*, 253.

42 Nicolson to Stamfordham, 14.11.1911, RA PS/PSO/GV/C/M/346/5.

43 A.K. Benckendorff to Neratov, 22.11./05.12.1911, AVPRI, f.340, op.812, d.10, ll.68 ob.

44 A.K. Benckendorff to Iswolsky, 03.12.1911, AVPRI, f.340, op.835, d.30, ll.7–9 ob.

45 Nicolson to Stamfordham, 29.11.1912, RA PS/PSO/GV/C/M/346/3.

which was discussed during Haldane's mission to Berlin.[46] Sazonov was angry about the concession he had to make and Benckendorff replied: 'I agree that our coming to Grey's rescue looks somewhat weird, but the public opinion here was against him'. He tried to impress Sazonov by building a chain of far-fetched events which would follow the fall of 'Grey's government': a Conservative government would be formed, but because it would be called into existence for no other reason than the popular rejection of the Liberal foreign policy, they would at once abrogate the Entente and would be ousted from power. The next government would sign an Anglo-German agreement.[47]

He derived this conviction from Grey's words: 'The day when our cooperation and mutual aid becomes difficult, the convention will become obsolete. The break-up of this convention would lead to that of the Entente. Once the Entente collapses, English policy will have to look for an entirely new orientation, and then no one should be astonished at the swiftness with which public opinion will shift'.[48] Grey reminded Sazonov of the value of the convention to Russia, while Benckendorff reinforced his view of Russia's obligations to Britain: as Russia faced more problems in the northern zone, than Britain in the southern, Russia needed to consult Britain more often than Britain consulted Russia.[49]

Shuster left after Britain had ceased to defend him but Russia made another significant concession: it agreed that Russian troops would not remain in Persia and to curb chaos a Swedish-commanded gendarmerie was organized in 1911. As Morgan Shuster travelled back to the US via Britain in 1912, the Persian Committee organized public welcome meetings in Manchester and London, condemning Grey's cooperation with Russia. At the same time in Russia, Ivan A. Zinoviev, a former ambassador to Constantinople, published an attack on Iswolsky's policy of non-intervention in Persian domestic affairs. He wrote that Iswolsky made this concession to the British who did not have any direct contact with Persia and could afford not to intervene. Now that Russia's hands were tied, there was chaos in Persia.[50] Benckendorff adhered to Hardinge's view that, with the chaos in Persia, 'what would have happened [between Russia and Britain] without the Anglo-Russian agreement, heaven only knows'.[51] But Zinoviev accused Iswolsky and Benckendorff of having chosen Britain's friendship over Russia's interests and security and in this way allowed the chaos to reign.

Grey and Sazonov tried to maintain the convention in Persia by removing the officials who failed to cooperate with the other side. In June 1914 Etter passed on to Sazonov Benckendorff's criticism of the new Russian minister at Teheran: 'lack

46 A.K. Benckendorff to Sazonov, 28.01/10.02.1912, AVPRI, f.138, op.467, d.707/756, l.197.

47 A.K. Benckendorff to Sazonov, January 1912, BC2, box 14.

48 M. Soroka, 'Debating Russia's Choice', 6.

49 A.K. Benckendorff to Neratov, 29.10/11.11.1911, in *The Entente Diplomacy*, 115.

50 *Les carnets de Georges Louis*, 10.01.1912, 1: 224–5.

51 Hardinge to A.K. Benckendorff, 14.05.1912, BC2, box 13.

of [British] confidence, Korostovetz a European diplomat at Teheran'. Sazonov promised that he would replace all the staff at Teheran to put an end to frictions with the British,[52] but asked Benckendorff to keep it secret. He feared to be accused of kowtowing to the British.

The Foreign Office, privately, thought that the Persians were incapable of ruling themselves; that Russia was steadily advancing; and that in order to check Russia's advance to India and the Gulf the Anglo-Russian convention was essential. Nicolson held that, instead of scolding Russia for her methods, the British should ensure a free hand for themselves, 'not only in our sphere but also throughout the South of Persia', which made the partition of Persia a question of time.[53]

Benckendorff and Sazonov

Very soon, Benckendorff came to feel that the new minister kept him uninformed and complained: 'The ministry has forgotten that there is a tradition: Buchanan's telegrams to Grey must be confirmed by your telegram to me'. In Nicolson's (that is, Iswolsky's) times it had not been necessary, but now there were so many misunderstandings between Petersburg and London that he wanted to learn first hand about Sazonov's discussions with Buchanan. Sazonov had written to him that he was sending him copies of documents confidentially, not to share the information with the British and the French. Benckendorff disagreed, because 'it would mean that other powers will exchange information and we shall be excluded from these exchanges'.[54]

A leak of the Potsdam convention draft text to a London newspaper contributed to the agitation around the Russo-German talks. Sazonov had to resort to the customary diplomatic practice: he rewrote the draft and denied the authenticity of the published document.[55] Benckendorff blamed the German embassy in London,[56] never suspecting that his embassy had a German spy on staff.

The general atmosphere at Chesham House was relaxed; no suspicion of spying crossed the diplomats' minds. The worst that might happen would be an indiscretion. Even so, in 1909 Poklevsky was sufficiently alarmed to ask the Director of the Russian Chancellery to let him know urgently and secretly how many lithographed copies of diplomatic correspondence had been despatched to

---

52 Etter to A.K. Benckendorff, 29.06.1914, BC2, box 16.

53 Nicolson to Hardinge, 11.06.1914, *The Mirage of Power*, 473–4.

54 A.K. Benckendorff to Sazonov, 30.01/12.02.1911, AVPRI, f.340, op.812, d.10, ll.9–14.

55 E.G. Kostrikova, *Rossiiskoe obshestvo i vneshna'ia politika nakanune pervoi mirovoi voiny, 1908–1914* (Moscow, 2007), 162–3.

56 A.K. Benckendorff to Sazonov, 30.01/12.02.1911, AVPRI, f.340, op.812, d.10, ll.9–14.

the embassy.[57] In the next letter he explained that he had not found the lithographs in their usual place but later it turned out that they had been misplaced.[58] The incident was dismissed, but Savinsky marked the paragraph with a red pencil, whether to mark the happy ending or his concern about the sloppy ways of the London embassy.

Early in 1911 Benckendorff complained to Cambon that he had never been so uneasy since the beginning of his mission. He blamed Sazonov for impatience: 'He likes to solve a situation. He sees a situation, he deals with it ... But his entente with Kiderlen is a draft, it can be modified'. Benckendorff read to Grey and Cambon, Sazonov's confidential letter and Cambon dictated to the Russian ambassador the changes which the French expected Sazonov to make in the Russo-German agreement. Grey remarked, hopefully, to Cambon that if Sazonov insisted on these changes and clarifications in the treaty text, Russo-German relations would worsen instead of improving.[59]

Cambon's letters of the period show that Benckendorff saw himself as an independent political entity, more authoritative than Sazonov, and closer to Cambon and the Foreign Office than to St Petersburg in his views. The new minister's moves made the ambassador feel excluded from St Petersburg's decisions, so he advised the French and the British to pressure Sazonov to comply with the Entente interests. The ambassador spoke about 'the atmosphere of suspicion' around him at St Petersburg, because his reputation as Grey's *alter ego* deprived him of Sazonov's trust.

Pressure on Benckendorff from the Foreign Office and Cambon continued. Nicolson reminded him that the Anglo-Russian convention was based on Persia; after Sazonov let Germany into Persia the arrangement seemed to have lost its point. The British government saw only one way out of the situation created by Sazonov: the internationalization of the Baghdad railway. Benckendorff defended himself by saying that he had warned Sazonov that the Potsdam convention would allow Germany to press Russia out of Persia entirely. He told Cambon: 'I keep writing this to Sazonov and it seems, from his letters, that he still has some confidence in me, but I believe that he is beginning to find me a little overbearing'. The ambassador predicted Sazonov's fall because of the Potsdam affair. He told Cambon that as Sazonov was weak and blind to the implications of his own actions, someone had to explain to Nicholas II the danger of German interference. He complained that much as he would like to go to Paris to talk to Iswolsky, he did not do it for fear that Sazonov might suspect them of plotting his fall.[60]

The Foreign Office considered the situation serious enough to follow up on Benckendorff's advice to influence Nicholas II, and in December 1910 the Tsar promised Buchanan that he would not conclude any arrangements with Germany

57 Poklevsky to Savinsky, 20.03/02.04. 1909, AVPRI, f.340, op.806, d.14, ll.106 ob.
58 Poklevsky to Savinsky, 31.03/13.04. 1909, AVPRI, f.340, op.806, d.14, 107 ob.
59 Paul Cambon to Pichon, 16.01.1911, DDF, XIII: 212–14.
60 Paul Cambon to Pichon, 07.02.1911, DDF, XIII: 261–5.

without informing the British government.[61] In March 1911, on the eve of Britain's joining the German-Turkish Baghdad railway conversations, George V warned Nicholas II against Germany's attempt to isolate France which Nicholas II was to keep in mind during the Russo-German negotiations. The British monarch reassured Nicholas II about the 'absolutely private' character of William II's visit to England and reminded him about the commitment to inform each other about any discussions with Germany or Turkey regarding the railway.[62]

The Potsdam meeting; the passivity of the French government due to a governmental crisis and what Cambon described as lack of seriousness of the British cabinet, made Cambon, Benckendorff and Nicolson in the winter of 1910–11 worry about the break-up of the Entente.[63] In April 1911, Benckendorff's daughter Nathalie married a member of a prominent Conservative family, Jasper Ridley. Iswolsky used the wedding invitation as a pretext for conferring with Benckendorff.[64] Together, they pushed Sazonov to demonstrate his loyalty to the Entente. As Grey was scheduled to speak in the Commons, Iswolsky wanted Sazonov also to make a public speech and asked Benckendorff to 'give him a *hint*, for example, by telegraphing that it is the opinion of Sir E. Grey'.[65]

Sazonov fell dangerously ill in April 1911 and took the first of his prolonged leaves, which caused further concerns among the Entente diplomats. Benckendorff at once warned the acting minister, Anatoly Neratov, about the priority of the Russian foreign policy: Britain did not take up Germany's invitations to make a general agreement only out of consideration for Russia and France, so Neratov should court Britain's favour.[66] He instilled in Neratov such fear that he had to reassure him: 'Do not worry about the Anglo-German relations … Only an obvious abandonment of the entente by Russia would lead to an Anglo-German entente'.[67]

It is hard to say whether Benckendorff believed in what he repeatedly told his superiors in St Petersburg about Britain being constantly on the verge of abandoning the convention. He certainly wanted to prevent such an occurrence, but one had to be blind not to see that Britain had many good reasons to maintain the convention. If he knew of such reasons, he never referred to them, which leads one to the conclusion that Grey's complaints about the difficulties and even inconveniences for the Liberal government of maintaining the convention (e.g. in Persia) were Benckendorff's sole premise in advising St Petersburg.

---

61 Buchanan to George V, 15.12.1910, RA PS/PSO/GV/C/P/284a/1.

62 George V to Nicholas II, 15.03.1911, GARF, f.601, op.1, ed.hr.1219, l.37 ob.

63 Paul Cambon to Pichon, 28.2.1911, *Correspondance*, 2: 312.

64 Iswolsky to A.K. Benckendorff, [n.d.], BC2, box 13.

65 Iswolsky to A.K. Benckendorff, 23.01.1911, BC2, box 13.

66 A.K. Benckendorff to Neratov, 16/29.03.1911, AVPRI, f.340, op.812, d.10, l.15–16 ob.

67 A.K. Benckendorff to Neratov, 30.03/12.04.1911, AVPRI, f.340, op.812, d.10, l.17.

Neratov complied and kept Grey abreast of the Russo-German negotiations, especially since Germany chose to reactivate them at the time of the Agadir crisis, making it difficult for Russia to appear strictly neutral. In May Neratov received the German counter-draft of the agreement[68] and sent it to Benckendorff, asking the ambassador to let him know if the text was liable to be misinterpreted in London.[69] Pourtalès had told him that an Anglo-German agreement was imminent and Neratov was anxious to obtain from the Entente governments a confirmation that the pledge to discuss the final agreement among the four was still binding.[70]

Paul Cambon wrote to his son in May that the Russian foreign ministry did not exist any more: due to the minister's inexperience the system had collapsed.[71] Such an impression in the circles close to Iswolsky and Benckendorff, both derived from and encouraged the Russian diplomats' attempts to conduct their own pro-Entente policies in Paris and London. The French cabinet, worried about the weakening of the Entente, decided that the Russo-French alliance had to be extended to apply to more situations[72] and such a situation, developed during Sazonov's absence.

The Agadir Crisis

In May France occupied Fez, violating the Algeciras Act. It counted on open British and Russian support, but neither of the two was disposed to go to war for Morocco, so a minister of the French government entered secret negotiations with the German embassy. At the beginning of the conflict, all Russian political factions unanimously decided that Russia had too much to do at home to interfere and spoil Russo-German relations.[73] Neratov was happy to hear from Benckendorff that London was also going to observe neutrality favourable to France.[74] When in June Spain suddenly occupied two ports in Morocco, it looked as if Spain and France were going to partition Morocco without any thought for Germany and the German Foreign Secretary, von Kiderlen-Wächter, decided to push the French government into serious negotiations. On 1 July 1911 a German warship, *The Panther*, came to Agadir and Germany demanded compensation.[75]

France appealed to Britain and Russia to make a stand against what it naturally tried to present as Germany's assault on the Entente. Germany had no intention of going to war or occupying Agadir, and Kiderlen's motives were prestige and

68 Neratov to A.K. Benckendorff, 05/18.05.1911, BC2, box 14.

69 Neratov to A.K. Benckendorff, n.d., BC2, box 14.

70 Neratov to A.K. Benckendorff, 24.05/07.06.1911, BC2, box 14.

71 Paul Cambon to his son, 31.05.1911, DDF, XIII: 607–8.

72 *Les carnets de Georges Louis*, 1: 162.

73 *Les carnets de Georges Louis*, 1: 168.

74 A.K. Benckendorff to Neratov, 13/26.05.1911, AVPRI, f.340, op.812, d.10, ll.19–22 ob.

75 Geoffrey Barraclough, *From Agadir to Armageddon*, 102–5.

influence, but Nicolson and Eyre Crowe, the rising star of the British diplomatic establishment, sounded the alarm, drawing misjudged comparisons between the 1905 crisis and the 1911 one.[76] If Britain failed to show support to France, the latter might abandon the Entente and go over to Germany. Russia would follow.

The French almost at once countermanded their request for a joint Anglo-French naval demonstration and went back to negotiations with Germany, but both sides continued the waiting game, neither making an offer. France's manoeuvres made Britain fear that it was about to 'barter away' British interests; it did not want to see Germany in Morocco because of its strategic position on the British line of communications.[77] Grey told Benckendorff that the negotiations on the Morocco issue would be collective (he had already put in a claim for compensation, too) and that he would not make concessions on Britain's political interests. He said he would have liked to be even blunter about it, but had to take into account the Germanophile cabinet radicals.[78] In reporting on Grey's readiness to face Germany, Benckendorff wanted to encourage St Petersburg to show equal determination. He did not seem to doubt that Grey would overcome or overrule the cabinet's refusal to oppose Germany's action in Morocco.

Two weeks later, Germany again bluffed, by demanding the French Congo as compensation. Confused by the continuing German refusal to explain its goals and by the wildly exaggerated reports from Paul Cambon and Sir Francis Bertie, the Foreign Office came to the conclusion that this crisis was an Anglo-German one, rather than Franco-German.[79] Paul Cambon described to his son how he got around the opponents of intervention in the British cabinet:

> The English went up like rockets when they heard that Kiderlen claimed all of the French Congo with *the potential deriving rights on the Belgian Congo.* This last point, perhaps, was not what Kiderlen had in mind, but I formulated it to Bertie last Tuesday and his despatch detonated an explosion. It had been agreed [with the Germans] that the negotiations would remain secret. It is, of course, too bad that we have spoken, but as a result of the indiscretion we have woken the English up.[80]

The Foreign Office claimed that Britain's determination was being tested and the possible action with regard to the present crisis was viewed with the Bosnian crisis in mind.[81]

---

76 Ibid., 114–5.

77 Geoffrey Barraclough, 122.

78 A.K. Benckendorff to Neratov, 22.06/05.07.1911, AVPRI, f.340, op.812, d.10, ll.23–5.

79 Grey to Bertie, 20.07.1911, FO 800/141, 270.

80 Paul Cambon to his son, 24.07.1911, DDF XIV: 108–9.

81 William Tyrrell to Hardinge, 21.07.1911, *The Mirage of Power*, 434.

On 21 July 1911 Grey told the German chargé d'affaires that Britain would not remain passive if the negotiations broke, and later, on Grey's approval, Lloyd George, the chancellor of the Exchequer, made a belligerent public speech about maintaining Britain's place and prestige among the great powers at all hazards.[82] What began as a colonial squabble became an issue of prestige – first for Germany and then for Britain.

Even the French ambassador admitted that it was hard to insist on Russia's intervention since she had absolutely no interests in Morocco.[83] Stolypin and Neratov blamed both sides for stubbornness. To Benckendorff's exhortations to demonstrate Russia's unhesitating support of the Entente, Neratov answered that, according to Russian information, Germany did not want war and probably would not insist on compensation in the Morocco region, which should be acceptable to all parties, including Britain. The crisis would end in extended negotiations, in which Russia, fortunately, would not need to participate.[84] But Benckendorff wanted Russia to be fully involved in the crisis. So, he pointed out to Neratov, now that Germany had agreed to collective negotiations about Morocco, Russia had an opportunity to demonstrate her loyalty to the Entente by making obvious her solidarity with Britain in Persia[85] against Germany.

At the end of July the director of military operations, Sir Henry Wilson went to Paris, as he had since 1906, and discussed with the French staff the plans for joint military action, involving the deployment of a British expeditionary force in case of war.[86] At the same time, Iswolsky infuriated the French and the British by talking about settling the issue by arbitration.[87] The Entente did not want an arbitrated settlement, they wanted Germany's retreat. Grey told Benckendorff on 6 August that Russia should let Berlin know her readiness to give military support to France. Benckendorff informed Neratov and Iswolsky made his reassuring declaration in Paris on 14 August.[88]

The war scare was growing in Britain in proportion to the tension in France and even the members of the cabinet who had been seen as 'dubious or uncertain factors' now were the most determined to have a showdown with Germany.[89] At the historical meeting of the CID on 23 August the government members heard Wilson's exposition of the war office's plans to send British forces to France

82 Grey of Fallodon, *Twenty-Five Years*, 1: 217.

83 Louis to de Selve, *Memorandum*, 07.07.1911, DDF, XIV: 38–9.

84 Neratov to A.K. Benckendorff, 30.06/13.07.1911, BC2, box 14.

85 A.K. Benckendorff to Neratov, 22.06/05.07.1911, AVPRI, f.340, op.812, d.10, ll.23–5.

86 John W. Coogan and Peter F. Coogan, 'The British Cabinet and the Anglo-French Staff Talks, 1905–1914' in *The Journal of British Studies*, 24, 1 (January 1985): 121.

87 Bertie to Grey, 8.08.1911, BD, 7: 467.

88 *Les carnets de Georges Louis*, 1: 204.

89 Nicolson to Hardinge, 17.08.1911, *The Mirage of Powers*, 434.

against German advance.[90] The letters between Churchill and Lloyd George in August 1911 spoke of fleet movements in response to German war preparations, of securing Belgium's consent to a British landing and an Anglo-Belgian army. Lloyd George wanted Grey to ascertain what Russia would and could do in the event of war:

> It is true that Iswolsky dropped a casual observation … that Russia would give material support to France if war were declared. We ought to have a much more formal or definite assurance than that … We ought to know what Russia is capable of before we trust the fortunes of Europe to the hazard.[91]

If Russia owed any explanations, it was to France, so Lloyd George's insistence on 'the right to know' might seem naive, particularly since Britain, with respect to Russia, had always stood firmly by its tradition of never discussing eventualities. But it was in line with Benckendorff's conviction that Russia ought to offer every possible reassurance to Britain. Lloyd George urged on Grey the need for a triple alliance with Russia and France to safeguard the independence of Belgium, Holland and Denmark.[92] Grey reassured his colleagues regarding Russia's loyalty to France.[93] All the while, the Russian government hoped that the French would accept a compromise for the sake of European peace. Buchanan told Neratov that the British were advising Paris to moderate its position and Neratov heartily approved, writing that Iswolsky also reminded the French that they had to act soberly, considering their long-term interests.[94]

Benckendorff was insistent that Russia could not waste such an opportunity to be useful to Grey. The German-Russian railway agreement, ratified at the height of the Agadir crisis, undermined Britain's intention to intimidate Germany with a united Entente front. Neratov suggested to Benckendorff that it was Russia's contribution to a Franco-German settlement: Germany's diplomatic success might incline her to be more flexible in the Morocco negotiations.[95] Benckendorff was annoyed with the Russian disengagement from the crisis at the time when Britain was determined not to allow Germany's triumph in Morocco. He replied that the

---

90 Keith Jeffery, 'Wilson, Sir Henry Hughes, baronet (1864–1922)' in Oxford Dictionary of National Biography (ed. H.C.G. Matthew and Brian Harrison) (Oxford, 2004).

91 D. Lloyd George to W. Churchill, 25.08.1911, House of Lords Record Office, LG/C/3/15/6.

92 W. Churchill to Grey, 30.08.1911, Parliamentary Archives, LG/C/3/15/7.

93 Grey to Churchill, 30.08.1911, Parliamentary Archives (copy), LG/C/3/15/7.

94 Neratov to A.K. Benckendorff, 25.08.1911, BC2, box 14.

95 Neratov to A.K. Benckendorff, 11/24.08.1911, BC2, box 14.

Russo-German treaty did not extend to a general political agreement and therefore the Germans did not see it as a diplomatic triumph.[96]

While the British preparations in September went as far as discuss 'all the details, trains, landing, concentration, etc'.[97] in case of war, Iswolsky reflected the general St Petersburg mood when he told the French that France could expect no more from Russia than France and Britain had done for Russia during the Bosnian crisis. The British, became alarmed again that the Russian government was 'shaky on the issue',[98] and Benckendorff shared their concern. To Neratov's remark that France had to show more flexibility for the sake of general peace, Benckendorff retorted that when France's national pride was at stake, there was no point in speaking of general European interests. He blamed Russian diplomacy for allowing Berlin to count on Russia's moral support and repeated the British opinion that Germany was seeking hegemony and therefore Russia had to join Britain in pressuring Berlin.[99] His advice throughout the crisis reflected all the moods and shifts of the Foreign Office and it is striking to find this man, whose abhorrence of war had been noted by his acquaintances and repeatedly stated in letters, so disposed to push his government into a confrontation. Benckendorff was completely taken over by the London alarmist mood, which dissipated as suddenly as it emerged: in September Germany dropped its most onerous claims, and an agreement would have been signed much earlier than November, had it not been for France's intransigence.[100]

Long before that the Agadir nearly disappeared from the ambassador's correspondence because of a new crisis. Italy chose the moment when the powers were absorbed by the Moroccan crisis, for claiming its share of North Africa. In 1900, 1902 and 1909 it had secured the consent of France, Britain and Russia respectively, to seek compensation in Tripoli. Italy counted on Germany's and Austria-Hungary's support as a member of the Triple Alliance.

The Italo-Turkish war began in late September by Italy's attack on Turkey in Tripoli and an attempt to force the Dardanelles. Iswolsky gave a wise warning to the Italian ambassador in Paris: 'Be careful not to find yourself suddenly faced with the break up of Turkey and the necessity of a European intervention in the Balkans'.[101] Then he gave in to his gambler's nature. In Sazonov's absence, Iswolsky and Tcharykow (now Russian ambassador at Constantinople) persuaded Neratov to take advantage of the situation to resolve the Straits issue. In October

---

96 A.K. Benckendorff to Neratov, 17/30.08.1911, AVPRI, f.340, op.812, d.10, ll.29–31.

97 Richard A. Cosgrove, 'A Note on Lloyd George's Speech at the Mansion House, 21 July 1911' in *The Historical Journal*, 12, 4 (December 1969): 698.

98 Goschen to Nicolson, 08.09.1911, BD VII: 480.

99 A.K. Benckendorff to Neratov, 30.08/12.09.1911, AVPRI, f.340, op.812, d.10, ll.38–44.

100 Freiherr von Schoen, 153.

101 Geoffrey Barraclough, 145.

Neratov informed Benckendorff that the Bosnian crisis tandem was in charge of the negotiations with the French and Ottoman governments. Russia only asked for the Entente's and Turkey's consent to the passage of Russian warships through the Straits in exchange for Russian assistance to the Turkish government in the maintenance of the existing Straits' regime. Russia's support in the Tripoli and Morocco issues would compensate Italy and France for their support. When the Turkish government crisis was over and Tcharykow returned to the charge, Benckendorff was to request Britain's support. In exchange for England's statement of disinterest in the Straits, Russia could offer her compensation in Egypt or Arabia. Russia might also accept Grey's formula of 1908 about the equality of rights of belligerent powers in the Straits. There was no reason for Britain to fear Turkish hostility in case of her favourable attitude to Russia because Russia was offering Turkey real guarantees. Turkey was more favourable than ever to Russian overtures; the diplomatically isolated Turkish government even spoke of an alliance.[102] France and Britain refused the Turks' requests of assistance for fear of alienating Italy, as did the Triple Alliance.[103]

This letter crossed with the one from Benckendorff reporting that the Foreign Office knew everything from Buchanan and Cambon, so he had spoken to Grey without waiting for an authorization. The French and British advice to him was to wait and see which faction would come to power in Turkey.[104] Nicolson and Cambon obviously knew of Russia's 'secret' convention with Italy, because they told Benckendorff that the convention and Russia's declaration of neutrality made a wartime agreement with Turkey impossible. As for the chance of a British favourable attitude in case of Turkey's acceptance, he wrote: 'Discussions of eventualities and contingencies with the British government lead nowhere. The London cabinet makes decisions only when a situation is well-defined'.[105]

Meanwhile Tcharykow obtained the Turkish government's acceptance of his proposal on condition that Britain would become the third party in the agreement. Britain refused.[106] The Foreign Office said that the Straits issue could only be resolved by a conference and the timing was wrong. If Turkey accepted the Russian proposal, she would face the opposition of all other powers.[107] Neratov wrote to Benckendorff in despair that the most he expected was to get out of Grey was a somewhat better formula than that of 1908.[108] On 24 November/7 December the Turkish government officially rejected Russia's proposals. Nicolson informed

102 Neratov to A.K. Benckendorff, 06/19.10.1911, BC2, box 14.

103 Geoffrey Barraclough, 146.

104 A.K. Benckendorff to Neratov, 10/23.10.1911, AVPRI, f.340, op.812, d.10, ll.52–5 (copy).

105 A.K. Benckendorff to Neratov. 12/25.10.1911, AVPRI, f.340, op.812, d.10, ll.60–4 (copy).

106 Oleg Airapetov, 544.

107 Nicolson to Lord Stamfordham, 07.12.1911, RA PS/PSO/GV/C/M/346/4.

108 Neratov to A.K. Benckendorff, 20.10/02.11.1911, BC2, box 14.

the king that the Foreign Office only partially and indirectly knew the details of the 'strange' Russian move and that Benckendorff seemed to be perfectly ignorant about Tcharykow's action.[109] On 26 November/9 December, Sazonov, on the way from his Swiss cure, learned about the attempt in Paris and at once disavowed Tcharykow in an interview with a French newspaper.[110] Whatever his other flaws may have been, Sazonov had never been a Straits' issue addict.

Benckendorff reported that Grey had promised to support Russia under more favourable circumstances and that the British desired to extend the convention because Anglo-Russian positions coincided, especially in the Near East. He wrote of a wider understanding, covering Constantinople, the Balkans and perhaps Asia Minor, in exchange for Britain's freedom of action in Egypt. Then he pointed out an unforeseen result of the Anglo-Russian convention: it had been based on Persia and everyone expected that difficulties in Persia would lead to its abrogation, and yet it was gathering strength despite Persia.[111]

When late in 1911, Sazonov recovered enough to return to Russia via Paris. Iswolsky alerted Benckendorff that Sazonov had no intention of visiting Britain, despite Iswolsky's warning that it would upset Benckendorff and give rise to speculations.[112] On 5 December Benckendorff rushed over to Paris. On his return, he could assure the British that the Anglo-Russian convention remained the cornerstone of Sazonov's course and that he would not allow any frictions in Persia. The count also told the Foreign Office that he thought Sazonov was too ill to remain in his post for much longer. At this moment, Georges Louis, the French ambassador at St Petersburg, was registering rumours about Benckendorff's advice not being welcome at the foreign ministry because the objectivity of his reports was suspect. He cited Sazonov's refusal to go to Britain as proof of Benckendorff's weak position.[113] The French ambassador recorded wistful remarks at the Russian foreign ministry that Nicolson should be brought back at St Petersburg to strengthen the Anglo-Russian rapprochement.[114]

After what he described as 'harassment and nervous explanations' from Iswolsky and Benckendorff in Paris – almost certainly, about the Constantinople demarche – Sazonov took the Express du Nord to St Petersburg via Berlin. To the surprise of the counsellor of the Russian embassy in Berlin, the minister arrived in a calm and sober mood and spoke about the need to maintain good relations with Germany. As he was still convalescent, he excused himself from official visits and had purely private meetings with the German state secretary

109 Nicolson to Lord Stamfordham, 07.12.1911, RA PS/PSO/GV/C/M/346/4.

110 *Rossiia i Tchernomorskie prolivy, XVIII– XX stoleti'ia* (eds. A.V. Ignatiev and L.N. Nezhinsky) (Moscow, 1999), 282.

111 A.K. Benckendorff to Neratov, 26.10/8.11.1911, AVPRI, f.340, op.812, d.10, ll.68–9.

112 Iswolsky to Benckendorff, 11/24.11.1911, BC2, box 13.

113 *Les carnets de Georges Louis*, 1: 218–19.

114 *Les carnets de Georges Louis*, 1: 221.

during his stay. The Russian embassy counsellor, Nikolai Schebeko, called his attention to the fact that the situation at the embassy was impossible 'because the ambassador has been non-existent for a long time'.[115] Baron N.E. Osten-Sacken, never an outstanding diplomat, by 1911 had collapsed physically and mentally, and his inaction combined with Benckendorff's and Iswolsky's constant lobbying, reinforced the pro-Entente direction in Russian foreign policy.

An odd combination of nervousness and neglect characterized Russian diplomacy towards Germany. Iswolsky had neglected the Berlin embassy, relying on his own contacts with the German ambassadors. Nicholas II considered that the needs of Russo-German relations were served by the presence of his 'personal representative', General Ilya Tatishchev, at the Berlin court and the 'Willy-Nicky' telegram exchanges. It was known in diplomatic circles that 'the [Russian] ambassador [in Berlin] is a fiction' and that 'the Germans are extremely nervous about everything relating to … [Russia's] relations with Britain',[116] for the paralysis of the Russian embassy in Berlin showed up the constant drive of the London embassy for Russia's further integration into the Entente. Benckendorff's efforts were so well noticed that in 1912 Schebeko twice explained to the director of the minister's Chancellery that not only would Benckendorff not be acceptable to Berlin as the next Russian ambassador,[117] neither would any former member of Benckendorff's staff. He wrote that Sevastopoulo, Benckendorff's first secretary, did not qualify for several reasons: 'What could have been an advantage in London, in the way of buying meals for and giving presents to old duchesses, is of no use in Berlin … As for politics, Sevastopoulo's earlier activity, his closeness to Poklevsky, Benckendorff and London in general … will make his work here very difficult, if not impossible'.[118] The reputation of the London embassy had been Benckendorff's doing, thanks to his known anti-German views being obligatory for his staff. Shebeko's other criticism addressed the type of diplomat whom the Benckendorff couple preferred to see around them.

The Balkan League

Seeing Turkey suffer defeats from Italy, the Balkan states began to prepare to attack it, too. In December 1911 Sazonov warned the allies that if the Italo-Turkish war continued into the spring there would be disorders in the Balkans. He suggested that France could lead the powers' conciliating efforts and asked

115 N.N. Schebeko to M.F. Schilling, 30.10/13.11.1911, GARF, f.813, op.1, ed.hr.445, 38–9 ll.ob.

116 Schebeko to Schilling, 20.1/02.02.1912, GARF, f.813, op.1, ed.hr.445, 47–50 ll. ob.

117 Schebeko to Schilling, 08/21.06.1912, GARF, f.813, op.1, ed.hr.445, 73–4 ob.

118 Schebeko to Schilling, 10/23.03.1912, GARF, f.813, op.1, ed.hr.445, 58–9 ob.

for Britain's support.[119] Grey wanted to protect Britain's relations with Turkey and refused to intervene in Constantinople unless all five powers agreed to apply pressure to Italy.[120] The war continued. In spring Sazonov wanted London and Paris to warn the Turks that an unjustified closure of the Straits would be a hostile action against the neutrals.[121] The British tried to exercise some informal pressure on the Turkish ambassador to avert the closure,[122] but it did not help. The debates about whether the demarches should be made in Constantinople or Rome and who should initiate them continued till the spring of 1912, when Turkey closed the Straits during the Italian bombardment. They were reopened in May, but the threat loomed over Russian trade until October 1912.

During the turmoil created by the Italo-Turkish war, Serbia, Bulgaria, Greece and Montenegro formed a secret Balkan League under the aegis of Russia with the support of France.[123] The initial idea, that appeared almost simultaneously in Hardinge's and Benckendorff's private letters, had been that Turkey would also adhere and the League would become an obstacle to Austrian expansion. But the actual League took on an anti-Turkish character. When Turkey was defeated by Italy and a new wave of unrest arose in Macedonia, the League saw its chance to get territorial concessions from the weakened Turkey. Sazonov realized that now a war in the Balkans was imminent and the Straits might change hands without giving any advantage to Russia.

Rumours of Iswolsky's Recall

Benckendorff's life in Britain continued its pleasant course: he visited Windsor, dined at Mrs Keppel's whose claim on his friendship was her liaison with the late King Edward, and made daily visits to the French embassy. After King Edward's death, Benckendorff's private letters increasingly quoted Cambon's opinions. This circumstance, coupled to the information about Iswolsky which he got from his former subordinate Sevastopulo (now posted to Paris)[124] and probably what he gathered from his Foreign Office friends about Sir Francis Bertie's growing feud with Iswolsky, made the count see his friend in a less

119 Sazonov to A.K. Benckendorff, 15.27/12.1911, AVPRI, f.184, op.520, d. 1428, ll.14–16.

120 Grey to A.K. Benckendorff, 28.02.1912, AVPRI, f.184, op.520, d.1428, ll.30–31.

121 Sazonov to A.K. Benckendorff, 19.04/02.05.1912, AVPRI, f.184, op.520, d.1428, l.35 ob.

122 A.K. Benckendorff to Sazonov, 12/23.04.1912, AVPRI, f.138, op.467, d.707/756, l.277 ob.

123 *Rossi'ia i Tchernomorskie prolivy, XVIII– XX stoleti'ia*, 283–5.

124 A.K. Benckendorff to S.P. Benckendorff, 06/19.09.1912, GARF, f.1126, op.1, ed. hr.153, ll.93–4 ob.

flattering light. He wrote to his wife that Iswolsky was losing professionalism in Paris: 'What's the use of being an intelligent man? He collects local gossip …'[125] The ambassador imagined that he might receive a request to go to Paris to put things right,[126] which would bring him into a conflict with Iswolsky and interfere with his London activities.

Iswolsky, according to Raymond Poincaré's memoirs, bungled his task by embroidering his instructions and by misrepresenting the French government's statements in his reports to Sazonov in an attempt to steer Russian foreign policy.[127] Like Benckendorff, he blackmailed St Petersburg with the threat of France's abandoning the alliance unless St Petersburg took the steps which he suggested. The French government wanted Iswolsky removed,[128] but Sazonov did not have the firmness either to discipline his former chief or to replace him. Benckendorff wrote to his wife about the repercussions of Iswolsky's possible recall for himself:

> It is quite mysterious how Mac [Iswolsky] has completely bungled his task and the situation. And from Russia, France and Germany I hear rumours which are posting me there, they are growing in a very unpleasant way. I have no need to reassure you. Never. But this may be more difficult to deal with than I thought. But I will make no bones about my arguments; I will not even be modest. I am needed here …[129]

In July 1912 the Franco-Russian naval convention was signed. In August, Anglo-French naval conversations began (which culminated in an Anglo-French naval agreement in March 1913). The French Prime Minister Poincaré visited Russia[130] where on 12 September 1912 the Franco-Russian convention was ratified: in case of a German mobilization, France and Russia would mobilize at once, with no prior consultation. The convention stipulated the scale and the speed of their respective mobilizations.[131]

---

125 A.K. Benckendorff to S.P. Benckendorff, 03/15.06.1912, GARF, f.1126, op.1, ed. hr.153, ll.50–51 ob.

126 A.K. Benckendorff to S.P. Benckendorff,18.07/01.08.1912, GARF, f.1126, op.1, ed.hr.153, ll.79–80 ob.

127 Raymond Poincaré, *The Memoirs of Raymond Poincaré* (London, 1926), 159–61.

128 Ibid., 150–52.

129 A.K. Benckendorff to S.P. Benckendorff, 13/26.06.1912, GARF, f.1126, op.1, ed.hr.153, ll. 55–7 ob.

130 N.P. Evdokimova, S.V. Vivatenko, *Raymond Poincaré: President Frantsii* (St Petersburg, 2006), 49.

131 V. Krasnov, V. Daines, *Russkii voenno-istoricheskii slovar* (Moscow, 2002), 522–3.

The Balkan Wars

In September, Benckendorff returned from Russia earlier than expected because Sazonov was due to come to Britain and he was surprised to find that the Foreign Office was calm[132] while St Petersburg was expecting a Balkan war to break out any moment.[133]

The count wrote to his wife: 'To think of you all alone, weighed heavily on my mind. But I still feel that I could not let Sazonov down at London. I know that alone he will achieve nothing …'.[134] Sazonov came to England to secure Britain's support in averting a Balkan war; to ask about Britain's position in case of a European conflict and to settle Asian problems.[135]

Persian affairs were at the core of the discussions. Grey suggested that Russia should withdraw the troops from her zone, replacing them with Persian soldiers under Russian command. In this case, the British would protect the trade routes in the neutral and British zones using Persian soldiers under British command. Grey agreed that eventually the British and Russian railways in Persia would be aligned and that both parties should secure concessions from the Persian government for the future constructions. They compromised in the affair of Greenway-Lynch syndicate which was trying to start railway construction in the neutral zone, in clear conflict with the interests of the Societé d'Études. British initiatives in Persia indicated to Sazonov that they planned to absorb the neutral zone. To avoid further frictions he even proposed partitioning it, but Grey refused. As for the Balkans, Britain would not support pressure on Turkey and in case of a Balkan war Britain would do everything to localize it.[136]

Benckendorff echoed the satisfaction of the British government with the results of the Balmoral conversations: 'Sazonov is as good as he should be: *no fuss* ... pleasant after Mac [Iswolsky] …'. At the end of the visit he concluded: 'Much work done in the past 5–6 days, though the war [in the Balkans] was not averted, but it was *hopeless*. Since the day when the [Balkan] foursome had formed an alliance … this outcome was to be expected …'.[137]

Pleased with himself and with Grey, he did not mention that happy results were achieved by Sazonov's concessions. In the 1920s Sazonov referred to it, saying that 'the Russian government put an extremely high value on the 1907 convention which had cost us many efforts and we were ready for certain sacrifices in order to

132 A.K. Benckendorff to S.P. Benckendorff, 03/19.09.1912, GARF, f.1126, op.1, d.153, ll.95–8 ob.

133 Etter to Sazonov, 15/28.08.1912, AVPRI, f.340, op.812, d.141, ll. 7–8 ob.

134 A.K. Benckendorff to S.P. Benckendorff, 30.08/12.09.1912, GARF, f.1126, op.1, ed.hr.153, ll.93–4 ob.

135 A.V. Ignatiev, *Vneshna'ia politika Rossii 1907–1914* (Moscow, 2000), 145.

136 A.V. Ignatiev, 146–7.

137 A.K. Benckendorff to S.P. Benckendorff, 27.09/10.10.1912, GARF, f.1126, op.1, ed.hr.153, ll.127–9 ob.

preserve it, because we considered that it had a political significance transcending … [Persia] which had been the subject of the convention'.[138] On Poincaré's advice, Sazonov also tested the assumption of the convention's European dimension by asking Grey: what assistance would the British navy give to Russia in the Baltic Sea in case of a German attack? The French fleet, as stipulated by the Franco-Russian convention, would bar the way into the Straits to the Austro-Hungarian navy. Would Britain assist Russia in the north? Grey said that the British would strike as hard as they could at the German fleet in the North Sea, but they would hardly be able to enter the Baltic for joint naval operations. First Grey and then George V confirmed that Britain was committed to come to France's aid on sea and on land.[139] But Sazonov did not get a clear promise or guarantee from the British for Russia, and he wrote in his memoirs that he did not then foresee any urgent need to press Britain for a commitment and was satisfied with the British answer.[140]

After his departure the British felt that Sazonov might have begun to question the usefulness of the convention to Russia. Nicolson was worried: 'It is of essential importance that no possible cloud should come over our relations with Russia …'.[141] He urged the king to write to Nicholas II about his satisfaction with the conversations and with the friendly relations between Britain and Russia. He was to introduce the phrase 'as the emperor is the all-important factor' and avoid mentioning the anti-Russian campaigns in Britain because 'His Majesty is not supposed to be conscious of them'. Nicolson had done his best to persuade Sazonov that the anti-Russian faction was politically of no importance.[142] The opposition to the Anglo-Russian convention was too vocal to omit, so the king tactfully introduced the subject: 'I am glad to tell you that with regard to Our Foreign Policy the opposition are in full agreement with the Government, whose only opponents are a small and insignificant number belonging to their own extreme left, and nobody pays any attention to them whatever'.[143]

War or no war in the Balkans, the ambassador prepared to return to Sosnovka and only waited for the last bag from Paris, 'Paris, on which war or peace hinges', where Sazonov was discussing Balkan affairs with Poincaré. Benckendorff wrote: '[Despite] my little faith in the last moment diplomatic efforts … I wanted to send a telegram to Sazonov, telling him that I would postpone my departure'.[144] Instead, Sazonov's telegram arrived from Paris:

---

138 Sazonov, 62.

139 S.D. Sazonov, *Extract from Report to Nicholas II*, AVPRI, f.138, op.467, d.323/327, ll. 5–6 ob.

140 Sazonov, 66.

141 Nicolson to Stamfordham, 02.10.1912, RA PS/PSO/GV/C/M/456/8.

142 Ibid.

143 George V to Nicholas II, 06.10.1912, GARF, f.601, op.1, ed.hr.1219, l.41 ob.

144 A.K. Benckendorff to S.P. Benckendorff, 23.09/06.10.1912, GARF, f.1126, op.1, ed.hr.153, ll.112–15 ob.

'Friendly advice postpone departure to avoid recriminations'.[145] Russia received French assurances of firm support in case of Austrian military action in the Balkans and the two empires began to prepare.

Throughout the summer, Russian newspapers stirred public emotions by loud warnings that Russia would not tolerate a second Bosnian crisis and publicized the provocative visits of the members of the Russian opposition to the Balkan capitals.[146] The foreign ministry's – and Benckendorff's – main concern was that Serbia might provoke a conflict with Austria, and 'for an issue which has nothing to do with the Slav or Greek liberation our sister [country] may push Russia into an absurd situation'.

Aware of Bulgaria's ambitions, he blamed Sazonov for the situation and was concerned about the Straits: '... it is a dream ... but the question imposes itself in a negative way ... [By promoting the Balkan League] Saz[onov] created an infinitely worse situation for us than the Turks. Think what Bulgaria is ... and will become, and what her probable political orientation will be'.[147] He excused Austria's belligerence by her near collapse, but wrote that the French were pouring oil onto the fire by publishing the confidential official telegrams exchanged by the European chancelleries: 'I read the telegrams in the papers before I receive them here. The Balkan governments knew what the powers thought and it is not surprising that they began to act – the French are to blame'. His closing words were: 'Just think what a war, a European war might represent at this moment for Russia. Just think of Sosnovka! There are many Sosnovkas in Russia'.[148] He explained to Sofia Petrovna Russia's position:

> We cannot – unless there is an extreme case and unforeseen circumstances – repeat 1878. The situation is quite different. There was no Bulgaria then ... – now it is here. We had an alliance with Rumania – now we do not. The Balkan war would begin under the eyes of the Triple Alliance which did not exist in those times, strictly speaking. I think the Bulgarians realize it and will not go to the end. No one would aid them.[149]

He was mistaken: despite Sazonov's warning in the autumn of 1912, the rebellions in Albania and Macedonia pushed the Balkan states towards war. Benckendorff explained to his wife that the existence of the Ottoman Empire was at stake:

---

145 Telegram enclosed in GARF, f.1126, op.1, ed.hr. 153.

146 *Rossi'ia i tchernomorskie prolivy*, 285.

147 A.K. Benckendorff to S.P. Benckendorff, 23.09/06.10.1912, GARF, f.1126, op.1, d.153, ll.112–15 ob.

148 A.K. Benckendorff to S.P. Benckendorff, 27.09/10.10.1912, GARF, f.1126, ed.hr.153, ll.127–9 ob.

149 A.K. Benckendorff to S.P. Benckendorff, 27.09/10.10.1912, GARF, f.1126, op.1, ed.hr.153, 130–33.

> It began to get excited and agitated after the Bosnia-Herzegovina affair, The Morocco [Crisis] contributed to the unrest and finally this war with Italy – all this created a situation in which Turkey cannot afford to make concessions … to the four Christian Balkan countries, it has to fight … At the bottom of it, naturally, is the fact that they never went through with the reforms promised to the Berlin Congress. But this is already ancient history. There are two facts which have gone to the heads of the four countries. First, this Italian war which is paralyzing Turkey completely and second, their sudden unanimity, which up to now they have never managed to achieve.[150]

A member of the Russian Duma's military committee, who heard Sazonov's and war minister's explanations of the events, reminisced that Sazonov answered evasively the questions of 'how the states which had been always at loggerheads with each other now managed to form a league', but the budget lists of emergency expenses of the war ministry indicated that soon after the Balkan mobilization considerable amounts of weaponry and food had been sent to the southern Slavs: the Russian government handed over to them part of its own emergency reserves. He concluded: 'It was already a violation of neutrality. Sazonov realized it, but his excuse was that it had been the sovereign's desire'. It was not an 'excuse', but it well described Sazonov's weakness.[151]

Grey refused to support joint demands at Constantinople, fearing for Anglo-Turkish relations and Benckendorff defended it as a legitimate British concern.[152] At the last moment, Russia and Austro-Hungary attempted to avert the war by issuing a joint declaration in favour of the *status quo*. Benckendorff wrote: 'Everything occurring now has its good side. All the powers have become terrified of war. But this is not enough. There may arrive a moment when governments will become paralyzed'.[153] And so they did, when in October the Balkan League, disregarding Russia's warnings, attacked Turkey. By the end of October the Bulgarian army was closing in on Constantinople. Austria and Russia mobilized. Russia warned and cajoled the Bulgarian government to let the Sultan retain his sovereignty over the zone between Constantinople and the Black Sea coast. Benckendorff repeated Grey's and Nicolson's arguments which he made his own:

> Only coercion would be effective … It is impossible to foresee its consequences. Besides, no one will allow a Great Power to enter Constantinople. In order for Russia to establish herself there, first there would have to appear

150 A.K. Benckendorff to S.P. Benckendorff, 21.09/04.10.1911[1912?], GARF, f.1126, op.1, ed.hr.153, ll.44–7 ob.

151 N.V. Savich, 107.

152 A.K. Benckendorff to S.P. Benckendorff, 25.09/08.10. 1912, GARF, f.1126, op.1, ed.hr.53, ll.123–4 ob.

153 A.K. Benckendorff to S.P. Benckendorff, 01/14.10.1912, GARF, f.1126, op.1, ed.hr.153, ll.139–40 ob.

> another Napoleon I who would begin by defeating the rest of the world. I would not play this card … But neither can we allow the emergence of a Great Bulgaria which would include Constantinople … The same applies to Greece. Therefore if the Slavs are lucky in war we shall have to stop them from entering Constantinople. What an attractive ending … The only way of averting a general conflagration now … is to declare to all the belligerents that they are free to continue to wage war on each other, but that none of them will gain anything from it whatever the outcome …[154]

The Russian government asked Poincaré to organize a joint protest by the four powers to stop Bulgaria. Another closure of the Dardanelles loomed and the Russian press loudly protested that the diplomats were doing nothing to prevent this catastrophe which would stop Russian grain exports from reaching the markets. Benckendorff feared that if the Dardanelles were closed it might end in a war.[155] He wrote that Grey's position was similar to the Russian; he would not oppose any changes in the Balkans as long as no one occupied Constantinople and Austria did not enter the hostilities. Through Benckendorff, Grey dangled the old carrot in front of Sazonov: if now Russia declared her lack of interests in the Balkans, Britain would create no difficulties later in the Straits issue and Khanekin question.[156]

As usual, the French and the British refused to join Russia in pressing Bulgaria for fear of pushing her towards the Triple Alliance. Besides, they had no intention of keeping Bulgaria out of Constantinople only to have Russia take it.[157] To Sazonov's reproach to Britain for supporting Turkey, Benckendorff protested that Grey was giving a minimum of support to the Sultan because he chose his entente with Russia over Turkey's interests in Europe. Therefore, Russia owed it to Grey not to let Russian troops enter Teheran.[158]

Benckendorff wrote that Bulgarian victories produced an enormous impression on the British public: 'No one says anymore that it is a squabble among *rotten little nations*'. Benckendorff, as usual, came to share the latest British opinion. Now he said that old prejudices blinded Europe to the fact that the Balkan states had worked incessantly and became stronger while

154 A.K. Benckendorff to S.P.Benckendorff, 21.09/04.10.1911 [1912?]. GARF 1126, ed.hr.153, ll.44–7 ob.

155 A.K. Benckendorff to S.P. Benckendorff, 05/18.10.1912, GARF, f.1126, ed. hr.153, ll.145–7 ob.

156 A.K. Benckendorff to Iswolsky, 15/28.10.1912, AVPRI, f.340, op.835, d.30, ll.1–4.

157 *Rossi'ia i tchernomorskie prolivy*, 287.

158 A.K. Benckendorff to Sazonov, 09/22.10.1912, AVPRI, f.138 op.467, d.707/756, ll.304–8.

the Young Turks had been destroying the Ottoman Empire.[159] Benckendorff wrote: 'Everyone is stunned. An English newspaper all of a sudden ended an article with a mention of St Sophia!. I confess, I am also excited … It is very beautiful …'[160] He believed that Constantinople would become Bulgarian if Russia did not intervene and if the Bulgarian army did not become exhausted. The discord between Russia and Britain regarding the situation was growing. Benckendorff privately explained to Iswolsky that the Balkan allies' success made them popular with the British public but the Liberal party was concerned with the possible European outcomes of their successes. Grey told him that he wanted Russia to show her leadership of the Balkan allies by proposing an absolutely disinterested programme acceptable to Austria. Poincaré and some of the Russian military thought Europe was on the verge of a catastrophe[161] and Benckendorff was just as worried:

> If Ferdinand [of Bulgaria] entered Constantinople he would be acclaimed in London. We want to protect Constantinople, conserve it for the Turks. I suspect that we shall do it, there is nothing wrong about them keeping it … In London everything is very strange. It is odd that Austria also abandoned the Turks … It is more concerned about the relations with the Balkans than with Turkey. What will happen back home if the Bulgarians enter Constantinople? I am glad I am not the Master … It is impossible to prevent their entry or make them leave. There is only one remedy. And it would tempt me so strongly that I would succumb.[162]

He repeated to his wife Cambon's observation: '1) Crises always occur in the autumn; 2) Europe has never been as united as now and yet we have never been as ready for war'.[163]

Benckendorff explained to his wife that for Russia to let Bulgaria have the Straits would mean putting 'this real key to Russia into the hands of a power which has … already many times been our enemy'. If it happened, Russia would have to side with Turkey against Bulgaria. He imagined that Britain would support them but he was not sure about other powers.[164] Russia was all agog, junior and senior

159 A.K. Benckendorff to S.P. Benckendorff, 13/26.10.1912, GARF, f.1126, op.1, ed. hr.153, ll.150–53 ob.

160 A.K. Benckendorff to S.P. Benckendorff, 14/27.10.1912, GARF, f.1126, op.1, ed.hr.153, ll.154–5 ob.

161 A.K. Benckendorff to Iswolsky, 15/28.10.1912, AVPRI, f.340, op.835, d.30, ll.1–4 ob.

162 A.K. Benckendorff to S.P. Benckendorff, 19.10/02.11.1912, GARF, f.1126, op.1, ed.hr.153, ll.163–4 ob.

163 A.K. Benckendorff to S.P. Benckendorff, 24.09/07.10.1912, GARF, f.1126, op.1, ed.hr.153, ll.119–22 ob.

164 A.K. Benckendorff to S.P. Benckendorff, 23.10/05.11.1912, GARF, f.1126, op.1, ed.hr.153, ll.165–8 ob.

diplomats received letters from their friends back home asking for explanations. Benckendorff wrote to Empress Maria Feodorovna a defence of Britain's position:

> It is clear and legitimate that Russia will not tolerate any questioning of the result of the magnificent campaign of the Balkan allies against the Turkish yoke [the position of the Russian press which in reality infuriated the ambassador] … Britain would support us if we decided to go to war, but only for a great and noble cause. What if a war breaks out? Supporting Russia [by promising unconditional support] would mean giving arms to all our enemies, in and out of Russia … England's position is infinitely more complicated than ours. They have little interest in the Balkans …[165]

This letter was to prepare the imperial family indirectly for the news of Britain's refusal to support Russia's Balkan interests. Benckendorff wrote to Sazonov that even though in London they expected an Austrian attack on Serbia, 'for Britain it is not enough reason for war and therefore Russia's participation would not be received sympathetically'. In fact the British blamed Russia for Serbia's stubborn position in the negotiations.[166] To his wife, he put it more frankly, reverting to the popular British stereotype of 'rotten little nations': 'Now it is not about the Balkans or Slavs or the Turkish Empire in Europe. Now it is paltry Serbian pretensions, absolutely unjustified. Supported by our press, they lost their head and are pushing Europe into war'.[167] To his question about Britain's position in case of an Austrian attack, Grey replied that it depended on the attitude of other powers.[168] Even though he conceded that Grey and Nicolson did not always see eye to eye, Benckendorff thought that Nicolson's words to Cambon meant that if the Triple Alliance engaged Russia and France in war, Britain would take part.[169] He expanded in another letter: Britain's intention was to remain uncommitted, but from Grey's various utterances he concluded that Britain would not enter a continental war unless France was actively engaged and the other side must be clearly the aggressor. He added, that to have Britain's backing in case of a war, Sazonov should do everything to demonstrate that Russia was not pursuing any interests of her own.[170]

The louder the Russian press campaign for a strong Russian stand for Serbia and Montenegro, the more concerned Sazonov became. He saw the growing anger

---

165 A.K. Benckendorff to Empress Maria Feodorovna, 16/29.11.1912, GARF, f.642, op.1, ed.hr.918, ll.34–40 ob.

166 A.K. Benckendorff to Sazonov, 07/20.11.1912, AVPRI, f.138, op.467, ed.hr.707/756, ll.316–18.

167 A.K. Benckendorff to S.P. Benckendorff, 31.10/13.11.1912, GARF, f.1126, op.1, ed.hr.153, ll.177–80.

168 A.K. Benckendorff to Sazonov, 01/14.11.1912, in *The Entente Diplomacy*, 399.

169 A.K. Benckendorff to Sazonov, Ibid.

170 A.K. Benckendorff to Sazonov, 07/20.11.1912, in *The Entente Diplomacy*, 404.

in Vienna and at the same time the groundswell of support for Slavs in Russia robbed him of freedom of manoeuvre. Grey also realized that public opinion would not let Sazonov retreat if the Austrian army invaded Serbia.[171] Benckendorff wrote to Sazonov: 'I did not defend the Russian press at the Foreign Office, it is too horrible'.[172] He was echoed by another Russian diplomat, writing from Bucharest that the *Novoye Vremya* was pushing Russia into war by their attacks on Sazonov: 'They would sink Russia through their desire to succour the Slavs'.[173] Benckendorff himself became the target of the Russian press' attacks. While there were many faults to be found with the ambassador, the journalists blamed him for one of which he was innocent: pro-German sympathies. Lichnowsky and Mensdorff, German and Austrian ambassadors to London, were his relatives and this caused snide comments. Lichnowsky recalled his cousin Benckendorff at the time as a man 'always at pain to avoid a brusque attitude'.[174]

The Ambassadors' Conference in London

An armistice was arranged on 20 November/3 December 1912. The issues to settle were an autonomous Albania under Turkish suzerainty and everything else partitioned according to war conquests between Bulgaria, Serbia and Greece, with Salonica free and open. The thorniest issues were Constantinople and Serbia's claims of a port in Albania which Austria opposed.[175] On 7 December Vienna mobilized half a million soldiers. St Petersburg reciprocated by delaying demobilization of the soldiers in the European zone of Russia and in the Caucasus until 1 January 1913. Both powers put their navies on alert.[176] On the eve of the Ambassadors' conference in London, the Triple Alliance was pointedly renewed and Bethmann-Hollweg declared that Germany would support Austria-Hungary militarily if a third power attacked her.[177]

The London conference began with Bulgaria demanding Adrianople and Russia supporting the claim. Benckendorff wrote to Sazonov in a new tone, assessing Russia's situation in case of war: Germany promised support to Austria-Hungary and the Foreign Office wondered whether St Petersburg and Paris would make challenging moves. Benckendorff, torn between his dream of Russia in Constantinople and his loyalty to Grey, was suddenly concerned that Grey's vacillating attitude might

171 N.V. Savitch, 109.

172 A.K. Benckendorff to Sazonov, 09/22.10.1912, AVPRI, f.138, op.467, ed.hr 707/756, ll.304–8.

173 Schebeko to Schilling, 11/24.10.1912, GARF, f.813, op.1, ed.hr.445, ll.79–80 ob.

174 K. Lichnowsky, *Heading for the Abyss: Reminiscences* (New York, 1928), 56.

175 A.K. Benckendorff to S.P. Benckendorff, 27.10/09.11.1912, GARF, f.1126, op.1, ed.hr.153, 172–7 ob.

176 Airapetov, 563.

177 John F.V. Keiger, 101.

prevent him from 'saying the decisive firm words' which would make Berlin stop and reconsider before launching a war. He warned that there was no sympathy for Russia's desires and Russia should not intervene. If war broke out despite Britain's efforts, Grey hoped Russia would be moderate and disinterested,[178] which meant that Russia should think twice about going to war for no gain.[179]

Early in 1913, when the Young Turks' coup and rejection of the peace terms made the resumption of the war merely a question of time, he reminded Sazonov of his pledge not to allow the Balkan war to degenerate into another Bosnian crisis and advised that if Russia went to the end, it should be for an important issue.[180] A conflict was averted in January when Francis Joseph II cancelled Austrian preparations for an invasion of Serbia and Russian diplomats persuaded the Montenegrin ruler to evacuate the Turkish Adriatic port of Skutari. Benckendorff told the German ambassador that military measures taken in Russia at the time were much slower than in Germany and even than in Austria-Hungary and that Sazonov, though apt to fly into passion and use sharp words, was absolutely pacific. Russia did not want a war because it would bring a revolution in its wake.[181] Again and again Benckendorff very simply and frankly stated his main concern: to avoid a replay of 1904–5 in Russia. This 'remarkable clearness and comprehensive vision'[182], to use Benno von Siebert's praise of his chief in 1921 was common among the Russian gentry badly shaken by the first revolution.

The Collapse of the Armistice and Resumption of the London Conference

After the Balkan armistice collapsed, Benckendorff's suggestion was to try and agree with Germany on a course of action. He believed that Grey had hoped for a resumption of the war; after Adrianople was taken it would be possible to go back to the negotiations. Nicholas II made a derisive note on the margin of this letter where Benckendorff explained Grey's attitude: 'What an appalling incomprehension of the situation on the Balkan Peninsula! He imagines that the allies will agree to go back to the London babbling!!!'[183] When the Bulgarian advance faltered, the Bulgarians sent an extraordinary mission to St Petersburg, asking for Russia's naval support in exchange for handing over the Straits to Russia. But St Petersburg,

178 A.K. Benckendorff to Sazonov, 21.11/04.12.1912, AVPRI, f.340, op.467, d.707/756, ll.322–6.

179 A.K. Benckendorff to S.P. Benckendorff, 31/10/13.11.1912, GARF, f.1126, op.1, ed.hr.153, ll.177–80 ob.

180 A.K. Benckendorff to Sazonov, 1913, AVPRI, f.138, op.467, d.707/756, ll.330–32.

181 K. Lichnowsky, 163–4.

182 *The Entente Diplomacy*, xii.

183 A.K. Benckendorff to Sazonov, 16/29.01.1913, AVPRI, f.138, op.467, ed.hr. 707/756, ll.334–5 ob.

fearing a European war, refused the assistance and from this moment Bulgaria ceased to count with Russia and began to look to Austria for support.[184] Russia opposed European control of Turkish finance suggested by Britain: it would make Turkey completely subservient to France, England and Germany. The hostilities resumed in February and in March Bulgaria took Adrianople. In Russia, the split between the confused government and the delirious public could not be greater. As the Bulgarian military mission, led by General R. Dmitriev, was leaving Petersburg empty-handed, the Russian Duma met with a standing ovation the news of the Bulgarian occupation of Adrianople and sent a collective telegram of congratulations to the Bulgarian parliament.[185]

The Russian government once again discussed landing in the Straits, but the military told the council of ministers that the Black Sea fleet had no resources and the finance minister Kokovtzeff asked them angrily what the point had been of their agitating since 1896 about the capture of the Straits. It only made enemies for Russia.[186]

After a collective naval demonstration by the powers, the Bulgarian advance came to a halt and the discussions of peace terms resumed, though with Montenegro again refusing to accept them. Benckendorff fell gravely ill with influenza and Etter took over his duties. He reported privately to Sazonov:

> The doctors are sending him to the South for two-three weeks, but because of the situation he refuses to listen to them or to the countess. I am trying to do my best but sometimes I am confused, so please be tolerant if I blunder. I will be extremely glad when Count Benckendorff resumes work but, at the countess' request I do not hurry him.[187]

In April Benckendorff was back and passed on to Sazonov Grey's complaint about Hartwig's active encouragement of the Serbian government's demands which contradicted Russia's position at the conference and undermined Sazonov's authority. The count reported to Sazonov that he had replied that he could not accuse a colleague behind his back and that Buchanan would be in a better position to do so at St Petersburg.[188] Privately, Benckendorff told Cambon that he had already advised Sazonov to get rid of Hartwig.[189] He had long considered the man to be a threat to the pro-Entente course because of his belief that Russia's interests could be served by supporting the governments of his accreditation rather than

184 N.V. Savich, 109.

185 N.V. Savich, 112.

186 M. de Taube, *La politique russe*, 307.

187 Etter to Sazonov, 13/26.03.1913, AVPRI, f.340, op.812, d.141, ll.9–13 ob.

188 A.K. Benckendorff to Sazonov, 27.03/09.04.1913, AVPRI, f.138, op.467, d.707/756, l.349.

189 Paul Cambon to Jules Cambon, 14.11.1912, *Correspondance*, 2: 27–8.

the Entente's interests.[190] Benckendorff reported to St Petersburg, perhaps as an excuse for the lack of a breakthrough, that because of a weak cabinet, in the spring of 1913 Grey practically headed the government, and his foreign policy was tied up by domestic problems. The Foreign Secretary was so busy in parliament that he only rarely came to the Ambassadors' conference, he hastily made a decision and insisted that a peace treaty be signed then and there.[191] But the others resisted and the 'babbling' went on.

Almost at once after the peace was signed in London, another war broke out in June, when Bulgaria attacked her former allies who were preparing to open hostilities. Rumania and the Ottomans joined Bulgaria's enemies. The Turks re-took Adrianople.

Finally, in August 1913, by the Treaty of Bucharest, most of Bulgaria's land claims (Macedonia and Thrace) were divided between Serbia and Greece. Serbia and Montenegro doubled in size. Greece got Salonica and Romania, Dobrudja. Bulgaria asked for Russian diplomatic support once again, but Sazonov and Nicholas II believed that there was no point in alienating a pro-Russian Serbia and potentially friendly Romania for the sake of the unreliable Bulgaria. The Entente politicians in their post-1918 memoirs blamed each other for Bulgaria's 1913 resentment which brought her to the German side in 1914, as if with their experience and knowledge of history they indeed believed that governments based their vital decisions on gratitude or vindictiveness.

With unusual unanimity the Russian diplomacy worked for peace, as acknowledged by the representatives of the Triple Alliance.[192] The erratic Iswolsky for once received praise from the harshest critics – his own subordinates – for leaving behind all petty personal motivations.[193] Lichnowsky cooperated with Grey and under Germany's pressure Austria became more conciliatory. Grey also applied pressure to Serbia to the same effect. He confided to Lichnowsky that above all he wanted to avoid a repetition of the Bosnian crisis because he was convinced that Russia would not beat a retreat a second time.[194]

Observing the behaviour of the great powers during the conference, Benckendorff concluded that both Britain and Germany were eager to settle the conflict, while Austria vacillated under the influence of her war party and Russia, although it did not have a war party, was under the sway of excited public opinion which mistakenly thought that the Serbs' national dignity was at stake. He wrote that of all the powers only France looked forward to a war.

---

190 A.K. Benckendorff to Iswolsky, 07/20.11.1912, AVPRI, f.340, op.835, d.30, ll.5–6 ob.

191 A.K. Benckendorff to Sazonov, 21.05/03.06.1913, AVPRI, f.138, op.467, ed.hr. 707/756, ll.358–60 ob.

192 F. von Pourtalès to Betthmann-Hollweg, 06.05.1913, GP, v 34, 2: 810–11.

193 Sevastopoulo to Schilling, 25.10/07.11.1912, GARF, f.813, op.1, ed.hr.406, ll.34–7 ob.

194 K. Lichnowsky, 167.

Cambon assured him that Britain would go to war to prevent France's defeat and that Churchill, the First Lord of the Admiralty, told him that the Royal Navy was in combat readiness. Benckendorff compared Russia's and France's situations: unlike France, Russia would have to fight two armies along an extended frontier, and to protect herself she needed an alliance with Rumania, 'both now and for the sake of a future eventuality'.[195] These future eventualities seemed unavoidable to most of the people he knew. His brother Pavel wrote in 1913:

> I do not believe that there will be peace in the Balkans, it is going to flare up again, and everyone [in St Petersburg] is of this opinion. You are right to speak of the Emperor's pacific disposition. But he does not realize that peace and war are not solely dependent on his disposition. Neither Sazonov nor Kokovtsev managed to pull him out of lethargy.[196]

Benckendorff largely misunderstood Grey's policy, but he was right in his assessment of the confident French mood. Between 1908, when Clemenceau drummed into the heads of all the British statesmen of his acquaintance that Britain needed to prepare for a continental war and explained to Edward VII the consequences for Britain of a German invasion of France,[197] and 1913, France had increased her military potential and obtained increased military commitments from Russia (formal) and from Britain (informal). Cambon congratulated himself on this unprecedented security of his country, while others painfully realized the flaws in their own networks of alliances. At the time of the Ambassadors' conference, Cambon wrote to his brother in Berlin about the encouraging change in the British attitude to the European situation: Prince Henry of Prussia, visiting his cousin George V, heard from the latter that under certain circumstances Britain would enter a war between Austria-Hungary and Germany on one side and Russia and France on the other because she considered herself honour-bound to her friends even if there was no formal alliance. According to Cambon, Grey approved of this reply, and said it was similar to what Haldane had told Lichnowsky.[198]

The evolution of Anglo-Russian relations from 1907 to 1914 confirmed Benckendorff's conviction about Russia's need for the understanding. In 1905 he promised that a settlement with Britain would open France's and Britain's financial markets to Russia, and so it did, stimulating Russia's industrialization and railway construction and rearmament programmes. After the initial breakthrough of 1905 Russia's political modernization was slowly moving ahead. At the same time, frequent international crises kept the Russian government in constant tension. The

195 A.K. Benckendorff to Sazonov, 12/25.02.1913, AVPRI, f.138, op.467, ed.hr. 707/756, ll.333–43.

196 P.K. Benckendorff to A.K. Benckendorff, 12.09.1913, BC2, box 19.

197 Philippe Erlanger, *Clemenceau* (Paris, 1968), 386.

198 Paul Cambon to Jules Cambon, 21.01.1913, Correspondance, 2: 35–6.

members of the Duma noticed that Sazonov's explanations of his policy were becoming more and more nebulous, especially when it came to the Balkans. After the Balkan wars he lost all his optimism: Bulgaria was lost to the Entente and from 1913 on, Russia could only count on Serbia in the region.

His pessimism was particularly noticeable when he spoke to the Duma committee on foreign affairs in January 1914. Germany was completing its large re-armament programme after having legislated emergency taxation, as if it wanted to meet a deadline; Austria-Hungary was preparing to assert its influence in the Balkans by weakening Serbia. Russia was not ready for war and Sazonov wanted to accelerate Russia's military and naval programmes in order to discourage the central powers from aggressive designs.[199]

In the last pre-war years Benckendorff's and Sazonov's fear was that Russia might become embroiled in a Balkan conflict. Sazonov's only 'policy' rationale was keeping Russia out of confrontations. As for Benckendorff, who philosophically considered that any policy might result in war, he feared that Russia would be drawn into a conflict for reasons of no importance to the Entente, as had happened during the Bosnian crisis, and might have to face the Triple Alliance alone. His reasoning was always the same: a diplomatic or military defeat would produce an anti-Entente shift in Russian foreign policy, culminating in a revolution. He consistently sided with Cambon and Grey against Sazonov because without the Entente's support the latter's attempts to conduct a Balkan policy were doomed, and Russia's every new failure created more tension between her and the Entente.

199 N.V. Savitch, 116.

Chapter 9
The Price of an Alliance, 1914–1917

Benckendorff misinterpreted the consequences for Russia of the developments of 1907–14 partly because he saw Russia's position through the eyes of Cambon and Grey, and partly because he had always ignored all but the great powers' relations. He hoped that fear of an all-European conflagration was a sobering element in all great powers' policies. The count believed that by tying Russia to the Entente, the convention would contribute to the balance of power in Europe and consolidate Russia's internal situation at the same time. But, ultimately, his efforts in this direction contributed to an increasingly tense European situation which made it impossible for the two coalitions to negotiate their way out of the Sarajevo crisis in 1914. When his French colleague in St Petersburg, Maurice Paléologue in a similar way opposed all French intents to welcome Germany's attempts to improve the bilateral relations, his words may have been taken out of Benckendorff's or Nicolson's mouth. Paléologue warned that Germany's friendly moves were attempts to introduce a wedge into the Entente and detach France from Russia: 'We cannot let Germany into our system which would at once collapse'.[1]

Seven Years of the Anglo-Russian Convention: Results

Regional events brought Asian issues, which Benckendorff considered little more than pretexts for the convention, to the forefront of Anglo-Russian relations in 1911–14. Benckendorff praised the convention for the lack of conflicts with the Anglo-Japanese alliance in Asia after 1907, but Russia's post-1905 weakness would have imposed the need to avoid confrontations even without a general arrangement with Britain. As it happened, thanks to the non-intervention of the British and Russian governments, the Manchurian rulers occupied Tibet militarily. In April 1910 the Indian government took steps to prevent a Chinese invasion of Tibet by taking under its protectorate the Himalayan state of Bhutan. Benckendorff defended this violation of the convention as a necessary pragmatic measure which did not create a threat to Russia.[2] Later Sazonov was careful to avoid straining the Anglo-Russian convention by responding to the Dalai Lama's appeals for help.[3]

1 John Keiger, 'Jules Cambon and Franco-German Détente, 1907–1914' in *The Historical Journal*, 26, 3(1983): 651.

2 A.K. Benckendorff to Iswolsky, 21.07/03.08.1910, *Au service*, 2: 289–92.

3 Nikolai II to Dalai Lama, 10.11.1910, *Rossi'ia i Tibet*, 166.

In 1912, as Benckendorff and Iswolsky had hoped, Mongolia became a Russian protectorate, and in the same year, following the Chinese revolution, Tibet proclaimed its independence. Britain's recognition of Tibet's independence would make it a British protectorate and would require a revision of the Anglo-Russian convention on Tibet.[4] When Sazonov pointed out that some of the articles of the Simla convention of Tibetan, British and Chinese representatives contravened the Anglo-Russian convention Grey promised that he would not use the new advantages without coming to an agreement with the Russian government.[5] The consul general in Calcutta, K.D. Nabokoff, considered that Britain was obviously gaining control over Tibet, and Russia should concede freely Britain's right to enter Tibet in exchange for compensatory adjustments of the convention regarding the Afghan border.[6]

The Anglo-Russian rapprochement, in combination with the French alliance, made an unfavourable impact on Russia's relations with the Triple Alliance, at times making Russia's European policy too reckless and at times depriving it of flexibility. Russia had been the dominant partner in the French alliance because of the French need for the Russian army, so prior to 1904–5 Lamsdorff still referred to Russia as a marriageable girl whose favours were disputed by several wooers, Benckendorff shared this opinion[7] and Russia's relations with Germany, while never easy, were close. An idea of a Russo-German war seemed improbable to the Russians. After 1908–9 it was no longer the case, although some (including Nicholas II) remained unaware of it.

Russia achieved the Potsdam compromise with Germany on the issue of the Baghdad railway by abandoning the idea of four-party negotiations which Britain upheld. This shift did not substantially improve Russo-German relations because Russia refused to negotiate a general agreement, always keeping in mind its pro-Entente orientation. It reinforced the Entente's suspicions of Russia's good faith, while Germany came to treat Russia as the weakest link of the hostile Entente.

Russo-German relations were further complicated by the French pressure through Théophile Delcassé and Maurice Paléologue, posted to St Petersburg respectively in February 1913 and January 1914, and by the disarray at the Russian foreign ministry. Sazonov was often ill and absent from his post. Iswolsky and Benckendorff did their best to tie Russia closer to the Entente, hoping to accelerate political reforms in Russia, ensure Russia's place on the winning side in the looming European war and, last but not least, protect Russia's Near Eastern interests. Austria-Hungary and Germany were building up their presence

4 L.H.Reveliotti to Neratov, 01.06.1912, *Rossi'ia i Tibet*, 179–82.

5 British embassy at St Petersburg, *Memorandum for S.D. Sazonov*, 10/23.05.1914, *Rossi'ia i Tibet*, 209–10.

6 K.D. Nabokov to Neratov. 27.12.1912/09.01.1914, *Rossi'ia i Tibet*, 189–91.

7 A.K.Benckendorff to Lamsdorff, 27.03/09.04.1901, GARF, f.568, op.1, ed.hr.326, ll.25–6.

in the Near East and it was clear that Russia would have to reassert its interests there. It was inevitable not just for strategic considerations, like the Straits, or the economic considerations, like the grain exports, or hegemonic ambitions, like expansion in the Balkans. It was not only because 'to preserve ... its hold over its subjects the Russian state could [not] ... afford ... to seem weak'[8]. Russia had a terrible reminder of the fate of a former great power in the Ottoman Empire; she was torn asunder by her neighbours, exploited by the French, German and British capital and manipulated by the powers. After the Russo-Japanese War, Russia's foreign policy had, among others, the goal of preventing the empire's slide into the category of the powers' prey.

Russian envoys in the Balkans tried to strengthen the ties of the Balkan states to Russia, assuming that in this case Austrian expansion would be neutralized and Russia would be able to wait patiently for the collapse of the Ottoman Empire. N. Hartwig, A. Nekliudov and N. Schebeko did not press for the solution of the Eastern Question, but they were encouraging the volatile Balkan governments to resist Austria-Hungary's pressure and form a barrier to the 'Germanization of the Balkans'. Benckendorff, who had not been concerned about any but the great powers' interests, resented the 'paltry little nations' and condemned the activities of his colleagues posted in them, for their dangerous potential consequences, but his efforts to contribute to the Entente's version of a safer Europe also contributed to the antagonism of the blocs. No matter what policies Sazonov may have conceived, their implementation depended on his stubborn envoys, most of whom had their own ideas of what was best for Russia and Europe.

Sharing Benckendorff's and Iswolsky's view that Russia could count only on England and France in maintaining her status and achieving her goals, Sazonov pressed for a further rapprochement with the Entente, through a closer tie to Britain. Grey did not see any possibility or pressing need for closer relations with Russia. On the other hand, the more strained Russia's relations with the Triple Alliance were, the riskier it was for Britain to give Russia guarantees of support.

The Foreign Office saw no harm in symbolic gestures of goodwill. In January 1912 a large British parliamentary deputation visited St Petersburg, attracting much attention in the press as a new proof of Russia's growing closeness with Britain. Typically, Benckendorff's main concern about the visit was that Sazonov should pay particular attention to Lord Salisbury's youngest son and Asquith's inveterate enemy, Lord Hugh Cecil, whom he admiringly described as a 'high Tory'.[9] Benckendorff was confident that the 'high Tories' of his acquaintance would form the next government and the Anglo-Russian convention would then be in good hands. The counsellor of the Russian embassy in Berlin wrote that the Petersburg raptures over the British visitors, coupled with the aggressively anti-

8 D.C.B. Lieven, *Russia and Origins of the First World War* (London, 1983), 153.

9 A.K. Benckendorff to Sazonov, 04/17.01.1912, AVPRI, f.138, op.467, d.707/756, ll.180–82.

German tone of the *Novoye Vremya* and the imprudent speeches by the hosts and the visitors, made a very bad impression in Germany.[10]

Yet Benckendorff did not tire of pointing out that Berlin counted too much on Russia's support,[11] always encouraging less consideration for German views. His staff made a great joke out of their anti-German reputation; Poklevsky boasted in 1908 that he was accused of anti-German intrigues because 'the ambassador and I are now painted with the same brush'.[12] In Paris, Iswolsky – or the French foreign ministry[13] – made Russia's position *vis-à-vis* Germany more difficult by leaking to the French press Sazonov's confidential letters,[14] with instructions for supporting France against Germany.

Russia's Position in the Balkans in 1913–1914

Russia's Balkan initiatives left her in a precarious position: the 1912–13 Balkan wars demonstrated that St Petersburg could not stop the Balkan states from going to war. Largely because of the Straits issue, Russia's relations with the Ottoman Empire remained tense. Russia's 1908 and 1912 attempts to force on Turkey negotiations about a change in the Straits' regime failed without the Entente's support. Sazonov once again saw the lack of sympathy from the Entente during the Liman von Sanders affair in November 1913–January 1914, when Russia's fear of Turkey's stronger and better organized armed forces under German control forced her to bring pressure on the Turkish government and also in Berlin to revoke a German general's appointment to the command of the First corps of the Turkish army stationed in Constantinople.

Paul Cambon referred to the Russian request for support as Iswolsky's 'ridiculous note regarding a German general in Constantinople', adding indignantly: 'Russian government demands *a collective demarche* of the Triple Entente in Berlin'.[15] On 31 December 1913, the Russian government discussed whether Russia was able to stand up to the Triple Alliance in case of a Turkish refusal to comply with the Russian demand. V.N. Kokovtsev, the head of the government, insisted that Russia could not face a European conflict, which led Sazonov to explain that Russia had

10 Schebeko to Schilling, 20.01/02.02.1912, GARF, f.813, op.1, ed.hr.445, ll.47–50 ob.

11 A.K. Benckendorff to Neratov, 30.08/12.09.1912, AVPRI, f.340, op.812, d.10, ll.38–44.

12 Poklevsky to Savinsky, 25.05/10.06.1908, AVPRI, f.340, op.706 ed.hr.13, ll.324–5.

13 Irwin Halfond, 'Maurice Paleologue: The Diplomatist, the Writer and the Man' (PhD Dissertation, Temple University, 1974), 198.

14 M. de Taube, *La politique russe d'avant-guerre et la fin de l'empire des tsars,* 311–12.

15 P. Cambon to Fleuriau, 02.01.1914, *Correspondance*, 2: 61.

two options only: demonstrate to its allies its readiness to go to war or leave them with a dangerous impression that Russia would concede anything in order to avoid war. It would make them lose interest in Russia's friendship and Russia would end up in political isolation.[16]

After a compromise with Germany settled the incident, Sazonov angrily told Buchanan that the Turks would have given in if they had seen a united Entente behind Russia. Now Turkey believed that Russia would never fight. Not for the first time he said that the Entente powers, because of their '... dread of war ... will one day suddenly find that they have brought war upon themselves'.[17] Nevertheless, in the wake of the affair, he defended Britain in the Duma insisting that the British would not stay neutral in case of a Russo-German war, even though they did not have an alliance with Russia. He only feared that the British would intervene too late to prevent the success of the German coalition.[18]

Benckendorff failed to get Grey's support for Russia and explained to Sazonov at great length that the Entente's collective representations involved a risk of war, as Germany would then defend Turkey as a point of honour. A Russo-German conflict would have no sympathy in Britain unless it was preceded by negotiations. He had to admit that the Triple Entente was not united but tried to present it as an advantage, arguing that the absence of formal commitments allowed Britain to help Russia more effectively: 'Thanks to England's special position we avoided a war'.[19]

Fears of a Conflict with Germany

At that time, several prominent statesmen and diplomats (S.Yu. Witte, P.N. Durnovo, V.N. Kokovsev, R. Rosen, M. Taube, L. Kasso, K. Goubastov and P. Botkin), most of them Benckendorff's erstwhile supporters, agreed that the pro-Entente policy was leading Russia to a war with Germany that Russia could not sustain. They attempted a conspiracy to replace the Anglophile Sazonov with another former subordinate of Benckendorff's, Petr S. Botkin. Nicholas II received a barrage of lectures with historical analogies, reports and memoranda which warned him of the dangerous consequences of the Entente orientation for Russia's domestic and international condition.[20] From Taube's description, it seems that Nicholas II closed his eyes to the importance of the issue and dismissed the campaign as a cabal of a power-hungry clique. The group became known as 'the Germanophiles'

16 V.A. Emets, *Otcherki vneshnei politiki Rossii 1914–1918: Vzaimootnosheni'ia voiny* (Moscow, 1977), 60.

17 Buchanan to George V, 25.12.1913, RA PS/PSO/GV/C/P/284a/10.

18 Savich, 116.

19 A.K. Benckendorff to Sazonov, 04/17.12.1913, AVPRI, f.138, op.467, d.707/756, ll. 377–9.

20 M.A. Taube, *Zarnitsy*, 169.

and, with the help of the Entente diplomats, they were shut out of Russian politics in 1914–17.[21]

St Petersburg's Attempts to Form an Alliance with Britain

From the beginning of 1914, Sazonov and Nicholas II had repeatedly spoken to Buchanan and Paléologue about getting Britain's formal pledge of support in Europe.[22]

Sazonov believed that Russia's full and formal alignment with Britain and France would deter Turkey and the Triple Alliance from challenging Russia. Did not Germany back down in the Morocco crisis after England made her position clear? Sazonov blamed England's vacillations for imperilling European peace, and asked Benckendorff: 'What will happen if the Turks occupy the Ionian Islands and, of course, the Triple Alliance refuses to coerce them? A new Balkan war?' Then England would have to enter the war whether she liked it or not, and at a moment dictated by others. 'It is foolish and dangerous to be aware of one's superior strength and capitulate to those who are weaker but better organized and more united'.[23] In principle, the ambassador agreed with Sazonov. At the time of the Bosnian crisis, Grey recorded Benckendorff's opinion of Britain's role in a European crisis:

> … should such a crisis arise, [Benckendorff] was optimistic enough to think that sharp, decisive action on our part would keep the peace. The British government were at once to ask for a vote of credit from the House of Commons, he thought that would make the whole difference.[24]

Benckendorff explained Grey's behaviour by his absorption in Britain's internal political problems. He assured Sazonov that the British military were for a formal entente with Russia and so were his counterparts at the Foreign Office, 'Nicolson, Hardinge, Mallet, Buchanan and the novice, Eyre Crowe'. Grey could not side with Russia because of public opinion, which the count tactfully called 'the isolationist mood'. He quoted Grey's words that Britain would not conclude an alliance, not even with France.[25]At the same time, he reminded Sazonov of the important 'indirect fruits', of the convention and advised him to be more generous with England in discussing Tibet and Persia: the British then would

21 Grey to Buchanan, 01.08.1916, FO 800/75, 339.

22 Buchanan to Grey, 18.02.1914, FO 800/74, 260–71.

23 Sazonov to A.K. Benckendorff, 06/19.02.1914, AVPRI, f.138, op.467, d.323/327, ll.7–8 ob.

24 Grey to Nicolson, 10.11.1908, FO 800/73, 136–7.

25 A.K. Benckendorff to Sazonov, 29.04/12.05.1914, in *The Entente Diplomacy*, 716.

accept the Trans-Persian railway which would bring an Anglo-Russian alliance in its wake.[26]

If it is true that by mid-1914 Grey and his influential private secretary W. Tyrrell were more concerned about improving Anglo-German relations than about coming closer to Russia and the pro-Russian Nicolson was 'of no account' and his policy was questioned,[27] Sazonov did not hear about it. Benckendorff never changed his upbeat tone when referring to his conversations with Grey regarding the future of Anglo-Russian convention.

Anglo-Russian Convention in Asia

Benckendorff hoped to offset British lack of support for Russia's interests in Europe by progress on the issue of the Trans-Persian railway and blamed the unpopularity of the idea in Britain on the tactless Russian press which 'spoilt it all for Grey'.[28] The British attitude to the alignment of the railway systems was the touchstone of their attitude to the Anglo-Russian convention[29] and both sides knew that it had a symbolic dimension to it. In 1912–14, the Societé des Études, formed by the French and British financiers under the aegis of the Foreign Office, discussed the enterprise. The Russian ambassador did his best for the cause by suggesting Lord Revelstoke as an intermediary for Russia[30] and confidently waited for the fruition of the project after the completion of the Persian railway network.[31]

In February 1914 Sazonov proposed to Buchanan the long-discussed alignment of the Trans-Persian railway, implying that, if the British continued to procrastinate, Russia would undertake the project alone in the Russian and the neutral zone. Since 1910 the Foreign Office had realized that Russia would sooner or later build railways to the boundary of their zone and there would have to be a corresponding railway system on the British side, despite the fears of the Indian government.[32]

As the Anglo-Russian convention was coming up for revision, the 'pro-Russians' in the Foreign Office wanted a more binding arrangement to make it impossible for Russia to turn to Germany.[33] Grey was delaying the revision of

26 A.K. Benckendorff to Sazonov, 12/25.02.1914, AVPRI, f.138, op.467, d.323/327, ll.9–14 ob.

27 Keith Neilson and T.G. Otte, *The Permanent Under-Secretary for Foreign Affairs, 1854–1946* (New York, 2008), 146.

28 A.K. Benckendorff to Sazonov, June/July 1912, AVPRI, f.340, op.812, d.10, l.275–9.

29 Paul Cambon to Pichon, 07.12.1910, DDF, XIII: 121–5.

30 A.K. Benckendorff to Sazonov, 30.01/12.02.1912, AVPRI, f.138, op.467, d.707/756, ll.204–10.

31 A.K. Benckendorff to Neratov, 30.03/12.04.1911, AVPRI, f.340, op.812, d.10, l.17–18 ob.

32 David McLean, *Britain and Her Buffer State*, 116–17.

33 D.W. Sweet and R.T.B. Langhorne, *Great Britain and Russia, 1907–1914*, 252.

the convention because Britain wanted Russian concessions in Tibet and Persia but had nothing to offer in exchange. A Trans-Persian railway would be a *quid pro quo*.[34] On 19 March 1914, the British cabinet accepted the alignment of the Trans-Persian railway with a terminus at a port east of Bunder Abbas. The British minister at Teheran wrote that, since Britain wanted the whole of the neutral zone under its control, the British *quid pro quo* would be supporting Russia over Serbia.[35] The need for revising the 1907 convention was now even more obvious than before.

The Foreign Office asked George V to obtain Nicholas II's favourable influence over Sazonov during the pending discussions. The king was to suggest 'a frank and friendly exchange of views on Persia'. Nicolson recommended to George V to open his letter with 'I know my dear Nicky that I can count on your friendship'. On the other side of Nicolson's draft, the king jotted his own: 'My dear Nicky, you will remember the very satisfactory conversations we had last year in Berlin. Now – my anxiety about the present unsatisfactory state of affairs in Persia …'.[36]

Two months later, the war interfered with these plans. In late 1914 Turkey invaded Persia. Russian troops ousted the Turks from Tabriz and Persian Azerbaijan, and remained stationed there, though they still refrained from occupying Teheran, thus preserving the semblance of Persian sovereignty as agreed with the British. In 1915, when Sazonov complained about the British minister, Grey decided that the latter would go if the Russian minister was also removed[37] and Nikolay S. Etter replaced Ivan Korostovetz in Teheran. The nomination of another of Benckendorff's subordinates reaffirmed the Russian foreign ministry's continuing goodwill towards the British. Nicholas II spoke to Etter about a partition of Persia 'in 10 or 15 years' time'; Sazonov was calm but pessimistic about Persia because Russia lacked troops to send there and the Russian bank was nearly broke. Persia did not matter any more. Like Poklevsky, Etter asked Benckendorff to recommend to him the course to follow.[38]

In 1915 Russia promised to give the neutral zone to the British in exchange for British consent to Russia's control of the Straits following the defeat of the Ottoman Empire. This meant a partition of Persia. Late in 1916 Ivan Korostovetz prepared a memorandum for the pending revision of the Anglo-Russian convention to incorporate the changes of 1907–16. It was prompted by the

34 Grey to Buchanan, 18.03.1914, FO 800/74, 282–4.

35 Keith Wilson, 'Imperial Interests in the British Decision for War, 1914', in *Empire and Continent: Studies in British Foreign Policy from the 1880s to the First World War* (London, 1987), 160–61.

36 Nicolson's draft for George V. [n.d] and the king's draft, 16.06.1914, RA PS/PSO/GV/C/M/624/3.

37 W. Tyrell, 16.01.1915, FO 800/92, 19–20.

38 Etter to A.K. Benckendorff, 18.05.1915, BC2, box 16.

Persian government's proposal to sign an alliance with Russia and Britain. The three-sphere arrangement had not worked for Russia because Britain regarded the neutral zone as its own and even exercised a restraining action on Russia's actions in her zone (Teheran). Russia could not pressure the hostile central government because of the British insistence on non-interference, and so the provincial authorities felt free to obstruct Russian interests. Korostovetz thought that in the future, Russian policy should encourage decentralization of the provincial administration,[39] taking a page from the British policy in the south. He also suggested some useful changes to the boundary line and spoke of the need for parity of issue rights for the Russian and British banks in Persia and of Franco-British financial support for the Russian Trans-Persian railway. He suggested starting the construction without delay, to protect at least part of the Russian market in Persia from the consequences of the completion of the Baghdad railway. The railway, when completed by the British after the war, would be aligned with Britain's Indian and African colonies, but Russia still controlled strategically important Persian Azerbaijan. He wrote that it would be to Russia's advantage if British consular officials in Persia would report to London instead of India – probably because the Foreign Office had shown more interest in conciliating the interests of the two sides than the Indian government. Korostovetz believed that the British would agree to make non-political concessions to Russia in the matter of border relations with Afghanistan.[40]

The multiple reasons which had called the Anglo-Russian convention into being in 1907 had undergone changes in the decade that followed; but they had not disappeared. No matter how unnatural the convention seemed to its critics, it created a habit of reluctant cooperation in Asia. The European content of the convention prevailed over the local interests to the degree that averted the collapse of the Anglo-Russian understanding while presiding over the collapse of the Persian Empire.

Benckendorff's pressure on the foreign ministry to be conciliatory in the regional relations with Britain for the sake of the European goal was successful: the idea of coexistence in Asia gradually took root in Russian minds. Specific details of Anglo-Russian cooperation were criticized, but not the general policy. Given another decade, the instinctive antagonism and mistrust would have subsided as the younger generation of Russian diplomats knew only a world in which Anglo-Russian friendship was one of the staples of Russian policy. In 1916 the Russian government took for granted post-war cooperation with Britain in Asia, even though the Triple Alliance's anticipated defeat would bring about a new stage in the relations of the great powers in Asia.[41]

---

39 David McLean, *Britain and Her Buffer State*, 140.

40 I. Korostovetz, *Memorandum Relating to the Revision of the Anglo-Russian Convention of 1907*, 25.10.1916, AVPRI, f.138, op.467, d.632/653, ll.1–11 ob.

41 Ibid.

Attempts to Consolidate the Entente

In March 1914, Sazonov wrote to Benckendorff and Iswolsky that Russia's most urgent diplomatic goal was to consolidate, and if possible transform, the so-called Triple Entente into a Triple Alliance. The French promised to help Iswolsky tackle the issue during King George V's forthcoming visit to Paris.[42] Iswolsky was going to suggest that Grey should inform Russia about the terms of the Anglo-French arrangement.[43] Benckendorff worried that another failed Russian initiative might damage Anglo-Russian relations and tried to change Sazonov's mind or at least postpone the step which would probably end in a disappointment. He reminded the minister that the days of the Liberal government were numbered (an election was due in 1915) and speculated on the chances of an Anglo-Russian alliance under their Conservative successors.[44]

Poincaré accepted Iswolsky's request for support, although pointing out that the French could not ask from Britain for Russia what they did not have themselves – an alliance. Paris put Cambon in charge of persuading the British to agree to Anglo-Russian naval conversations. Grey told him that only a naval arrangement was feasible because the Russian and the British armies could never act together, and added that he foresaw trouble on that issue with his party and public opinion.[45] The irritated Cambon wrote to his brother that Sazonov's complaints about the 'drifting' of the Triple Entente were groundless because his own erratic political steps caused it. In other words, Sazonov's attempts to find support in Paris and London, exposed the Entente's lack of unity.

Iswolsky submitted to Grey a draft of an Anglo-Russian naval convention to secure British support of Russia in the Baltic,[46] an echo of Sazonov's conversation with Grey in 1912. Nicholas II also told Buchanan that he looked forward to formalizing Anglo-Russian friendship because if the looming Greco-Turkish war resulted in another closure of the Straits, Russia would have to use force to open them. Then, if Germany sided with Turkey, war would break out. He wanted Buchanan and also the French government to explain to Grey that an Anglo-Russian entente would prevent Germany's assistance to Turkey.[47]

A week after Grey's return from Paris, the cabinet accepted the Russian proposal. Cambon informed Benckendorff of the content of his exchange with Grey, and the Russian ambassador reported as his own Grey's idea that Anglo-Russian talks should take place in London between the Admiralty and the Russian

42 Sazonov to A.K. Benckendorff, 20.03/02.04.1914, AVPRI, f.138, op.467, d.323/327, ll.15–16 ob.

43 Sazonov to Iswolsky, 20.03/02.04.1914, AVPRI, f.138, op.467, d.323/327, l.18 ob.

44 A.K.Benckendorff to Sazonov, 25.03/03.04.1914, AVPRI, f.138, op.467, d.323/327, ll.19–23 ob.

45 P.Cambon to J. Cambon, 29.04.1914, *Correspondance*, 3: 65–6.

46 Freiherr von Schoen, 171.

47 Paleologue to Doumergue, 11.04.1914, AVPRI, f.138, op.467, d.323/327, l.31 ob.

naval attaché.[48] When necessary, the naval attaché would make inconspicuous lightning visits to St Petersburg for consultation. [49]

Grey's risky step was urged on him by the French and his assistants at the Foreign Office. If it became known it might topple his government, because, as Goschen wrote to Nicolson at that time, 'It is extraordinary to see how many people even including our own countrymen, fail to see the importance of our maintaining our *Entente* with Russia'.[50]

When Benckendorff despatched to St Petersburg his copies of the Grey-Cambon exchange, he added that he was told most emphatically that there was no Anglo-French alliance, only a preliminary agreement.[51] Russia, therefore, could expect no more. The form in which Grey agreed to satisfy Russia's wish did little for Russia because Britain's secret and limited commitment would not have been a deterrent to the Triple Alliance. Benckendorff told Grey that he opposed the idea of an alliance, considering the existing relations safer, since without pledges there would be no bickering about who had to follow whom. Grey warned Buchanan that Benckendorff's view, which the Foreign Secretary shared, was to be kept secret from Sazonov.[52]

Benno von Siebert at once informed the Germans about the naval conversations. The German foreign ministry, worried by Britain's readiness to cooperate with the Franco-Russian alliance, arranged leaks to the German press.[53] At the same time, the *Manchester Guardian* published news about an alleged Anglo-Russian Straits agreement. Grey made a carefully-worded denial that the government 'had no secret engagements committing this country to action; and that we had not engaged, were not now engaged, and were not likely to engage in any negotiation that would make that statement less true than it was when made by the P[rime] M[inister]' some time earlier. Having agreed with Benckendorff that the German *Berliner Tageblatt* must have got wind of the conversations from Paris, Grey nevertheless pointed out that, despite the Quai d'Orsay's reputation for indiscretion, 'the Military and Naval conversations with the French Authorities had not leaked out, nor the letter to Cambon'. So he was inclined to blame Iswolsky.[54] As usual, Benckendorff repeated it all to Sazonov as his own conjectures.[55] Despite

48 Viscount Grey of Fallodon, K.G., *Twenty-Five Years, 1892–1916* (New York, 1925), 1: 267.

49 A.K. Benckendorff to Sazonov, 02/15.05.1914, AVPRI, f.138, op.467, d.323/327, l.38 ob.

50 *The Diary of Edward Goschen*, 23.05.1914, 58.

51 A.K. Benckendorff to Sazonov, 06/19.05.1914, AVPRI, f.138, op.467, d.323/327, ll.39–40 ob.

52 Grey to Buchanan, 07.05.1914, FO 800/74, 275–7.

53 Stephen Schroeder, Ausgedehnte Spionage – Benno von Sieberts geheime Zusammenarbeit mit dem Auswaertigen Amt (1909–1926) in *Militargeschitchliche zeitschrift*, 65 (2005): 459.

54 Grey to Buchanan, 10.06.1914, FO 800/74, 282–4.

55 A.K. Benckendorff to Sazonov, 19.06/02.07.1914 in *The Entente Diplomacy*, 732.

Sazonov's insistence on their immediate resumption, the naval conversations were postponed till August when Prince Louis Battenberg, the First Sea Lord and the Tsar's brother-in-law, would visit Tsarskoe Selo.[56]

At the end of June, in anticipation of the convention revision, Sazonov asked for all the Anglo-Russian treaties, including Russian guarantees for India, to be prepared. He expected that Benckendorff and Buchanan would be able to bring the pending negotiations to a successful conclusion. The minister expected to spend all July 1914 at Tsarskoe Selo and wanted to see Benckendorff there on his way from Sosnovka to London.[57]

July 1914 in Europe

By 1914 fear of Germany had accumulated in the Entente foreign ministries because of what they knew of German military plans, read in the German press and observed in William II's personal diplomacy. It gave more definite shape to the fatalistic expectation of a general European war routinely mentioned in the correspondence of the statesmen and their entourages. George V wrote to Nicholas II in 1912 that it would be a disaster if the attempts to localize the Balkan war failed and general war ensued.[58] In June 1914 he reminded the emperor about their 1913 conversation in Berlin about 'friendship between our two countries to secure peace in Europe'[59] making it clear that in his eyes the Anglo-Russian convention was about Europe. Since 1909 Benckendorff and Paul Cambon had expected a European war to break out every August after the harvest.[60]

All European governments wanted peace, but none thought of the preservation of peace as being their foremost national interest, superseding all others. They were always quick to point out to other governments that in order to save peace they had to curb their ambitions. Germany moderated Austrian ambitions; Russia pressed Montenegro and Serbia to accept the powers' decisions for the sake of peace; Britain and France practised wise prudence at the expense of Russia's interests and, as Russians bitterly felt, prestige. These situations arose when Russian foreign policy in the last pre-war years attempted to assert its claims or promote its interests in the Near East and encountered resistance, usually encouraged by one of the great powers. In 1909, 1912 and January 1914, Russia and Europe benefited from this Entente selfishness. Britain and France refused Russia support which, had it been given, would have led a weak and unprepared Russian Empire onto 'the path of honour' and an even earlier demise.

---

56 Buchanan to Grey, 25.06.1914, FO 800/74, 285–6.

57 Etter to A.K.Benckendorff, 29.06.1914, BC2, box 16.

58 George V to Nicholas II, 06.10.1912, GARF, f.601, op.1, ed.hr.1219, l.41 ob.

59 George V to Nicholas II, 16.06.1914, GARF, f.601, op.1, ed.hr.1219, l.48 ob.

60 Constantine Benckendorff, *Half a Life: The Reminiscences of a Russian Gentleman* (London, 1955), 149.

Nicholas II and his government, as always, acted in discord, ignoring or contradicting each other's plans. By 1914 the Tsar had ceased to receive yearly ministerial reports and mostly based his judgments on brief summaries and a daily selection of telegrams and letters presented by Sazonov. The minister loosely coordinated his actions with the Tsar and periodically faced him with a *fait accompli*. The French and the British ambassadors preferred to deal with Nicholas II, bypassing Sazonov, because they usually managed to bend the Tsar to their will. Whenever Nicholas II's impromptu decisions threw a matter off course, Sazonov had to request a second audience and ask him to reconsider his concession. The minister's job became especially hard and thankless after Stolypin's assassination in 1911. Stolypin was the last prime minister capable of keeping in check the government, the Duma and, to a degree, the Tsar himself. It did not help that Sazonov was by 1914 barely able to withstand the physical strain of his duties. He looked forward to Benckendorff's retirement when he would replace his old chief in London.[61] Benckendorff was also tired[62] and complained that the golden age of his embassy was in the past.[63] He had accomplished his dream, the Anglo-Russian convention. Without Edward VII, London was not the same and even Grey could not replace the late venerated king in Benckendorff's affections.

May-June of 1914 in London was marked by a third successful *Saison Russe*, which the Benckendorffs attended, surrounded by their London friends. Lady de Grey, Diaghilev's patron and Countess Benckendorff's distant relative, had the Russian actors give a performance at her country house, Coombe Court, where she was entertaining Empress Maria Feodorovna, Queen Alexandra and the Benckendorffs. It was at Coombe that the ambassador learned of the Sarajevo assassination.[64] Benckendorff was not the only one to be alarmed:[65] Russian statesmen had never left Germany or Austria in doubt as to their attitude: an attack on Serbia would be a *casus belli*. European diplomats equally understood that if Russia stepped back now she would lose all influence in the Balkans[66] and her standing with the Entente.

Sazonov attempted to avoid a confrontation with the Triple Alliance. After the Austro-Hungarian ultimatum to Serbia was sent to all the powers on 24 July, Buchanan told Sazonov that Britain was not directly involved in Serbia and therefore would not intervene. He offered Britain's mediation in inducing Austria-Hungary to extend a delay to Serbia and Sazonov accepted, despite the protests

---

61 Georgy N. Mikhailovsky, *Zapiski: Iz istorii rossiiskogo vneshnepoliticheskogo vedomstva, 1914–1920* (Moscow, 1993), 1: 75–8.

62 Wesselitsky to A.K. Benckendorff, 12.11.1914, BC2, box 15.

63 D.I. Abrikossov, *Revelations*, 202.

64 *Dnevniki imperatritsy Marii Fedorovny, 1914–1920, 1923 gody* (Moscow, 2005), 18.

65 Sir George Frankenstein, *Facts and Features of My Life* (London, 1939), 146.

66 K. Lichnowsky, *Heading for the Abyss: Reminiscences* (New York, 1928), 16.

of the French ambassador that there was no time for that. Buchanan reported that Sazonov seemed less belligerent than Maurice Paléologue,[67] (who, as it turned out later, misinformed his chief regarding the atmosphere at St Petersburg and was pushing Sazonov to defy Austria-Hungary).[68]

Benckendorff warned Grey that mediation would look as if France and England were distancing themselves from Russia. Grey argued that, if both the Entente and Germany clearly stayed out of the Russo-Austrian conflict, these two might find a compromise. Benckendorff was not convinced, and asked Grey to indicate to Germany that Britain would not stand aside if there were a war. Grey replied in his customary way which had served him so well in 1905–14 that he had never given any indication that Britain *would* stand aside. He also told Lichnowsky that as long as it was an Austro-Serbian quarrel Britain would not intervene.[69] He was dealing with the situation in the same way he had dealt with previous Balkan crises.

The next day, in the hope that Austria-Hungary would retreat, Sazonov issued a conventional warning communiqué, stating that Russia would not remain indifferent to Serbia's fate. At the same time, he told the Entente ambassadors that Russia would not take aggressive measures unless forced: the emperor had approved a partial mobilization, leaving it to Sazonov to set the date. Buchanan protested that a Russian mobilization would make Britain's mediation impossible, while Paléologue then and there pledged France's absolute support – without an authorization from Paris.[70] At that point, the word 'mobilization' did not particularly impress anyone, as Austria and Russia had mobilized before 1914, and nothing happened.

Benckendorff had often told his cousin Lichnowsky that neither Nicholas II nor anyone who counted in Russia was anti-German. And despite Austria's unpopularity, no one in Russia would dream of going to war in order to seize part of the Habsburg Empire.[71] In July 1914 Lichnowsky asked the state secretary von Jagow to keep this in mind, adding that Sazonov and Nicholas II were so pacific that they even resented Poincaré's July visit as a provocative demonstration.[72] Jagow answered: 'I am ready to believe your cousin Benckendorff about them not being anxious to fight, but as they will grow stronger they will become more anti-German'. Still, von Jagow said, he was glad to hear that Russia was unprepared: her protests, then, would not amount to much.[73] Even here Benckendorff's good intentions did more harm than good.

When the terms of the Austro-Hungarian ultimatum became known, on 25 July Sazonov through Benckendorff asked Grey to communicate to the Austrian

67 Irwin Halfond, 235–6.
68 Ibid., ii.
69 Viscount Grey of Fallodon, 1: 306–7.
70 Irwin Halfond, 241–2.
71 K. Lichnowsky, 378.
72 Ibid., 382.
73 Von Yagow – Lichnowsky, 18.07.1914, K. Lichnowsky, *Heading for the Abyss*, 381.

government his 'unequivocal and firm' condemnation of their policy. He added that unfortunately, its actions against Serbia Austria counted on Britain's remaining uninvolved.[74] Benckendorff privately warned Lichnowsky that Russia could hardly advise the Serbs to accept the ultimatum because it would be the end of Serbia's sovereignty.[75] Still, Serbia, on Russia's advice, accepted practically all of Austria's terms.

As for Grey, he deplored the Austrian ultimatum when Count Mensdorff brought it and on the same day, 24 July, he told Lichnowsky that a local war between Austria and Serbia did not concern Britain, but it would be different if Russian public opinion forced the government to declare war on Austria-Hungary. Then he described to Lichnowsky the horrors of a European war, clearly saying that it would be a continental war of 'four powers',[76] – that is, without Britain.

While the German ambassador reported to Berlin Grey's reassuring words, Benckendorff wrote to Sazonov a day later: 'Although I cannot offer you a formal guarantee of Britain's military assistance, I have noticed no sign in Grey or the king or any other influential person that Britain seriously believes in the possibility of remaining neutral'.[77] In the following days, Benckendorff sent telegrams to Sazonov confirming that Grey was urging Berlin to accept mediation.

On 26 July, after the ultimatum expired, Austria did not launch an immediate attack and Grey called for a conference[78] which Russia accepted but Germany rejected. To the ambassador's words that Britain was increasing the risk of war by letting Vienna and Berlin think that she would stand aside, Grey answered that Britain could only promise diplomatic support, but at the same time he wrote to Buchanan that the orders to the First Fleet not to disperse for manoeuvre leave ought to give a warning to the powers.[79]

Sazonov instructed Russian ambassadors in European capitals to continue negotiations with Austria-Hungary, even if the latter opened hostilities, thereby precluding the communication between him and the Austrian ambassador. After the Austrian attack on Serbia on July 14/27 and 15/28, Sazonov telegraphed Benckendorff and other ambassadors asking for British or any other mediation to solve the conflict and to exert influence in Berlin.[80] On 28 July Sazonov telegraphed Benckendorff that the next day Russia would order a partial mobilization because of the Austrian declaration of war on Serbia.[81] Benckendorff told his son Konstantin, on a holiday in London, to go back to Russia because war was inevitable: 'I think

74 *Istori'ia diplomatii* (Moscow: AST, [1947] 2006), 807.

75 K. Lichnowsky, 387.

76 *Istoria diplomatii*, 807–8.

77 *Istoria diplomatii*, 808.

78 Irwin Halfond, 243.

79 Grey to Buchanan, 27.07.1914, *Collected Diplomatic Documents*, 41.

80 P.L. Bark, 'I'iul'skie dni 1914' in *Vozrozhdenie*, 91 (1959): 28.

81 Sazonov to A.K. Benckendorff, 28.07.1914, *Collected Diplomatic Documents*, 55–6.

this time we are in for it … And I really do not know what England will do'.[82] On 29 July Grey told the German ambassador that Britain could only remain neutral while France and Germany did not join the conflict. Grey's words produced a storm in Berlin because of their earlier conviction that Grey would restrain Russia and France by declaring to them that Britain would remain neutral.

The Benckendorffs' son-in-law, Jasper Ridley, circulating between the City, the House of Commons and the Russian embassy, recorded the all-European rise of food prices in preparation for war, the continuing indecision at Downing Street, the postponement of the Irish Amending Bill debate and the rollercoaster moods at the Russian embassy where everyone waited with bated breath for telegrams from St Petersburg.

On the 29 July Benckendorff declared at dinner that diplomats had done all they could and any attempt to keep France and Germany out was bound to end in failure. Ten days before a statement by Grey that Britain would intervene 'in certain eventualities' would have prevented the whole thing but by now Austria had gone too far to pull back and Germany, following suit, had decided to strike at Russia.[83]

The German Chancellery, realizing the danger, on the night of 29–30 July attempted to make Austria soften its demands to Serbia and accept Grey's mediation, but Austria declined and then the German general staff took over from the diplomats.[84] The Germans spoke of nothing but Russia's mobilization, although they knew that it would take six weeks and was more of a deterrence gesture than actual preparation for war.

Under the circumstances, Grey decided that he could not ask Sazonov to cancel the mobilization because then, if attacked, Russia might expect Britain to come to its rescue.[85] Grey's hedging which had served him well before, misfired: the French and the Russians were alarmed by Britain's lack of support, while the Triple Alliance was alarmed by Britain's refusal to restrain Russia and France.

Nicholas II wrote to George V that, despite the insistence of the military on a full mobilization, he wanted a partial one and only accepted their opinion after the Austrian mobilization was over and Belgrade was bombed.[86] On 30 July Benckendorff repeated to Grey that Sazonov would accept any proposal of Grey's in order to preserve peace, but wrote to Sazonov that, after the mobilization, which Benckendorff considered 'the only possible answer for a great power', Russia's position with regard to Germany was compromised,[87] making Grey's mediation useless. At the embassy, on 31 July Grey's secretary

82 Constantine Benckendorff, 149–50.

83 Jasper Ridley's diary, 29.07.1914. Private collection, Ridley family.

84 *Istori'ia diplomatii*, 809–10.

85 Grey of Fallodon, 307.

86 Nicholas II to George V, 01.08.1914, RA PS/PSO/GV/C/Q/2551/2.

87 A.K. Benckendorff to Sazonov, 17/30.07.1914, *Collected Diplomatic Documents*, 288–9.

Louis Mallet talked about Britain's going in at once war was declared. The *Times'* headlines indicated that Britain began to realize the danger of the moment: 'Close the Ranks. The Amending Bill Postponed. Agreement in face of National Danger'.[88]

The First Day of the Great War

In July 1914 Nicholas II passed from judging Sazonov too easily frightened, because surely no great power would think of making war for a Balkan issue,[89] to writing increasingly nervous letters to George V and William II. In a letter to George V of 16/29 July, after a paragraph written in his usual unemotional style he broke down and exclaimed: 'It is awful!' because '... a war at the present moment would be a dreadful calamity'. William II's mediation was his only remaining hope.[90]

With hours remaining until the expiry of the German ultimatum to Russia, Grey faced a cabinet in which a majority led by Lord Morley was against entering the war. On 1 August Grey told Benckendorff that he asked Lichnowsky to accept the Russian proposal in the hope that no one would open hostilities before considering Sazonov's formula.[91] He did not tell the Russian that he also offered Germany to guarantee Britain's and France's neutrality, provided Germany did not attack the latter.[92] He hoped to induce France to abandon her ally, but the French rejected this proposal. George V appealed to the Kaiser through the latter's brother Prince Henry of Prussia. But the reply from Berlin on 30 July was that France was preparing, Russia was taking '... equal to mobilization measures' and that therefore William II had to protect his people. Berlin suggested that the king should use his influence to keep France and Russia neutral.[93] Grey told Lichnowsky on 31 July that Austria should accept Sazonov's condition of stopping short after occupying Belgrade; only then could he bring pressure on Paris and St Petersburg.[94]

Nicholas II telegraphed George V on 1 August that he would have accepted Britain's proposals but Germany had declared war on Russia. It had caught him by surprise as he had promised William II that, despite the mobilization, Russian troops would not move so long as the mediation efforts continued. His telegram

---

88 Ridley, 31.07.1914.

89 Bark, 18.

90 Nicholas II to George V, 16/29.07.1914, RA PS/PSO/GV/C/Q/1549/1.

91 A.K. Benckendorff to Sazonov, 19.07/01.08.1914, *Collected Diplomatic Documents*, 292.

92 *Die Deutschen Dokumente zum Kriegsausbruch 1914* (Berlin, 1927), B.II, No 562, in *Istori'ia diplomatii*, 814.

93 Henry of Prussia to George V, 30.07.1914, RA PS/PSO/GV/C/Q/1549/5.

94 K. Lichnowsky, 409–11.

ended with the strongest plea which Nicholas II was capable of formulating: 'I trust that your country will not fail to support France and Russia in fighting to maintain the balance of power in Europe'.[95]

On the same day George Lloyd, a Liberal Unionist MP and an expert on Near Eastern trade, and Leo Maxse, the editor of the *National Review*, came to Jasper Ridley 'in a great stew', about the cabinet's indecision. They thought Grey was 'absolutely weak' because Britain had given undertakings to France and persuaded her to delay mobilization and now 'we are going to leave her in the lurch'. Maxse asked Ridley to tell Benckendorff to take 'an extremely strong line' with Grey at their one o'clock meeting. Benckendorff told his son-in-law that Grey had told him that he would try to persuade the Cabinet sitting this morning. He also said that Russia had twice agreed to Grey's proposals for conference and mediation, and Germany meanwhile had been preparing for war.

Countess Benckendorff and Maurice Baring discussed with Ridley the need to put a statement of the Russian position in the press, because Germany and Austria had been twisting the situation into a Russian aggression. Sevastopoulo telephoned his former chief from Paris about the German ultimatum to France. Ridley concluded that 'to refuse to go in now is madness and folly and wickedness not only towards our obligations but towards our own skin as a nation'.

Alarmed by a rumour emanating from Cambon that the Unionists were not for war, Ridley went to see Balfour, the only Tory in town at the moment. He found at Balfour's Cecil Spring Rice, then the ambassador to Washington, and the Duke of Devonshire. Balfour said that the Tories considered 'that if it was purely a question of Servia, they were against war; if it was the … European issue, they were for it to a man'. When Ridley spoke about Britain's obligations and future position in Europe, Balfour quickly said that there were no obligations. Ridley replied that the French and Russian nations felt very strongly that Britain was bound to them. 'Yes, that's just the difficulty', Balfour said, 'and it's what has sometimes made me feel that real obligations would be wiser'. He asked Ridley to explain to Benckendorff the Tory attitude.

Back at Chesham House the ambassador told Ridley that after Cabinet that morning Grey told him that England was asked and refused to promise neutrality to Germany.[96] In the evening, when the news came out that Germany had declared war on Russia, the editor of the pro-war *Times,* H.W. Steed, called at the Russian embassy, hoping to learn about the attitude of the British government. Benckendorff told him that he had no idea of the British attitude. He said: 'Sazonov keeps telegraphing me every few hours instructing me to beg Sir Edward Grey for some assurance of support, but Grey will not say a word or give any clue whatsoever to his thoughts. At St Petersburg poor Buchanan is sitting in his embassy while 50,000 Russians are singing *Rule Britannia* outside.

95 Nicholas II to George V, 01.08.1914, RAPS/PSO/GV/C/Q/2551/2.

96 Ridley, 1.08.1914.

I have a feeling at the bottom of my heart that Grey is straight. That is not much, but it is something'.[97]

The French government received on 1 August the German notice about the ultimatum to Russia and a demand to pledge their neutrality. The French were given 18 hours to answer. In case France accepted, the next German demand was for France to let the German army occupy two French fortresses (Verdun and Thoule) as guarantees, for the duration of the war against Russia. It was a foregone conclusion that France would reject the demands.

At midnight the French foreign minister telephoned Cambon, shouting: 'Nom de nom de … que ces c … d'Anglais se decident donc … Sinon la paix est foutu! Courez chez le roi, sacré nom …'[D-! These d-d English have to make up their mind, otherwise the peace is over! Go see the king, d- it!'] When Cambon replied that the king was surely already in bed, the minister ordered: 'Wake him up!' Cambon obeyed the order, but the king only promised that he would pass his words to Grey.[98]

On 2 August while the ambassador, his family and staff attended a service at the small Orthodox church to pray for Russia's victory, Cambon was at the Foreign Office, asking Grey what Britain would do now that the Germans invaded Luxemburg: Britain was a signatory to 1867 guarantees. Grey replied that it was a collective guarantee and if one of the signatories violated it, it became void for all the others. Still, he promised Cambon that the British would not let the German navy enter the English Channel. It was the least Cambon expected Britain to do, as in fulfillment of its obligations deriving from the naval staff talks with the British, the French fleet had long been stationed in the Mediterranean.

Posters in London streets were getting excited. In the evening of Sunday the 2nd August the Ridleys went to see Mallet, one of the Foreign Office's known Germanophobes and a frequent guest at the Russian embassy. They drove Mallet to the Foreign Office to ask Sir Arthur Nicolson about the latest developments. As they arrived cabinet members began to emerge from 10 Downing St and drove away cheered by the crowd that filled the street. Mallet went in, reappeared and after having Ridley swear that he would not tell the Benckendorffs, told him the good news: Britain pledged to protect the French north coast. Ridley drove Mallet to his house and went home. But soon Benckendorff rang his daughter to say that the Triple Alliance was waking up and some time later the ambassador showed up at the Ridleys' house accompanied by Mallet who had dined at the embassy! The evening papers announced that the navy was mobilized and all naval reserves called out. Mallet had heard at the FO of a possible coalition government and a credit of £50 million to be approved by the House of Commons.[99]

97 Henry Wickham Steed, *Through 30 Years, 1892–1922: A Personal Narrative* (Garden City, NY, 1925), 2: 12–13.

98 Jules François Blondel, *Ce que mes yeux ont vu: Recit d'un diplomat: De 1900 à 1950* (Paris, 1960), 2: 90–92.

99 Ridley, 02.08.1914.

On the 3rd August a considerably relieved Benckendorff waited for the outcome of the credit vote at the Commons and for the reports about German invasion of Belgium. All the talk around the Benckendorffs' table concerned the situation. One of the secretaries said that there had been a telephone call from the US embassy promising Russia support if they got into hot water with Japan: an offer that came ten years late. Benckendorff said his cousin Lichnowsky's exaggerated reports of English friendliness had encouraged Germany to promote this war.[100]

The Triple Entente Becomes the Triple Alliance

Under considerable pressure from Grey, the cabinet took the decision for war on the grounds of the Entente policy.[101] In the morning of 4 August the newspapers published Grey's statement and there was a marked hostility to Germany in press reports. In the evening Grey's secretary Sir William Tyrrell let the ambassador know that the German embassy informed the Foreign Office that at 7 pm Goschen was given his passports at the German foreign ministry and that Britain would declare war at 11 pm. Close to midnight the Ridleys, Countess Benckendorff and the counsellor, N. Etter drove to Trafalgar Square, saw a large crowd, then drove on and watched Buckingham Palace.[102]

When Benckendorff announced to his staff that Britain entered the war there was no excitement. Jasper Ridley thought it was because by this time it was a foregone conclusion.

Sceptics in Russia were surprised,[103] but Benckendorff and Cambon felt vindicated.

At the grill of a Hyde Park hotel near the French embassy where the diplomats used to have lunch, the Austrian ambassador complained to a French colleague about his embarrassing position: his country was practically at war with Britain, but he had accepted many weekend invitations from his British friends and now he was not sure whether to renounce his social or political duties.[104]

George V wrote to Nicholas II in August 1914 that they had both done everything to prevent the war which all had feared for years; they were fighting for justice and right, their consciences were clear.[105] Petr Benckendorff's Horse Guards were among the first Russian regiments to start for the front. His older

100 Ridley, 3.08.1914.

101 Keith Wilson, 'The Cabinet's Decision for War, 1914' in *The Policy of the Entente* (Cambridge, 1985), 135–47.

102 Ridley, 04.08.1914.

103 Georgy N. Mikhailovsky, 1: 31.

104 Abel Thierry, *L'Angleterre au temps de Paul Cambon* (Paris: La Palatine, 1961), 113.

105 George V to Nicholas II, 13.08.1914, GARF, f.602, op.1, d.1219, l.53.

brother Konstantin re-enlisted in the navy.[106] Jasper Ridley, Benckendorff's son-in-law, and Maurice Baring, the family's closest friend, went to France with the British Expeditionary Force.

The War and the Old Diplomacy

Three days into war, the king passed on to the ambassador Scotland Yard's request. The Count was to ask Grand Duke Michael, the Tsar's cousin who was resident in Britain, to take precautionary measures against his German butler.[107] Wartime spy fever began to overtake Britain, yet the German spy at the Russian embassy remained. In January 1914 Siebert became a supernumerary attaché to avoid being transferred from London[108] and until 1918 he remained in the embassy. In 1916 on Benckendorff's recommendation, Barings hired this reliable and intelligent man.[109]

In an Entente gesture of solidarity, on 5 September the allies signed the Pact of London whereby they pledged not to conclude a separate peace. Europe was split into what Sazonov described as the continental groupings of 'la triple alliance, la triple entente et la triple attente'[110] – Bulgaria, Greece and Italy, who were preparing to sell their allegiance to the highest bidder.

Most of Benckendorff's family and friends on both sides reacted to the war with despair. Unlike the crowds in the streets, they knew from the first how absurd and unnecessary it was. To paraphrase Benckendorff's reference to the Russo-Japanese war, in 1914 unreason triumphed over reason.[111] His brother wrote from St Petersburg: 'This is what we have feared for 40 years. I wish I had not lived to see the obliteration of European civilization'.[112] On the day when Germany declared war on Russia, Benckendorff's cousin Lichnowsky sent him a hurried note, ending with an exclamation: 'This war is a crime against humanity!'[113] Grey wrote to the departing Austro-Hungarian ambassador about his sorrow and swore his unchanged personal friendship.[114]

The diplomats felt as if a disaster not of their making had temporarily interfered with their peaceful and fruitful activity. But they believed that they would soon be in charge of the peace negotiations, and, ignoring the war hysteria,

106 K.A. Benckendorff to A.K. Benckendorff, 09/22.08.1914, BC2, box 17.

107 Lord Stamfordham to A.K. Benckendorff, 08.08.1914, BC2, box 14.

108 B.A. von Siebert to Schilling, 20.12.1913/02.01.1914, GARF, f.813, op.1, ed. hr.256, ll.1–2 ob.

109 Stephen Schroeder, 432.

110 Georgy N. Mikhailovsky, 1: 67.

111 A.K. Benckendorff to Lansdowne, 03.09.1905, FO 800/141, 198–200.

112 P.K. Benckendorff to A.K. Benckendorff, 28.07/10.08.1914, BC2, box 19.

113 K.M. Lichnowsky to A.K. Benckendorff, 02.08.1914, BC2, box 16.

114 Grey to A. Mensdorff, 12.08.1914, FO/800/41, 329–31.

were already looking for the threads which might lead the governments out of the labyrinth. In November 1914 Benckendorff's old colleague, Fyodor A. Budberg, wrote that despite the successful mobilization he shared Benckendorff's gloomy premonition about Russia's prospects. He thought that his position as the dean of the diplomatic corps in neutral Madrid and his personal friendly relations with the Austro-Hungarian and German ministers, ('put on ice for the present'), might ease the imminent task of opening peace negotiations.[115]

Maurice Paléologue panicked when there was no talk of peace by December 1914.[116] In September 1915 Grey considered that the Germans were financially at the end of their tether and soon would accept the Entente's peace terms,[117] but two weeks later George V had issued an order to the army saying that the end was not in sight yet.[118] After these disappointments, Benckendorff settled into waiting for the peace conference which would firmly lock a liberalized Russia in the European community of nations.

No one as yet had blamed the war on 'the old diplomacy'. In fact, no one had ever blamed diplomats for wars, for it was common knowledge in Europe that governments led nations into wars for various reasons, some honourable and some not, but diplomats patched up the quarrels which governments started and which armies fought. Diplomats were the most civilized and pacific representatives of their nations.

In the summer of 1914 they had not done anything different from what they had always done in crises, and their responsibility for what happened was no greater than for the Crimean war or the Franco-Prussian war or the Italo-Turkish war. During the Anglo-Boer war there was a moment, in 1900, when Germany, Russia and France seemed to be on the verge of intervening to make Britain sign peace. But, as a French government official wrote: strategic interests, humanitarian considerations and public opinion sympathetic to the Boers failed to outweigh the three powers' political interests, prudence and expediency. Much as their public opinion sympathized with the Boers, the governments backed away from a confrontation, resigning themselves to the fact that 'England will swallow the two poor little nations without being disturbed or distracted'.[119] A major conflict was avoided.

In July 1914 the inability to think beyond the status and strategy considerations deprived the European cabinets of real alternatives and diplomacy was pushed aside while the military advised the heads of governments. When the unforeseen

115 F.A. Budberg to A.K. Benckendorff, 17/20.11.1914, BC2, box 12.

116 Irwin Halfond, 291.

117 A.K. Benckendorff to Sazonov, 29.08/11.09.1915, AVPRI, f.134, op.473, d.107, l.7–8.

118 A.K. Benckendorff to Sazonov, 9./22.10.1915, AVPRI, f.134, op.473, d.107, l.23.

119 Abel Combarieu, *Sept ans à l'Elysée: Avec le président Emile Loubet – De l'affaire Dreyfus à la conférence d'Algéciras 1899–1906* (Paris, 1932), 53.

duration and scope of the war became clear, the wrath of the nations fell on their governments, which sought the most plausible scapegoat and deftly passed the blame on to the diplomats. By 1918 the 'old diplomacy', roundly condemned for its undemocratic, secretive and inefficient character, had been demoted to the rank of a handmaiden to the pure-minded monarchs, prime ministers and presidents of the powers whose inherently pacific intentions had been so poorly served by their elitist and hawkish foreign offices.

Military Strategy and Diplomatic Strategies

Keith Neilson wrote that British wartime decisions regarding Russia were shaped by military considerations.[120] On the Russian side, coalition loyalty considerations largely prevailed over others. Nicholas II's usual comment on the proposals submitted for his approval was: 'Harmonize our actions with the allies'.[121] Had this been always the case on all sides, the war may have been over before 1918, but long-term political calculations complicated the military decisions.

Soon after the war broke out, it became clear that Britain's financial help, and therefore her leadership, was decisive to Russia and France in pursuing the war. Travel between Russia and France and Britain was now difficult, so to expedite the process of coordinating the action – which in many cases would entail Russia's acquiescence – Sazonov proposed to concentrate the discussion of all political issues in London.[122] But the minister increasingly turned to Buchanan and Nicholas II as better channels than Benckendorff for getting Russia's requests over to the Foreign Office. Benckendorff was sidelined for various reasons. His failing health, his grief over the loss of his younger son in June 1915 and his age, combined with the fact that bilateral relations centred on the military goals and their conduct largely passed from the diplomats to the wartime cabinets and financial and military experts.

Numerous military representatives and agents, Russian and British, reported directly to the military command (and in Russia, to the monarch), so it was convenient, from time to time, to entrust them with settling even financial issues, as it happened in the summer of 1916, when brigadier-general W.H-H. Waters talked to Nicholas II during a visit to the Russian headquarters.[123] In 1916, after the Austro-German troops defeated Serbia, Nicholas II asked George V to help

120 Keith Neilson, *Strategy and Supply: The Anglo-Russian Alliance, 1914–1917* (London, 1984), 305.

121 Georgy N. Mikhailovsky, 75–8.

122 Sazonov to A.P. Iswolsky and A.K. Benckendorff, 07/20.11.1915, AVPRI, f.134, op.473, d.107, l.51.

123 Brigadier General Waters to George V, 22.08.1916, RA PS/PSO/GV/C/Q/832/288.

evacuate Serbian troops from Albania to Corfu.[124] When at the end of 1916 Russia wanted to have the Straits treaty of 1915 published in the Allied capitals, it was through Nicholas II that the foreign ministry asked the British government to confirm their support of Russia's possession of Constantinople and the Straits.[125] Last but not least, Sazonov was often exasperated by having to defend Russia's case not only against Buchanan but also against Benckendorff.

The ambassador's position was so obviously impaired that in August 1916, Grey felt it necessary to tell a member of the Russian parliamentary delegation that 'it would be most disagreeable' to the British government if the count were replaced.[126] Benckendorff felt his growing irrelevance and complained in a roundabout way, writing that people wanted to know what was happening in Russia, but he lacked information: 'Since I know almost nothing, I cannot offer explanations, and many people might consider this suspicious'.[127]

But the count was not idle. He reported in minute detail the royal audiences, the royal health and the rumours about changes in the British cabinet, as he had done all his life, concentrating on familiar and comforting details, such as exchanges of awards and medals between the British and the Russian military. He did not miss an opportunity to help his friend Revelstoke. He proposed Barings as the intermediary in the Russian loans in England, for which Barings got a hefty commission. When conscription was introduced in 1916, he helped Revelstoke retain his best employees by providing him with a letter for the City of London tribunal, asking on behalf of the Russian government that confidential correspondence would continue to be handled by the same staff as before 1914.[128]

Wartime unreason did not change his principles and sense of personal duty. He maintained correspondence with his numerous relatives and friends on both sides of the conflict and meticulously acted on the requests to find out the fate of German or Austrian relatives captured by Russians. He repeatedly interceded with Scotland Yard for the interned and imprisoned German Count Wolff-Metternich.[129]

The War Aims

The largest issue which the war presented to Russian foreign policy was that Russai fought in isolation, for Turkey's entrance in war on Germany's side closed the Straits for merchant vessels and cut the communication lines between

124 Nicholas II to George V, 08/21.01.1916, RA PS/PSO/GV/C/Q/1550/298.

125 Nicholas II to George V, 13/26.09.1916, RA PS/PSO/GV/C/Q/2527/3.

126 Grey to Buchanan, 26.06.1916, FO 800/75, 309.

127 A.K. Benckendorff to Sazonov, 8/21.09.1915, AVPRI, f.134, op.473, d.103, l.12.

128 Philip Ziegler, *The Sixth Great Power: Barings 1762–1929* (London, 1988), 322.

129 Christina Metternich to A.K. Benckendorff, 20.10.1916, BC2, box 13.

Russia and her allies through the Mediterranean. The German navy dominated the Baltic and the Far Eastern Vladivostok port was too remote and its turnover capacity was low. The remaining communications were through the White Sea port Arkhangel'sk (Archangel) which froze in winter, or through the evidently unreliable Rumania, Serbia and Greece. In late 1915, the Austro-German offensive on Serbia cut this line, too.

To continue the war Russia needed more and more financial help and military supplies. Russian armies were fighting alone while the strategic planning was made with coalition priorities in mind. It created tensions and arguments between the military and the diplomats. In time it also led to a bitterness and disenchantment in Russian society. Another permanent complication was the divergent attitudes towards the Balkan and Mediterranean states between Russia and the Entente. When, in April 1915, the Entente agreed that Russia would get the Straits and Constantinople after the defeat of the central powers, Russia began to view Greece, Italy, Bulgaria and Rumania not just as potential allies but also as real contenders for the Straits. Britain and France were anxious not to allow Russia to become the dominating power in Europe after the war; only two months before the Straits Treaty was signed Aristide Briand and Lloyd George discussed the ways of converting the Balkans into 'a barrier to Russian omnipotence and possession of Constantinople and to all the exclusive advantages which such possession would give to Russia'.[130] These factors determined the main topics in Anglo-Russian diplomatic communications, and Benckendorff smoothed over the disagreements, allaying Russian suspicions of bad faith and defending the British position at St Petersburg.

On 14 September 1914 Sazonov gave Buchanan a draft proposal of the Allied war aims, which he composed in collaboration with the French ambassador Paléologue. They were to destroy German domination of Europe and implement postwar territorial changes on the basis of nationality. Russia would annex the lower course of the Nieman, Eastern and Western Galicia, eastern Posen and Silesia; France would recover Alsace-Lorraine and annex the Palatinate and the Rhineland; England, France and Japan would divide German colonies in Asia; Belgium would be increased in size; Denmark would recover Schleswig; the kingdom of Hanover would be restored; Serbia would get Bosnia-Herzegovina, Dalmatia and northern Albania; Bulgaria would get Macedonia, Greece would get southern Albania, except for Valona which would go to Italy. Austria-Hungary would become tripartite, with Bohemia. Austria-Hungary and Germany would pay indemnities. Nicholas II made corrections in the draft: he wanted Austria-Hungary dismembered, Armenia to get autonomous status and Constantinople to be an international city.[131]

Grey rejected all of the Russian official proposals except for the idea that Austrian and German Poland would go to Russia to form an autonomous state,

130 Francis Bertie, *Memorandum*, 05.02.1915, FO 800/172, 55–7.

131 Irwin Halfond, 283, 288.

Alsace-Lorraine would go to France and Bosnia-Herzegovina to Serbia. He wanted to maintain Germany and Austria-Hungary as great powers, and would not agree to their dismemberment for the benefit of Serbia[132] or Russia.[133]

It does not seem that Benckendorff set a great store by Sazonov's war aims. On 18 September, the Benckendorffs and Asquiths dined at 18 Gloucester Place, the house of Jasper and Nathalie Ridley. After dinner, the prime minister and the Russian ambassador sat over a map of Europe, discussing the postwar changes. Benckendorff agreed with Asquith that Poland should be reconstituted and Austria-Hungary should continue to exist because it consisted of too many small parts that could not exist as sovereign states. Benckendorff supported the idea by pointing out that there was a Hapsburg loyalty in Austria.[134]

The Straits Issue and the War

Initially, the idea of the Straits was not prominent in Sazonov's thoughts and Russia tried to secure Turkey's neutrality,[135] offering her generous wartime guarantees which Grey pared down in the Anglo-Russian proposal of 18 August.[136] After the German defeat on the Marne in September 1914 Germany offered Turkey a loan on condition of her immediate entrance in the war and Turkey accepted. The Russian Black Sea ports were bombed on 29–30 October and with great reluctance Russia, followed by Britain and France, declared war on Turkey. Britain had abandoned the principle of Ottoman integrity in Europe or Asia on 2 October, but already on 27 September Benckendorff reported that Grey proposed to substitute Constantinople and the Straits for Russia's other war aims.[137] Three days later the king repeated Grey's offer to Benckendorff of Constantinople to Russia and also seemed to approve of dismemberment of the German Empire.[138] It pointed to vacillations in the British cabinet and made Sazonov all the more anxious to have their firm promises because the Russians took it for granted that the Allies would make peace with the central powers as soon as they secured their own interests, when it would be too late for Russia to demand their help in the Straits issue.[139]

132 C.Jay Smith Jr., 'Great Britain and the 1914–1915 Straits Agreement with Russia: The British Promise of November 1914' in *American Historical Review*, 70, 4 (1965): 1024.

133 Wesselitsky to A.K. Benckendorff, 12.11.1914, BC2, box 15.

134 Ridley, 18.09.1914.

135 B.E. Nol'de, *Daleko'ie i blizkoe* (Paris, 1930), 72.

136 C.Jay Smith Jr., 1017.

137 C.Jay Smith Jr., 1024–5.

138 A.K. Benckendorff to Sazonov, 31.10/13.11.1914, *Constantinople et les detroits. Livre premier. Documents secrets de l'ancien Ministère des Affaires Etrangères de Russie* (Paris, 1930), 148–9.

139 Neratov, *Memorandum*, [1914], *Constantinople et les detroits: Livre premier*, 102–6.

Following Grey's proposal, in October 1914 the foreign ministry formulated its goal: Russia should claim sovereign and exclusive rights over Constantinople and a strip of land on the Asiatic and European coasts, and the Dardanelles, with the same zones, as well as an international guarantee of the Straits' closure for warships, excepting Russian ones.[140] In November, Grey informed Sazonov through Buchanan about the British decision to annex Egypt, and Sazonov gladly accepted it as a quid pro quo for the British memorandum[141] concerning the solution of the Straits issue according to Russia's wishes.[142] The Straits acquired the status of a prize and all other issues to be settled between the Entente and Russia were complicated by Sazonov's efforts not to lose the promised prize.

Sazonov reluctantly gave his assent to the Entente's negotiations with the Young Turks in 1915: a separate peace with Turkey would ruin Russia's chances to get the Straits. Sazonov asked that the negotiations be conducted in general terms because Russia's public opinion (that is, the government) counted on the future possession of the Straits.[143] Later, during the Dardanelles campaign, Sazonov, expecting the Allied occupation of the Dardanelles, wanted to make public the Allies' pledge to Russia. He asked Paris and London to prepare their public opinion by disseminating the idea that the post-war arrangement should secure Russia's interests even if it was acting in a separate theatre of war.[144] When Sazonov spoke to the Duma about Russia's 'definite occupation of Constantinople', Grey had to explain it to the Commons.[145] He evasively stated that the British government sympathized with Russia's desire to achieve the political and economic advantages accruing from a successful offensive on the Russo-Turkish front.[146] Contrary to Sazonov's expectations, Grey emphasized that Russia could only rely on its own military success to reach the Straits. Benckendorff defended Grey: 'You should not expect him to say more than you and he agreed on'.[147] But Russia's participation was vital to the Entente and Grey privately confirmed to Benckendorff that 'whatever the

---

140 Georgy N.Mikhailovsky, 1: 86–8.

141 Sazonov to A.K. Benckendorff, 3/16.11.1914, *Constantinople et les detroits: Livre premier*, 152.

142 Sazonov to A.K. Benckendorff, 5/18.11.1914, *Constantinople et les detroits: Livre premier*, 152–3.

143 Sazonov to A. K. Benckendorff, 01/14.02.1915, *Constantinople et les detroits: Livre premier*, 159–60.

144 Sazonov to A.K. Benckendorff, 17.02/02.03.1915, *Constantinople et les detroits: Livre premier*, 166.

145 A.K. Benckendorff to Sazonov, 12/25.02.1915, *Constantinople et les detroits: Livre premier*, 162.

146 Ibid., 162–3.

147 A.K. Benckendorff to Sazonov, 18.02/03.03.1915, *Constantinople et les detroits: Livre premier*, 170–72.

theatre of war where various powers act, at the time of peace the totality of the rights of each of them will be taken in consideration'.[148]

Italy, Greece and the Entente

Italy, having declared its neutrality in August 1914, had at once begun negotiating the terms of joining the Entente or the Triple Alliance. Even Benckendorff was alarmed when in February 1915 he heard that Italian war aims included a Greek Constantinople and internationalized Straits.[149] Sazonov wrote: 'I believe that Italy's demands are greater than the help it will give'. He correctly foresaw that Italy would engage only against Turkey without breaking with Austria but to make gains both in the Ottoman Empire and in Austria. He insisted that Italy should act not only against Turkey but, especially, side by side with Russia, against Austria-Hungary.[150] He was also trying to ensure the post-war advantages of the Balkan states which traditionally were Russia's clients. Grey appealed to Sazonov not to deprive the Entente of Italy's cooperation because it was morally important for drawing Bulgaria and Rumania to the Entente side.[151]

During the preparation of the Dardanelles operation, Italy insisted on participating and the Allies hoped initially that Greece would participate too. Benckendorff sided with Grey, repeating that 'participation of neutral Balkan states is extremely important for the war … if Greece is the first to join [the Dardanelles operation] others will follow. The Admiralty seems to need the Greek navy and even troops in Gallipoli'. He emphasized that it was a military opinion[152] which diplomats ought to accept. Sazonov strongly opposed it,[153] for fear of the Greeks claiming Constantinople as their price. He offered a way out. On 4 March he formally requested recognition of Russia's claims in exchange for recognizing British claims in other regions of the Ottoman Empire and elsewhere.[154] He added that in case of the Entente's continuing opposition to Russia's control of the Straits,

148 A.K. Benckendorff to Sazonov, 18.02/03.03.1915, *Constantinople et les detroits: Livre premier*, 172–4.

149 A.K. Benckendorff to Sazonov, 04/17.02.1915, *Constantinople et les detroits: Livre premier*, 246–7.

150 Sazonov to A.K. Benckendorff, 23.02/08.03.1915, *Documents diplomatiques secrets russes 1914–1917 d'après les archives du Ministère des affaires étrangères à Petrograd* (Paris, 1928), 228.

151 British embassy at Petrograd, *Memorandum for S.D. Sazonov, Constantinople et les detroits: Livre premier*, 271–2.

152 A.K. Benckendorff to Sazonov, 25.02/07.03.1915, *Constantinople et les detroits: Livre deuxième*, 117–8.

153 A.K. Benckendorff to Sazonov, 19.02/04.03.1915, *Constantinople et les detroits: Livre deuxième*, 108–9.

154 K. Robbins, 307.

he will have to resign, and he might be replaced by a person who would adhere to the 'old system of the Three Emperors' League'.[155]

He put forward four conditions on Greece's participation at the Dardanelles: the Greeks had to volunteer for it; they had to be informed beforehand that they would not get any territorial gains close to the Straits; they would operate in the locations indicated by the Allied command; and under no circumstances would Greek troops enter Constantinople. [156] Three days later, the instability which had plagued Greece since the beginning of the war ended with the resignation of the warlike pro-Entente government. The King of Greece maintained his neutrality.

Benckendorff took it on himself to rebuke Sazonov, saying that the unacceptable conditions which Russia placed on Greek participation in the war caused the fall of the Venizelos government.[157] Grey nevertheless said that he understood Russia's position and promised that the cabinet would soon make a decision on the Straits issue.[158]

As the future borders in the Balkans were being rearranged at the Foreign Office during the negotiations between the Entente and the Balkan states, Sazonov reminded Benckendorff to insist on observing the principle of national self-determination, to avoid more bloodshed later.[159] Benckendorff balked at causing unpleasantness to the Foreign Office, and Sazonov wrote increasingly stiff and hostile letters to him:

> It is my duty to call your attention to the very negative points of the present situation. There are many Italian demands, like those regarding Asia Minor, for example, to which Russia has no objections. But as they touch upon the interests of Russia's allies, I would think that it is my duty to give the maximum support to my allies' interests. But Grey, who succeeded in declining firmly Italian claims to the regions which are of interest mostly to England and France, not only has shown an excessively conciliatory spirit where it was in our interest to curb Italy's claims, but even, it seems, revealed to the Italian ambassador that Russia objected to an agreement on those points.

He pointed out to Buchanan that Russian public opinion would condemn the concessions made to Italy at the expense of the Serbs, Slovenes and Croatians. If it became known that Britain fully backed the Italian domination of the Adriatic

155 *Istori'ia diplomatii*, 830.

156 Sazonov to A.K. Benckendorff, 21.02/07.03.1915, *Constantinople et les detroits: Livre deuxième*, 116.

157 A.K. Benckendorff to Sazonov, 26.02/11.03.1915,*Constantinople et les detroits: Livre deuxième*, 121.

158 A.K. Benckendorff to Sazonov, 25.02/10.03.1915, *Constantinople et les detroits: Livre premier*, 202–4.

159 Sazonov to A.K. Benckendorff, 09/22.11.1915, AVPRI, f.134, op.473, d.117, l.19.

Sea, Russian public opinion would turn against Britain.[160] Benckendorff's way of excusing his own ineffectiveness and Grey's opposition was to blame it all on Asquith who made decisions in Grey's absence. But even Asquith was not to be blamed too much because personally he sympathized with Sazonov's views, 'but on the other hand he believes that at this point an alliance with Italy … is indispensable'.[161]

The Treaty of London

Sazonov finally gave in because he did not want Italy to break off the talks because of the Russian position;[162] but he still wanted Italy to promise to enter the war within a month of signing the agreement. Asquith complained that he spent most of an April afternoon at the Foreign Office seeing the Italian, French and Russian ambassadors in turn. He 'pressed Benck to make it easier for … [the Italians] by dropping a not very important Russian requirement'.[163] Benckendorff agreed that the Russian requirement was not important, but Sazonov did not. He insisted that Italy's adhesion to the Entente should be made public.[164] Benckendorff pressed for the minister's capitulation, citing the opinion of the celebrated military authority, the Secretary for War Kitchener, that an Entente with Italy had to be concluded immediately.[165] The Foreign Office used the tried method of having the king privately ask Nicholas II to give way,[166] with Poincaré doing the same.[167] Sazonov's next letter to his former chief was even angrier:

> Count Aleksandr Konstantinovich,
> … You already know that for the reasons which I have recently explained to you and which I do not want to repeat, the Italian entente obtained in London is a complete failure from my point of view, and that I only agreed to sign

---

160 Sazonov to A.K. Benckendorff, 18/31.03.1915, *Documents diplomatiques secrets russes,* 233–4.

161 A.K. Benckendorff to Sazonov, 20.03/02.04.1915, *Documents diplomatiques secrets russes*, 234–5.

162 Sazonov to A.K. Benckendorff, 18/31.03.1915, *Documents diplomatiques secrets russe*s, 237.

163 H.H. Asquith to Venetia Stanley, 1.04.1915, *Letters to Venetia Stanley* (Oxford: Oxford University Press, 1982), 469.

164 Sazonov to A.K. Benckendorff, 04/17.04.1915, *Documents diplomatiques secrets russe*s, 238–9.

165 A.K. Benckendorff to Sazonov, 07/20.04.1915, *Documents diplomatiques secrets russes*, 240.

166 *The Duff Cooper Diaries, 1915–1951*, 20.04.1915, (ed. J.J. Norwich) (London, 2005), 5–6.

167 President of the Republic to Nicholas II, 19.04.1915, *Documents diplomatiques secrets russes*, 239–40.

> it under the insistent pressure of our allies ... The articles of the treaty were prepared by ... [Grey] and Cambon without our participation and when they were communicated to me they had already been accepted by them ... The result ... is ... a complete capitulation of the three Great powers to Italy's demands and even without a guarantee of the latter's entry into the war any time soon ... I find it necessary ... to write you all this because this incident makes me fear for the future. If the negotiations about the end of the war have been so unsatisfactory now, with only three powers participating, what will happen when Italy also takes part in them?

He finished sarcastically expressing a hope that Benckendorff 'will find a way of explaining to Grey that in the future he should pay more attention to Russia's desiderata when joint decisions are taken'.[168] The embassy counsellor, K.D. Nabokov, recalled that Benckendorff's relations with the foreign minister suffered during the 1915 negotiations when Sazonov wrote to the ambassador a very strong criticism of his action and Benckendorff shrugged and affected indifference but was deeply hurt.[169]

Benckendorff received instructions to sign the document, but after this he was to give Grey and Cambon a note stating that none of the decisions relating to the future peace which were taken by the three Allies before Italy's adhesion would be subject to revision and that Italy had to accept this condition. Benckendorff also had to formulate a written reservation protecting the interests of Montenegro on the Adriatic coast.[170]

Sazonov's resistance imposed on the Allies the need to compensate Russia. On 25 April 1915, Asquith, overcoming the resistance of his cabinet, signed the Treaty of London with Benckendorff. Russia got the Straits and Constantinople with the proviso that the Straits would be open to international commerce and Constantinople would remain a free city.[171] At the end of the war Russia would get her claim pending the Allied victory and an agreement between the three about the French and British gains in the Ottoman Empire and elsewhere.[172] The Treaty of London also stipulated the partition of Austria-Hungary. Benckendorff put his signature to the document, but made it known that he had not participated in its preparation.[173] Sazonov achieved what Benckendorff and Iswolsky had dreamed of and in the process had to fight Benckendorff's eagerness to comply with Grey's needs.

---

168 Sazonov to A.K. Benckendorff, 08/21.04.1915, *Documents diplomatiques secrets russes*, 242–3.

169 C. Nabokoff, *The Ordeal of a Diplomat* (Salisbury, NC, 1976), 37.

170 Sazonov to A.K. Benckendorff, 07/20.04.1915, *Constantinople et les detroits: Livre premier*, 273–4.

171 K. Robbins, 308.

172 H.G. Asquith to Lord Stamfordham, 10.03.1915, RA PS/PSO/GV/C/M/969/1.

173 Georgy N. Mikhailovsky, 1: 98.

The Bribing of the Balkans

The Entente tried to induce Bulgaria and Greece to maintain neutrality by promises of post-war rewards, but, when Bulgaria attacked Serbia, her ally Greece began to mobilize and the only route for taking supplies to Serbia was through Greece,[174] where the Entente representatives became ever more deeply involved in the domestic political struggle.[175] In order to guarantee the passage of their supplies to Serbia, Britain promised Italy Albanian autonomy under Italian protectorate. Russia learned about it *post factum* and protested that bribing Italy with new promises beyond those stipulated in the April treaty would not get more Italian support, but that including Christian minorities into Muslim territory would cause international conflicts later.[176] With Serbia's fall, Russia's remaining communication line with the Allies was cut and Sazonov complained that, despite promises, England failed to help Serbia which undermined the Entente's credibility. He asked Benckendorff to 'express these ideas to Grey energetically',[177] something which Benckendorff refused to do. Instead, he offered Sazonov his excuses for Grey: he may have made promises to Serbia based on a treaty with Greece and after the Greek defection it was more difficult to take military measures.[178] He explained decisions unpopular with Russia by parliamentary interference or by Grey's absence. Overall, as in the past, Benckendorff considered that as long as Britain remained Russia's ally, Russia had no reason for complaints.[179]

Next came the turn of courting Rumania which had been getting British loans for its neutrality[180] and now got from the Allies promises of Russia's territorial concessions for the same;[181] it was demanding a higher price through the Rumanian Queen Marie, a cousin of George V. The Foreign Office prevented another lengthy argument between Benckendorff and Sazonov by agreeing with Buchanan that further concessions would show Rumania that Russia was weak and would induce more blackmail.[182]

---

174 A.K. Benckendorff to Sazonov, 03/16.10.1915, AVPRI, f.134, op.473, d.107, l.19–20.

175 Hardinge to Bertie, 02.09.1916, FO 800/172, 142–3.

176 Sazonov to A.K. Benckendorff, 09/22.11.1915, AVPRI, f.134, op.473, d.117, l.19.

177 Sazonov to A.K. Benckendorff, 26.11/09.12.1915, AVPRI, f.134, op.473, d.117, l.24.

178 A.K. Benckendorff to Sazonov, 27.11/10.12.1915, AVPRI, f.134, op.473, d.117, l.25.

179 A.K. Benckendorff to Sazonov, 28.11/11.12.1915, AVPRI, f.134, op.473, d.117, ll.26–7.

180 Lord Stamfordham, *Memorandum*, 15.01.1915, RA PS/PSO/GV/C/Q/733/1.

181 B. Arsen'iev to Sazonov, 08/21.02.1915, *Dnevniki i dokument'y iz lichnogo arkhiva Nikola'ia I* (Minsk, 2003), 285.

182 Buchanan to Grey, 05.11.1915, FO 800/75, 171–4.

Russia's Post-War Interests

Sazonov was already planning for post-war when Russia would need security in the Far East in order to turn her attention to Europe, so he wanted an alliance with Japan.[183] In December 1914 Sazonov wanted to have the Quadruple Entente formalized[184] so that Japan could formally join Allied military operations. Grey opposed formalization and also Japanese troops coming into Europe[185] because of the effect on the British prestige in the colonies. He did his best to dissuade the Japanese,[186] and told Benckendorff that the question of military cooperation with Japan regarded only Russia.[187] In October 1915, after having agreed that Japan would be informed about the Straits agreement and, in general terms, about the promises to Italy[188], Benckendorff, Grey and Cambon exchanged notes with the Japanese ambassador about Japan's adherence to the Entente's Declaration of 5 September.[189] Sazonov's diplomacy, coupled to Russia's military successes in late 1915, brought about Japan's proposal to Russia to open discussions,[190] and in the summer of 1916, Russia and Japan signed an alliance treaty, which finally put to rest Russia's concerns about the Anglo-Japanese alliance of the previous decade.

The Munitions Crisis on the Russian Front

While political issues were setting everybody's nerves on edge, the munitions crisis was gathering strength in Russia. As early as 30 December 1914 the Russian military agent in Britain was shocked by a telegram that insufficient supplies of ammunition might soon paralyze the Russian army's operations. He asked Kitchener, the secretary of state for war, to supply the Russian army and give Russia's orders priority in neutral countries. Kitchener promised to do this for Russian orders placed in Canada and the US. After consultation with Benckendorff, the Russian military decided to form a committee under the ambassador's chairmanship to coordinate the orders for supplies and contacts with the British Board of Trade which issued authorizations for exports.[191] As chairman of the Supplies Committee, Benckendorff resisted Sazonov's instructions to

183 Sazonov to A.K. Benckendorff, 10.09.1915, AVPRI, f.134, op.473, d.96, ll. 21.

184 V.S. Vasiukov, *Vneshnay'ia politika Rossii nakanune Fevral'skoi revolutsii. 1916–fevral' 1917 g.* (Moscow, 1989), 101–4.

185 K. Robbins, 312–3.

186 Iswolsky to Sazonov, 24.08/06.09.1915, AVPRI, f.134, op.473, d.96, l.7.

187 A.K. Benckendorff to Sazonov, 10/23.09.1915, AVPRI, F.134, op.473, d.633, l.24.

188 Ibid.

189 A.K.Benckendorff to S.D. Sazonov, 27.09/10.10.1915, AVPRI, f.134, op.473, d.96, l.31.

190 V.S. Vasuikov, 117.

191 A.M. Nikolaev, *Pol-veka tomu nazad* …, 88.

demand more weapons for the Russian army, because Kitchener had told him that Britain had no reserves until the American weapons arrived. Expecting Sazonov's disbelief Benckendorff wrote that the Russian military attaché in London would confirm his opinion: 'England does not have what we demand of her … Therefore I see no possible way of returning to this subject'.[192]

Sazonov, in despair at Russian army's retreat, made Nicholas II send two telegrams in two days asking about the decisions of the Calais conference and reiterating Russia's need of rifles.[193] Benckendorff defended the British from Sazonov's reproaches of putting their interests in Egypt before those of the war: 'The situation in Asia is critical as you know'.[194] With Benckendorff Britain's needs always took precedence over Russia's, which was an odd position for a Russian envoy, perhaps explained by his emotional distancing from Russia over many years.

The British did for Russia what they reasonably could, but in 1918, faced with the recent military and political events on the Continent, the well-informed CID secretary Sir Maurice Hankey bitterly regretted the fact that Britain's assistance had not been greater. If the opening phrase of this letter is an emotional overstatement, the description of the Russian army's situation seems accurate and explains the urgency of Sazonov's requests which Benckendorff hated to take to the Foreign Office. Hankey wrote:

> We ought to have equipped Russia before we equipped our own Armies, because had we done so, the Russians would never have sustained the appalling losses they did in putting pikes against rifles and machine-guns. This was the real reason of the Russian catastrophe – the appalling casualties and the inability of the old regime to supply armaments on a modern scale. Had this been our policy, I believe the War would have been won long ago …[195]

Plans for Future Friendship

Relations between the Allies were necessarily growing closer and this seemed to augur well for Anglo-Russian post-war relations. Benckendorff's early preoccupation was with the future peace settlement, probably taking his cue from Grey. He argued that for the sake of a profitable post-war arrangement Russia needed to come to the peace conference on the best terms with Britain. Everything

---

192 A.K. Benckendorff to Sazonov, 17/30.10.1915, AVPRI, f.134, op.473, d.107, l.41–2.

193 Nicholas II to George V, 25.11/08.12.1915, RA PS/PSO/GV/C/Q/2551/4.

194 A.K. Benckendorff to Sazonov, 28.11/11.12.1915, AVPRI, f.134, op.473, d.107, l.61–2.

195 Lt-Colonel Sir Maurice Hankey to Admiral Sir John Fisher, 21.02.1918, *Fear God and Dread Nought*, 3: 512–4.

had to be subordinated to this goal. In December 1915 he reported that Cambon presented to the British government a formal French proposal to begin discussions of a post-war economic rapprochement between England and France and that he told Nicolson that it was also the desire of the Russian government.[196] But in March 1916, as Buchanan was using the perspective of a post-war Anglo-Russian political rapprochement in order to make Nicholas II amenable to Britain's wartime needs,[197] Benckendorff advised Sazonov not to mention an economic rapprochement at the Paris conference because he now heard that the British considered it premature before the industrialists and financiers had expressed their opinion.[198]

He hoped that wartime trade might form the base for the future commercial treaties and in November 1916 supported Grey's idea that the Russian government should send commissioners to Canada and Australia to discuss the terms of future trade relations.[199] Benckendorff focused on attending Anglo-Russian friendship meetings and conferences. On 29 November 1916 he presided at an inaugural luncheon at the Savoy Hotel of the Russo-British chamber of commerce. This was one of the bricks with which the post-war Anglo-Russian entente would be built.[200]

Benckendorff looked forward to political changes in Russia, for they would forestall the eruption of violent political struggle. He warned Sazonov: 'We must particularly take care to counter the idea that [separate] peace will be brought about by our domestic circumstances'.[201] Like Buchanan,[202] he wanted to see changes in Russia which would encourage British postwar government to form closer ties to Russia. Domestic reforms would dispose British public opinion towards Russia and reassure the British government regarding the country's stability. The most urgent issue to tackle was, therefore, the one which irritated US and British public opinion: the Jewish laws. During the visit to Britain of the Russian Duma members, Aleksandr D. Protopopov, the vice-president of the Duma and the soon-to-be Empress Alexandra's and Rasputin's last candidate for the ministry of interior, discussed the need for domestic reforms with a sympathetic Benckendorff. Then he asked Grey to authorize Buchanan to assist the Russian opposition with advice on the emancipation of the Russian Jews. Grey declined,

196 A.K. Benckendorff to Sazonov, 10/23.12.1915, AVPRI, f.134, op.473, d.107, l.66.

197 Buchanan, *Memorandum*, 03/16.02.1916, FO 800/75, 240–48.

198 A.K. Benckendorff to Sazonov, 28.02/12.03.1916, AVPRI, f.134, op.473, d.107, l.29.

199 A.K. Benckendorff to B.V. Sturmer, 11/24. 11.1916, AVPRI, f.134, op.473, d.144, l.75.

200 'Death of Count Benckendorff: A Maker of the Entente', *The Times*, 12.01.1917, 9.

201 A.K. Benckendorff to Sazonov, 8/21.09.1915, AVPRI, f.134, op.473, d.103, l.12.

202 Buchanan, *Memorandum*, 03/16.02.1916, FO 800/75, 240–48.

saying that Britain's involvement in Russian domestic affairs would compromise the Russian opposition's efforts.[203]

The mood in Britain seemed to favour Benckendorff's intention of improving Russia's public image. On Hardinge's recommendation, Russia's consul-general in Calcutta, Konstantin D. Nabokov, came to London as the embassy counsellor in 1915. His eligibility is clear from his description of his earlier task in India:

> … to persuade the Russian government that our interests are in every way identical with those of Great Britain, and that … the strengthening of British influence in the countries bordering on Hindustan not only does not endanger the interests of Russia, but affords the best guarantee of peaceful progress and neighbourly intercourse.[204]

In wartime England Nabokov's main function became addressing meetings to raise funds for the emerging chairs of Russian language at British universities.[205] In 1915 a Russia Society was set up 'to expand the alliance through dissemination of knowledge about Russia and promote the interest of the British public in Russian art and literature'.[206] One of the first pieces of information which the society spread was that in 1914–15 the Allies' fate had depended on Russia. If Russia had remained inactive or suffered a serious defeat, she could have opted for a position war for which a relatively small army would have sufficed. In this case all the German forces would have been thrown against the French, the British and the Belgians. 'Russia's gigantic effort', the society's manifesto said, 'cost her more lives than those lost by all the other Allies together'.[207]

Two centres of help to Russian prisoners of war were founded in London, one chaired by the librarian of London Public Library C.H. Wright, sent books to the prisoners; the other, chaired by Countess Benckendorff, was supported by Lord Derby and Sir Louis Mallet. On the pages of *The Times*, Countess Benckendorff appealed to Russians resident in Britain and to the British public to help Russian prisoners of war in Germany who could not receive food parcels from Russia and suffered near-starvation. The public rallied: in the first four months of war the committee received close to £34,000[208] and through international charitable agencies in neutral countries it regularly sent parcels with bread and warm clothing to nearly 100,000 Russian soldiers in a dozen German and Austrian camps. The countess, as well as her helpers in the Russian colony, like the famous Oxford medievalist Sir Paul Vinogradoff, repeatedly thanked the British donors for their

203 Grey to Buchanan, 26.06.1916, FO 800/75, 309.

204 C.Nabokoff, 20.

205 C.Nabokoff, 42.

206 A.M.Nikolaev, 97.

207 A.M.Nikolaev, 97.

208 Pavel Vinogradov, 'Angli'ia i russkie voennoplenny'e' in *Rossi'ia na rasput'ie: Istoriko-publitsisticheskie stat'i* (Moscow, 2008), 361–2.

generosity in speeches and through the press. The countess also quietly arranged for her British and French acquaintances to send money and parcels to their German and Austrian relatives captured by the Russian army through her sister Princess Dolgorouky.

War Fatigue

As the Entente suffered enormous losses without seeing the end of the war come any nearer, the press in every country reflected the growing suspicion that the war had not been necessary and that one's allies were not pulling their weight. In England wartime propaganda and censorship did not entirely obliterate the old idea that a despotic barbarian Russia was not a suitable ally for Britain. The British felt that the allies did not appreciate their effort. Lloyd George suggested in January 1915 that Kitchener should release to the press the numbers of the British troops so that the French and the Russians would realize the enormous British war effort: the government's policy before the outbreak of the war was to keep up six divisions as an expeditionary force; by January 1915 they had practically had as many casualties as that force.[209]

Two days later, Sazonov, interviewed by the *Sunday Times*, reproached certain [British] journalists who believed that there was an unbridgeable gulf between Britain and Russia because of Russia's lack of a developed parliamentary system and promised that after the war greater changes would take place in Russia than anywhere else, increasing the scope for Anglo-Russian friendship.[210]

In April 1915 Benckendorff also complained that Russian public opinion failed to appreciate the positive change in the British attitude: before the war the change in Russia's favour had been mostly for political reasons, but after 1914 'the desire to trust Russia and to appreciate her more seriously and more objectively … is growing every day'. He attributed Grey's new attitude to the Straits issue to the growing popularity of the Anglo-Russian entente in England.[211] Benckendorff's assistant and admirer Wesselitsky disagreed. The journalist wrote that the Entente reluctantly admitted the value of Russia's cooperation but they were still hostile:

> You will tell me that our entente is so perfect that there is no need to consolidate it, that we do not need exaggerated compliments which are dispensed to the others. Perhaps it is so as far as the cabinet is concerned, but what about the public?

209 Lord Stamfordham, *Memorandum*, 15.01.1915, RA PS/PSO/GV/C/Q/733/1.

210 'Russia and England' (a typewritten copy of the interview in *The Sunday Times*), 17.01.1915, AVPRI, F.134, op.473, d.103.

211 A.K. Benckendorff to Sazonov, 19.02/04.03.1915, *Constantinople et les detroits: Livre premier*, 181–3.

He quoted Benckendorff's words about the need for fairness in judging Britain and pointed out that Britain did not show fairness to Russia. English society already worried that German hegemony on the continent would be replaced by Russian. The British spoke of preserving a diminished Austria to use in future combinations against Russia and of a Polish state as a buffer between Germany and Russia.[212]

In Russia, the idea of perfidious Albion began to gain strength as Russia's human losses and her financial debt to Britain mounted. After a series of military defeats, Russians were becoming angry with their government and with the Allies. The ambassador did not see any place for improvement on the British side and was anxious to correct the Russian attitudes. In the summer of 1915 Benckendorff wrote that the British were concerned that Russia did not appreciate their sacrifice in the Dardanelles and in France.[213] Further indications of Russia's growing resentment of Britain led to an exchange of letters between Nicholas II and George V and to Benckendorff's reassurances to the king regarding Russia's continued friendship for Britain,[214] but the mood in Russia did not change. Benckendorff reported to Sazonov in January 1916 that journalist Stanley Washbourne published a letter in *The Times* about the 'diminished sympathies for England in Russia'. It provoked a debate in the press and Benckendorff recommended 'subsidies' to the Russian papers for writing articles favourable to Britain. Benckendorff explained his preoccupation: 'The issue will be even more important during the peace talks where the nations' mutual sympathies will determine the strength of support which our governments will give each other'.[215]

As a propaganda effort, in 1916 Russian journalists were brought to see Britain's war effort and to disseminate this knowledge in Russia, but disillusionment was gaining ground even at the highest level of Russian administration. When a parliamentary delegation came to London, Benckendorff heard Baron Roman Rosen, his former colleague, declare to the embassy staff that the pro-Entente course had been a mistake and that Constantinople was a pipedream. Rosen was a senator and Benckendorff, a stickler for etiquette, designated him as the head of the delegation. The rest of the delegates protested on the grounds of Rosen's 'pro-German' views and the offended Rosen locked himself in his hotel room for the rest of the visit.[216]

Sazonov's Dismissal

Boris Sturmer, a protégé of Empress Alexandra, became the head of the Russian government in January 1916. To quell the rumours of Sturmer's pro-German

212 G. Wesselitsky to A.K. Benckendorff, 12.11.1914, BC2, box 15.

213 A.K. Benckendorff to Sazonov, AVPRI, f.134, op.473, d.103, ll.8–9.

214 A.K. Benckendorff to Sazonov, AVPRI, f.134, op.473, d.117, l.10–12.

215 A.K. Benckendorff to Sazonov, 19.12.1915/01.01.1916, AVPRI, f.134, op.473, d.117, l. 25–6.

216 C. Nabokoff, 52.

orientation, Sazonov spoke in the Duma about Russia's determination to fight the war to the end and defended the Entente's Balkan policy.[217] To turn the tide of anti-British opinion, Sazonov had wanted prominent members of the cabinet, like Reginald McKenna or Austen Chamberlain, to come to Russia in the early summer 1916 with the popular Kitchener to discuss the finances at Petrograd;[218] but luckily they did not, as Kitchener's ship was sunk by a German submarine on the way to Russia.

Stürmer took the foreign ministry over in July, despite Buchanan's attempts to dissuade Nicholas II from firing Sazonov.[219] V.S. Vasiukov says that Sazonov had been doomed ever since he had opposed Nicholas II's decision to assume the chief command of the army in 1915,[220] but there may have been another reason. The *Novoye Vremya* reflected a growing trend in Russian society when it welcomed Stürmer's appointment and hoped that he would curb the influence of the Entente ambassadors on the foreign ministry.[221] Nicholas II warned George V about the excessive involvement of Entente diplomats in the internal affairs of Greece which undermined the king's authority.[222] (His own representative, Elim Demidov, had quarrelled with the French mission in Athens for this reason).[223] The Tsar may have had the same forebodings with regard to Buchanan's and Paleologue's influence on Sazonov.

Russian Monarchy's Meltdown

When the telegram announcing Sazonov's resignation and Stürmer's appointment reached London, the ambassador said to his subordinates: 'C'est de la demence'. [This is madness] Abandoning all discretion, he rejoiced when he heard about the attacks on the new minister in the Duma and at the court.[224] Iswolsky shared his dislike of Sazonov's successor. It was not his alleged pro-German orientation which the two friends feared: they knew that, like Rosen's 'pro-Germanism', it was dictated by the concern about falling under the sway of the Entente rather than fondness for Germany. But Iswolsky and Benckendorff saw the appointment as a death knell to domestic liberalization.[225] It also revealed an internal instability which, they wrongly thought, might force the government to accept German offers of separate peace. Benckendorff should have been able to dispel the British and

217 V.S. Vasiukov, 28–9.
218 G. Buchanan to Lord Stamfordham, 23.06.1916, RA PS/PSO/GV/C/P/284a/24.
219 G. Buchanan to Nicholas II, 06/19.06.1916, *Dnevniki i dokumenty*, 129–30.
220 V.S. Vasiukov, 208.
221 V.S. Vasiukov, 216.
222 Nicholas II to George V, 04/17.08.1916, RA PS/PSO/GV/C/Q/2551/7.
223 Sevastopoulo to A.K. Benckendorff, 1916 (after 6/19.10), BC 2, box 14.
224 C. Nabokoff, 37.
225 Iswolsky to A.K. Benckendorff, 21.08.1916, BC2, box 13.

French fears of Russia making separate peace. Many memoirists quote the Tsar saying that he wanted to hand Russia over to his son with the same structure and laws that he had received in 1896. It was generally condemned as the blindness and obtuseness of a man who did not take into consideration the changing world. But this very obtuseness was the Entente's best guarantee that the emperor would keep his promise to continue the war. He was incapable of taking into account his country's condition.

Benckendorff pressed Stürmer for an immediate official confirmation of Russia's commitment to the Entente course. Condescending to the ignorance of the new minister, Benckendorff explained: 'This international custom is so universally accepted that silence would provoke puzzlement'.[226] Stürmer obliged, emphasizing the Anglo-Russian friendship in a press statement [227] and in a personal message he confirmed to Grey that 'Russian policy remains unchanged and all my efforts will be focused on consolidating the ties which unite us to England'.[228]

In August 1916 Grey authorized Buchanan to tell the new foreign minister that the British government considered Petr Botkin pro-German and that his appointment as deputy minister would damage relations between Russia and the Entente.[229] Instead of Botkin, Anatoly Neratov became the deputy foreign minister. In September, Benckendorff insisted again on the need to reassure the allies: Britain's loyalty to Russia had been demonstrated. Russia's loyalty had to be reaffirmed after the change of the foreign minister.[230] Stürmer promised, but did nothing. The new minister wanted the Allies' consent to making the Straits agreement public.[231] Russian public opinion was increasingly anti-war and anti-Entente, and with the concern that the Allies might try to wriggle out of the promise always present, the government thought that the declaration would solve both problems.[232] The allies were reluctant, thinking about the effects of such a declaration on Muslim opinion and public opinion in the Ottoman Empire.[233] George V asked Nicholas II to wait until the final victory.[234] In the end, the Russian government limited itself to a governmental declaration to the Duma without having the treaty simultaneously published in the Entente capitals.[235]

---

226 A.K. Benckendorff to B.V. Sturmer, 13/26.07.1916, *Dnevniki i dokumenty*, 130–31.

227 V.S. Vasiukov, 222.

228 A.K. Benckendorff to Grey, 02.08.1916, FO 800/75, 333–5.

229 Grey to Buchanan, 01.08.1916, FO 800/75, 339.

230 A.K. Benckendorff to B.V. Sturmer, 01/14.09.1916, *Dnevniki i dokumenty*, 131–4.

231 V.S. Vasiukov, 246–9.

232 Nicholas II to George V, 13.09.1916, RA PS/PSO/GV/C/Q/2527/3.

233 A draft by Lord Carnock (Sir Arthur Nicolson), 26.09.1916, RA PS/PSO/GV/C/M/969/5.

234 George V to Nicholas II, 05.10.1916, GARF, f.601, op.1, ed.hr.1219, l.72.

235 Neratov to A.K. Benckendorff and A.P. Iswolsky, 16/29.11.1916, *Constantinople et les detroits: Livre premier*, 425.

Buchanan spoke to Nicholas II at the beginning of 1916 about the lack of trust in the Russian government and Stürmer's reputation as a reactionary.[236] Stürmer was dismissed in November, after Pavel Miliukov, the leader of the Constitutional Democrats had attacked him in a speech in the Duma. Empress Alexandra described the incident in a letter to her husband, blaming the British ambassador for instigating the attack.[237] A few days later she calmed down and passed on to her husband Rasputin's pragmatic advice to compromise and replace Stürmer at the foreign ministry while leaving him as the head of the government.[238] Two days after, on 11/24 November Sturmer was replaced by the finance controller, Nikolai Pokrovsky. To this Benckendorff said only: 'At least this one is an honest man'. The Russian ambassador had lost all hope in Russia even before the Allied powers.[239]

English letters from Russia in 1916 spoke of the government's weakness and of German propaganda in favour of separate peace. They need not have worried: the Russian government would never go back on its pledge. As the French ambassador said in 1906, in Russia foreign policy was not influenced by the domestic situation: only the emperor's will determined Russia's course. First Nicholas II and then the Provisional Government chose to face the collapse of Russia rather than desert their allies. But the cost of such loyalty was proving too high. Among the diplomats, the dejection manifested itself in growing personal tensions and quarrels, sometimes conducted by correspondence. In August 1916 Iswolsky, not for the first time, complained to Benckendorff about the offensive behaviour of the British ambassador. Lord Bertie, a malicious bully at all times,[240] was losing self-control and he attacked Iswolsky in the French press. Iswolsky complained to Benckendorff that his main concern was that it would mar the coming peace if the Russian and British ambassadors were not on speaking terms during the peace conference.[241] Bertie did not apologize; the Foreign Office's opinion of Iswolsky's importance was not high and they let things rest. After August 1916, the two Entente embassies in Paris communicated through the counsellors.

In October, Iswolsky's counsellor Sevastopoulo sent his former chief Benckendorff a copy of Iswolsky's reprimand to the Russian minister in Greece, Elim Demidov. Iswolsky accused his old friend and colleague of sowing doubts in the coalition camp at the time of Sazonov's fall and catering to the Petrograd circles which hoped that Russia would break free from France and England and assert her independence, 'which neither Benckendorff at London nor myself at

236 Buchanan, *Memorandum*, 03/16.02.1916, FO 800/75, 240–48.

237 Empress Alexandra to Nicholas II, 04/17.11.1916, *Letters of the Tsaritsa – to the Tsar, 1914–1916* (London: Duckworth & Co, 1923), 433.

238 Empress Alexandra to Nicholas II, 09/22.11.1916, *Letters of the Tsaritsa – to the Tsar, 1914–1916*, 437.

239 C. Nabokoff, 52–7.

240 Joseph Caillaux, 135–6.

241 Iswolsky to A.K. Benckendorff, 05.08.1916, BC2, box 13.

Paris [allegedly] succeeded in maintaining or defending'. His bitter reproach: 'given the tendencies which at present prevail at Petrograd ... your language will make more impression than mine',[242] meant that Iswolsky and Benckendorff knew that the policy which they promoted was unpopular even among their Russian colleagues. Sevastopoulo warned Benckendorff about the anti-British mood in Russia, which he also noticed in the Russians visiting Paris: 'In Russia people talk a little too much about the English governess having replaced the German nanny'. He mentioned the indignation among the Russians regarding the rumour that Russia had pledged not to buy supplies from any country but Britain.[243]

When the Russian Supplies Committee was organized in London, to coordinate all Russia's purchases abroad, the British government stipulated that all Russian military orders abroad would be negotiated through this committee, and in this way the British could influence the purchases. As the munitions bought in North America were brought to Russia by sea, they were convoyed by the British navy. The British government suggested that all the Russian merchant fleet should be controlled by British freight companies, in order to improve the organization. Nicholas II and his staff approved of the idea, but on 2 January 1916 the chairman of the Duma protested against such slavery, calling it 'unworthy of a great nation and an ally', and warned Buchanan and the military agent that if the Tsar accepted this claim he would speak about it to the Duma. The British retreated,[244] but the discussions continued behind the scenes, although the offensive phrase about the British officers supervising Russian transportation was omitted.[245]

As the strain was growing, something inconceivable and out of character happened. In late 1916 Benckendorff quarrelled with his longtime colleague Paul Cambon. The document referring to the incident is filed in the French National Archives as the case of the Russian ambassador accusing France of having wanted this war and Paul Cambon's reply, which made an acrimonious reference to Russia's 1905 Björko treaty with Germany.[246]

A concerned British resident in Russia suggested to the Foreign Office that the Entente needed to become an *Entente Eclatante* and dazzle the dejected Russians by royal visits.[247] Hardinge, who replaced the retired Nicolson at the Foreign Office, dismissed the idea: the next Allied peace conference would be held in Petrograd

242 Sevastopoulo to A.K. Benckendorff, 1916 (after 6/19.10), BC 2, box 14.

243 Sevastopoulo to A.K. Benckendorff, 11/24.10.1916, BC2, box 14.

244 M.V. Rodzianko, *Krushenie imperii* (Moscow: Fond Sergei'a Dubnova, 2000), 182.

245 Sazonov to A.K. Benckendorff, 26.03/08.04.1916, AVPRI, f.134, op.473, d.144, l.37.

246 Castelnau to Ribot, 1917. Available at: www.archivesnationales.culture.gouv.fr/chan/chan/pdf/ap/563.

247 Adrian Simpson to Sir George Arthur, 06.11.1916, RA PS/PSO/GV/C/Q/995/2.

and it would have a positive effect on Anglo-Russian relations.[248] The Foreign Office hoped too that the conference would take place at the general headquarters where Nicholas II could be present.[249] At least part of the reason must have been his known malleability.

Benckendorff was to preside over the conference in Petrograd in January 1917.[250] His appointment was Nicholas II's gesture to confirm Russia's loyalty to the Entente. But the count felt increasingly lonely: his closest colleague, Iswolsky, lost heart and remained at Paris only because of financial considerations;[251] in May 1916 Nicolson retired and Grey left in December, when Lloyd George became prime minister. Grey's departure was long-overdue in the opinion of many of his colleagues and subordinates. Bertie had discussed with Curzon, 'Grey's weakened health which has increased the pacifism in his nature'; both agreed that pacifism would be detrimental in the future peace negotiations.[252] Benckendorff wrote a farewell letter to which Grey replied with a long one of his own, probably the last one the Russian ambassador received. The tenor of Benckendorff's letter is clear from Grey's response:

> As you say we failed to prevent war, but the Balkan Conference showed that war could have been prevented. The machinery and personelle in London were effective and absolutely trustworthy. You, Cambon, Imperiali, Lichnowsky, Mensdorff and myself could and would have settled any European crisis honourably [...] and fairly [if] the difficulty had been referred to us.

Grey probably was answering his own soul-searching as well as Benckendorff's bitter self-accusations and the criticisms which his political opponents were already addressing to him and other veterans of the old diplomacy. He insisted that it had been the criminal plan of the 'Prussian Military party' to break the Entente and leave Britain isolated, so as to dominate the world. Germany had left the Entente no choice but war. But, Grey concluded:

> Providence which has its own intentions as to the evolution of the human race and whose ways are beyond our understanding, intended the world to go through this awful trial. 'It must needs be that offences come', all we can certainly do is to make sure that it is not through us that they come. This at any rate you and I and the Ambassadors with whom we worked in London, including Lichnowsky and Mensdorff, certainly did, and more we could not do.

---

248 Hardinge to Lord Stamfordham, 13.11.1916, RA PS/PSO/GV/C/Q/995/5.
249 Foreign Office to Lord Bertie, 07.11.1916, RA PS/PSO/GV/C/Q/1200/8.
250 M.A. Taube, *Zarnitsy*, 204.
251 Iswolsky to A.K. Benckendorff, 05.08.1916, BC2, box 13.
252 Lord Bertie, *Memorandum*, 12.04.1916, FO 800/175, 45–6.

'So much for failure. Now for success', Grey wrote briskly and tried to raise Benckendorff's spirits by pointing out that the Entente succeeded in frustrating Germany's plan of a blitzkrieg in France and a separate peace with Russia. Although the issue of the war was still in doubt, Germany was exhausted; if they held for a few more weeks the Allies would get much better peace terms. He ended: 'In spite of anxiety about the war, which must continue for some weeks yet, I cannot help enjoying life. I am attending to private affairs, neglected for 11 years, arranging books and papers, going out alone with gun and a dog ...'[253] This was the British talent for taking life a day at a time which Benckendorff clearly lacked in 1916. In 1915 to Grey's condolences on his son's death the ambassador answered that his son and other soldiers died 'not only for their country but for something even higher on which sooner or later international relations will come to rest';[254] but in 1916 this hope for a secure and peaceful European order seemed too remote to serve as a consolation.

The 'few weeks' of war which Grey optimistically foresaw were decisive to Russia's survival. Letters which flew from London to Petrograd and to the general headquarters at this point were all concerned with the rumours of German attempts to induce Russia to make a separate peace. Russia's collapse was also a possibility. British estimates of Russia's condition wildly differed. Buchanan saw the depressed mood in Petrograd; General Hanbury Williams attached to the Russian headquarters, assured the king that Nicholas II's popularity was growing as he became better known after assuming the command of the army and that Brusilov, the best Russian general, gave the Germans '... six months on the result of this year's harvest – then 2 months very badly off for food and supplies – and during the next three months – the end'.[255] George V urged Nicholas II to continue fighting to the end.[256] Nicholas II's New Year order to the army confirmed his determination on victory. So did his last letter to George V, after the Petrograd conference, dwelling on the transport difficulties which created food crises in cities. He concluded:

> Everything is being done to ameliorate this state of things which I hope will be overcome in April. But I never lose courage and egg on the ministers to make them ans those under them work as hard as they can.[257]

The Ambassador's Last Message

Benckendorff fell ill with Spanish influenza at the end of December and five days later he was dead. As he was used to frequent illness, he did not realize

253 Grey of Fallodon to A.K. Benckendorff, 22.12.1916, BC2, box 12.
254 A.K. Benckendorff to Grey, 14.06.1915, FO 800/75, 114–15.
255 Hanbury Williams to George V, 14.11.1916, RA PS/PSO/GV/C/Q/722/32.
256 George V to Nicholas II, 10.01.1917, GARF, f.601, op1, ed.hr.1219, l. 74.
257 Nicholas II to George V, 04/17.02.1917, RA PS/PSO/GV/C/Q/2551/8.

the gravity of his situation and to the last moment attended to his work.[258] King George V wrote to his mother about the suddenness of Benckendorff's death, saying: '... he will be a great loss to me, as he was the only one I could talk to, quite openly, about Russia'.[259]

Letters of condolence poured into the Russian embassy – from Lansdowne, Revelstoke, Queen Alexandra, Lady Emma Rothschild and other British friends. Letters from Russians were markedly few. In his memoir Nabokov quoted Paul Cambon's formal condolences:

> I was, perhaps, a better judge than anyone else of Count Benckendorff's great and charming qualities. His death is a loss not only to Russia, but to France as well. He was educated in France. France knew how much experience, wisdom and sagacity he displayed in the most difficult negotiations which were conducted in London.[260]

The incongruous combination of the 'great' with 'charming' eloquently expresses Cambon's opinion of a courtier diplomat, which Benckendorff had always been in his eyes. His use to France was in being malleable and France appreciated it, though without being blinded by gratitude. *The Times*' publications dedicated to Benckendorff's memory reminded the readers of the ambassador's two traits: his great, unswerving devotion to Britain to which he served by disclosing to the Foreign Office Russia's condition and intentions; and the twin feeling of deep disenchantment with the Russian state which he had represented for most of his life. The two were intimately connected and grew apace.

The Times' leader dedicated to Count Benckendorff, as was the custom, spoke of his distinguished personality and his sincere liking for England which had moved him to promote the 1907 convention and the wartime cooperation. They praised his fine intelligence, wide culture and his charm, 'born of goodness of heart and readiness to help every worthy cause'.[261] Three days later, under the sensationalist title 'Anxious Days in Russia: Count Benckendorff's Forebodings', *The Times* reproduced an article from a small Russian newspaper, describing a conversation between the imperial ambassador and a well-known feuilletonist, Aleksandr Amfiteatrov. In 1916 Amfiteatrov spent two weeks in London and became party to what he later much more vaguely called 'cautious apprehensions among the staff of the Russian embassy' regarding the political situation in Russia.[262] According to Amfiteatrov's 1917 article the ambassador

258 C. Nabokoff, 52–7.

259 George V to Queen Alexandra, 13.01.1917, RA GV/PRIV/AA37/69.

260 C. Nabokoff, 58–9.

261 'Count Benckendorff' (editorial), *The Times*, 13.01.1917, 9.

262 A.V. Amfiteatrov, *Zhizn cheloveka, neudobnogo dl'ia seb'ia i dl'ia mnogih* (Moscow, 2004), 2: 207.

was not cautious in talking to him, for he said: 'Either I am becoming old and stupid or else an epidemic of some mysterious kind of mental aberration prevails in diplomatic circles in Petrograd'. He called Stürmer a man who damaged Russia's reputation and honour in Europe. Benckendorff confessed to 'inexpressible sufferings seeing Russia pushed to the edge of the abyss and ended by saying:

> Of course I am Liberal in comparison with those who are at present in power. I have spent all my life in Europe and I have formed ties of kinship with England, who enlightens and teaches. But there in Russia is blindness ... I wish Russia all good, but I must confess that every mail from Petrograd plunges me ever deeper into dismal pessimism.[263]

The article caught Benckendorff's mood in 1916 as recorded in his correspondence and Nabokoff's memoir. On the other hand, the near-omission of his visit to the embassy in Amfiteatrov's 1930s memoirs inspires some doubt as to the reliability of the 1917 article. It seems odd that Benckendorff would confide in a stranger, a Russian and a journalist – three qualifications which would not predispose the count to frankness. He could only have done so if he were in a state of nervous breakdown, which the article implies. Genuine or fantasized, this article became Benckendorff's posthumous service to the British, his last warning against relying on Russia.

The first consequence of Benckendorff's death was a British request to have Sazonov posted to the Russian embassy.[264] Nicholas II conceded the wish but Sazonov never came to London, for the February revolution overtook him. K.D. Nabokov was in charge of the embassy after the Provisional government came to power in Russia. In November 1917, after the Bolsheviks overthrew the Provisional government of the Russian Republic, the commissar of the foreign affairs L. Trotsky telegraphed an invitation to the Russian diplomatic service to serve the new Soviet government, but, with the exception of the Russian chargé d'affaires in Spain, Russian diplomats refused to recognize the legitimacy of the Soviet regime. The staff of the London embassy, first drawing on the remaining funds and later unpaid, served the needs of the Russian White Armies and looked after the Russian emigrants in Britain. The terms of the lease made the ambassador's widow the sole lease-holder of Chesham House and the countess refused to surrender it to the Soviet representatives when Britain established diplomatic relations with the Soviet Union in 1924. When the lease expired, the former staff of the Russian imperial embassy left Chesham House, taking with them what they did not want the enemy to have: boxes upon boxes

263 'Anxious Days in Russia. Count Benckendorff's Forebodings', *The Times*, 16.01.1917, 9.

264 George V to Nicholas II, 17.01.1917, GARF, f.601, op.1, ed.hr.1219, l.76.

of diplomatic correspondence, which contained the record of Anglo-Russian relations during Benckendorff's embassy.

Conclusion

> ... it is difficult to be progressive ... in Russia, for every progressive man here becomes, without realizing it, a peaceful revolutionary, that is, he peacefully prepares the ground for the un-peaceful or irreconcilable ones.
>
> Konstantin Leonti'iev (1880s)

The timing of Benckendorff's death tempts one to slide into clichés and speak of the passing of an epoch in diplomacy or of the demise of the Russian Empire, but it was one among the millions caused by the Spanish influenza. Also, like his colleagues, he had become increasingly irrelevant long before he died: when the war which, by the diplomats' accounts, was to be the Third Balkan war turned out to be the First World War and diplomats began to be scathingly called 'the old diplomacy'.

The significance of Benckendorff's role had nothing to do with the quality of his mind but mostly with the number of his initiatives. Rather like Nicholas II, his private correspondence highlights the disproportionate input of an average intellect into the foreign policy of an empire. His career and activity, besides completing the picture of Anglo-Russian interactions in 1902–17, is an example of how a diplomatic representative of one country becomes an agent of influence of others.

Aleksandr Benckendorff was a man of great tact, of the highest personal ethics and culture. He was a kind and magnanimous man who commanded loyalty from his subordinates. He thought of serving his government rather than using his government's services for personal satisfaction. During the European war he rejected the general chauvinism and vindictiveness and answered pleas for help from both sides of the conflict, defending the victims of the anti-German hysteria in wartime Britain. From this point of view any diplomatic service in Europe could have been proud of such a representative.

But the personal virtues which Benckendorff had in such abundance could not replace the qualities which he lacked. He was unable to present to the world an open face and a closed mouth, a basic requirement in diplomacy.

He was only vaguely aware of the forces which drove the policies of the European powers, including Russia and England, relying mostly on his personal connections with the statesmen which these forces brought to the surface of political life. In his eyes, it was his colleague Cambon and two or three officials at Quai d'Orsay who 'made the weather' in French political life. He considered that he had done everything for Russia by becoming the weekend guest of two successive British monarchs. He confused Curzon's or Grey's dinner conversations with policy declarations, Revelstoke's and Rothschild's parties with having his finger on the pulse of the City and Asquith's bridge partnership with close ties to the Liberal government. From this angle Benckendorff's remark to his wife that his letter to the foreign minister, Lamsdorff, was practically indistinguishable from the one he wrote to her on the same subject,[1] does not speak so much of frankness as lack of seriousness.

He had a high opinion of his own worth and felt justified in following his own judgment if it came into conflict with his instructions. He served a government which he despised and which drove him – and many other Russians – into despair towards the end of his life. His disappointment in the Russian government grew apace with his admiration of the British. Both feelings made him cling to the friendship and support of the British political establishment. As he switched his loyalty from the outmoded and ineffective autocracy to a modern, rational constitutional monarchy, he also switched it from Russia to Britain without noticing it. His duty was to represent the Russian emperor, but he chose to serve the interests of Russia in his own way, freely interpreting or ignoring his instructions. By so acting he further diminished the already insufficient consistency of Russian foreign policy.

Like many other Russians, Benckendorff dreamed of guiding Russia's political course towards stability and prosperity and saw a shift in foreign policy as a universal cure for all Russia's ills. He wanted the Russian state to sacrifice all other interests for the sake of an Anglo-Russian alliance. He was certain that once Russia proved her good faith by harmonizing all of her policies with the Foreign Office and by granting all British desires in the areas where their interests met, the latter would take the Russian Empire into its fold. With Russia within Britain's orbit, a gradual modernization would take the Russian state towards a constitutional regime similar to the Western European ones, resulting in 'national cohesion' and internal stability. He was convinced that Britain's friendship was vital to Russia, and therefore the onus of preserving it lay on Russia.

He consistently refused to attempt to influence the position of the Foreign Office and focused his efforts on trying to modify the Russian position. It led to a growing estrangement from his colleagues at St Petersburg and in other Russian diplomatic missions. That was the origin of the jokes about Count Benckendorff whose reports began always in the same way: 'Grey m'a dit …' But the results were not what Benckendorff expected.

His fear of losing Britain's friendship made him oppose all efforts at improving Russo-German relations. His contribution to distancing Russia from Germany was made in all innocence for the sake of earning Britain's trust and goodwill. He set himself a goal of bringing about an Anglo-Russian 'marriage of true minds', and fought against the negative stereotypes of each other existing in the British and Russian public opinion. As a result, from 1902 to 1914 Russia did not have an ambassador in Britain so much as a cultural attaché while Britain had two ambassadors to Russia, one at St Petersburg and one in London. Benckendorff dreamed of a European Union structure with a different membership: parliamentary constitutional Britain, France and Russia would be the founding members.

1 A.K. Benckendorff to S.P. Benckendorff, 17.04.1903, f.1126, op.1, ed.hr.151, ll.16–17.

In politics, success often depends on the ability to take advantage of the opportunities. Benckendorff's weaknesses made his posting to London a welcome opportunity for his Entente colleagues, and they made use of it. Benckendorff thought that he could induce Russia to follow Britain on this path and the Foreign Office, much more realistic in its expectations, encouraged his efforts because they advanced the immediate interests of the British foreign policy. How much it benefited the Entente in the long run, is open to debate. As far as Russia is concerned, he worked steadily and zealously toward an impossibility.

Benckendorff was not the only near-sighted diplomat in Europe, but he was one of the most active. Not only he misinterpreted his information and misinformed his government about the British policies, but he interfered in Russia's relations with Germany, the Balkans, Austria-Hungary and Persia. All these human failings might have been checked in a better administrative system. But the Russian system suffered from nepotism, indiscipline and disillusionment among the diplomatic representatives of the empire. There is always a gap between the views of any foreign ministry and its foreign service at any time, but the Russian foreign ministry failed to bring together the good, the bad and the indifferent to work for one purpose, formulating and serving Russia's interests.

Count Benckendorff was one of those lofty-minded and naive Russian noblemen who entered the state service to serve the interests of their country but acted as anarchists. When individual civil servants feel that they are better than the institution they serve, their best-intentioned efforts will destroy the institution, especially in the absence of a strong central authority. That was the case in the Russian foreign ministry (and Russian government) between 1896 and 1917.

List of Characters

Abrikossov, Dmitry I. (1876–1951) – Russian diplomat, attaché of the London embassy (1904–8).

Aehrenthal, Alois Lexa von (1854–1912) – Austro-Hungarian ambassador to Russia, (1899–1906) and Foreign Minister (1906–12).

Amfiteatrov, Aleksandr V. (1862–1938) – Russian journalist and author.

Asquith, Herbert Henry (1852–1928) – Liberal Prime Minister of Great Britain (1908–16).

Balfour, Arthur James (1848–1930) – Conservative Prime Minister (1902–5) and Foreign Minister (1916–19).

Barclay, George Head – British diplomat, minister to Persia (1908–12).

Baring, Maurice (1874–1945) – Journalist and author, a Russian scholar and translator, Countess Benckendorff's friend.

Benckendorff, Konstantin A. (1880–1959) – The ambassador's elder son, a naval officer.

Benckendorff, Konstantin K. (1817–58) – The ambassador's father, Russian military agent in Wurtemberg and Berlin.

Benckendorff, Natalia A. (Ridley) (1886–1968) – The ambassador's daughter.

Benckendorff, Pavel K. (1853–1921) – Chamberlain at the court of Nicholas II, the ambassador's brother.

Benckendorff, Pyotr A. (1882–1915) – The ambassador's younger son, a guards officer.

Benckendorff, Sofia P. (1859–1928) – The ambassador's wife.

Berchtold, Leopold von (1862–1942) – Austro-Hungarian ambassador to Russia (1906–12), Foreign Minister (1912–15).

Bertie, Francis Leveson (1844–1919) – British ambassador to France (1905–18).

Bethmann-Hollweg, Theobald von (1856–1921) – German Chancellor 1909–17.

Bompard, Louis Maurice (1854–1935) – French civil servant, diplomat. Posts: Tunisia, Montenegro, ambassador to Russia (1902–7), ambassador to the Ottoman Empire (1908–14).

Botkin, Petr S. (1861–1933) – Russian diplomat. Posts: Washington, Brussels, London, Morocco. Minister to Portugal.

Brodrick, St John (1856–1942) – Secretary of State for War (1900–1905), Secretary of State for India (1903–5).

Buchanan, George William (1854–1924) – British diplomat. Posts: Tokyo, Switzerland, Darmstadt, Italy, Germany, Bulgaria, Netherlands. British ambassador to Russia (1910–18).

Bülow, Bernhard von (1849–1929) – German Chancellor and Prussian Prime Minister during 1900–1909.
Caillaux, Joseph (1863–1944) – French Minister of Finance (1899–1902, 1906–9), Premier (1911–12).
Cambon, Jules (1845–1935) – French diplomat, minister to the US, ambassador to Spain, ambassador to Berlin
Cambon, Paul (1843–1924) – French diplomat, ambassador to the Ottoman Empire, ambassador to London (1898–1920).
Cassini, Arthur Pavlovich (1835–1919) – Russian diplomat. Posts: Hamburg, China, the US, Spain.
Chamberlain, Joseph (1836–1914) – British businessman, radical politician and imperialist, Liberal Unionist, member of the Conservative cabinet (1895–1902).
Charykow, Nikolai V. (1855–1930) – Russian diplomat. Posts: Bulgaria, Germany, Vatican, Serbia, Netherlands. Deputy Minister of Foreign Affairs (1908–10), ambassador to Constantinople (1910–12).
Chirol, Valentine (1852–1929) – Journalist and author, foreign editor of *The Times* (1899–1912).
Churchill, Winston (1874–1965) – Member of the Liberal government, First Sea Lord (1911–15).
Clemenceau, Georges (1841–1929) – French statesman and journalist, Interior Minister and Premier (1906–9).
Cranley, Viscount – Son of the 4th Earl of Onslow, official of the British embassy at St Petersburg, private secretary to Sir Arthur Nicolson at the Foreign Office.
Curzon (of Kedleston), George Nathaniel (1859–1925) – Viceroy of India (1898–1905).
Delcassé, Théophile (1852–1923) – French Foreign Minister (1898–1905) and 1914–15), ambassador to Russia in 1913.
Demidov-San Donato, Elim P. (1868–1943) – Russian diplomat. Posts: Britain, Paris, Greece.
Etter, Nikolai S. (1865–1935) – Russian diplomat, Counsellor of the London embassy (1908–1915), minister to Persia (1915–17).
Feodorovna, Aleksandra (1872–1918) – Empress of Russia, consort of Nicholas II.
Feodorovna, Maria (1847–1928) – A princess of Denmark, consort of Alexander III, sister to Queen Alexandra, mother of Nicholas II.
Fisher (of Kilverstone), John (1841–1920) – Second Sea Lord (1902–4), First Sea Lord (1904–10 and 1914–15).
Goschen, William Edward (1847–1924) – British diplomat. Posts: Serbia, Denmark. Ambassador to Austria-Hungary (1905–8), Germany (1908–14).
Goubastov, K.A. (1845–1919) – Russian diplomat. Posts: Constantinople, Austria-Hungary, Montenegro, Vatican, Serbia. Deputy foreign minister (1906–7).

Graevenitz, Grigory – Counsellor of the Russian embassy in London (1899–1905).

Guiccioli, Alessandro (1843–1922) – Italian statesman and diplomat, Benckendorff's brother-in-law.

Hardinge, Arthur (1859–1933) – British minister in Persia.

Hardinge, Charles (1858–1944) – British diplomat, ambassador to Russia (1905–6). Permanent under-secretary for foreign affairs (1906–10 and 1916–20), Viceroy of India (1910–16).

Hartwig, Nikolay (1855–1914) – Russian diplomat, director of the first department of the Russian foreign ministry, minister in Persia (1906–8), minister in Serbia (1909–14).

Iswolsky, Aleksandr P. (1851–1919) – Russian diplomat. Posts: Vatican, Tokyo, Denmark (1903–6), foreign Minister (1906–10), ambassador to France (1910–17).

Knollys, Lord Francis (1837–1924) – Courtier, private secretary of King Edward VII.

Kokovtsev, Vladimir N. (1853–1943) – Russian statesman, finance minister (1904–6), chairman of the Council of Ministers (1911–14).

Komarov, Nikolai – Employee of the *Novoye Vremya*, recruited by Count Benckendorff.

Korostovets, Ivan Ya. (1862–1933) – Russian diplomat and orientalist. Posts: China, Persia.

Lamsdorff, Vladimir N. (1844–1907) – Official of the Russian Foreign Ministry, Foreign Minister (1900–6).

Lansdowne, Henry Charles Keith Petty-Fitzmaurice (1845–1927) – British diplomat, Viceroy of Canada and of India, Secretary for War and Foreign Secretary (1900–6) in the Conservative cabinet.

Lessar, Pavel M. (1851–1905) – Russian explorer of Central Asia, diplomatic agent in Bukhara, counsellor of the London embassy, Russian minister to China.

Lichnowsky, Karl Max (1860–1928) – German ambassador to Britain (1912–14), Benckendorff's cousin.

Louis, Georges – French diplomat, civil servant, ambassador to Russia (1909–13).

Mallet, Louis – Foreign office official, private secretary to Lansdowne and to Grey, head of the Eastern department.

Marling, Charles M. – British minister to Persia (1912–18).

Mensdorff-Pouilly, Albert von (1861–1945) – Austro-Hungarian diplomat. Posts: France, London. Ambassador to Britain (1904–14), appointed at the request of King Edward VII, Benckendorff's relative.

Nabokov, Konstantin D. (1874–1927) – Russian diplomat. Posts: Washington, Belgium, India. Counsellor of thc London Embassy and Chargé d'affaires (1915–20).

Nekliudov, Anatoly V. (1856–1934) – Russian minister to Bulgaria and Sweden.

Nelidov, Aleksandr I. (1835–1910) – Russian diplomat, ambassador to the Ottoman Empire (1883–96), Italy (1897–1903), France (1903–10).

Neratov, Anatoly A. (1863–1938) – Official of the Russian foreign ministry, acting minister of foreign affairs (1911), deputy minister of foreign affairs (1916–17).

Nicolson, Arthur (1849–1928) – British diplomat. Posts: Germany, China, the Ottoman Empire, Greece, Austria-Hungary, Bulgaria, Morocco. Ambassador to Russia (1906–10), Permanent Under-Secretary of State at the Foreign Office (1910–16).

Obolensky-Neledinsky-Meletsky, Valerian (1848–1907) – Deputy Minister of Foreign Affairs (1900–6).

Onslow, William Hillier (1853–1911) – Politician and colonial governor, Undersecretary of State for India (1895–1901), the Colonies (1900–3) and President of Board of Agriculture and Fisheries (1903–5).

Osten-Sacken, Nikolai D. (1831–1912) – Russian diplomat. Posts: Netherlands, Spain, Switzerland, Parma, Darmstadt, Bavaria. Ambassador to Germany (1895–1912).

Paléologue, Maurice-Georges (1859–1944) – French diplomat. Posts: Morocco, Rome, Germany, Korea and Bulgaria. Ambassador to Russia (1914–17).

Poincaré, Raymond (1860–1934) – Prime minister of France and foreign minister (1912–1913). President (1913–20).

Poklevsky-Koziell, Stanislav A. (1868–n.d.) – Russian diplomat, counsellor of the London embassy, minister to Persia (1909–1912).

Pourtalès, Friedrich von (1853–1928) – German diplomat. Posts: Austria-Hungary, Netherlands, France. Ambassador to Russia (1907–1914).

Revelstoke, John Baring (1863–1929) – Head of Barings Bank (1901–29), mostly concerned with major transactions and close to the political establishment, with A.J. Balfour and Lord Lansdowne his clients, Benckendorff's banker and friend.

Rosen, Roman R. (1847–1921) – Russian diplomat. Posts: Japan, USA, Mexico, Serbia, Japan, Bavaria, Greece, USA. Senator, member of the State Council.

Sablin, Evgueny V. (1875–1949) – Russian diplomat. Posts: Serbia, Morocco, Persia. First Secretary of the London embassy (1915–17).

Sanderson, Thomas Henry (1841–1923) – Civil servant, permanent under-secretary of state at the foreign office (1894–1906).

Savinsky, Aleksandr A. (1868–1934) – Russian diplomat, Director of the Minister's Chancery under V.N. Lamsdorff and A.P. Iswolsky. Posts: Sweden and Bulgaria.

Sazonov, Sergei D. (1860–1927) – Russian diplomat. Posts: London and Vatican. Deputy Foreign Minister (1909–10), Foreign Minister (1910–1917).

Scott, Sir Charles Steward (1838–1924) – British ambassador to Russia (1898–1904).

Schebeko, Nikolai N. (1863–1953) – Russian diplomat. Posts: Germany, Rumania. Ambassador to Austria-Hungary (1913–14).

Sevastopoulo(s), Matvei M. (1868–1943) – Russian diplomat. Posts: Rumania. second secretary, later first secretary of the London embassy (1905–12), France (1912–16), minister to Egypt (1917).

Siebert, Benno von (1876–1928) – Russian diplomat. Posts: Belgium, USA. second secretary, later attaché of the London embassy (1908–16), German agent since 1909.

Spender, John Alfred (1862–1942) – Journal editor and writer, editor of the Liberal *Westminster Gazette* (1896–1922).

Spring-Rice, Cecil Arthur (1859–1918) – British diplomat. Posts: USA, Germany, the Ottoman Empire, Persia, Russia, Sweden, USA. Secretary of the St Petersburg embassy (1903–6), minister to Persia (1906–8).

Stamfordham, Arthur John Bigge (1894–1931) – Courtier, private secretary to Queen Victoria and King George V.

Stead, William Thomas (1849–1912) – Newspaper editor, spiritualist and pacifict. Advocated radical foreign policies, including an Anglo-Russian entente.

Steed, Henry Wickham (1871–1956) – Journalist, authority on European diplomacy, head of the foreign department of *The Times* (1913–19).

Stolypin, P'yotr A. (1862–1911) – Russian statesman, interior minister and prime minister (1906–11).

Suvorin, Aleksei S. (1834–1912) – Editor and owner of the *Novoye Vremya.*

Taube, Mikhail A. (1869–1961) – Legal adviser of the Russian foreign ministry.

Wallace, Donald Mackenzie (1841–1919) – Journalist, Russian expert and *The Times'* leading foreign affairs authority.

Wesselitsky-Bozhidarovich, Gavriil (1841–1930) – Political journalist, (pen name Argus), after 1882 the *Novoye Vremya* London correspondent. Publications: *The Problem of Asia*, *The Russian Problem*, *Anglo-Russian Relations*.

Witte, Sergei Yu. (1849–1915) – Russian statesman, minister of finance (1892–1903), chairman of the Council of Ministers (1905–6).

Wolff Metternich zur Gracht, Paul (1853–1934) – German ambassador to Britain (1901, 1903–12).

Yermolov, Nikolai S. (1853–n.d.) – Orientalist, explorer of Central Asia, Russian military agent in Britain in 1891–1905 and 1907–17.

Zinov'iev, Ivan A. (1835–1917) – Russian diplomat and orientalist. Posts: Rumania, Persia, Sweden, the Ottoman Empire. Author of a critique of the Anglo-Russian convention *Russia, England and Persia* (1912).

Bibliography

Manuscript Sources

Arkhiv Vneshnei Politiki Rossiiskoi Imperii [*Archive of the Foreign Policy of the Russian Empire*]

F.133 Kantsel'ariia ministra [The Minister's Chancellery].

F.134 Arkhiv 'Voina' [Collection 'The war'].

F.138 Sekretnyy arkhiv ministra [The Minister's secret archive].

F.151 Politicheskii arkhiv (POLITARHIV) [Political affairs archive].

F.159 Departament lichnogo sostava i khoz'aistvennykh del [Staff and household department].

F.184 Rossiiskoe posol'stvo v Londone [Russian embassy in London].

F.340 Kollektsiia dokumental'nykh materialov chinovnikov Ministerstva Inostrannykh Del [Private documents of the foreign ministry officials].

Bakhmetev Archive. Private papers of Benckendorff family, Part II Private papers of Prince Urusov.

Gosudarstvennyy Arkhiv Rossiiskoi Federatsii [*State Archive of the Russian Federation*]

F.1126 Benckendorff'y, Alopeus'y, Shuvalov'y [Benckendorff, Alopeus and Shuvalov family].

F.1127 Pavel K. Benckendorff.

F.559 A.P. Iswolsky.

F.568 V.N. Lamsdorff.

F.642 Imperatritsa Maria Feodorovna [Empress Maria Feodorovna].

F.601 Imperator Nikolai II [Emperor Nicholas II].

F.813 M.F. Schilling.

F.597 S.P. Tatischev.

House of Lords Record Office, Lloyd George Papers [Minister of Munitions].

The National Archives

Foreign Office Private Collections, Various Ministers and Officials 1824–1949.

FO 800/51, 72–76 Sir Edward Grey's Papers.

FO 800/92 Sir Edward Grey's Papers.

FO 800/140–145 Lord Lansdowne's Papers.

FO 800/173–175 Sir Francis Bertie's Papers.

FO 800/ 337 Sir Arthur Nicolson's Papers.

Royal Archives

Diary of George V.

Letters from Nicholas II to Edward VII.

Letters and telegrams from Nicholas II to George V.
Letters from British ambassadors to Russia to Edward VII and George V.
Letters and memoranda from members of British Cabinets to Edward VII and George V, 1900–1917.
Correspondence of Lord Francis Knollys.
Sir Adam Ridley's Family Papers
Jasper Ridley, 1914 Diary.
Russian State Library, Manuscripts Department
Sofia Petrovna Benckendorff, Diary.
Surrey History Centre, Woking, UK
Earls of Onslow of Clandon Park, Records.

Printed Documents

Adamov, E.A. *Constantinople et les detroits. Livre premier. Documents secrets de l'ancien Ministère des Affaires Etrangères de Russie*. Paris: Les éditions internationales, 1930.
British Documents on the Origins of the War, 1898–1914. London: His Majesty's Stationery Office, 1927.
Collected Diplomatic Documents Relating to the Outbreak of the European War. London: Harrison and Sons, 1915.
Documents Diplomatiques Français, 1871–1914. 2e Serie. Paris: Imprimerie nationale, 1931.
Documents Diplomatiques Secrets Russes 1914–1917 d'après les archives du Ministère des affaires étrangères à Petrograd. Paris: Payot, 1928.
German Diplomatic Documents, 1871–1914 (trans. E.T.S. Dugdale). London: Methuen & Co. Ltd., 1931.
Dmytryshin, B. (ed.) *Imperial Russia: A Source Book, 1700–1917*. New York: Harcourt Brace Jovanovich College Publishers, 1990.
Glushkov, V.V. and Cherevko, K.E. *Russko-iaponska'ia voina 1904–1905 gg. v dokumentakh vneshnepoliticheskogo vedomstva Rossii: Fakty i kommentarii* [*Russo-Japanese War of 1904–1905 in Documents of the Russian Foreign Ministry: Facts and Comments*]. Moscow: IDEL, 2006.
Korennye interesy Rossii glazami ee gosudarstvennykh dey'atelei, diplomatov, voennykh i publitsistov. Dokumental'na'ya publikatsi'ia [*Russia's National Interests Through the Eyes of Statesmen, Diplomats, Military and Political Analysts*]. Moscow: RAN Institut Rossiiskoi Istorii, 2004.
Krasnyi Arhiv, 1924, vv. 6 and 7.
Lepsius, J., Mendelsohn Bartholdy, A. and Thimme, F. (eds) *Die Grosse Politik der Europaischen Kabinette, 1877–1914*. Berlin: Deutsche Verlagsgesellschaft für Politik und Geschichte MBH, c.1924.

Lowe, C.J. and M.L. Dockrill (eds) *The Mirage of Power: British Foreign Policy 1902–22, Vol. 3: The Documents*. London and Boston: Routledge and Kegan Paul,1972.

Lieven, D. (ed.) *British Documents on Foreign Affairs – Reports and Papers from the Foreign Office Confidential Print. Part I, from the mid-nineteenth century to the First World War. Series A, Russia, 1859–1914*. Frederick, MD: University Publications of America, c.1983.

Rossi'ia i Tibet. Sbornik russkikh arkhivnykh dokumentov: 1900–1914 [*Russia and Tibet: Collection of Russian Archival Documents: 1900–1914*]. Moscow: Vostochnay'a literatura, 2005.

Perepiska Imperatora Aleksandra II s velikim kniazem Konstantinom Nikolaevichem Dnevnik Velikogo Kniazia Konstantina Nikolaevicha [*Correspondence of Emperor Aleksandr II with the Grand Duke Konstantin Nikolaevich: The Diary of the Grand Duke Konstantin Nikolaevich*]. Moscow: Terra, 1994.

Schreiner, G.A. *Entente Diplomacy and the World Matrix of the History of Europe, 1909–1914: Translated from the Original Texts in his Possession by B. de Siebert, Late Secretary of the Imperial Russian Embassy at London. Edited and Annotated by George Abel Schreiner*. New York and London: The Knickerbocker Press, 1921.

Works of Reference

Almanach de Gotha. Gotha, 1903, 1911.

Raskin, D.I. (ed.) *Ministerskaya sistema v rossiiskoi imperii* [*Russian Imperial Ministries*]. Moscow: ROSSPEN, 2007.

Oxford Dictionary of National Biography.

Printed Primary Sources

Abrikossov D.I. *Revelations of a Russian Diplomat*. Seattle: University of Washington Press, 1964.

Asquith, H.H. *Letters to Venetia Stanley*. Oxford: Clarendon Press, 1982.

Au service de la Russie: Alexandre Iswolsky, Correspondance diplomatique, 1906–1911. Paris: Les Editions Internationales, 1937.

Au temps de l'alliance franco-russe. Correspondance entre le grand-duc Nicolas Mikhailovitch de Russie et Frédéric Masson. Paris: Bernard Giovanangeli, 2005.

Baring, M. *Russian Essays and Stories*. London: Methuen, 1909.

Baring, M. *The Puppet Show of Memory.* London: Cassell [1937] 1987.

Bark, P.L. 'I'iul'skie dni 1914'. [July 1914] In: *Vozrozhdenie*, No.91 (1959), 28.

Benckendorff, C. *Half a Life: The Reminiscences of a Russian Gentleman*. London: The Richards Press Ltd, 1955.
Blondel, J-F. *Ce que mes yeux ont vu: Récit d'un diplomat – De 1900 à 1950*. Paris: Hachette, 1960.
Bompard, M. *Mon ambassade en Russie, 1903–1908*. Paris: Librairie Plon, 1937.
Botkin, P.S. *Kartinki diplomaticheskoi zhizni* [*Sketches of a Diplomat's Life*]. Paris: izd-vo E. Si'al'skoi, 1930.
Brett, M.V. (ed.) *Journals and Letters of Reginald Viscount Esher*. London: Ivor Nicholson and Watson Limited, 1934.
Bülow, Prince von. *Memoirs 1903–1909*. London: Putnam & Co, 1931–2.
Bülow, Prince von. *Letters of Prince von Bülow*. London: Hutchinson & Co, Ltd, n.d.
Byng, E. (ed.) *The Letters of Tsar Nicholas and Empress Marie*. London: Ivor Nicholson and Watson, 1937.
Caillaux, J. *Mes memoires, 1863–1909*. Paris: Librairies Plon, 1942.
Cambon, P. *Correspondance 1870–1924*. Paris: Editions Bernard Grasset, 1940.
Chambrun, C. de. *L'esprit de la diplomatie*. Paris: Editions Correa, 1944.
Combarieu, A. *Sept ans à l'Elysée: Avec le président Emile Loubet: De l'affaire Dreyfus à la conférence d'Algéciras 1899–1906*. Paris: Librairie Hachette, 1932.
Dnevnik Alekseia Sergeevicha Suvorina [*Diary of Aleksei Sergeevich Suvorin*]. London: The Garnett Press; Moscow: Nezavisimaya Gazeta, 2000.
Dnevniki i dokument'y iz lichnogo arkhiva Nikola'ia II [*Diaries and documents from Nicholas II's private archive*]. Minsk: Harvest, 2003.
Dolgorukov, P. *Peterburgskie ocherki: Pamflety emigranta, 1860–1867* [*St Petersburg Sketches: An Emigrant's Pamphlets, 1860–1867*]. Moscow: Novosti, 1992.
Gibel' imperii [*The collapse of the empire*]. Moscow: Fond Serge'ia Dubnova, 2000.
Goschen, E. *The Diary of Edward Goschen, 1900–1914*. London: Offices of the Royal Historical Society, 1980.
Grey of Fallodon. *Twenty-Five Years, 1892–1916*. New York: Frederick A. Stokes Company, 1925.
Guiccioli, A. *Diario di un conservatore*. Milano: Edizioni del Borghese, 1973.
Gwynn, S. (ed.) *The Letters and Friendships of Sir Cecil Spring Rice: A Record*. London: Constable, 1929.
Hardinge of Penshurst. *Old Diplomacy: The Reminiscences of Lord Hardinge of Penshurst*. London: John Murray, 1947.
Jusserand, J.J. *What Me Befell: The Reminiscences of Jean J. Jusserand*. Freeport, NY: Books for Libraries Press, n.d.
Kessler, Count Harry. *The Diaries of a Cosmopolitan, 1918–1937*. London: Weidenfeld & Nicolson, 1999 [1971].
Lamsdorff, V.N. *Dnevnik 1891–1892* [*Diary 1891–1892*]. Minsk: Harvest, 2003.

Lamsdorff, V.N. *Dnevnik 1894–1896* [*Diary 1894–1896*]. Moscow: Mezhdunarodnye otnosheniia, 1991.

Lee, S. *King Edward VII: A Biography*. London: Macmillan, 1925.

Letters of the Tsaritsa – to the Tsar, 1914–1916. London: Duckworth & Co, 1923.

Lichnowsky, K. *Heading for the Abyss: Reminiscences*. New York: Payson and Clarke, Ltd, 1928.

Louis, G. *Les Carnets de Georges Louis (directeur des affaires politiques au ministère des affaires étrangères, ambassadeur en Russie) tome premier 1908–1912*. Paris: F. Biered et Cie, Editeurs, 1926.

Marder, A.J. (ed.) *Fear God and Dread Nought: The Correspondence of Admiral of the Fleet Lord Fisher of Kilverstone*. London: Jonathan Cape, 1952–1959.

Memuary grafa S.D. Sheremeteva [*Count S.D. Sheremetev's Memoirs*]. Moscow: INDRIK, 2001.

Meyendorff, A.F. (ed.) *Correspondance diplomatique de M. de Staal (1884–1900)*. Paris: Librairie Marcel Rivière, 1929.

Mikhailovskii, G.N. *Zapiski: Iz istorii rossi'iskogo vneshne-politicheskogo vedomstva, 1914–1920* [*Reminiscences: From the History of the Russian Foreign Ministry, 1914–1920*]. Moscow: Mezhdunarodny'ie otnosheni'ia, 1993.

Nabokoff, C. *The Ordeal of a Diplomat*. Salisbury, NC: Documentary Publications, 1976.

Nekludoff, A. *Diplomatic Reminiscences Before and During the World War, 1911–1917*. New York: E.P. Dutton & Company, 1920.

Nikolaev, A.M. *Pol-veka tomu nazad: Vospominani'ia o sluzhbe ofitsera imperatorskogo general'nogo shtaba v dolzhnosti pomosh'nika voennogo agenta v Londone i voennogo agenta v Vashingtone vo vrem'ya pervoi mirovoi voiny 1914–1918* [*Half a Century Ago: Reminiscences of an Officer of the Imperial General Staff, an Aide to the London Military Agent and the Military Agent in Washington During the First World War, 1914–1919*]. New York: Izdanie Severo-Amerikanskogo Otdela Russkogo Obshevoinskogo Soyuza, 1968.

Nol'de, B.E. *Daleko'ie i blizkoe* [*The Past and the Present*]. Paris: Sovremenny'e zapiski, 1930.

Norwich, J.J. (ed.) *The Duff Cooper Diaries, 1915–1951*. London: Weidenfeld and Nicolson, 2005.

Onslow, R.W.A., the 5th Earl. *Sixty Three Years: Diplomacy, the Great War and Politics, with Notes on Travel, Sports and Other Things*. London: Hutchinson, 1944.

Perepiska Vilgel'ma II s Nikolaem II: 1894–1914 [*William II and Nicholas II: Correspondence, 1894–1914*]. Moscow: Gosudarstvennaia publichnaya istoricheska'ia biblioteka Rossii, 2007.

Poincaré, R. *The Memoirs of Raymond Poincaré*. London: William Heinemann, 1926.

Rediger, A. *Istori'ia moei zhizni: Vospominani'ia voennogo ministra* [*My Life Story: Memoirs of a War Minister*]. Moscow: Kanon-press-Z, 1999.
Rozanov, V. *Literaturny'ie izgnanniki: Vospominani'ia.Pis'ma* [*Literary Exiles: Memoirs, Letters*]. Moscow, 2000.
Savich, N.V. *Vospominani'ia* [*Memoirs*]. St Petersburg: Logos, 1993.
Savinsky, A.A. *Recollections of a Russian Diplomat*. London: Hutchinson & Co., n.d.
Sazonov, S.D. *Vospominani'ia* [*Memoirs*]. Minsk: Harvest, 2002.
Schebeko, N. *Souvenirs: Essay historique sur les origines de la guerre de 1914*. Paris: Bibliothèque, 1936.
Schoen, Freiherr von. *The Memoirs of an Ambassador: A Contribution to the Political History of Modern Times*. New York: Brentano's, 1923.
Spender, J.A. *Life, Journalism and Politics*. London: Cassell and Company Ltd, 1927.
Steed, H.W. *Through 30 Years, 1892–1922: A Personal Narrative*. Garden City, NY: Doubleday, Page & Company, 1925.
Stolypin, P.A. *Perepiska* [*Correspondence*]. Moscow: ROSSPEN, 2004.
Taube, M. de. *La politique russe d'avant-guerre et la fin de l'empire des tsars (1914–1917)*. Paris: Librairie Ernest Leroux, 1928.
Taube, M.A. *Zarnitsy: Vospominani'ia o tragicheskoi sud'be predrevolutsionnoi Rossii (1900–1917)* [*Early Warnings: Memoirs About the Tragic Fate of the Old Russia (1900–1917)*]. Moscow: ROSSPEN, 2007.
Tcharykow, N.V. *Glimpses of High Politics*. London: Allen & Unwin Ltd., 1931.
The History of the Times: The 20th Century Test, 1884–1912. London: The Office of *The Times*, 1947.
Thierry, A. *L'Angleterre au temps de Paul* Cambon. Paris: La Palatine, 1961.
Vinogradov, Pavel. 'Angli'ia i russkie voennoplenny'e', in *Rossi'ia na rasput'ie: Istoriko-publitsisticheskie stat'i* ['England and Russian prisoners of war', in *Russia on the Crossroads: Historical and Political Essays*]. Moscow: Territori'ia budushego, 2008.
Witte, S.Yu. *Vospominani'ia* [*Memoirs*]. Tallinn-Moscow: Skif Aleks, 1994.

Secondary Sources

Airapetov, O. *Vneshn'aia politika Rossiiskoi imperii, 1815–1914* [*The Foreign Policy of the Russian Empire, 1815–1914*]. Moscow: Evropa, 2006.
Astaf'iev, I.I. *Russko-Germanskie diplomaticheskie otnosheni'ia 1905–1914: Ot portsmutskogo mira do potsdamskogo soglasheni'ia* [*Russo-German diplomatic relations in 1905–1914: From the Peace of Portsmouth to the Potsdam Agreement*]. Moscow University Publishers, 1972.
Barraclough, G. *From Agadir to Armageddon: Anatomy of a Crisis*. London: Weidenfeld & Nicolson, 1982.

Berberova, N. *Liudi i lozhi: Russkie mason'y XX stoleti'ia*. Kharkov: Kaleidoskop, 1997.

Bickers, R. and Tiedemann, R.G. (eds) *The Boxers, China and the World*. New York: Rowman & Littlefield, 2007.

Bridge, F.R. *From Sadowa to Saraevo: The Foreign Policy of Austria-Hungary, 1866–1914*. London and Boston: Routledge and Kegan Paul, 1972.

Hinsley, F.H. (ed.) *British Foreign Policy Under Sir Edward Grey*. Cambridge: Cambridge University Press, 1977.

Cambon, H. *Paul Cambon: Ambassadeur de France (1843–1924) par un diplomate*. Paris: Librairie Plon, 1937.

Chaudordy, Cte. Jean Baptiste Alexandre Damaze de. *La France en 1889*. Paris: Librairie Plon, 1889.

Churchill, R.P. *The Anglo-Russian Convention of 1907*. Cedar Rapids, IA: Torch Press, 1939.

Degoev, Vladimir. *Bolsha'ia igra na Kavkaze. Proshloe I nastoiaschee* [*The Great Game in the Caucasus: Its Past and Present*]. Moscow, Mezhdunarodnye otnosheni'a, 2003.

Delcassé et l'Europe à la veille de la grande guerre: Actes du colloque tenu à Foix les 22–23–24–25 Octobre 1998. Archives départementales de l'Arriège, 1999.

Emets, V.A. *Otcherki vneshnei politiki Rossii: Vzaimootnosheni'ia voyn'y, 1914–1918* [*Essays in Russian Foreign Policy: Wartime Diplomacy, 1914–1918*]. Moscow: Nauka, 1977.

Evdokimova, N.P. and Vivatenko, S.V. Raymond Poincaré: President Frantsii [*Raymond Poincaré: President of France*]. St Petersburg: University Publishers, 2006.

Hughes, M. *Diplomacy Before the Russian Revolution: Britain, Russia, and the Old Diplomacy, 1894–1917*. Basingstoke: Macmillan Press Ltd, 2000.

Ignatiev, A.V. *Russko-angliiskie otnosheniia nakanune Oktiabr'skoi revolutsii, fevral–oktiabr' 1917* [*Anglo-Russian Relations on the Eve of the October Revolution, February–October 1917*]. Moscow: Nauka, 1966.

Ignatiev, A.V. *Vneshna'ia politika Rossii v 1905–1907* [*Russia's Foreign Policy in 1905–1907*]. Moskva: Nauka, 1986.

Ignatiev, A.V. *Vneshn'aia politika Rossii, 1907–1914: Tendentsii, Sobyti'ia, Liudi* [*Russia's Foreign Policy in 1907–1914: Trends, Events, Persons*]. Moscow: Nauka, 2000.

Khvostov, V., Tarle, E. and Mintz, I. *Istori'ia diplomatii* [*History of Diplomacy*]. Moscow: AST, 2005.

Kazemzadeh, F. *Russia and Britain in Persia, 1864–1914: A Study in Imperialism*. New Haven: Yale University Press, 1968.

Khariukov, L.N. *Anglo-russkoie sopernichestvo v Tsentral'noi Azii i ismailism*. Moscow: Izdatel'stvo Moskovskogo universiteta, 1995.

Kostrikova, E.G. *Rossiiskoe obshestvo i vneshn'a'ia politika nakanune pervoi mirovoi voiny, 1908–1914* [*Russian Society and Foreign Policy on the Eve of the First World War, 1908–1914*]. Moscow: RAN, Institut Rossiiskoi Istorii, 2007.

Lieven, D.C.B. *Russia and the Origins of the First World War*. Basingstoke: Macmillan Press Ltd, 1983.

Lieven, D.C.B. *Russia's Rulers Under the Old Regime*. New Haven: Yale University Press, 1989.

McDonald, D.M. *United Government and Foreign Policy in Russia, 1900–1914*. Cambridge, MA: Harvard University Press, 1992.

McLean, D. *Britain and Her Buffer State: The Collapse of the Persian Empire, 1890–1914*. London: Royal Historical Society, 1979.

Milza, P. *Les relations internationales de 1871 à 1914*. Paris: Armand Colin, 1990.

Neilson, K. *Strategy and Supply: The Anglo-Russian Alliance, 1914–1917*. London: George Allen & Unwin, 1984.

Neilson, K. *Britain and the Last Tsar: British Policy and Russia, 1894–1917*. Oxford. Clarendon Press, 1995.

Neilson, K. and Otte, T.G. *The Permanent Under-Secretary for Foreign Affairs, 1854–1946*. New York: Routledge, 2009.

Neton, A. *Delcassé (1852–1923)*. Paris: Academie Diplomatique Internationale, 1952.

Newton, T.L. *Lord Lansdowne: A Biography*. London: Macmillan and Co, 1929.

Nicolson, H. *Sir Arthur Nicolson, Bart., first Lord Carnock: A Study in the Old Diplomacy*. London: Constable & Co. Ltd, 1930.

Nish, I. *The Origins of the Russo-Japanese War*. London and New York: Longman, 1985.

Nish, I. and Yoichi Kibata, I. (eds) *The History of Anglo-Japanese Relations*. Basingstoke: Macmillan Press Ltd, 2000.

Nol'de, B.E. *Dalekoie i blizkoie* [*The Past and the Present*]. Paris: Izdatel'stvo sovremenny'e zapiski, 1930.

Ostal'tseva, A.F. *Anglo-russkoe soglasheni'ie 1907* [*Anglo-Russian Convention of 1907*]. Saratov: Izdanie Saratovskogo universiteta, 1977.

Ramm, A. *Sir Robert Morier: Envoy and Ambassador in the Age of Imperialism, 1876–1893*. Oxford: Clarendon Press, 1973.

Renouvin, P. and Duroselle, J.P. *Introduction to the History of International Relations*. New York: Frederick A. Praeger, 1967.

Robbins, K. *Sir Edward Grey: A Biography of Lord Grey of Fallodon*. London: Cassel, 1971.

Nezhninsky, L.N. and Ignat'iev, A.V. (eds) *Rossi'ia i tchernomorskiie prolivy (XVIII–XIX stoleti'ia)* [*Russia and the Black Sea Straits (18th–19th Centuries)*]. Moscow: Mezhdunarodnye otnosheni'ia, 1999.

Rybachonok, I.S. (ed.) *Rossi'ia: mezhdunarodnoye polozheni'ie i voennyi potentsial v seredine XIX–nachale XX veka* [*Russia: International Situation and Military Resources, 1850s–1914*]. Moscow: Institut rossiiskoi istorii RAN, 2003.

Ignat'iev, A.V., Rybachonok, I.S. and Sanin, G.A. (eds) *Rossi'iska'ia diplomati'ia v portretakh*. Moscow: Mezdunarodnye otnosheni'ia, 1992.
Itenberg, B. and Shelohaev, V. (eds) *Rossiiskie liberal'y* [*Russian Liberals*]. Moscow: ROSSPEN, 2001.
Rybachonok, I.S. *Soyuz s Frantsi'ei vo vneshnei politike Rossii v kontse XIX v.* [*The French Alliance in Russian Foreign Policy of the 1890s*]. Moscow: IRI RAN, 1993.
Searle, G.R. *A New England? Peace and War, 1886–1918*. Oxford: Clarendon Press, 2004.
Schroeder, Paul W. *Systems, Stability and Statecraft*. New York: Palgrave, 2004.
Shatsillo, V. and Shatsillo, L. *Russko-yaponskaia voina, 1904–1905* [*Russo-Japanese War, 1904–1905*]. Moscow: Molodaya gvardi'ia, 2004.
Taylor, A.J.P. *The Struggle for Mastery in Europe, 1848–1918*. Oxford: Oxford University Press, 1971.
Vasiukov, V.S. *Vneshnay'ia politika Rossii nakanune Fevral'skoi revolutsii. 1916–fevral' 1917* [*Russia's Foreign Policy on the Eve of the Revolution, 1916–February 1917*]. Moscow: Nauka, 1989.
Vinogradov, V.N. *Rossi'ia I Balkany: Ot Ekateriny Vtoroi do pervoi mirovoi voiny* [*Russia and the Balkans: From Catherine II to World War I*]. Lampeter, NY: The Edwin Mellen Press, 2000.
Kin'iapina, N.S. (ed.) *Vostochnyi vopros vo vneshnei politike Rossii: Konets XVII–nachalo XX vv* [*The Eastern Question in Russia's Foreign Policy: Late 17th-Early 20th Century*]. Moscow: Nauka, 1978.
Wallace, Sir D.M. *Russia*. London: Cassell & Company, 1905.
White, J.A. *Transition to Global Rivalry: Alliance Diplomacy and the Quadruple Entente, 1895–1907*. Cambridge: Cambridge University Press, 1985.
Wilson, K.M. *The Policy of the Entente: Essays on the Determinants of British Foreign Policy, 1904–1914*. Cambridge: Cambridge University Press, 1985.
Wilson, K.M. *Empire and Continent: Studies in British Foreign Policy from the 1880s to the First World War*. London and New York: Mansell Publishing Limited, 1987.
Zaionchkovskii A.M. *Podgotovka Rossii k voine v mezhdunarodnom otnoshenii* [*Russia's Diplomatic Preparation for the War*]. Leningrad: GIZ, 1926.
Ziegler, P. *The Sixth Great Power: Barings, 1762–1929*. London: Collins, 1988.
Zinov'iev, I.S. *Rossi'ia, Angli'ia i Persi'ia* [*Russia, England and Persia*]. St Petersburg, 1912.
Zorgbibe, C. *Delcassé: Le grand ministre des Affaires Etrangères de la IIIe République*. Paris: Editions Olbia, 2001.

Unpublished Sources

Halfond, I. *Maurice Paleologue: The Diplomatist, the Writer and the Man* (PhD Dissertation). Temple University, 1974.

Rakosin, M.E. *Les diplomates russes entre 1890 et 1914: Perception identitaire, activité professionelle et reflexions politiques PhD*. Paris: EHESS, 2003.

Articles

Cosgrove, R.A. 'A Note on Lloyd George's Speech at the Mansion House, 21 July 1911'. *The Historical Journal*, 12, 4 (December 1969): 698–701.

Klein, I. 'British Intervention in the Persian Revolution, 1905–1909'. *The Historical Journal*, 15, 4 (1972): 731–52.

Mulligan, W. 'From Case to Narrative: The Marquess of Lansdowne, Sir Edward Grey, and the Threat from Germany, 1900–1906'. *The International History Review*, 30, 2 (2008): 273–302.

Nish, I. 'Politics, Trade and Communications in East Asia: Thoughts on Anglo-Russian Relations, 1861–1907'. *Modern Asian Studies*, 21, 4 (1987): 667–8.

Renzi, W.A. 'Great Britain, Russia, and the Straits, 1914–1915'. *Journal of Modern History*, 42, 1 (1970): 1–20.

Schroeder, S. '"Ausgedehnte Spionage" – Benno von Sieberts geheime Zusammenarbeit mit dem Auswaertigen Amt (1909–1926)'. *Militargeschichtliche zeitschrift*, 65 (2005): 425–63.

Smith Jr., C. Jay. 'Great Britain and the 1914–1915 Straits Agreement with Russia: The British Promise of November 1914'. *American Historical Review*, 70, 4 (1965): 1015–34.

Soroka, M. 'Debating Russia's Choice between Great Britain and Germany: Count Benckendorff versus Count Lamsdorff, 1902–1906'. *The International History Review*, 32, 1 (2010): 1–24.

Sweet, D.W. 'The Baltic in British Diplomacy before 1914'. *The Historical Journal*, 13, 3 (1970): 451–90.

Williams, B.J. 'The Strategic Background to the Anglo-Russian Entente of August 1907'. *The Historical Journal*, 9, 3 (1966): 360–73.

Wilson, K. 'Directions of Travel: The Earl of Selborne, the Cabinet and the Threat from Germany, 1900–1904'. *The International History Review*, 30, 2 (2008): 259–72.

Index